PEOPLE WITH DISABILITIES
WHO CHALLENGE THE SYSTEM

This book is printed on recycled paper. ✪

PEOPLE WITH DISABILITIES WHO CHALLENGE THE SYSTEM

edited by

Donna H. Lehr, Ph.D.
School of Education
Boston University

and

Fredda Brown, Ph.D.
School of Education
Queens College, City University of New York

·P·A·U·L·H·
BROOKES
PUBLISHING CO

Baltimore • London • Toronto • Sydney

Paul H. Brookes Publishing Co.
Post Office Box 10624
Baltimore, Maryland 21285-0624

Typeset by PRO-IMAGE Corporation, York, Pennsylvania.
Manufactured in the United States of America by
The Maple Press Company, York, Pennsylvania.

Library of Congress Cataloging-in-Publication Data
People with disabilities who challenge the system / edited by Donna H. Lehr
  and Fredda Brown : foreword by Doug Guess.
      p.   cm.
    Includes bibliographical references and index.
    ISBN 1-55766-229-0
    1. Handicapped—Services for—United States.   2. Handicapped
  children—Services for—United States.   I. Lehr, Donna H.   II. Brown,
  Fredda.
  HV1553.P44   1996
  362.4'048'0973—dc20   95-39075
                                                                           CIP
British Library Cataloguing-in-Publication data are available from the British
Library.

Contents

Contributors

EDITORS

Donna H. Lehr, Ph.D., Associate Professor, School of Education, Boston University, 605 Commonwealth Avenue, Boston, Massachusetts 02215. Donna Lehr is Associate Professor of Special Education in the School of Education at Boston University. Her work focuses on educational issues and practices for students with complex health care needs and the inclusion of students with disabilities in general education settings. She has published articles and chapters on individuals with severe disabilities and was co-editor with Fredda Brown of the book *Persons with Profound Disabilities: Issues and Practices* (Paul H. Brookes Publishing Co., 1989).

Fredda Brown, Ph.D., Associate Professor, School of Education, Queens College, City University of New York, Special Education Program, 65-30 Kissena Boulevard, Flushing, New York 11367. Fredda Brown is Associate Professor and Coordinator of Special Education at Queens College, City University of New York. Her current work focuses on issues and practices for individuals with challenging behavior, with a specific focus on the relationship between challenging behavior, quality of life, and self-determination. Dr. Brown has published many articles and chapters in the area of severe disabilities and was co-editor with Donna Lehr of the book *Persons with Profound Disabilities: Issues and Practices* (Paul H. Brookes Publishing Co., 1989).

CONTRIBUTORS

❊ **Richard W. Albin, Ph.D.,** Associate Professor, University of Oregon, 1235 University of Oregon, Eugene, Oregon 97403-1235. Richard Albin is Associate Professor of Special Education at the University of Oregon. Dr. Albin's research has addressed instructional procedures for building generalized skills, strategies for reducing severe problem behaviors, and procedures for training teachers and staff in educational and behavioral procedures.

Marilyn Ault, Ph.D., Department of Special Education, University of Kansas, Lawrence, Kansas 66045. Marilyn Ault is Program Associate and Adjunct Professor in the Department of Special Education at the University of Kansas. Her recent work has focused on educational practices and issues pertaining to children and youth with significant disabilities and special health care needs. She is also involved in the development of multimedia instructional resources for people interested in individuals with profound disabilities. She co-directed with Barbara Thompson the U.S. Department of Education, Office of Special Education Programs project that produced and field-tested three videotapes pertaining to the Circle of Inclusion Project.

Barbara J. Ayres, Ph.D., Assistant Professor, College of Education and Human Services, Montana State University–Billings, 1500 North 30th Street, Billings, Montana 59101-0298. Barbara Ayres is Assistant Professor of Special Education at Montana State University–Billings. In addition to teaching undergraduate and graduate courses in special education, she spends time supporting families and educators as they work to promote inclusion in their schools and communities. Her other areas of focus include cooperative learning, adult teaming, and creating positive behavioral supports.

Diane Baumgart, Ph.D., Associate Professor, University of Idaho, College of Education, 113 Education Building, Moscow, Idaho 83844-0381. Diane Baumgart teaches undergraduate and graduate courses in special education. Her research focuses on curriculum development, personnel preparation, and strategies for enhancing language, communication, and social relationships for students with severe disabilities as well as other traditionally marginalized students. Dr. Baumgart has authored numerous articles, books, and video products on school reform, curriculum development, and communication. She is co-author with Jeanne M. Johnson, Edwin Helmstetter, and Chris Curry of *Augmenting Basic Communication in Natural Contexts* (Paul H. Brookes Publishing Co., 1996). She recently developed teaching technology to enhance distance education for special education and elementary science teachers and taught science to integrated classes of first through third graders, including students with and without disabilities.

Denise Berotti, M.A., Research Assistant, Department of Psychiatry and Human Behavior, University of Mississippi Medical Center, Jackson, Mississippi 39216-4505. Denise Berotti is a research assistant at the University of Mississippi Medical Center and is completing her doctorate in clinical psychology at the State University of New York at Albany. Her dissertation research is focused on the effects of preference and choice on severe behavior problems.

Joan Brinckerhoff, Ph.D., Director of Early Intervention, North Shore ARC, Danvers, Massachusetts 01923. Joan Brinckerhoff has developed and implemented early intervention and family support policy and practice at the local, state, and federal government levels. Dr. Brinckerhoff has administered and/or implemented grants for demonstrations in early intervention in the areas of severe disabilities, outreach for parent participation and curriculum development, and training for personnel preparation of interdisciplinary early interventionists.

John Butterworth, Ph.D., Judge Baker Center, Children's Hospital, Longwood Avenue, Boston, Massachusetts 02115. John Butterworth is Research Coordinator for the Institute for Community Inclusion (University Affiliated Program) at Children's Hospital and the University of Massachusetts at Boston. He is Director of the Massachusetts Natural Supports Project and Research Director for the Center on Promoting Employment (RRTC), and conducts research and training in the areas of transition, natural supports, and supported employment.

Nicholas J. Certo, Ph.D., Professor, San Francisco State University, Department of Special Education, California Research Institute, San Francisco, California 94132. Nick Certo is Professor in the Department of Special Education at San Francisco State University. He has specialized in developing service systems and strategies to ease the transition of adolescents and adults with severe disabilities into integrated employment, community living, and recreation for over 20 years as a federal official, national consultant, and university professor serving his local community.

Daniel W. Close, Ph.D., Associate Professor, University of Oregon, 1235 University of Oregon, Eugene, Oregon 97403-1235. Daniel Close is Associate Professor of Special Education at the University of Oregon and Training Coordinator for the University Affiliated Program. Dr. Close has pioneered models for providing residential support for people who have severe intellectual disabilities, and he has conducted research on training procedures for building functional community skills.

Daniel B. Crimmins, Ph.D., Director of Psychology, Westchester Institute for Human Development, and New York Medical College, Cedarwood Hall, Valhalla, New York 10595-1689. Daniel Crimmins is Director of Psychology at the Westchester Institute for Human Development/University Affiliated Program. He is also a member of the faculties of the Medical School and Graduate School of Health Sciences at the New York Medical College. Dr. Crimmins has worked extensively in developing strategies for educating students with severe disabilities and challenging behaviors. A major focus of his efforts over the last several years has been on assisting schools and agencies to develop their capacities to deliver positive behavioral supports through team training.

Kathy Doering, M.A., San Francisco State University, Department of Special Education, California Research Institute, San Francisco, California 94132. Kathy Doering teaches in the Department of Special Education at San Francisco State University and is active in systems change efforts at the preservice, inservice, and adult service system levels. She has served as project coordinator for several demonstration projects focusing on person-centered transition services, agency conversion, employment, relationship/friendship development, community building, and implementation of natural supports across work, home, and community environments for individuals with severe disabilities. In addition, she has provided numerous presentations and technical assistance to school districts and adult agencies, both nationally and throughout California.

Dianne L. Ferguson, Ph.D., Associate Professor, Specialized Training Program, University of Oregon, 1235 University of Oregon, Eugene, Oregon 97403-1235. Dianne Ferguson is Associate Professor in the Special Education/Developmental Disabilities Area of the Division of Special Education and Rehabilitation, University of Oregon. She is also a member of the Center on Human Development. She teaches courses in interpretivist methodology, prepares teachers to work in inclusionary settings with students who have significant disabilities, and is the principal investigator in a number of funded research projects related to school inclusion, curriculum and teaching, and the experiences of families of individuals with developmental disabilities.

K. Brigid Flannery, Ph.D., Assistant Professor, University of Oregon, 1235 University of Oregon, Eugene, Oregon 97403-1235. Brigid Flannery is Assistant Professor of Special Education at the University of Oregon. Her research focus has been on communication systems, educational inclusion, and reduction of problem behaviors. Dr. Flannery directs the Oregon Transition Systems Change effort.

H.D. Bud Fredericks, Ph.D., Research Professor, Teaching Research, Western Oregon State College, 345 North Monmouth Avenue, Monmouth, Oregon 97361. Bud Fredericks is Research Professor at Western Oregon State College. He is a former president of the Association for Persons with Severe Handicaps, a parent of a son with disabilities, and the founder of an array of service models, including early intervention, educational instruction, residential support, treatment for youth who have engaged in sexual offenses, and residential support for medically fragile individuals. Dr. Fredericks is recognized internationally for his leadership and innovation in the field of special education and developmental disabilities. Bud Fredericks currently directs TRACES, the national technical assistance project for children and youth who are deaf-blind. He has established residential enviroments for individuals with the most challenging behaviors. As part of that endeavor, he is researching integrated and coordinated community projects that provide wraparound services for troubled youth.

Michael F. Giangreco, Ph.D., Research Assistant Professor, University of Vermont, College of Education and Social Services, 499C Waterman Building, Burlington, Vermont 05405-0160. Prior to joining the faculty at the University of Vermont in 1988, Michael Giangreco spent several years working directly with people with disabilities as a counselor in community residential services, as a special education teacher, and as a special education coordinator. His research and teaching efforts have focused primarily on teamwork and coordination of related services, curriculum planning and adaptation, and other strategies to facilitate inclusive education. Dr. Giangreco has authored or co-authored several publications. He is a co-author of *Choosing Options and Accommodations for Children: A Guide to Planning Inclusive Education* (Paul H. Brookes Publishing Co., 1993) and author of *Vermont Interdependent Services Team Approach* (Paul H. Brookes Publishing Co., 1996).

Lori Goetz, Ph.D., Professor, San Francisco State University, Department of Special Education, California Research Institute, 612 Font Boulevard, San Francisco, California 94132. Dr. Goetz is currently Professor in the Department of Special Education at San Francisco State University, Coordinator of Area Programs in Severe Disabilities, and Director of the California Research Institute. She is a co-author of several books, has completed a 3-year tenure as Associate Editor of the *Journal of The Association for Persons with Severe Handicaps,* and has served as Director of several federally funded research projects. She has published widely in the areas of communication, program evaluation, and sensory functioning with students with severe disabilities. Currently, she directs a major federal demonstration project for students who are deaf-blind and a minority recruitment and retention personnel training grant. She also currently serves as a board member of The Association for Persons with Severe Handicaps (TASH).

Carole R. Gothelf, Ed.D., Director of Education, The Jewish Guild for the Blind, 15 West 65th Street, New York, New York 10023. Carole Gothelf is Director of Education at The Jewish Guild for the Blind in New York City and is Co-Director of the New York State Technical Assistance Project serving children and youth who are deaf-blind. As a consultant to a wide range of state and local organizations, she provides training and technical assistance for planning and programming for students of transition age and for designing and implementing educational interventions for individuals who are deaf-blind and have severe behavior problems. Her recent work focuses on curriculum practices that support choice and self-determination.

Lora Tuesday Heathfield, Ph.D., Department of Pediatric Psychology, Children's Seashore House, Philadelphia Center for Health Sciences, 3405 Civic Center Boulevard, Philadelphia, Pennsylvania 19104-4388. Lora Tuesday Heathfield is a clinical associate in pediatrics at Children's Seashore House in Philadelphia. Her research has focused on generalization technology and social development.

Deborah L. Hedeen, Ph.D., Assistant Professor, Department of Special Education, College of Education, Idaho State University, Box 8059, Pocatello, Idaho 93209-8059. Deborah Hedeen is Assistant Professor in the Department of Counselor Education and Special Education at Idaho State University. Her educational efforts have been in the areas of inclusive education and advocacy for individuals with moderate and severe disabilities.

✳ **Robert H. Horner, Ph.D.,** Professor, Special Education, University of Oregon, Specialized Training Program, 1235 University of Oregon, Eugene, Oregon 97403-1235. Rob Horner is Professor of Special Education at the University of Oregon and Director of the Research and Training Center on Positive Behavioral Support. His research has addressed instruction procedures for students with severe disabilities, techniques to promote generalization, supported employment, and, most recently, research on severe problem behaviors.

Carolyn Hughes, Ph.D., Assistant Professor, Department of Special Education, Box 328, Peabody College, Vanderbilt University, Nashville, Tennessee 37203. Carolyn Hughes is Assistant Professor of Special Education at Vanderbilt University and Project Director of the Tennessee High School Project. Her research is in the areas of self-management among people with disabilities, the transition from school to adult life, and models of social support.

✝ **Craig H. Kennedy, Ph.D.,** Assistant Professor, University of Hawaii. Craig Kennedy's research focus is on systems for building social relationships, educational inclusion, functional equivalence, and stimulus control among people with disabilities.

William E. Kiernan, Ph.D., Director of Rehabilitation, Developmental Evaluation Clinic, Director of Community and Support Services, The Children's Hospital, 300 Longwood Avenue, Boston, Massachusetts 02115. William Kiernan is Director of the Institute for Community Inclusion, a University Affiliated Program, and Rehabilitation Research and Training Center at Children's Hospital in Boston. He has published extensively in the area of disability and employment and has served as a national and international expert in the area of administration and public policy in rehabilitation. He is Adjunct Professor in the Graduate College of Education at the University of Massachusetts and is on the faculties of the School of Public Health at Harvard University and the Graduate School of Health Studies at Simmons College. He is President of the American Association on Mental Retardation (AAMR).

Mellanie Lee, Educational Consultant, University of Hawaii University Affiliated Program. Mellanie Lee is currently Educational Consultant for the Federated States of Micronesia through the University Affiliated Program at the University of Hawaii. She has worked for the California Research Institute at San Francisco State University since 1987. Ms. Lee has also been a corporate liaison for a federally funded demonstration project exploring employer support models for youth in transition and has also served as a consultant on the implementation of a diversified work force for companies and adult service providers.

Gwen Meyer, M.S., Research Assistant, Specialized Training Program, University of Oregon, 1235 University of Oregon, Eugene, Oregon 97403-1235. Gwen Meyer is a research assistant with the Schools Projects in the Specialized Training Program at the University of Oregon. She is a former teacher and is currently involved in research on school restructuring and reform, particularly in the areas of curriculum design and instructional strategies developed to accommodate a broad range of student learning.

Luanna H. Meyer, Ph.D., School of Education, Syracuse University, 150 Huntington Hall, Syracuse, NY 13244. Luanna Meyer is Professor of Education, Chair of the Doctoral Program in Special Education, and Coordinator of the Inclusive Elementary and Special Education Program at Syracuse University. Her research has focused on inclusive schooling, children's peer relationships, nonaversive behavioral intervention, and educational change. She has published more than 100 books, book chapters, and journal articles and has lectured extensively in the United States as well as in Canada, New Zealand, Poland, Israel, and Australia. She currently co-directs the New York Partnership for Statewide Systems Change and is Director of the Consortium for Collaborative Research on Social Relationships.

✳ **Robert E. O'Neill, Ph.D.,** Assistant Professor, University of Utah, Salt Lake City, Utah 84112. Robert O'Neill is Assistant Professor of Special Education at the University of Utah. His research has focused on the development and use of communication in young children with disabilities, procedures for reducing severe problem behaviors, and instructional procedures for building functional, generalized skills.

Frank R. Rusch, Ph.D., Director, Transition Research Institute, University of Illinois at Urbana-Champaign, Champaign, Illinois 61820. Frank Rusch is Professor of Special Education and Director of the Transition Research Institute at the University of Illinois. He has published extensively in the areas of supported employment, transition from school to adult life, co-worker support for employees with disabilities, and self-instructional strategies.

Martha E. Snell, Ph.D., Professor, Curry School of Education, Department of Curriculum, Instruction, and Special Education, Ruffner Hall, Room 236, 405 Emmet Street, University of Virginia, Charlottesville, Virginia 22903. Martha Snell is Professor of Education in the Curry School of Education at the University of Virginia. Part of her time is devoted to the preparation of teachers of students with severe disabilities and preschoolers with disabilities. She also writes about and studies inclusion in schools and teaching approaches. She is a past president of TASH.

Jeffrey R. Sprague, Ph.D., Assistant Professor, University of Oregon, 1235 University of Oregon, Eugene, Oregon 97403-1235. Jeffrey Sprague is Assistant Professor of Special Education at the University of Oregon. Dr. Sprague is the former Director of the Institute on Inclusion at Indiana University. He is widely published, and he has made major contributions through his research on instructional technology, communication systems, educational models, and reduction of severe problem behaviors.

Barbara Thompson, Ph.D., Department of Special Education, University of Kansas, Lawrence, Kansas 66045. Barbara Thompson is Associate Professor and Coordinator of the Early Childhood Program Area in the Department of Special Education at the University of Kansas. Her recent work has focused on systemic change that supports the development of inclusive early childhood services for young children with significant disabilities and the preparation of early childhood educators to function effectively in inclusive early childhood education/child care settings. Since 1985, she has been Director of the Circle of Inclusion research and demonstration projects described in Chapter 2, and she currently directs a related national outreach training project.

Jacquelyn Waite, M.S., Ticonderoga Central School District, Ticonderoga, New York 12883. Jacquelyn Waite is currently a kindergarten teacher and Building Leadership Team Co-Chairperson of Ticonderoga Elementary School. She has interests in research regarding the inclusion of students with severe disabilities into general education classrooms, multi-age education, and the education of students labeled gifted and talented, particularly females.

Jane Wegner, Ph.D., Department of Speech, Language, and Hearing, University of Kansas, Lawrence, Kansas 66045. Jane Wegner is Director of the Schiefelbush Speech, Language, and Hearing Clinic and Adjunct Professor in the Department of Speech, Language, and Hearing at the University of Kansas. She has a long-standing interest and expertise in augmented communication, as well as in the transdisciplinary approaches to training individuals to support the needs of individuals with significant disabilities in preschool, school, and community settings. From 1988 through 1992, she was Co-Investigator with Barbara Thompson for the Kansas Early Childhood Research Institute Project 2.2, which was designed to investigate the transition of children with significant disabilities from special education preschool programs to inclusive community early childhood programs.

Donna Wickham, Ph.D., Department of Special Education, University of Kansas, Lawrence, Kansas 66045. Donna Wickham is Program Associate and Adjunct Professor in the Department of Special Education at the University of Kansas. She is the coordinator of several federal projects directed toward inclusive education for elementary school–age children with significant disabilities. Her current research interests pertain to systemic change, staff development, and investigating approaches for training para-educators to function in inclusive settings. She has been actively involved in research and program development related to the Circle of Inclusion Project since 1987.

Christopher Willis, M.S., Special Education Specialist, Aberdeen School District, 311 Sunset Drive, Hoquiam, Washington 98550. Christopher Willis has been a research assistant with the Schools Projects in the Specialized Training Program at the University of Oregon. He was Project Coordinator for the Including Exceptions Systems Project, from which the information for his chapter was generated. Mr. Willis worked with the Schools Projects for 6 years. He works for the Aberdeen School District in Aberdeen, Washington.

Foreword

READING THE CHAPTERS that were prepared for this book gave me a much-needed "jolt" to really appreciate the transformation that has taken place in the provision of services for persons who pose the most significant challenges to our educational and adult service agencies. Our progress does not reflect a linear, gradual change process in which each advancement is just an extension of a preceding finding or thought. Kuhn (1970) has diminished this illusion by showing us that science itself does not advance in this way. To the contrary, major scientific breakthroughs and advances are explosions, so to speak, that rearrange and significantly perturb the otherwise flat landscapes where we conduct our human endeavors. The current status of educational and social services for persons with severe disabilities is similar to this phenomenon.

Our field has undergone massive reorganization (or even self-organization) since the early 1990s, as evidenced by the work and thinking of the distinguished authors who have contributed to the content of this book. The transformation in our perceptions of persons with severe disabilities is depicted clearly in how these authors have identified "self-determination" as a quality inherent in the dignity of individuals who challenge the system, along with the more inclusive and holistic procedures for achieving dignity in our relationships with them.

Our current best practices represent major departures from previous approaches to the education and treatment of people with severe disabilities, even though vestiges of early procedures are still much evident—especially in the terminology sometimes used to describe these practices. Also, I am still aware of (and appalled by) some existing practices that have not changed since the 1970s—for example, students with severe disabilities spending much of their day in isolated rooms where adults use bits of food to reinforce compliance with such nonfunctional tasks as "stand up" and "touch your nose," view smile rate as evidence of "happiness," and derive individualized education programs (IEPs) from duplicated forms of laboriously reduced, task-analyzed segments of behavior taught out of context, with the IEPs being selected with total disregard for what the individual might want to know or learn. Furthermore, these and similar practices promoted procedures that some current educators (e.g., Kohn, 1993) perceive as resulting in long-term damage both to the development of positive values and to intellectual achievements, especially creativity and the ability to solve problems. In the main, however, these earlier practices have now been abandoned in large part because they were ineffective in producing *substantive* changes in adaptive behavior and development.

We no longer perceive challenging behaviors as deviant expressions from dysfunctional persons or deaf-blindness and other profound disabilities as conditions that require massive intercession from instructional procedures that allow little room for the expression of preference and choices. Compliance training has been replaced by strategies for promoting self-determination. Most people now agree that systematic instruction emanating from diverse theories and approaches should be used to enhance learning, not to control the lives of vulnerable individuals who receive it. Friends, support groups, and case managers replace behavior modifiers, and individuals with disabilities who challenge the system are now acknowledged as having their own agendas in life. We now pursue such concepts and practices as "quality inclusion," "collaborative teaming," "supported living in the community," "natural supports in the workplace," and "participatory instruction in the classroom." The chapters in this book herald these accomplishments, as should the people for whom it was written. Drs. Lehr and Brown and all of the contributors to this project are to be commended for elucidating innovative practices within a genuinely positive philosophy that accentuates our best efforts to extend quality-of-life opportunities to people with significant disabilities who do challenge the system and all of us working in it.

Doug Guess, Ed.D.
Professor, Department of Special Education
Senior Scientist, Schiefelbusch Life Span Institute
University of Kansas

REFERENCES

Kohn, A. (1993). *Punished by rewards.* Boston: Houghton Mifflin.
Kuhn, T.S. (1970). *The structure of scientific revolutions* (2nd ed.). Chicago: University of Chicago Press.

Preface

IN 1989, we co-edited a book entitled *Persons with Profound Disabilities: Issues and Practices* (Paul H. Brookes Publishing Co.). It was our goal in that book to provide a resource for professionals and families who were involved in the lives of individuals with the most profound disabilities. The purpose was to provide readers with information specifically aimed at a population of individuals whose needs we felt were not adequately addressed in the literature. In that book, we included chapters to help the reader more meaningfully apply concepts developed for individuals with less severe disabilities to individuals with more significant disabilities.

There are several reasons why we considered a second book to be necessary. Although the basic guiding principles of the field have not changed (e.g., normalization, quality of life, inclusion), the application and interpretation of these principles have changed. For example, integrating students into regular school buildings is no longer the ideal; we want educational and social inclusion in general education classes. We no longer accept congregate living in the community; we strive for individualized supported living arrangements in the community.

What has not changed, however, is that we continue to see individuals who present significant challenges to the systems designed to serve them. These individuals are often excluded from participating and benefiting from the current models of service delivery. Indeed, they are rarely the targets or beneficiaries of innovative research designed to advance our knowledge base in the area of severe disabilities. What has become apparent to us is that not only have individuals with profound disabilities been omitted from consideration, but so have others with intensive and unique needs.

It was with these issues in mind that we decided this book was needed. Here we focus on those individuals who present the greatest challenges to the system, so we have titled the book *People with Disabilities Who Challenge the System*. It is designed to present the foundations (legal, theoretical, and philosophical) of our current practices for these and other people with severe disabilities as well as to offer illustrations of exemplary practices specific to individuals whom we have observed to present the greatest challenge to our systems: individuals who have profound mental retardation, who are deaf-blind, who demonstrate significant behavioral challenges, or who have special health care needs.

Although contributors to this book provide a variety of perspectives and approaches to support individuals with disabilities who challenge the system, common themes recur across all chapters. First, it is clear that one reason individuals may be considered a challenge to the system is that their needs are complex and there are no simple solutions. The intensity of needs and uniqueness of the individuals preclude the development of standard solutions. The development of individualized systems of support must be the foundation of best practice. One individual may need intensive behavioral consultation and supports to learn to appropriately communicate his or her activity preferences instead of exhibiting self-injury. Another may need support from a specially trained health care aide to provide suctioning as needed in the classroom. Yet another may need a carefully developed and coordinated individualized family service plan (IFSP) to procure supportive services from several agencies.

Second, many authors emphasized that the uniqueness of the individuals requires flexibility in the determination of meaningful outcomes. Outcomes for one individual may include competitive work, independent performance of daily living skills, and independent mobility in the community. Outcomes for another individual may include acceptance within a kindergarten classroom, and for yet another they may include access to community recreation programs.

A third theme that was evident was that educational and habilitative planning is most effective when addressed through the process of team decision making. Team representation should be broad, including sufficient professional expertise and, most important, those most affected by the decisions: the individuals and their families. Because most individuals who challenge the system have concomitant problems with communication, nontraditional methods of communicating must be acknowledged as an individual's way of contributing to the team. Thus, a fourth theme across the chapters is an emphasis on analysis of how the system must accept nonverbal behavior as an indication of preferences and decisions. For example, Hedeen, Ayres, Meyer, and Waite (Chapter 6) describe how one student's school program discovered that some problem behaviors communicated a preference to pack everything from her desk into her backpack to take home at the end of the day. Once this preference was discovered and respected, her support staff simply arranged for her to have a specific folder where papers to go home would be kept throughout the day.

The final theme expressed across chapters is the need for support strategies that are practical, not just possible through demonstration projects or specially funded research projects. Thus, each author felt it critical to describe practices that, although based in theory and research, can be implemented on an ongoing basis within natural settings.

The book is organized into six sections: Young Children Who Challenge the System, Challenges at School, Challenges Within the Community, Challenges at Work, Challenging the System with Self-Determination, and Future Challenges. In turn, each section is then divided into one to four chapters. The first chapter in each section provides an overview of the philosophical and theoretical bases of practices within the topical area. The focus of these chapters is an overview of relevant literature and a summary of current trends and issues in that area. Each of these chapters is then followed by chapters that focus on "practices" relevant to individuals who have profound cognitive disabilities, who are deaf-blind, who have behavioral challenges, or who have complex health care needs. Each of these chapters provides practical approaches to implementation of these current trends and is based upon the authors' vast experiences in supporting individuals who challenge the system.

The first section, Young Children Who Challenge the System, contains two chapters focusing on the youngest members of our communities. In Chapter 1, Lehr and Brinckerhoff provide an overview of many critical issues facing families and professionals as they support young children with the most severe disabilities. In Chapter 2, Thompson, Wickham, Wegner, and Ault provide examples of effective practices for educating young children who have a variety of severe disabilities. The second section, Challenges at School, is made up of four chapters. The first chapter in this section, by Lehr, discusses the challenges that students with special health care needs bring to the system and specific practices that have been successful in addressing these challenges (Chapter 3). Baumgart and Giangreco (Chapter 4), based on their experience including *all* students with disabilities, summarize the critical components of inclusive educational experiences. This is then followed by "practices" chapters. Ferguson, Willis, and Meyer (Chapter 5) focus on practices that have been successful in including students with severe and profound multiple disabilities in school, and Hedeen, Ayres, Meyer, and Waite (Chapter 6) describe school inclusion for students with severe behavioral challenges.

Evolving philosophies and practices related to individuals with disabilities as they move into adulthood are discussed throughout the next two major sections, Challenges Within the Community and Challenges at Work. There are three chapters within each of these sections. Brown and Gothelf (Chapter 7), in their introduction to community living, discuss the continuing development of a philosophy of community life for all individuals who challenge the system, from the days when institutions were the conventional method of care to our current commitment to the development of individualized supports focused on quality of life as the critical outcome. Fredericks (Chapter 8) and Horner and his colleagues (Chapter 9) describe a variety of innovative approaches and practices to supporting individuals with challenging behaviors and who are deaf-blind to live in homes in the community. In the fourth section, Challenges at Work, Butterworth and Kiernan (Chapter 10) provide a comprehensive and historical review of the laws and foundations of employment services and opportunities for individuals with disabilities. This chapter is followed by individual chapters addressing specific challenges and practices related to individuals who are deaf-blind (Goetz, Certo, Doering, & Lee, Chapter 11) and who exhibit challenging behaviors (Hughes & Rusch, Chapter 12). Each of these chapters provides exciting demonstrations of how such individuals can participate in meaningful work experiences in their communities.

The fifth section is Challenging the System with Self-Determination. Although this section does not neatly parallel the earlier format of divisions by setting or age, we felt it was necessary to highlight self-determination to underscore its importance. Brown and Gothelf (Chapter 13) introduce this section by reviewing the concept of self-determination and discussing current educational and behavioral strategies within this framework. Gothelf and Brown (Chapter 14) and Crimmins and Berotti (Chapter 15) continue this topic by applying the concept of self-determination to individuals with challenging behaviors who are deaf-blind. These chapters provide practical strategies and approaches to support individuals in developing skills related to self-determination.

The book concludes by describing future challenges with a chapter by Snell (Chapter 16). Based on current literature and research in the field and the philosophies and practices described within the chapters of this book, Snell shares her insights on where we have been and where we seem to be going.

SUMMARY

This book was designed to provide readers with information that will enable them to understand and meet the challenges that they encounter as individuals with the most severe disabilities enter early intervention, school, community living, and vocational systems. Individuals who have profound cognitive disabilities, who are deaf-blind, who have behavioral challenges, or who have special health care needs are people who often do not receive the best, or even appropriate, programs for their unique needs. It is hoped that readers will gain specific information about meeting the special needs of these individuals, while realizing the possibilities for accomplishing that goal within normalized settings.

In a 1993 issue of *JASH*, Felix Billingsley hauntingly described a nightmare he had. His nightmare was that in the name of inclusion, that which is necessary to meet the unique needs of students who have severe disabilities would be lost and that, ultimately, students with severe disabilities would be identified as being unable to benefit from the existing educational programs. This book was motivated by a similar concern, but one that has been revealed not only in our dreams but also in reality. We too have often talked with professionals trained in the field who said they were so challenged by some individuals that they 1) discussed their uncertainty and confusion about their underlying professional and personal beliefs of support as applied to these individuals, 2) questioned their ability to address the needs of these individuals, and 3) raised the question of the individuals' abilities to benefit from their programs of support. It is hoped that this book provides some information to those professionals that will enable them to more confidently and effectively meet the needs of individuals who challenge the system.

REFERENCE

Billingsley, F. (1993). Reader response: In my dreams: A response to some current trends in education. *Journal of The Association for Persons with Severe Handicaps, 18,* 61–63.

Acknowledgments

WE WISH TO acknowledge the support of our children, Jessica, Geoffrey, Grayson, and Lea, who are terrific about sharing us with our work, and our husbands, Greg and Chris, who always understand. We would also like to acknowledge not only the professional support we have given to each other for so many years but also the personal friendship that also supports our continued work together and the enjoyment of this work together. We are confident that we will continue to find synergism in each other's ideas.

*To the generations of
professionals and advocates
who have taught us that there
is always more that can be done,
and that it can always be
done better.*

People with Disabilities Who Challenge the System

I

YOUNG CHILDREN WHO CHALLENGE THE SYSTEM

1

Bases of Practice for Young Children with Disabilities Who Challenge the System

DONNA H. LEHR

AND JOAN BRINCKERHOFF

A child is born and is immediately diagnosed as having multiple physical anomalies. The hospital staff members suggest that the family not hold the child. They suggest that it would be best if the family locate a pediatric nursing home in which to place the child and that they not bond with the child. They say this will ease the separation. They assure the family that they will be able to assist them in locating a suitable home and that doing so would be the best for the family and the child.

A SCENE FROM the past or from a Third World country? No. It took place in Boston, Massachusetts. Well, in that case, this must have happened years ago. No . . . !!! 1992! 1992? How could that be? Don't we do things differently now? Don't we have support programs for families of newborns with significant disabilities? Don't we provide complete information to families to enable them to decide what to do in times like this?

The most succinct answer to this question of what happens to young children with disabilities is "It depends." The purpose of this chapter is to discuss *on what it* depends—what affects the services that children receive, or don't, and why.

This chapter discusses young children with disabilities who present significant challenges to our medical, educational, and social services systems. More specifically, the chapter addresses the challenges that are faced when there is clear evidence, very early on, that a child faces significant risks to his or her development. Often, such children have multiple physical or sensory anomalies that present themselves before, at, or soon after birth.

This chapter begins with a description of the legislative history of support for early educational and medical intervention for these children. However, a chapter on the bases of practice for young children with disabilities cannot focus exclusively on laws and regulations. Laws themselves do not deliver services; people do. Consequently, this chapter also examines some of the ways that knowledge and attitudes affect the access to and quality of educational and medical services for this population of young children.

PUBLIC POLICY

Federal policy during the past 25 years has resulted in impressive, progressive changes and improvements in this country's educational services for young children with disabilities (Hebbeler, Smith, & Black, 1991). Early legislation was aimed at the development and dissemination of model educational programs, the provision of technical assistance and training, and the creation of incentives for states to provide educational programs to young children with disabilities. These efforts ultimately resulted in a legislative mandate to states to provide educational services for some young children with disabilities and for their families. Other legislation was designed to protect newborns with disabilities from medical discrimination and to ensure access and accommodations for individuals with disabilities. Major legislative milestones are discussed in the following sections.

1968—Handicapped Children's Early Education Act (PL 90-538) HCEEA authorized the establishment of HCEEP to develop model demonstration programs to serve young children with disabilities and also to serve their families. With Congress having recognized the need for services for these children, funded programs were designed to provide models of effective service delivery and to stimulate the development of new local programs.

The Handicapped Children's Early Education Program (HCEEP; part of HCEEA), now known as the Early Education Program for Children with Disabilities (EEPCD), was seen as highly successful and was expanded to include outreach programs that provided technical assistance and training to programs and agencies interested in replicating model services to young children with delays and disabilities and their families. Funding was also appropriated to develop early childhood research institutes to add to the base of knowledge on intervention and education.

Although these programs were considered to be tremendously successful (Hebbeler et al., 1991), most of the model demonstration and research programs have focused on young children with mild and moderate disabilities, not those with the most severe disabilities (Bricker & Kaminski, 1986; Farran, 1990). Consequently, few models have been available to local agencies to guide program developers in meeting the unique needs of children who present greater challenges.

1972—Economic Opportunities Amendments (PL 92-424) The Head Start program was enacted under the Economic Opportunity Act of 1964 (PL 88-452). This program was designed to provide preschool intervention for 3- and 4-year-olds who were considered to be economically disadvantaged. Amendments to the act in 1972 required that at least 10% of the children enrolled in these programs must have disabilities.

Most of the children in Head Start programs identified as meeting the 10% mandate have mild speech and language delays (Wolery, Werts, & Holcombe, 1994). Young children with more severe disabilities had little access to this program. This limitation was recognized by the Senate Appropriations Committee in 1993 when it increased the Head Start budget dramatically to expand the service base. The committee urged the Administration of Children and Families to increase technical assistance to Head Start programs to enable them to better serve this population of children. The impact of this recommendation is not yet known.

1975—The Education for All Handicapped Children Act (PL 94-142) This act authorized the provision of free appropriate public education for children between the ages of 3 and 21 who have special education and related service needs. However, in the original act, states were required to provide services for 3- to 5-year-olds (and 18- to 21-year-olds) only if their state laws required it. PL 94-142 requires that parents be permitted to be involved in their child's program planning, but the focus of the law was intervention directed at children. Included within the law was a preschool incentive grant program that provided some, albeit minimal, funding of services for children between the ages of 3 and 5 who had disabilities and were already being provided with an educational program. By 1986, only 24 states mandated special education programs down to age 3 (Safer & Hamilton, 1993), and programs for infants and toddlers were even more sparse.

Consequently, while a stated priority of PL 94-142 was the education of the unserved population of children, which included many children with severe disabilities, the mandated age range did not result in an assurance that all very young children with severe disabilities would be provided educational services. Whether or not a child received educational services was a function of local initiatives.

1984—Amendments to Child Abuse Prevention and Treatment Act (PL 98-457) The 1984 amendments to the Child Abuse Prevention and Treatment Act of 1974 (PL 92-247) were designed to have an impact on the lives of infants with disabilities. These amendments were intended to end medical discrimination against infants with disabilities. Prior to this act was a period of intense nationwide publicity around several cases in which infants with disabilities were denied surgery that infants without disabling conditions would have been routinely provided (U.S. Commission on Civil Rights, 1989). The act required that all medically indicated treatment be provided and specified that failure to do so would be considered neglect. The exceptions were cases in which any of the following held true:

(i) The infant is chronically and irreversibly comatose;
(ii) The provision of such treatment would merely prolong dying, not be effective in ameliorating or correcting all of the infant's life threatening conditions, or would otherwise be futile in terms of the survival of the infant;
(iii) The provision of such treatment would be virtually futile in terms of the survival of the infant and the treatment itself under such circumstances would be inhumane. (Part 1340, Sec. 1340.15, p. 14888)

Coulter (1991) stated that although there are limitations to the act, "the legacy of the rules is that there is now a presumption in favor of continued treatment in most cases" (p. 556). However, it appears that the vagueness of its language and the weak provisions for enforcement have caused the act to be ignored. According to Coulter (1991), decisions are once again between parents and physicians in delivery rooms, and it is likely that at least some of those decisions do not comply with the act.

1986—Education of the Handicapped Act Amendments (PL 99-457) To offer further incentive to provide services, Congress passed landmark legislation that funded services for all preschoolers (ages 3–5) by 1991 and provided seed money to states to develop a system to support comprehensive, coordinated interagency programs for infants and toddlers. The preschool portion of this legislation required states to extend PL 94-142 downward to children age 3; originally, PL 94-142 encouraged states to serve students under 5 years of age, but did not *require* that they serve these young children.

Recognizing the need for intervention to begin even before the age of 3, and the fact that only six states had mandates for children with disabilities from birth, Congress enacted Part H of the Education of the Handicapped Act to stimulate the development of programs for these children. Part H made a distinction between young children with *established risk* for developing disabilities and those *at risk.* States were required to develop plans to serve children with *established risk,* and each state was to develop its own criteria for developmental delay and to choose whether to serve the *at-risk* population of children. *Established risk* is defined as "a diagnosed physical or mental condition which has a high probability of resulting in developmental delay" (PL 99-457, Sec. 672). Many young children with severe disabilities would logically be considered to have an established risk, including such conditions as chromosomal abnormalities, genetic or congenital disorders, severe sensory impairments, inborn errors of metabolism, disorders reflecting disturbance of the nervous system, congenital infections, and severe attachment disorders. Additional evidence of Congress's interest in young children with significant disabilities can be detected in one of the originally stated purposes of the 1986 statute: to design supports that enable children with significant disabilities to reside with the family, not in an institution.

Part H provides financial assistance to states to support families in keeping an infant or a toddler with disabilities in a natural environment. The new, unique feature of the Part H program is the emphasis on support to families, not just to the child. Instead of the development of individualized education programs (IEPs) focused on the child as required by PL 94-142, individualized family service plans (IFSPs) are developed that focus on the family's priorities, concerns, and needed resources. Part H requires that service needs, outcomes, and strategies be identified and coordinated across providing agencies within the context of a family-directed approach. Specifically, Congress stated that the purpose was to "develop and implement statewide, comprehensive, coordinated, multidisciplinary, interagency program of early intervention services for handicapped infants and toddlers and their families" (PL 99-457, Sec. 671). The stated goals were to "enhance development" and "minimize risk of developmental delay," lessen costs to society by reducing "need for special education and related services," decrease risk of institutionalization and "maximize potential for independent living," and "enhance the capacity of families to meet the special needs of their infants and toddlers" (PL 99-457, Sec. 671).

Part H of PL 99-457, now reauthorized, amended, and included in the Individuals with Disabilities Education Amendments of 1991 (PL 102-119), has been and continues to be difficult to implement and has resulted in uneven implementation (Gerry & McWhorter, 1991). Challenges relate to 1) the establishment of criteria for eligible children, particularly within the "at-risk" category of children, and 2) coordination of services across agencies. At the core of the difficulty is the necessity to coordinate funding streams at the federal, state, and local levels.

All 50 states have elected to participate in the federal program; however, as of 1995, the states are at various points in terms of the required phasing in of the requirements of the law (LRP Publishing Co., 1994). Thirty-nine states have assured full implementation of all requirements of Part H, and 13 states are fully implementing all requirements of the law.

Consequently, whether young children with severe disabilities have a right to services under the law depends on the following: 1) if they are between 3 and 5 and have significant disabilities, they have the right to services regardless of where they live; 2) if they are under the age of 3, their access to service depends on where they live.

In addition to location, another factor affecting the delivery of services is how well an individual service coordinator can perform the coordination functions required under Part H. Children and families facing multiple challenges require a number of services and supports from multiple agencies. The service coordinator must possess not just knowledge of available services and supports for families, but also considerable skill to obtain, create, and coordinate the needed services or supports across agency lines and multiple providers. (A further discussion of the knowledge and skills required is found later in this chapter.)

1990—The Americans with Disabilities Act (PL 101-336) The Americans with Disabilities Act (ADA) has provisions that relate to services for young children with disabilities, despite the fact that most people associate the ADA with employment access. Relevant to young children is the requirement that cities, states, school districts, parks and recreation programs, and other public agencies make their services accessible. Also included are child care centers and family child care. However, the extent of the accommodations that must be made are not yet clear. The wording of the act states that "reasonable" accommodations must be made, but what is considered reasonable will be the focus of legal maneuvering for some time. For example, it is possible for a child care program to exclude a child with a severe disability if inclusion would result in "undue hardship" on the part of the care provider, but it is not yet clear as to what would constitute an "undue hardship."

Summary of Public Policy

The Handicapped Children's Early Education Program (HCEEP), now EEPCD, has provided model demonstration programs for educating young children with disabilities and their families, although few of the models have focused specifically on young children with profound disabilities. Public Law 94-142, now reauthorized as the Individuals with Disabilities Education Act (IDEA), PL 101-476, has not ensured that all children less than 3 years of age in all states would be provided with an education. The requirement that Head Start enrollment include a minimum of 10% children with disabilities did not result in services to all children with severe disabilities. The Child Abuse and Neglect Protection and Treatment Act has included some protection for infants with disabilities. PL 99-457 did assure service to age 3, but below that, services are still spotty, and, at present, Congress has allowed a 2-year extension for states to fully implement all components of Part H of this law. The ADA has the potential to increase educational opportunities provided by public agencies to young children with severe disabilities; however, the law is relatively new and hence untested. However, it is likely that the clause related to reasonable accommodations will be challenged by agencies faced with the delivery of extensive supports often necessary for the youngest children with profound disabilities.

So, even under a strict interpretation of the law, whether a child receives services depends on several factors, discussed in the following section.

PERSONAL INFLUENCES

Many educational and medical practices for young children with disabilities are framed within the current laws and regulations, which set forth general parameters within which people work. People bring to their interactions with young children who have severe disabilities personal influences that can affect how these services will be delivered within those parameters. This section discusses some of these influences. Some additional factors upon which services to these children depend include beliefs about the inherent qualities of young children with severe disabilities, knowledge of the purposes of early intervention, and the experience, knowledge, and skill of care providers charged with responsibility for these young children.

Personal Characteristics

Effective early intervention is provided as a result of a team of individuals working together. Thorp and McCollum (1994) remind us that "*relationships* [italics added] lie at the heart of early intervention service delivery" (p. 175). Thorpe and McCollum point to the critical underlying need for individuals involved in early intervention to demonstrate such personal characteristics as flexibility, maturity, independence, and self-knowledge. Through a process of expert validation, West, Idol, and Cannon (1989) identified a number of personal characteristics considered to be essential for successful collaboration in the delivery of special education services. These include such areas as the "ability to be caring, respectful, empathic, congruent, and open"; the ability to "maintain positive self-concept and [an] enthusiastic attitude"; "willingness to learn from others"; ability to manage stress and maintain calm, flexible, and resilient; and the ability to "respect divergent points of view, acknowledging the right to hold different views and to act in accordance with personal convictions" (pp. 299–300).

These personal traits are the basis of relationships between families and professionals who are working together to provide necessary supports for these young children and their families. Such personal traits as flexibility and commitment produce approaches that create best practices and challenge the field to bridge the gap between best practices and standard practices.

Beliefs Regarding People with Severe Disabilities

Coulter (1991) discussed the ideal world of medical care for people with disabilities. He stated that in that world, the provision of "medical treatment would be provided without any reference to the presence or absence of a severe developmental disability" (p. 553). Treatment would be provided based on three ethical principles: beneficence, autonomy, and justice. The treatment would be in the best interest of the child, decisions regarding treatment would rest with the individual and the family, and resources would be available to provide the treatment (Coulter, 1991). Coulter is describing his ideal world in terms of medical treatment, but the same description can be applied to early or educational interventions.

As Coulter also points out, however, ours is not an ideal world. Answers are not always clear, resources are limited, and the people responsible for developing answers and providing resources have differing points of view about who should provide what medical services to whom. Young children with severe disabilities, because of their complex needs, raise multiple questions that must be answered by parents and professionals, who may have varying points of view.

Obviously, what one thinks about people with severe disabilities can affect both interactions with these individuals and service delivery decisions made for them; an optimistic professional is likely to make different decisions than a pessimistic one (Siperstein, Wolraich, & Reed, 1994). A parent or professional who assumes that a life with a disability is a life not worth living may provide care different from that provided by one who makes no such assumption. One who believes a person with a disability is less than human may act differently toward an individual with a disability than one who believes in the inherent humanness of all people. One who believes that a person with a severe disability is incapable of learning will make different decisions than one who believes the opposite. These perspectives and the ways that they can have an influence are discussed in the following sections. These various perspectives can be in the back or the forefront of individuals' minds as they make decisions about providing medical and educational services and supports for young children with severe disabilities.

A number of very popularized, so-called "Baby Doe" cases have made it clear that, in the medical community, the issue of predicted quality of life of infants with disabilities has had a direct bearing on decisions regarding the provision of care. In Baby Doe cases, infants with disabilities were denied medical treatment that would have been provided to infants who did not have obvious disabilities (U.S. Commission on Civil Rights, 1989). These decisions can be traced to physicians' views about the quality of life of individuals with disabilities. Fost, Chairman of the Committee on Bioethics of the American Academy of Pediatrics, is cited in *Medical Discrimination Against Children with Disabilities* (U.S. Commission on Civil Rights, 1989) as stating the following:

> A profound handicap may be a compelling reason for allowing a patient to die. Ever improving technology makes it possible to keep such patients alive for longer periods. Some live in intensive care units for years or at home at enormous expense. This treatment clearly has medical benefit—it maintains respiratory functions and prevents the complications of respiratory arrest—yet too often seems to serve no interest of the patient, who cannot appreciate any of the joys of living. (p. 32)

This comprehensive study of medical discrimination against infants with disabilities also reveals the following:

> One of the most common justifications given for denying treatment to children with disabilities is that there are circumstances in which it is in the children's best interests to spare them a life of unacceptably poor quality. (U.S. Commission on Civil Rights, 1989, p. 32)

This attitude is not uncommon. Many professionals involved with children with severe disabilities have listened to stories from parents about the difficulty that they have had persuading their child's physicians to provide treatments that the parents thought would enhance their child's life. Parents have been told, directly or indirectly, "What difference would it make if Barry could see better with glasses? He can't understand what he sees anyway." "Why bother continuing to work on oral motor development? The tube feeding is going fine." The family's interpretation was that the physician's actions were based on a presumption that the child was so disabled that the treatment would make no difference or that the extra expenditures would not be worthwhile or cost-effective.

The case of *Timothy W. v. Rochester, New Hampshire, School District* (1989) points to the "why bother" question as related to the issue of the provision of education to students with severe disabilities. Despite the fact that PL 94-142 is permeated with the language "*all* handicapped children" [italics added], Timothy's school district administrators contended that Timothy was so severely mentally retarded that he was not able to benefit from an education and was therefore not entitled to one. The case, which was heard before the First Circuit Court of Appeals, was decided in favor of Timothy. The judge determined that the law was unequivocal on the matter of *all,* that Congress's intent was that *all* students with disabilities were entitled to a free appropriate public education, not just certain students.

Although the ruling established a precedent regarding exclusion of students, it is likely that there will continue to be questions, either public or private, about the education of young children with severe disabilities. How often is extra effort not given to the development of a communication system for a young child, based on the assumption that the youngster is too mentally retarded to communicate anything? Or how often do parents and professionals get frustrated due to lack of observable progress on the part of the child and so reduce their efforts?

Some observers question the appropriateness of using precious resources on these children when perhaps greater gains could be realized by investing in children with lesser disabilities or even gifted children. Some have questioned the mandatory requirement in PL 99-457 to serve those with established risk and the permissive option to serve those at risk.

Guess et al. (1984) discussed the utilitarian theorists as supporting practices of euthanasia and infanticide on the basis of "society's interests and well-being preced[ing] those of the individual" (p. 9). The utilitarian theorists recognize the high fiscal and emotional costs associated with providing care to children with significant disabilities and the limited likely return on the investment. On this basis, they question the appropriateness of such expenditures.

Baer (1986), who supports education of all children, regardless of their level of mental retardation, discusses the point of view of those who believe "A dollar spent on them [students with severe disabilities] is a dollar not spent on me" (p. 159).

Shaw (1977, 1988) proposed the use of the formula QOL = NE × (H + S) to determine an individual's quality of life. In this formula, quality of life (QOL) was based on the child's natural endowment (NE) multiplied by the support that can be provided by the home (H) and society (S). The formula has been used to help determine which children born with disabilities should receive medical treatment (Gross, Cox, Tatyrek, Pollay, & Barnes, 1983).

Will It Benefit the Common Good? Some see the value of intervention as not necessarily for the individual with severe disabilities but rather for the benefit of the common good. Although institutional review boards have worked to prevent the misuse of these individuals as subjects for purposes of experimentation, newborns continue to be vulnerable. Some professionals see premature, extremely low-birth-weight newborns as providing an opportunity to test the limits of neonatal technology (Kolata, 1991).

Baer (1986) points to the benefit for others in teaching those who are the most difficult to teach, discussing what we can learn about learning in general from students for whom learning is difficult. He contrasts this with typical learners who "too often . . . cheat us of the opportunity to learn completely how the trick is done, because they do some of it for us, and they do it privately" (p. 154).

We Must Provide Services Veatch (1986) writes that justice for individuals with profound disabilities is served when they are given priority, not just equal access. He believes that the same priority must be given to infants—persons who have not yet had the benefits of living their lives. Thus, he believes that infants with profound disabilities should receive our greatest attention.

Sanctity of life is the belief that the value of a life should not be relative to the quality others perceive in that life or in the potential contribution of the individual. Proponents of medical services for individuals with disabilities will point to this perspective as a rationale in support of the provision of medical treatments for infants with profound congenital anomalies. Guess et al. (1984) argue that the quality of life for all individuals, those with and without disabilities, is affected by society's decisions regarding the sanctity of life of individuals with disabilities.

The rationale, duration, and intensity of commitment to young children with severe disabilities varies among parents and professionals. Brown (1991) describes differences in commitment to these children in the following manner:

Some come—sell their kits—make their money—leave.
Some come—tire—find something less demanding.
Some come—lose interest—try something else.

Some come—have no agenda—won't step aside.
Some come—take a break—return to fight again.
Some come—want to stay—but are taken.
Some come—fight—realize they can never leave—keep going.
(p. xxv)

Some observers do believe that we have to do all we can. Why? For reasons that have not been systematically studied, some "come—fight—realize they can never leave" and "keep going." They believe that *we have to do whatever we can to care for and educate young children with the most severe disabilities.*

That decision makers may well hold differing points of view on this issue is disturbing. If a physician in a delivery room thinks that the life of an infant born with disabilities is less valuable than that of a child with no evident disability, the infant may be denied access to medical treatment, despite the law. If a physician wants to try a new intervention, he or she may well do so—what is there to lose? If a teacher or administrator believes a child cannot learn, that student may attend school, but the instructional effort may not be sufficient for meaningful educational experiences and outcomes. A teacher with limited time and a large group of students in his or her class may decide that the available time would be most effectively used with those students who are likely to make the greatest gains. However, the teacher or physician who believes that it is these students who need their greatest efforts is likely to "fight—realize they can never leave [and] keep going" (Brown, 1991, p. xxv).

Beliefs About the Purposes and Processes of Early Intervention

Individuals involved with young children with severe disabilities bring to their interactions differing knowledge or beliefs about the purposes and processes of early intervention. These beliefs can affect the nature of the services delivered. This section discusses some of the differing ways that early intervention is viewed and some of the resulting implications.

Early Intervention as Early Interference Consider the following comments. "School for babies? But what can you teach a baby? Babies should be in a warm nurturing environment, with their families, not poked at, prodded, 'taught.' They should be loved and left alone to develop." Early intervention can be, as Cooper (1989) calls it, "early interference" (p. 34). Professionals who share this belief may not adequately inform parents of services and supports. Parents who have this view are not likely to avail themselves of services for which they are eligible.

A parent of a newborn with Down syndrome dropped by the office of one of the authors several years ago. The individual was a university employee from another part of campus who was directed to the Department of Special Education. After he paced back and forth outside the office door several times, he poked his head in and said, "Someone told me you know something about Down syndrome." He continued, "I just had a baby, and he has Down syndrome. My first son. We have three girls." He went on to ask what Down syndrome was and what his son would look like when he got older.

The author wondered why these questions had not yet been answered for the family. Why hadn't the medical staff counseled this man and his wife?

The father continued: "You know, we just had him 3 weeks ago, and all my wife is doing is taking him for this test and that test." Immediately suspecting medical complications, the author asked about the tests. The father indicated that the physicians said that except for the Down syndrome, his son was healthy. He said they just wanted to study him. When asked about support through early intervention, he said yes, he and his wife were given names and addresses, but right now, "We just want to be left alone. We just want to love him."

These parents, expecting to have a "normal" baby like their three others, were not prepared for the swirl of activity that accompanied the birth of their newest child. They were not prepared to share their time with so many strangers. They were not prepared for so much exposure to doctors' offices, to hospitals, and to so many professionals. They elected, at least for the time being, to not participate in early intervention services.

Early Intervention as a Cure   Since the frequently stated goals of early intervention are to prevent or ameliorate disabilities, we wonder what effect the image of "fixing" has on services for young children with established disabilities for which prevention is too late and cures are not available. Physicians are trained to find a cure for their patients. How does knowing that a cure for the established disability is not available affect the services that they do deliver?

Teachers, while not aiming for "cures," do try to make their students independent. Teachers who do not see independence as even a long-range option for students with profound disabilities are sometimes left confused about what the direction of their educational efforts should be (Brown & Lehr, 1989, 1993). What can teachers select as important instructional goals? Although some attention is paid in the literature to outcome measures that are appropriate for individuals with profound disabilities (Evans & Scotti, 1989), no clear indicators have been established, and practitioners remain uncertain of standards to guide their decisions.

Even if there were clear goals for young children with profound disabilities, there would remain uncertainty about methods for attaining those goals; interventions successful for some students may not work for others. What impact do uncertainty and very difficult challenges have on the services that the children receive? What happens to teachers who use what has worked for other students, then try other approaches, and still find little success? Do they keep trying, or do their efforts subside? Does attention shift to other students for whom greater progress can be seen? We must provide information and support to teachers of young children with profound disabilities to ensure that these teachers are able to see and be encouraged by progress toward the unique outcomes identified for each child.

Teaching Babies or Supporting Families The brief history of early intervention has shown considerable change in the focus of efforts and the corresponding roles and responsibilities of those persons involved in such efforts (Johnson, 1994). What was initially a focus on education of the *child* by individual professionals from various disciplines has become a preference for support of the *family* through collaboration across many disciplines (Beckman, Robinson, Rosenberg, & Filer, 1994). These changes can be seen in Table 1. Although these changes were legislated for children age birth to 3 years of age, there are always gaps between recommended (or even legislated) best practices and implemented standard practices.

Differences in beliefs regarding the focus and roles of early intervention efforts can also result in considerable variation in the nature of the services received. Consider the likely differences in the nature of services for young children with severe disabilities provided by people with the following possible views:

- Early interventionist as direct service provider to child—The primary role of the teacher or therapist is to teach the child or provide direct therapy to the child.
- Early interventionist as teacher of parent—The primary role of teacher or therapist is to teach the parent to implement recommended interventions.
- Early interventionist as expert—The teacher or therapist's role is to transmit expert knowledge to the parent.

Table 1. Changes in orientation of early intervention services

Early efforts	Current trends
Teach child or teach parent to teach child	Support family
Unidisciplinary approach	Transdisciplinary approach
Professional as expert	Professional as collaborator
Specialized services	Natural supports and resources within the community

- Early interventionist as collaborator—The teacher or therapist's role is that of collaborator with family members and other professionals.
- Parent as recipient of information—The primary role of the parent is to receive knowledge from experts.
- Parent as trainee—The primary role of the parent is that of a student who is to be taught how to provide recommended interventions to his or her child.
- Parent as expert on his or her own child—The parent is seen as possessing expert knowledge about his or her own child and being a significant contributor to the child's development.
- Parent as collaborator—The parent is seen as a partner in the process of early intervention for the child.

There is also the problem of differences of opinion regarding the roles and responsibilities of individuals involved with the same child. What if parents and teachers both view themselves as *the* experts? What if the teachers view themselves as instructors of the parents and the parents see *themselves* as the experts? Recognizing these various perspectives and making the correct, collaborative adjustments are critical to the success of early intervention programs.

Knowledge Base

Parents and professionals must not only deal with their beliefs about the purposes or efficacy of early intervention for young children with profound disabilities, but they must also have considerable knowledge and skills to produce the desired outcomes. As Campbell (1990) points out, modern approaches to early intervention require new roles for personnel involved in early intervention. The focus is on not just children, as it had been in the past, but more on families. The focus is on working not just with professionals within one agency but on working across different agencies, all of which are providing services and supports to the family. All community supports and resources must be employed, not just formal services. Early interventionists are expected to be service coordinators who are responsible for coordinating, with the family, the provision of services and supports across agencies. This more modern approach to service coordination is not one that has been traditionally performed by early interventionists.

No single definitive list of necessary competencies for an early interventionist for children with severe disabilities exists, although several have been attempted by professional organizations and experts in the field of early intervention (Bruder & Nikitas, 1992; DEC Task Force on Recommended Practices, 1993). Frequently, the following areas of knowledge and skill are recommended:

- Assessment materials and procedures, both child- and family-centered
- Principles of family-centered practice
- Development of IFSPs
- Access to services and supports
- Methods of goal or outcome setting
- Instructional and intervention strategies
- Health and medical issues
- Models and methods of collaboration within and across programs, agencies, and community resources
- Models for service coordination

The nature or quality of support that a child receives is still a function, at least in part, of the knowledge base of the team members. The delivery of supports and services to young children with multiple challenges is not well established; it does not have an extensive database of best or standard practices, and colleges and universities specializing in training professionals in this area are not plentiful. Early intervention professionals may or may not have the necessary knowledge to reach the specific goals of early intervention, particularly for young children with the most severe disabilities; much continues to be unknown regarding the best strategies to help these children (Wolery, 1991). Once again, effective service delivery depends on the individuals delivering it.

SUMMARY

While legislative supports have been provided for early intervention for young children with disabilities, young children with the most severe disabilities may still not receive the services and supports that they need. What supports they do receive can be a function of where they live and the service delivery models used, and the personal characteristics and orientation of the individuals in a position to provide children and families with critical supports or to refer them to the proper agencies. Although variability in supports is desirable, the variability must be based on the individual needs and strengths of the children and their families, not on external factors beyond these families' control.

REFERENCES

Amendments to Child Abuse Prevention and Treatment Act of 1984, PL 98-457, Title 42, U.S.C. 5101.
Americans with Disabilities Act of 1990 (ADA), PL 101-336. (July 26, 1990). Title 42, U.S.C. 12101 et seq: *U.S. Statutes at Large, 104,* 327–378.

Baer, D.M. (1986). The issue of educability. In P.R. Dokecki & R.M. Zaner (Eds.), *Ethics of dealing with persons with severe handicaps* (pp. 147–160). Baltimore: Paul H. Brookes Publishing Co.

Beckman, P.J., Robinson, C.C., Rosenberg, S., & Filer, J. (1994). Family involvement in early intervention: The evolution of family centered service. In L. Johnson, R.J. Gallagher, M.J. LaMontagne, J.B. Jordan, P.L. Hutinger, J.J. Gallagher, & M.B. Karnes (Eds.), *Meeting early intervention challenges* (pp. 13–32). Baltimore: Paul H. Brookes Publishing Co.

Bricker, D., & Kaminski, R. (1986). Intervention programs for severely handicapped infants and children. In L. Blickman & D.L. Weatherford (Eds.), *Evaluating early intervention programs for severely handicapped children and their families* (pp. 51–78). Austin, TX: PRO-ED.

Brown, F., & Lehr, D.H. (Eds.). (1989). *Persons with profound disabilities: Issues and practices.* Baltimore: Paul H. Brookes Publishing Co.

Brown, F., & Lehr, D.H. (1993). Meaningful outcomes for individuals with profound disabilities. *Teaching Exceptional Children, 25*(4), 12–17.

Brown, L. (1991). Who are they and what do they want: An essay on TASH. In L.H. Meyer, C.A. Peck, & L. Brown (Eds.), *Critical issues in the lives of people with severe disabilities* (pp. xxv–xxvii). Baltimore: Paul H. Brookes Publishing Co.

Bruder, M.B., & Nikitas, T. (1992). Changing the professional practice of early interventionists: An inservice model to meet the service needs of Public Law 99-457. *Journal of Early Intervention, 16*(2), 173–180.

Campbell, P.H. (1990). Meeting personnel needs in early intervention. In A.P. Kaiser & C.M. McWhorter (Eds.), *Preparing personnel to work with persons with severe disabilities* (pp. 111–134). Baltimore: Paul H. Brookes Publishing Co.

Child Abuse and Neglect Protection and Treatment Act of 1974, PL 92-247. Title 42, U.S.C. 5101.

Cooper, M.L. (1989). Early interference. *Exceptional Parent, 15,* 34–37.

Coulter, D.L. (1991). Medical treatment. In L.H. Meyer, C.A. Peck, & L. Brown (Eds.), *Critical issues in the lives of people with severe disabilities* (pp. 553–558). Baltimore: Paul H. Brookes Publishing Co.

DEC Task Force on Recommended Practices. (1993). *DEC recommended practices: Indicators of quality in programs for infants and young children with special needs and their families.* Reston, VA: Council for Exceptional Children.

Economic Opportunity Act of 1964, PL 88-452. (August 20, 1964). Title 42, U.S.C. 2701 et seq: *U.S. Statutes at Large, 78,* 508–534.

Economic Opportunity Amendments of 1972, PL 92-424. (September 19, 1972). Title II, U.S.C. 688 et seq: *U.S. Statutes at Large, 86,* 688–705.

Education for All Handicapped Children Act of 1975, PL 94-142. (August 23, 1977). Title 20, U.S.C. 1400 et seq: *U.S. Statutes at Large, 89,* 773–796.

Education of the Handicapped Act Amendments of 1986, PL 99-457. (October 8, 1986). Title 20, U.S.C. 1400 et seq: *U.S. Statutes at Large, 100,* 1145–1177.

Evans, I.M., & Scotti, J.R. (1989). Defining meaningful outcomes for persons with profound disabilities. In F. Brown & D.H. Lehr (Eds.), *Persons with profound disabilities: Issues and practices* (pp. 83–107). Baltimore: Paul H. Brookes Publishing Co.

Farran, D.C. (1990). Effects of intervention with disadvantaged and disabled children: A decade review. In S.J. Meisels & J.P. Shonkoff (Eds.), *Handbook of early childhood intervention* (pp. 501–539). Cambridge, England: Cambridge University Press.

Gerry, M.H., & McWhorter, C.M. (1991). A comprehensive analysis of federal statutes and programs for persons with severe disabilities. In L.H. Meyer, C.A. Peck, & L. Brown (Eds.), *Critical issues in the lives of people with severe disabilities* (pp. 495–525). Baltimore: Paul H. Brookes Publishing Co.

Gross, R.H., Cox, A., Tatyrek, R., Pollay, M., & Barnes, W.A. (1983). Early management and decision making for treatment of myelomeningocele. *Pediatrics, 161,* 629–635.

Guess, D., Dussault, B., Brown, F., Mulligan, M., Orelove, F., Comegys, A., & Rues, J. (1984). *Legal, economic, psychological, and moral considerations on the practice of withholding medical treatment from infants with congenital defects.* Seattle: The Association for Persons with Severe Disabilities.

Handicapped Children's Early Education Act (HCEEA), PL 90-538. (September 30, 1968). Title 20, U.S.C. 621 et seq: *U.S. Statutes at Large, 82,* 901–902.

Hebbeler, K.M., Smith, B.J., & Black, T.L. (1991). Federal early childhood special education policy: A model for the improvement of services for children with disabilities. *Exceptional Children, 58*(2), 104–112.

Individuals with Disabilities Education Act of 1990, PL 101-476. (October 30, 1990). Title 20, U.S.C. 1400 *et seq: U.S. Statutes at Large, 104* (Part 2), 1103–1151.

Individuals with Disabilities Education Act Amendments of 1991, PL 102-119. (October 7, 1991). Title 20, U.S.C. 1400 et seq: *U.S. Statutes at Large, 105,* 587–608.

Johnson, L.J. (1994). Challenges facing early intervention: An overview. In L. Johnson, R.J. Gallagher, M.J. LaMontagne, J.B. Jordan, P.L. Hutinger, J.J. Gallagher, & M.B. Karnes (Eds.), *Meeting early intervention challenges* (pp. 1–12). Baltimore: Paul H. Brookes Publishing Co.

Kolata, G. (1991, September 20). Parents of tiny infants find care choices not theirs. *The New York Times,* p. 1.

LRP Publishing Co. (1994). *Early Childhood Report, 5*(10), 1–15.

Safer, N.D., & Hamilton, J.L. (1993). Legislative content for early intervention services. In W. Brown, S.K. Thurman, & L.F. Pearl (Eds.), *Family centered early intervention with infants and toddlers: Innovative cross-disciplinary approaches.* Baltimore: Paul H. Brookes Publishing Co.

Shaw, A. (1977). Defining the quality of life: A formula without numbers. *Hastings Center Report, 7*(5), 11.

Shaw, A. (1988). QOL revisited. *Hastings Center Report, 18,* 10–12.

Siperstein, G.N., Wolraich, M.L., & Reed, D. (1994). Professionals' prognoses for individuals with mental retardation: Search for consensus within interdisciplinary settings. *American Journal on Mental Retardation, 98*(4), 519–526.

Thorp, E.K., & McCollum, J.A. (1994). Defining the infancy specialization in early childhood special education. In L. Johnson, R.J. Gallagher, M.J. LaMontagne, J.B. Jordan, P.L. Hutinger, J.J. Gallagher, & M.B. Karnes (Eds.), *Meeting early intervention challenges* (pp. 167–184). Baltimore: Paul H. Brookes Publishing Co.

Timothy W. v. Rochester, New Hampshire, School District. 875 F.2d 954 (1st Cir. 1989).

U.S. Commission on Civil Rights. (1989). *Medical discrimination against children with disabilities.* Washington, DC: Author.

Veatch, R.M. (1986). Persons with severe mental retardation and the limits of guardian decision making. In P.R. Dokecki & R.M. Zaner (Eds.), *Ethics of dealing with persons with severe handicaps* (pp. 239–256). Baltimore: Paul H. Brookes Publishing Co.

West, J.F., Idol, L., & Cannon, G. (1989). *Collaboration in the schools.* Austin, TX: PRO-ED.

Wolery, M. (1991). Instruction in early childhood special education: "Seeing through a glass darkly . . . Knowing in part." *Exceptional Children, 58*(2), 127–135.

Wolery, M., Werts, M.G., & Holcombe, A. (1994). Current practices with young children who have disabilities: Placement, assessment, and instruction issues. *Focus on Exceptional Children, 26*(6), 1–12.

2

All Children Should Know Joy

Inclusive, Family-Centered Services for Young Children with Significant Disabilities

BARBARA THOMPSON, DONNA WICKHAM,
JANE WEGNER, AND MARILYN AULT

OUR EXPERIENCES with the Circle of Inclusion Project (CIP) at the University of Kansas have contributed to our interpretations of the issues facing families with infants, toddlers, and preschoolers who are just beginning to learn about the formidable barriers of an enormous and complex system. We do not really believe we are writing about "children who challenge the system." Instead we believe that we are writing about little children and their families who are challenged by the system—a system that is frequently unresponsive, often demeaning, sometimes rejecting, and occasionally cruel.

This chapter includes stories about children, results based on systematic data collection, and programmatic outcomes as well as reflections about our shared experiences over a 10-year period. All that we have to share is supported by rich empirical and theoretical literature about developmentally appropriate early childhood practices, effective early childhood special education practices, integration of children with and without disabilities, the roles of families in early childhood services, the value of the collaborative process, and issues of system change. This knowledge has now become "our knowledge" in the sense that it has evolved over time as a result of direct engagement with children, families, personnel, and programs in restructuring inclusive early childhood services for young children with significant disabilities and their families. Theories, principles, and practices acquired their meaning through genuine experience and prolonged engagement with the process we sought to understand.

In keeping with other discussions of CIP (Thompson, Wickham, Ault et al., 1991; Thompson et al., 1993), the first section of this chapter, *Children and Their Families: Stories of Our Pathfinders,* describes some of the children and families we have known through our work. The next section, *Our Work and Our Values,* provides an overview of the values, history, and activities of CIP. *Our Knowledge about Knowledge: A Summary of Results and Outcomes,* summarizes our strategies for understanding the process with which we have been associated and blends program outcomes, results of studies, and our experiences into thematic topics. The last section, *Final Comments and Recommendations: Features of an Exemplary Program,* offers a brief overview of the elements that we believe emerged as important for early childhood services for young children who "challenge the system."

CHILDREN AND THEIR FAMILIES: STORIES OF OUR PATHFINDERS

We are including stories of the children we have worked with and their families, because it was these children and their families' stories that taught us the most. With much difficulty we selected three children, Dana, Ashley, and Sheronda to illustrate important aspects of our experience.

Dana: The First Child

At the time of this writing, Dana is a sixth grader in an elementary school in Lawrence, Kansas. We met Dana, the first child in the program that was to evolve into CIP, when she was 3 years old. Dana is a beauty with enormous brown eyes, thick dark hair, olive skin, and a warm smile that speaks directly to the heart. She has multiple disabilities including mental retardation, spastic quadriplegia with very limited head control, and no ability to walk, sit unsupported, or speak. The quality of her vision is not known. These remarks reflect our earliest memories of Dana:

> When I met Dana she was three years old. She was lying on a mat in an overcrowded day room of an institution surrounded by people of all ages (mostly adults) with profound disabilities. The room was crowded and filled with the sounds and smells that occur when persons with profound mental retardation, significant physical disabilities, and serious medical

conditions are crowded together in a sterile, under-staffed, hospital-like environment in a state institution. The only speaking voices came from a large TV bolted to the wall about eight feet above the floor. (Thompson, Wickham, Ault, et al., 1991, p. 12)

Shortly after my visit I found myself thinking about my three year old granddaughter, Chelsea, and about the marked differences in Dana's and Chelsea's daily life experiences. A quotation which has been attributed to Nicholas Hobbs came to my mind. "All children should know joy." From where was Dana's opportunity to know joy to come? (Thompson, 1994, p. 3)

Within several months, Dana was welcomed into a wonderful foster family in the Lawrence, Kansas, community. Consequently, in the fall of 1986, we were looking for a community-based early childhood program whose staff would be willing to accept Dana. Initially there was no space in a special education preschool classroom, nor did the program accept children with severe multiple disabilities. Her foster parents believed (as did we) that it was important for Dana to have opportunities to be around other children and to be involved in preschool activities away from her foster home for a portion of the day.

We decided to contact one of the most respected programs in the community, Raintree Montessori School, a program that always has a long waiting list of children whose families are seeking early childhood education and child care. When we called Raintree, we began with a description of Dana. We also explained that a university student interested in the integration of preschoolers with disabilities would be available to assist Dana's Montessori teacher in meeting Dana's special needs and to enhance the adult-to-child ratio while Dana was in the classroom.

I was half expecting to be turned down and certainly assumed that I needed to do a real "sales" job on why the Raintree staff might want to consider accepting a child like Dana. As long as I live, I will never forget Pam Shanks' answer, "Lleanna McReynolds, our Program Director, and I are so excited you thought of us! We would love to have Dana. When would you like her to start?"

Just a few months later when I first saw Dana in Raintree Montessori School, her presence in this children's house was in such marked contrast with my memory of Dana in the institution that it evoked one of the most emotional experiences of my life. Dana looked valued, respected, and at home surrounded by other preschoolers who accepted her as one of them—which, of course, she was. (Thompson et al., 1993, p. 13)

Ashley: The "Dignity of Risk"

Ashley is a 6-year-old kindergartner. She is large for her age and quite striking. She wears her curly black hair in a braid pulled to the side with a bright ribbon. Her face is round and pretty with dark eyes and long lashes that accentuate her soft brown skin. We first knew her as a 2-year-old who had just suffered a spinal cord injury in a car accident in which she was a passenger without a seat belt. After months in a pediatric intensive care unit in which she was termed a "miracle child" for surviving such a significant injury, she returned home with full paralysis beginning at the first cervical vertebrae, a permanent tracheostomy, a respirator for assisted breathing, and a button gastrostomy.

Initially Ashley received home services from an early intervention program in which therapists and an early childhood special education teacher worked directly with Ashley, her mother, and a nurse. During her third year, Ashley's mother expressed a strong interest in having her attend preschool with other children. During the next 2 school years, she was placed in an excellent preschool located in an elementary public school building funded through Elementary and Secondary Education Act (ESEA), Chapter 1. She also attended a private Montessori preschool during the intervening summer. Ashley began by spending less than a full session for a few days a week. Within the first year, her attendance was increased to the full daily session for all 5 days per week.

Ashley brought with her the challenges of a medically complex condition and very significant physical disabilities. Fears about caring for Ashley were common across special education and general early childhood staff. Concerns were related to her breathing, suctioning procedures, and management of the range of physical problems associated with her condition. What was *not* a challenge was finding understanding peers who welcomed her into the classroom and, with some adult guidance, made the accommodations in their play needed to include her in activities.

We became used to pointing out that if Ashley was too fragile to be in an inclusive preschool classroom, she was too fragile to be in a special education classroom. Because there were risks for Ashley associated with her participation in a preschool program, some medical personnel had recommended she remain at home with 24-hour nursing care. Her mother's decision to involve her in an inclusive early childhood program was based on a commitment for Ashley to be an active participant in life. Ashley's participation taught the involved staff (teachers, therapists, paraprofessionals, and nurses) much about revising traditional beliefs about roles and responsibilities as well as about establishing consistent, reliable medical and emergency procedures within the context of a preschool classroom. Most important, it once again reminded those around Ashley of the importance of her right to be a child and to know joy.

Sheronda: From Medical Center to Kindergarten

Sheronda is currently doing well in a multi-age inclusive classroom for 5-, 6-, and 7-year-old children in an elementary building. She has a number of friends, several best friends, and a very best friend, Matt. While she still challenges her teachers to provide positive behavior supports, Sheronda is starting to talk quite a lot and is learning to read and write. When we first met Sheronda, she was a cute 3-year-old who participated in a self-contained special education preschool for children with autism that was housed within a university medical center. There were four children in the classroom, which was staffed by a teacher and two assistants.

Sheronda was nonverbal and had a number of challenging behaviors. One of her most problematic behaviors was running away. She was easily provoked into major tantrums when asked to comply or when a change occurred in a routine or in the environment. Sheronda sometimes attacked the other children by biting and slapping without obvious provocation.

During her second year in preschool, when Sheronda was 4, her program was moved from the medical center. She and her three classmates were placed in different inclusive preschool programs, and their teacher supported the teachers in these programs. Special education and related services were offered on a collaborative/consultative basis, and an additional paraprofessional with specialized training was added to each of the classrooms the children attended. The program in which Sheronda was placed offered full-day child care, which met important needs for her working mother and father. Despite these facts, there was considerable concern about her placement in this preschool classroom of 18 children. Her very challenging behavior and quick exits from home and classroom were viewed as major threats to a successful outcome.

The initial period of adjustment to this program was a stressful time for Courtney, Sheronda's early childhood special education teacher. It was a difficult transition from being the lead teacher with four beautiful children in her own classroom within a prestigious medical center to serving as an itinerant and collaborative teacher with four different early childhood teachers in community-based early childhood classrooms. Courtney likes to recall an early transformational experience when she entered Sheronda's classroom and was unable to find her. Courtney remembers her feeling of utter panic in her certainty that Sheronda had escaped the confines of the classroom and was wandering around the center or the urban neighborhood. She approached the classroom teacher, who calmly pointed to small group of children building with blocks. Courtney looked intently at the children and suddenly realized that Sheronda was one of them:

> It astounded me, because she blended into the group so well. It wasn't really that she was cooperatively involved with the children, but she was engaged and very near the children. She looked just like one of them. My eyes filled with tears until, once again, I couldn't see her. (C. Erickson, personal communication, October 12, 1992)

Sheronda needed a summer school placement for all 3 months, something that the program she had been attending did not offer. Consequently, in the summer before her fifth birthday, she moved to an all-day child care program in a private Montessori preschool. The same special education supports and services that were available in the previous school were made available to Sheronda in this program. Sheronda continued to progress and adjusted very well to the child-initiated work routine that was part of the program's method. It was during this time that she first spoke. Excited to hear about the details of this important event, we eagerly asked for the story:

> [What did she say? Who did she talk to? What was going on when she talked?]
> "Move, please [to a peer who was a little too close to her materials]."
> (J. Keating, personal communication, April 10, 1993)

Sheronda's mother was and remains closely involved with each of Sheronda's experiences and programs. Her mother faithfully attended biweekly and then monthly core team meetings on her day off from work in order to communicate with Sheronda's preschool staff and special education teacher. She visited the elementary school that Sheronda would attend and met with the principal and the multi-age classroom teacher in the spring before Sheronda's entry into primary education. Sheronda's mother is an involved parent in the school. She knows what she wants for her daughter and is comfortable planning and working with professionals as an equal member of a team.

Insights from the Stories

Many more stories could be related like these about Dana, Ashley, and Sheronda, stories that portray the powerful transformational moment that can occur upon first seeing a child with significant disabilities within an accepting inclusive setting. This is a moment when our assumptions about a child are unexpectedly suspended as we see them through a different frame of reference. The "Aha!" moment occurs when a shift in paradigms becomes possible (Covey, 1989; Kuhn, 1970) and one truly understands what it means to see a child with significant disabilities as a child with the same rights and needs for a joyful childhood as all children.

These stories offer evidence of what the participating adults have noted consistently: Young children do not view or respond to the presence of a person with disability as adults do. The stories offer powerful confirmation of the belief that early childhood is the most opportune time to begin breaking down the societal barriers and discrimination that confront those with disabilities and their families.

Our observations, however, do not suggest that the typically developing children are unaware of the differences presented by their friends with significant disabilities. Their countless questions related to disabling conditions of their classmates show that they are aware. Comments such as these offer evidence of their interest in and need to understand the differences they recognize in their peers: "I never knew a 5-year-old who wore diapers before," "I never knew a 5-year-old who couldn't walk on the bottom of the pool," "Why can't he say it with his mouth?" (i.e., talk), and "Why does he spit all the time?" (i.e., drool) (Thompson, Wickham, & Wegner, 1991).

Children's questions about their classmates with disabilities do not, however, reflect value judgments about individual worth, signal rejection, or suggest a questioning of a classmate's right to be part of the same setting (Shanks, 1990). It is common to hear a child repeat the content of an adult's response to explain something about the child with a disability to another classroom peer or to a new adult in the setting. A child may repeat this information even if he or she did not ask the question, but was present and listening when it was first answered. The role of informant, interpreter, and facilitator for a child with a disability is often naturally assumed by his or her typically developing friends who are 3–5 years of age. A child who has never asked a single question, but who has watched a classmate who experiences a disability with interest and openness, may offer an explanation like this:

> Jacob can't talk because his muscles don't work very well, but he knows all about the sound cylinders. He can't shake them . . . he nods his head if they are the same. He knows all about them.

OUR WORK AND OUR VALUES

As noted in the introductory section of this chapter, CIP has been directed toward the inclusion of young children with the most severe disabilities into a variety of early childhood programs that predominantly serve typically developing children. CIP has focused on initiating and implementing inclusive early childhood program services and on investigating and documenting important features of those services. The implementation of inclusive early childhood services has involved 1) starting the process, 2) preparing and then providing ongoing support for families and personnel, 3) accommodating the often intensive and individualized needs of children and families, and 4) providing ongoing facilitation of the social and instructional inclusion of children. This section describes CIP in greater detail.

A Value-Based Approach for Program Strategies

The strategies employed by CIP are grounded on an understanding and application of a milieu and naturalistic approach to meeting the needs of young children by embedding instruction and therapeutic services into existing activities and routines of the natural setting (e.g., home, child care center/preschool) (Bailey & McWilliam, 1990; Bricker & Cripe, 1992; Guess et al., 1978; Kaiser, Hendrickson, & Albert, 1991; Noonan & McCormick, 1993). In addition, attention has been directed to procedures that result in the meaningful inclusion of the children and their families. For example, strategies and variables have been investigated that support sustained positive reciprocal social interactions (friendships) among children and productive relationships among the families and personnel who are brought together within the context of these programs. Early in our work together, a value base was articulated in the form of seven value statements that guided CIP procedures and activities (see Table 1).

Emergence of the Circle of Inclusion Project

By 1992, 20 children with disabilities, two special education preschools, and four community early childhood programs had participated in CIP. The first 20 children to participate in CIP activities and investigations are described in Table 2, which provides information about these children at the time of their transition into inclusive preschool programs. As can be noted, the children were between the ages of 3 and 5 years, and all had diagnoses, medical conditions, and/or assessed developmental levels indicative of significant disabilities.

What had begun so informally in the fall of 1986 with one child, Dana, was merged into the service delivery systems of two public school districts beginning in the fall of 1992. Two applications were submitted for state grants to support efforts to restructure part of the early childhood service delivery system. Both projects were funded through Title VI-B Special Project state funding from the Kansas State Board of Education to implement programs of inclusive early childhood special education as a service delivery option within the two Kansas districts. The Lawrence, Kansas, project, Project LIM (Lawrence Early Education Program Inclusion Model), and the Kansas City, Kansas, Project WIN (Wyandotte Cooperative Inclusion Network), both focused on continuing to implement and expand components of the CIP and are described in Table 3.

Table 1. The Circle of Inclusion Value Statements

Value One
We reject the notion that children with disabilities must be "fixed" (frequently couched in terms of meeting certain criteria) before they are ready to take their place in families, neighborhoods, and community environments and experience the normal flow of everyday life and friendships available to children without disabilities. Specifically we are concerned that preschool children with severe disabilities and their families have the opportunity for inclusion in high-quality child care and preschool programs within the mainstream of community programs available to typically developing children and their families.

Value Two
We recognize that typically developing children must have an opportunity to develop relationships with children who experience disabling conditions, including children with the most significant disabilities. We acknowledge the importance of children learning to live in a pluralistic society and to accept individual differences at an early age. We believe that typically developing preschool children are at a critical readiness period for the experience of knowing a child with a disability and that their lives will be enriched by reaching out to friends who experience disabilities.

Value Three
We believe that a viable program must reflect involvement, input, and ongoing collaborative efforts from all participants, including the families receiving services and the special education and mainstream early childhood program personnel.

Value Four
We hold deep respect for the uniqueness and dignity of each child as an individual human being who merits our careful observation and response to his or her needs. We reject the application of any aversive procedures and believe that the acknowledgment of child preference and the development of choice-making skills, a sense of self, and personal autonomy are critical.

Value Five
We believe that inclusive programming efforts must incorporate exemplary practice approaches using developmentally appropriate activities and materials available to all children in a high-quality program. Objectives and activities must be guided by family priorities and developed via a team process with the family as the principal decision makers. The principle of partial participation should be used to maximize involvement when the child is not able to perform all aspects of an activity.

Value Six
We accept the concept of natural proportions and believe that it is best to place young children with severe disabilities in "mainstream" programs in accordance with realistic population distributions.

Value Seven
Our time and energy should be vested in investigating the variables that make inclusive endeavors work in the best possible way.

From Thompson, B., Wegner, J., Wickham, D., Shanks, P., Reinertson, B., & Ault, M. (1991). An investigation of the transition and integration of preschoolers with severe and profound multiple disabilities into a Montessori community preschool program: Program history, features, and research activities in progress, Circle of Inclusion Project. *Kansas Early Childhood Research Institute on Transition, Project 2.2, Working Paper No. 1.* Lawrence, KS: Schiefelbusch Life Span Institute, University of Kansas.

Recently, CIP components have been implemented, expanded, and disseminated via two U.S. Department of Education Office of Special Education Outreach Training Projects. One of the projects has been directed toward expanding aspects of the model for young elementary children with severe disabilities and autism, and the other project has

Table 2. Original participants in Circle of Inclusion Project at time of entry into inclusive community preschool

Child/ number	Inclusion transition date	Age in months	Gender	Diagnosed condition	Assessed development in months at entry into mainstream program[a]			
					Cognitive	Social	Language	Motor
DD 1	10/6/86	39	F	Deaf-blind Cerebral palsy	0–6[b]	6–18	0	g. 0–6 f. 0–6
CS 2	2/1/88	41	M	Cerebral palsy Microencephaly	1–6	8–15	e. 3–8 r. 3–9	g. 2–5 f. 1–4
MA 3	2/1/88	56	M	Deaf-blind	3–8	6–9	e. 4–6 r. 6–7	g. 5–6 f. 5–9
JF 4	2/8/89	39	M	Cerebral palsy	3–6	6–7	e. 6–7 r. 10	g. 3–6 f. 3
CA 5	2/8/89	35	M	Cerebral palsy	6–9	9–15	e. 4–6 r. 8–10	g. 6 f. 3–6
GM 6	4/3/89	46	M	Down syndrome	22–27	28–30	e. 28 r. 28	g. 24 f. 26
MA 7	4/3/89	51	F	Down syndrome	36–48	36–39	e. 34 r. 32–37	g. 26 f. 24
SD 8	9/28/89	52	F	Cerebral palsy Visual impairment	11–12	11–18	e. 8–9 r. 8–10	g. 6–15 f. 12–15
SB 9	9/10/90	60	F	Cerebral palsy Microcephaly	24–36	24–36	e. 19 r. 36	g. 18–21 f. 6–15
SW 10	9/10/90	56	F	Down syndrome	30–42	32–34	e. 19 r. 8–30	g. 18–21 f. 28
LB 11	4/18/91	65	F	Cerebral palsy	12–24	10–30	18–24	g. 12 f. 12–15

	Date		Sex	Diagnosis				
NA 12	9/3/91	52	M	Speech-language delay Hearing impairment	18–24	16–24	e. 4–12 r. 3–18	g. 12–24 f. 12–21
LW 13	9/16/92	45	F	Cerebral palsy Visual impairment	6–9	3–6	e. 3–24 r. 3–18	g. 12–24 f. 12–21
MG 14	9/17/91	60	M	Down syndrome	27–32	25–36	e. 18–21 r. 25	g. 18–41 f. 15–35
MB 15	11/27/91	62	M	Trisomy 6	9–18	6–18	e. 6–9 r. 3–6	g. 4–9 f. 4–7
BS 16	12/9/91	48	M	Cerebral palsy	0–9	0–9	e. 0–9 r. 0–9	g. 0–6 f. 0–9
DW 17	12/11/91	54	M	Meningitis Hydrocephaly	24	No score assigned	e. 28 r. 27	g. 19–24 f. 18–27
RH 18	1/1/92	38	M	Developmental delays	18–24	18–24	e. 16–18 r. 18–24	g. 12 f. 18–20
CB 19	2/4/92	64	F	DeMorsier's syndrome Cerebral palsy	6–9	6–9	7–8	g. 8–9 f. 8–9
TM 20	2/17/92	46	F	Cerebral palsy	1–15	0–6	e. 4–13 r. 4–13	g. 3–9 f. 3–9

Adapted from Thompson, Wickham, and Wegner (1991).

Note: e. = expressive language score; r. = receptive language score; g. = gross motor score; f. = fine motor score.

[a]Scores obtained from developmental assessments conducted by interdisciplinary professional team in special education program.

[b]Represents a range of subscores in months (e.g., 3–6 months).

Table 3. LIM and WIN Program Overviews

The Lawrence, Kansas, model (**Project LIM,** *Lawrence Early Education Program Inclusion Model*) has expanded inclusive services via interagency agreements with five community early childhood programs and involves services to children with a full range of delays and disabilities (i.e., mild to severe/profound). Approaches to services implemented in this model include 1) employment of an early childhood special education teacher in two community preschools that hold openings for placement of children with disabilities, 2) intensive itinerant early childhood special education services in Head Start and two additional community preschools that hold openings for placement of children with disabilities, and 3) intensive early childhood special education services provided to children in the program in which they were enrolled at the point they are identified as eligible for these services.

The Kansas City, Kansas, model (**Project WIN,** *Wyandotte Cooperative Inclusion Network*) includes children with severe and profound multiple disabilities and children with autism. Children previously served in segregated classrooms in the University of Kansas Medical Center are placed in classrooms with typically developing children that are 1) part of community service centers established as interagency community programs designed to meet the needs of families living in urban settings, 2) in private community preschool/child care centers, and 3) in Head Start programs.

been extended to community training teams to initiate and implement inclusive early childhood services that address the needs of children with the most significant disabilities.

By the end of the school year in 1994, early childhood teachers and child care professionals in 23 preschool classrooms within 10 community early childhood programs (including two Head Start Programs), primary general education teachers in 10 kindergarten programs, first-grade, and second-grade classrooms, as well as personnel from early childhood special education programs in two communities (Lawrence and Kansas City) received training to implement inclusive programs for young children with severe disabilities (Thompson & Wegner, 1993). At that point, more than 600 typically developing children and 35 children with severe disabilities had participated as members of inclusive classrooms that employed components of the CIP model.

OUR KNOWLEDGE ABOUT KNOWLEDGE:
A SUMMARY OF RESULTS AND OUTCOMES

Early in our work together in the implementation of inclusive early childhood services for preschool-age children with significant disabilities, we began documenting the experiences and reflections of all the participants. We kept field notes in which we recorded events and experiences as they happened, along with notes reflecting our thoughts and feelings in the role of participant-observers. We also periodically made audiotapes of interviews with the involved parents and professional so we could have verbatim transcriptions of their thoughts and recollections. Extensive videotape records of the children directly participating in inclusive classes, which now span 10 years, were also maintained and have been a rich source of data as well as a resource for training. In addition, we conducted a number of observational studies using internal and time-sampling approaches for data collection and single-subject experimental studies that validated and provided insight into what we believed we understood through our participation.

We became convinced that a combination of qualitative and quantitative approaches offers a particularly rich environment for understanding the development and evaluation of new program models within a system change endeavor. As already noted, our multifaceted approach has been grounded in observation, data gathering, reflection, and direct participation over 10 years of creating and maintaining inclusive and family-centered services. Inherent in such an approach is the means to flexibly adjust perspectives and units of analysis. A qualitative approach made possible a holistic view of a complex system and offered a means of addressing multiple components of the program and its impact. Linking a quantitative approach to this process offered opportunities to verify or reject impressions and to discover other factors of importance. Three studies primarily addressed qualitative components of our work (Perez, 1992; Stargardter, 1988; Thompson, Wickham, & Wegner, 1991). Six studies conducted as part of the project involved direct observation and coding of environmental, adult, and child variables; and several studies involved comparing a range of variables such as training procedures, equipment, adult style, and setting characteristics across programs, children, and personnel (Brooke, 1992; Kimura, 1991; Lit, 1993; Stegemann, 1993; Wegner, 1991; Wickham, 1993).

We focus on providing an overview of nine themes that emerged as meaningful for organizing results from specific studies, informative experiences, and outcomes of our program (Thompson & Wegner, 1993). The themes discussed in this chapter include 1) factors affecting program success, 2) evidence of participation of children and partners, 3) influence of adult on development of friendships among children, 4) accommodations for welcoming environments, 5) experiences and perspectives of parents of children with disabilities, 6) experiences and perspectives of parents of typically developing children, 7) transitioning for adults to inclusive services for children, 8) paraprofessionals as facilitators, and 9) preparation of adults to serve as a child's partner. While offering specific findings and impressions, liberty has been taken to interpret some of the results and to emphasize important implications.

Factors Affecting Program Success

Acceptance of the inclusion program and its overall success (long-term participation and quality implementation) seemed to be highly related to the extent to which *both* the director of a community program and the program's early childhood teachers held a consistent, articulated philosophy and a sense of mission centered around meeting the needs of children and families. Examples of the kinds of programs with which we have worked most successfully and that operate with an explicit philosophy and sense of mission are Montessori programs, Head Start programs, and National Association for the Education of Young Children (NAEYC) accredited programs. Other features of programs that we generally considered as having had an impact on success included program longevity and reputation in the community, employing of qualified teachers, low staff turnover, and a stable financial base for the program.

The education of children and youth with significant disabilities has a history of implementing teacher-directed approaches (Guess & Thompson, 1990; Thompson & Guess, 1989). Despite this fact, we have consistently found that classrooms with a child-initiated, child-centered approach to early childhood education grounded in developmentally appropriate practice (Bredekamp, 1991) seem particularly able to sustain the successful placement of young children with significant disabilities.

We have had long-term, successful experiences with the Montessori approach to early childhood education (Thompson, Wickham, Ault et al., 1991). For example, the initial placement site for our program, a private Montessori program accredited by the American Montessori Society, has increased its involvement over the past 10 years. One of the teachers was appointed as the coordinator for special education services to ensure optimal ongoing placement and coordination with the public school early childhood special education service program. This same teacher began and completed early childhood special education certification with a specialization in children with severe disabilities. By 1992, part of her salary was paid through a contract between the public schools and the private community program. Another teacher in the same program has begun graduate work in special education, and two additional teachers have worked actively with the multidisciplinary teams who serve children in their classrooms. This program also added ramps, purchased adaptive equipment (such as a toilet), installed a visual fire alarm, and altered the playground to increase accessibility.

A number of considerations make Montessori programs an attractive model for the inclusion of young children with significant disabilities (Thompson, Wickham, Ault et al., 1991). Certified Montessori teachers must meet rigorous performance standards and are well-qualified early childhood educators. In addition, Montessori environments have features associated with developmentally appropriate practice as articulated by NAEYC guidelines (Bredekamp, 1991). These features include mixed age groups, child-initiated focus of the classroom with a predictable structure, prepared classroom environments that enhance choice and autonomy, and a rich array of functional and interesting materials that can meet a wide range of developmental needs. A practical consideration relates to the relative consistency in the curriculum and method in quality Montessori programs, which enhances the probability of replicating effective procedures across multiple settings. (For other relevant features of the Montessori approach, see Chattin-McNichols, 1992; Krogh, 1982; Lillard, 1973; Loeffler, 1992; Safford, 1989; Thompson, Wickham, Ault et al., 1991; and Wegner, 1989.)

More recently, Head Start programs have become actively involved in the inclusion efforts of both districts we worked in, and eight Head Start classrooms in two communities have participated in our program quite successfully. The relationship with Head Start was facilitated by the Head Start regulations, which support collaborative arrangements with school districts and call for the inclusion of children with severe disabilities (Division for Early Childhood of the Council for Exceptional Children, 1993). Although Head Start classrooms may implement a variety of curriculums, two approaches that are frequently implemented and are particularly viable for inclusion include the High Scope program (Hohmann & Weikert, 1995) and Creative Curriculum (Dodge & Colker, 1992). Several noteworthy features of Head Start include the high level of involvement with families, the broad range of health and nutritional programs available to children and families, and ongoing required staff development activities.

It should be noted that the child care components of the inclusive community programs were consistently used by families and were often the reason they preferred one community program over another (Thompson & Wegner, 1993). As conveyed in the literature (Berk & Berk, 1982; Bristol, Reichles, & Thomas, 1987; Klein & Sheehan, 1987; Mense, 1990) and reflected in our experience, finding child care for children with significant disabilities is very difficult for families. By starting relationships with programs for inclusive early childhood education, doors were opened to many children for extended child care.

Finally, the issues of accessibility of a program for children with significant physical challenges has definitely been a factor in whether a program worked or not. While makeshift, temporary adaptations are often possible, some programs are located in buildings in which it is virtually impossible to safely include a child with significant physical challenges. This fact has important implications because accessibility has an impact on the safety of all young children.

Evidence of Participation of Children and Partners

Although we have documented countless touching personal observations of growing relationships among children with significant disabilities and their typically developing peers, we have also documented quantitative evidence of the children's experience. During a period of split enrollment in both an inclusive preschool and a special education preschool, three studies documented and compared aspects of the same children's communication, engagement in activities, and interaction with partners in both settings (Brooke, 1992; Stegemann, 1993; Wegner, 1991). The Brooke and Stegemann students used the CEVIT (Coding Environmental Variables and Interaction on Tape) (Kimura, 1991; Leon, 1992) to code interactions and environmental variables of the same three children in the two settings. Each student sampled different episodes during a similar time period. The Stegemann (1993) study used exactly the same video episodes as the Wegner (1991) study. The observational analysis conducted by Wegner involved the analysis of verbatim transcripts obtained from the video episodes. All three studies involved comparisons of data for statistical significance. The results indicated that an inclusive setting offers more desirable social and communicative environment for children with significant disabilities on both a quantitative and qualitative basis and can match a high-quality special education program on environmental adaptations. Some of the most interesting conclusions derived from these studies are summarized here:

- Children with severe disabilities had significantly more peer partners and more communicative interactions in the inclusive community preschool than in a special education preschool.
- The children initiated more frequently and took more participatory turns in the inclusive community preschool.
- The children interacted with more children in the inclusive community preschool than in the special education preschool.
- The children interacted with more adults in the special education preschool than in the inclusive community preschool.
- The length of time a child with a severe disability engaged in a single activity was consistently longer in the community preschool than in the special education class, although the difference was not significant. Furthermore, children with disabilities tended to spend more time on activities within a mainstream program over time.
- Accommodations (e.g., adaptive equipment for supporting positions, augmentative communication devices, and provisions for ac-

cessibility of materials) in an inclusive program were comparable
with those provided in high-quality special education classrooms.
In addition, children with significant disabilities spent more time
out of their wheelchairs and engaged in floor and table activities in
the inclusive program.

- When compared with adult partners in a special education program, adult partners in the inclusive community program were
  more facilitative of communication in their interactions with children with severe disabilities. Adults invited response, offered
  choice, redirected others to interact with the child, and interpreted
  the child's nonverbal responses as communicative significantly
  more often than did the partners in a special education program.
- When compared with adult partners in an inclusive program, adult
  partners in a special education program were more directive in their
  interactions with children with severe disabilities. They gave com-
  mands and instructions significantly more often than did the children's partners in a mainstream program.
- Peer partners in the inclusive community preschool initiated more
  frequently, took more turns, and used more redirections than did
  the peer partners in the special education preschool.

Influence of Adult on
Development of Friendships Among Children

The results of this project confirmed the importance of the role of the
adult partner in the development and maintenance of peer interactions
among children with significant disabilities and typically developing
children (Brooke, 1992; Lit, 1993; Stegemann, 1993; Wegner, 1991;
Wickham, 1993). Frequently, adults must mediate initial peer interactions by offering support for interaction. Successful strategies included 1) inviting participation, 2) answering questions and offering
content for interactions on behalf of the child with a disability, 3) assessing and providing for needed adaptations that allow participation
of the child with a disability, 4) assessing and ensuring facilitative
positioning of the child with a disability, and 5) teaching peers to interact directly with the child with a disability and fading from child-
to-child interactions when appropriate (Thompson et al., 1993).

Children with significant disabilities do form special relationships
(friendships) with some of their typical peers that appear to be mutually satisfying and are maintained when the children are in the classroom together. Evidence of such friendships includes reports of the
typically developing children's comments to their parents (Perez,
1992), invitations to play or attend parties (Stargardter, 1988; Thompson, Wickham, & Wegner, 1991), and consistent interactions over time
among the children as noted in observational records and videotaped

episodes that show the presence of peers (Brooke, 1992; Jenson, 1994; Kimura, 1991; Leon, 1992; Lit, 1993; Shanks, 1990; Stegemann, 1993; Wegner, 1991). Some of our conclusions and observations related to this process include the following:

- Preparation for first meeting the child with a significant disability, although often part of inclusion programs for school-age children, need not be extensive with very young children because their attitudes are still being formed rather than changed; and information is sought quite naturally (Shanks, 1990; Thompson et al., 1991).
- Although children are apt initially to place a child with severe multiple disabilities on a par with infants and toddlers, this view diminishes over time as information about the child and his or her disabling condition is offered to typical peers (Shanks, 1990; Stargardter, 1988; Thompson et al., 1991).
- Children with typical development or mild disabilities follow the model of adults in communicating with children with significant disabilities. If adults are facilitative partners, the children are more facilitative partners; if adults are directive partners, the children are more directive and more likely to refrain from involvement in cooperative activities with a child who has significant disabilities (Lit, 1993; Wegner, 1991).
- Same-age peers who are friends with children with significant disabilities learned to use supportive strategies that are related to physical assistance and facilitative support (e.g., supporting a friend's head, assisting a friend to grasp, supporting and moving a friend's hand and arm, supporting a friend's trunk, wiping saliva from a friend's chin, providing with assistance to eat, pushing a wheelchair, getting necessary positioning materials, presenting and handling materials, interpreting communications, selecting activities that their friend obviously enjoyed) (Jenson 1994; Lit, 1993; Stegemann, 1993; Wegner, 1991).
- Children responded fearfully to a child who was aggressive to them and noticed asocial and unusual behavior (e.g., stereotypy) (Thompson et al., 1993). They also accepted explanations of the communicative and/or coping nature of such behavior and the need for their peer to acquire new strategies. Typically developing children persisted in interactions with children whom they initially feared or avoided and assisted their classmate in practicing new strategies, generally but not always with adult support and encouragement.

Accommodations for Welcoming Environments

Environmental accommodations should be planned through ongoing environmental assessment, and the initial lack of adaptation *should not be used as a reason to reject placement in an inclusive program.* Our review of videotapes and direct observation consistently indicated that there was more focus in the inclusive settings on how accommodations would enhance participation than in the special education settings (Brooke, 1992; Stegemann, 1993; Wegner, 1991).

When children required specialized equipment and devices, many early childhood teachers found it helpful to explain and demonstrate equipment and devices as part of a large group activity in which its purpose and use were presented in a manner that was respectful to the child who would be using it and, to the extent possible, involved this child in the process. In addition, attention to replicating a typical child's position and keeping the child with a disability on a face-to-face level with his or her peers was important (Thompson et al., 1993).

The availability of ongoing support for assistive technology was a critical element in the degree to which assistive technology was used. Much time and considerable difficulty were involved in identifying appropriate assistive technology devices such as augmentative communication devices, as well as in programming the devices, identifying appropriate and functional child positions to facilitate effective use of the devices, and teaching children and staff to use the devices correctly (Thompson et al., 1993). The factors that interfered significantly with the availability and use of augmentative devices in an inclusive setting seemed very similar to the problems associated with these devices in self-contained special education programs.

Finally, the use of specific equipment does not appear to negatively affect interactions among children. In fact, using a device such as an augmentative communication device in an inclusive program offers many more opportunities for practice in using the device with speaking partners who are also peers in natural situations. Further, devices and special equipment often served as attractors for partners who were curious about them and interested in using them. In fact, one might venture to say that these devices sometimes took on a "status" quality. Pushing a child in a wheelchair was a highly valued activity. One 5-year-old who was negotiating with her classmates for how they might merit invitations to her birthday party was overheard approaching Shannon, who had just received a communication device. The child told Shannon that she could be one of the lucky invitees if she would "bring her box" to the party (D. Leon, personal communication, April 16, 1991).

Experiences and Perspectives of
Parents of Children with Disabilities

Our experiences over 10 years offered us some important insights into the experiences of parents. The concerns and fears expressed by parents of children with disabilities and personnel before transition into inclusive environments are consistent with a body of emergent literature (Hanline, 1993). Over the course of this project, we experienced a shift in parents' awareness of inclusion. Initially we had to invite parents to consider participating, whereas parents are now requesting, and sometimes insisting on, inclusive placements. Following are conclusions about the experiences and perspectives of parents and about strategies that were successfully implemented to facilitate the process of inclusion for the family (Thompson et al., 1993):

- Parents who had experience with special education preschool programs with high staff-to-child ratios sometimes expressed concern over their lack of contact with the regular education teacher.
- Some parents were less likely to attend general early education conferences and programs offered by the inclusive community program than those offered by the explicitly special education components of the program. Formal ways of linking these families with families of typically developing children who are in the program were needed to enhance the feeling of belonging for parents of children with severe disabilities.
- The parents and personnel tended to become more positive about the effects of inclusion on the children after direct participation in a program.
- Participation in an inclusive early childhood program appeared to affect the parent's placement preferences for inclusive school-age services. This result had an impact on the transition to school-age services (kindergarten and primary grades in elementary schools) and will ultimately have an impact on the nature of special education services through the life span.
- Whether or not parents requested the placement, activities and strategies for involving and informing parents were critical (e.g., tours of program, involvement in environmental assessment, small group meetings with veteran parents, a handbook). The MAPS, Making Action Plans or the McGill Action Planning System (Vandercook, York, & Forest, 1989), which is based on a futures planning approach that has been adapted for educational planning, was also useful for initiating the child's entry into a program and developing an individualized education program (IEP).
- A way of ensuring ongoing and frequent communication was very important. Daily notebooks were particularly useful for some families. The parent, early childhood teacher, and special education support team members all communicated in writing through the use of notebooks.

- Parents who participated as members of a core team that met bi-weekly or monthly to problem-solve and plan participatory strategies for the child in the classroom seemed most involved and empowered.
- Parents of children in an urban setting tended to demonstrate less confidence in advocating for their child with public school personnel. However, their interest in inclusive experiences and their need for child care were similar to that of the parents in more affluent, suburban communities.

Experiences and Perspectives of Parents of Typically Developing Children

Parents of typically developing children can be valuable resources. Although we did not sufficiently explore strategies for involving these parents, results suggested that parents of typically developing children should be educated and involved along with parents of children with disabilities and participating personnel. The following points all emerged from Perez's (1992) qualitative study of eight parents whose typically developing children had formed special relationships with their classmates who experienced significant disabilities:

- Parents of typically developing children supported the concept of integration at the preschool level and recognized that integration can be beneficial for their typically developing children, as well as for the children with disabilities. More specifically, parents stated that exposure to people with disabilities fostered acceptance and contributed to important changes in society.
- Without prompting by the interviewer and without responding to a specific question, all parents we formally interviewed brought up the role of the additional paraprofessional as an integration facilitator in the classroom. All these parents indicated that the addition of a knowledgeable person who could assist the teacher and the child with a disability was the most important factor in making the program work.
- Most parents indicated that while their children expressed acceptance and positive regard for their peers with disabilities, their children did not talk much about their peers with disabilities at home or describe any special type of relationship with them. Parents said that their children talked about the children with disabilities in the same way they spoke of other children in the school, although parents were also quite sure that their children were aware of the peers' disabilities. One parent noted that her little girl sometimes played "handicapped preschool" with her dolls.

- Conversely, the parents of a 5-year-old boy talked about the lengthy and detailed comments of their son about his friends with disabilities. This was consistent across 3 years of preschool. His parents attributed his close attachment to his friends with disabilities (three different children over a 3-year period) as instrumental to his adjustment and happiness in the program. Interestingly, these were also parents who expressed initial concern that the presence of children with disabilities would take too much teacher time away from their son.

- All of the parents indicated that they lacked specific knowledge about integration programs, but although they would like to know more about the program in which their child participated, this lack of information did not affect their positive attitude toward the concept of inclusion.

- In general, parents of typically developing children were open to and supportive of the inclusion of children with severe disabilities under the circumstances of CIP, in which the number of children with disabilities in a single classroom generally reflected the natural proportions in the population at large. Although parents did not use the term "natural proportions," they were clearly aware of this issue and spoke about ratios of children with typical development and children with disabilities.

Transitioning for Adults to Inclusive Services for Children

The immense power of the involved personnel to affect program success or failure must be recognized, and the need to educate and support these adults cannot be overemphasized. Although special education personnel working with children in inclusive settings initially expressed concern about their roles, most believed it was their responsibility to give their best effort for the sake of the children and were willing to sustain a period of discomfort to that end (Stargardter, 1988; Thompson, Wegner, et al., 1991). Conversely, the general early childhood staff indicated pleasure at the opportunity to participate in an inclusive program, but expressed concern about their ability to meet the needs of the child and about the degree of support and assistance they would receive. Fear of actually handling a child occurred consistently as a new program began including a child with significant disabilities.

As relationships with other professionals and families developed around addressing the needs of a child, most special education personnel became more positive and supportive of inclusive practices; and most general early childhood personnel became more comfortable and more interactive with the children. However, the search for strategies that fit this new paradigm from both special and general early childhood personnel seemed ongoing. Over 10 years we have encountered a number of issues related to the involved personnel and their work that merits discussion, including 1) competition among programs (special education preschools and inclusive community programs); 2) the confusion that confronted personnel undergoing changes in their role; 3) the lack of understanding that caused discomfort or conflict between the early childhood education personnel (program director, early childhood teacher, classroom assistant) and special education early childhood personnel (administrator, teachers, related service staff, paraprofessionals); and 4) the controversial role of the paraprofessional as a facilitator for a child with significant disabilities (Thompson et al., 1993; Thompson & Wegner, 1993), which are presented as a major theme in the next section.

When two or more service delivery models exist within a community, competition may occur between the two program staffs. For example, when the split program arrangement was used (children attended a special education classroom for half a day and a community preschool for the remaining half day), issues arose over which program was benefiting the child the most, although some professionals described this split as the best of both worlds (Stargardter, 1988). This underlying sense of competition also arose when one component of a school district early childhood special education program moved to an inclusive model and another component of the same program did not.

Role confusion and frustration are major factors that can negatively affect the satisfaction of all personnel. The need to invent some strategies to match the needs of a new program model was particularly disconcerting to some personnel. As the number of community programs increased, the need to tailor one's role to best fit the specific staff and children within the programs, each of which functioned quite differently, placed great demands on personnel to be flexible and inventive. For example, the way that many of the related service professionals scheduled their time did not really fit the needs of some programs and children. In some cases, scheduling related service professionals with children in an inclusive program for a less frequent but prolonged period, instead of scheduling more frequent and shorter periods, was found to be more productive for effective consultation, transdisciplinary training, and integrated therapy (e.g., an occupational therapist spending all morning with a child in a preschool program every 2 weeks instead of two or three 20- to 30-minute sessions per week).

In-service training related to teaming, collaboration, and problem solving were valued and constantly sought by participating personnel.

In retrospect, we believe we should have included more content related to understanding personality types and differing work styles as useful information for anticipating the reactions of some personnel to functioning in a program that requires inventiveness. A more thorough grounding in the process of system change would also have been desirable to assist individuals in anticipating their experiences and reactions.

One of the most common sources of confusion seemed to stem from a lack of understanding and respect for other program and personnel practices. Special education and related service staff needed to be informed about early childhood program models and procedures. Frequently these individuals did not have a background in early childhood education and in some cases lacked knowledge of child development. Personnel who were accustomed to working only with children with very significant disabilities within a segregated program setting sometimes had difficulty entering an inclusive childhood environment in a productive and respectful way.

As investigators with long histories of working in segregated special education settings, we were aware of the tendency for adults to talk to adults in a classroom in which none of the children are able to speak. One scenario with which we are all familiar is a special education teacher or therapist showing another adult how to work with a child and offering a clinical explanation of a procedure in the presence of everyone (children and adults) in the classroom. This was often viewed by the early childhood program staff as demeaning to the child, a way of negatively setting the child apart from his peers, and as rude and disruptive. (Need we mention professionals walking into a classroom with a coffee cup and engaging in personal conversations?) Another scenario with which we are also familiar is the self-contained preschool program for children with significant disabilities in which there as many (or more) adults as children present. We found it necessary to give considerable attention to minimizing the intrusion of specialized staff serving a child in an inclusive program.

Of course, early childhood educators and child care workers need to learn about the roles and contributions that related service personnel and special educators can make. They too must learn to adjust to becoming part of a team, opening their classroom to the expertise of other professionals and their suggestions about working with a child with significant disabilities. This collaborative attitude was hampered or enhanced to the degree that the early childhood program staff felt empowered as principal players on the team, valued rather than judged, and supported rather than intruded upon.

Paraprofessionals as Facilitators

The adult–child ratios for children in most early childhood programs (1 adult to 10–12 children) must be enhanced if a child with significant disabilities is to be included. Attention to the training of all classroom personnel and the investigation of a range of approaches for increasing adult support are still needed. One of the approaches used in CIP was to assign an additional assistant to the inclusive community classroom and to have the school district pay this person as a paraprofessional. This individual functioned in a variety of ways and was generally co-supervised by the district early childhood special education teacher assigned to work with the children and personnel in the community program and by the early childhood teacher in charge of the classroom. In some cases, this person functioned primarily as a classroom assistant across children and tasks. In many cases, however, this person functioned as a "facilitator" for the child with significant disabilities. This was most true when a child demonstrated very challenging behaviors and/or when a child had significant and multiple physical and sensory challenges that limited the ability to move or participate in an activity.

The explicit assigning of a paraprofessional to a specific child in an inclusive preschool had both advantages and disadvantages, and these issues have been raised by a number of individuals involved in inclusive programs (Giangreco & Putnam, 1991; York, Vandercook, Caughey, & Helse-Neff, 1988). The results of several studies indicated that an individual serving as an "integration facilitator" or an adult partner was beneficial to a child's communicative competence, as well as supportive of the child's meaningful participation in the settings (Stegemann, 1993; Wegner, 1991; Wickham, 1993). The strength of this approach included the presence of someone who was able to become extremely sensitive and "tuned in" to a child's nonverbal communication, thereby empowering the child to be heard and to be a more active communicator and social participant in the classroom. The facilitator's role could be compared with the role of an interpreter. In addition, the individual taking the role of the facilitator became very skillful in supporting a child's ongoing physical participation, which is critical for a child with extremely limited movement capabilities.

Adults with good skills in relating to young children attracted more partners for a child with significant disabilities (Lit, 1993), while still providing the intensity of support and instruction required by children with significant disabilities. As noted earlier, adults are initially the primary interpreter and are usually essential in facilitating new relationships between children. There remains, however, a significant need for more research about how adults can recognize when child-to-child interactions can be maintained without their support and how to fade from these interactions.

We also found problems associated with the assigning of a paraprofessional to a particular child. Our data indicated that paraprofessionals supporting the inclusion of children with disabilities sometimes appeared to negatively affect the frequency with which the regular early childhood teacher interacted with the child (Lit, 1993). It was fairly common for a facilitator to become overly attached to a child and to prevent the rest of the classroom staff from becoming meaningfully involved with the child. Another problem that sometimes arose was the tendency for some early childhood classroom teachers to turn over complete responsibility for the child to the paraprofessional facilitator. This result brought the loss of an appropriate teacher–child relationship and inhibited the child's true membership in the class group.

Preparation of Adults to Serve as Child's Partner

Individuals supporting the inclusion of a child are likely to miss opportunities to support interactions, instruction, and participation unless directly trained to do so (Wickham, 1993). Instruction on facilitative strategies that support child-to-child interactions for *all* adults who were involved with the program was necessary to ensure application of these strategies in the classroom. Direct training using videotaped episodes of children and paraprofessionals in inclusive classrooms that were part of CIP was conducted by Wickham (1993). The results of this study indicated that this training was an effective way to enhance the use of strategies that facilitate child-to-child interactions and specialized instructional procedures. Paraprofessionals in training viewed videotaped episodes of their interactions within a classroom, focused on observing specific strategies, and reflected on possible improvements with a specific trainer. The results were moderately encouraging in regard to generalization to other children and maintenance over time, but suggested that ongoing and direct training is important for a considerable length of time.

FINAL COMMENTS AND
RECOMMENDATIONS: FEATURES OF AN EXEMPLARY PROGRAM

Our prolonged involvement with CIP has contributed much to our perspective on the short- and long-term issues regarding inclusive services for young children with significant disabilities and the sustainability of emerging programs. Mindful that approaches to the development of service models should meet standards of exemplary practice, as well as reflect the unique characteristics of the community in which they are implemented, we have developed recommendations for features of an exemplary program (Thompson et al., 1993). These recommendations are designed to enable programs and personnel to move from the "believing" to the "doing" stage and to establish a lasting structure.

Embracing a Shared Value Base and Vision

The establishment of a set of values (see Table 1 on p. 31) to which a very diverse group of individuals ascribed made it possible to transcend a number of the differences in agency functions and procedures as well as in participating program approaches to early childhood education. These shared values and the vision of inclusive early childhood education and child care for all young children and their families provided the impetus to continue the program over a number of years.

Participation of Community-Based Early Childhood Programs

A broad number of "community-based programs" including private for-profit, private not-for-profit, and Head Start programs that predominantly serve typically developing children offer potentially excellent programs for the inclusion of young children with significant disabilities. One of the most compelling rationales for involving community programs is the opportunity for families to have the same options for selecting programs as do families of young children with typical development. Parents may have preferences based on a particular program approach and philosophy, location, and available services. Other children in the family may already attend a particular community program or may have attended a program with which the parents are comfortable.

Using Varied Approaches to Provide Inclusive Classrooms

A number of approaches offer communities ways to move toward establishing inclusive services for young children. These approaches include 1) contractual arrangements that support certified staff who are employees of the community programs; 2) blended classrooms, such as the emergent practice of blending Head Start and early childhood special education programs or arranging for team teaching between an early childhood teacher and special education early childhood teacher; and 3) use of a collaborative consultation model in which the early childhood special education teacher takes on an itinerant role and works with staff and children in several programs. In some communities, two or more of these models are used in combination as they were in the programs employing components of CIP.

Creative and Flexible Funding via Interagency Relationships

Sources of cost that are likely to be specifically associated with an early childhood inclusion program for young children with significant disabilities include child tuition and fees, additional personnel, facility accessibility adaptations, licensing adaptations, special equipment and materials, staff education programs, and numerous family programs. Administrative personnel involved in an early childhood inclusion program must have a good understanding of the potential resources available to the various agencies and individuals who might participate in the program. When several agencies work together (e.g., school district, Head Start, community preschool and child care centers), a creative and resourceful funding base can be built to support the program model that meets the unique needs of the community and is also responsive to the individual needs of families.

Linkage with Programs Offering Child Care Services

One solution to the problem of limited or nonexistent child care options for young children with significant disabilities is to assist service providers in existing child care programs to accept youngsters with severe disabilities and to assist families in gaining access to these services. A particularly viable application of this solution is to offer inclusive early childhood services in programs that offer full-day child care.

Providing High-Quality, Child-Centered
Programs with Developmentally Appropriate Practices

As Safford (1989) points out, there is inherent value in good early childhood practices for all children; and considerable benefit can derive from using child-specific adaptations and interventions with teaching approaches appropriate to all children. Characteristics of child-oriented programs that support active learning include 1) opportunities to practice developmental tasks, 2) teachers who understand developmental needs and characteristics of the children, 3) a curriculum that furthers cognitive development via concrete experiences, and 4) physical settings designed to encourage independence and motivate involvement (Day & Drake, 1986). Accreditation by NAEYC, AMS (American Montessori Society), or AMI (Association of Montessori International) generally are positive signs of a quality program.

Facilitating Membership Through Supported Placement

The use of a paraprofessional or another adult assigned as a classroom facilitator for a child with significant disabilities can offer the intensive support needed by children with severe disabilities within inclusive programs. In our experience, the inclusion facilitator plays a pivotal role in how well a child is accepted into a classroom because the facilitator often determines whether interactions occur or do not occur with other children and program staff. Interactions with young children with severe disabilities are fostered by teaching children to act as responsive and sensitive partners, by providing opportunities for meaningful interactions with peers, and by supporting a child in an interaction if he or she needs support. The person working directly with a child with a disability in an inclusive early childhood classroom must be a careful observer of children's behavior and must be sensitive to communicative attempts in order to promote interactions between children that are sustained, but not continuously supported by an adult. Using strategies that facilitate interactions among typically developing young children and their classmates with disabilities allows children to determine the content and direction of their interactions, encourages true communication, and fosters an environment in which friendships can unfold.

Establishing Collaborative Teams Based on Functional Tasks

Effective team functioning requires that all team members, including parents, share a common philosophy and commitment to the development of the whole child and be able to communicate openly and effectively with one another (Rainforth, York, & Macdonald, 1992; Swan & Morgan, 1993). An inclusive program model compounds the already complicated process of teaming because members often represent multiple community agencies, each with different administrative patterns, missions, and philosophies. Furthermore, the complex and intensive needs of children with significant disabilities and their families require an intensive effort on the part of the child and family team.

Joint Service Provider and Family Preparation

Change is stressful under the very best of circumstances. Staff and family preparation activities are absolutely critical to ensuring that each individual optimally approaches the shift to inclusive services (Klein & Sheehan, 1987). Participants must become acquainted with the nature of systemic change and the need to be proactive and inventive. The role confusion and negativity often experienced in a new program can be reduced by providing opportunities for participants to communicate with other members of the team about issues affecting their roles and by empowering participants with opportunities to affect their own role.

It is also essential that involved service providers show respect for individuals from programs and agencies that operate under different regulations and use different methods. Participants must learn how to enter a new system by suspending their assumptions about how things should be and follow the advice offered by Stephen Covey in his discussion of the habits of highly effective people: "Seek first to understand and then to be understood," and "Diagnose before you prescribe" (Covey, 1989). Service providers must learn this approach to work independently with each other and with families from diverse backgrounds and cultures. Ultimately, if we want individuals to work together in a collaborative and open manner, it is essential that we offer *joint,* not *separate,* education and development activities.

Family-Guided Decision Making and Family-Centered Services

A consistent frustration faced by families as they seek to establish exemplary services for their child and to maintain these services throughout the life span are the lack of a truly seamless service system, and professional resistance to empowering families and to the assertive stance taken by many families. Although family involvement is a principle espoused with the best of intentions by all early childhood interventionists (Bricker, 1989; Peterson, 1987; Raver, 1991), the processes and procedures that include the family in meaningful self-determined activities are still sorely lacking (Bailey & Wolery, 1989; Bricker, 1989; Whitehead, Deiner, & Toccafondi, 1990). Our experiences with the CIP project confirmed this reality. Changing the way professionals interact with parents continues to be one of our greatest challenges. Program procedures must be implemented that offer promise for empowering families and help service providers value the interdependent nature of their work with families.

SUMMARY

It seems fitting to conclude this chapter with one of our favorite anecdotes, not only because it is humorous, but also because an important concept is voiced so clearly by the words of a child:

> Five-year-old Shannon, a charmer with big brown eyes and a ready smile, experiences multiple disabilities. Shannon has a condition of microcephaly and cerebral palsy which is predominant on her left side. She is ambulatory, but non-oral. She also experiences intensive grand mal seizures which required that the community preschool have an emergency medical plan in place and included the immediate notification of an EMT unit. Finally, Shannon's condition is related to prenatal exposure to the cytomegalovirus (CMV). Although medical testing revealed that she was not currently shedding the virus, the community preschool personnel needed to take precautions related to infection control and limiting contact with pregnant staff and parents.

During the production phase of a video tape about the program of inclusion for young children with severe disabilities, four-year-old Sophie, also a charmer with blonde hair and blue eyes, was asked to comment about her classmate Shannon. One of the production crew members who was curious about what the children with typical development thought about the inclusion program was overheard asking, "Well, Sophie, do you think Shannon should be at Raintree or maybe do you think she should go to a preschool for other children just like her?" Sophie, after a short and what seemed as a reflective pause, responded. "No, she should go to Raintree, because—because, how would all the children know who the teacher was talking to—with everybody named Shannon in that school?" (Thompson et al., 1993, p. 25)

REFERENCES

Bailey, D.B., & McWilliam, R.A. (1990). Normalizing early intervention. *Topics in Early Childhood Special Education, 10*(2), 33–47.

Bailey, D.B., & Wolery, M. (1989). *Assessing infants and preschoolers with handicaps.* Columbus, OH: Merrill.

Berk, H.J., & Berk, M.L. (1982). A survey of day care centers and their services for handicapped children. *Child Care Quarterly, 11*(3), 211–214.

Bredekamp, S. (1991). *Developmentally appropriate practice in early childhood programs serving children from birth through age 8 (expanded).* Washington, DC: National Association for the Education of Young Children.

Bricker, D., & Cripe, J.J.W. (1992). *An activity-based approach to early intervention.* Baltimore: Paul H. Brookes Publishing Co.

Bricker, D.D. (1989). *Early intervention for at-risk and handicapped infants, toddlers, and preschool children* (2nd ed.). Palo Alto, CA: VORT Corp.

Bristol, M.M., Reichle, N.C., & Thomas, D.D. (1987). Changing demographics of the American family: Implications for single parent families of young handicapped children. *Journal of the Division for Early Childhood, 12*(1), 56–69.

Brooke, T. (1992). *A comparison of an integrated setting versus a special education setting using the CEVIT (coding environmental variables and interactions on tape).* Unpublished master's thesis, University of Kansas, Lawrence.

Chattin-McNichols, J. (1992). *The Montessori controversy.* Albany, NY: Delmar Publishers.

Covey, S. (1989). *The seven habits of highly effective people.* New York: Simon and Schuster.

Day, B., & Drake, K.N. (1986). Developments in experimental programs: The key to quality education and care of young children. *Educational Leadership, 44*(3), 24–27.

Division for Early Childhood of the Council for Exceptional Children. (1993). *New opportunities for collaboration: A policy and implementation resource and training manual for the Head Start regulations for children with disabilities.* Reston, VA: Author.

Dodge, D., & Colker, L. (1992). *The creative curriculum for early childhood* (3rd ed.). Washington, DC: Teaching Strategies, Inc.

Giangreco, M.F., & Putnam, J.W. (1991). Supporting the education of students with severe disabilities in regular education environments. In L.H. Meyer, C.A. Peck, & L. Brown (Eds.), *Critical issues in the lives of people with severe disabilities* (pp. 245–270). Baltimore: Paul H. Brookes Publishing Co.

Guess, D., Horner, R.D., Utley, B., Holvoet, J., Maxon, D., Tucker, D., & Warren, S. (1978). A functional curriculum sequencing model for teaching the severely handicapped. *American Association for the Education of the Severely and Profoundly Handicapped Review, 3,* 202–215.

Hanline, M.F. (1993). Facilitating integrated preschool service delivery transitions for children, families, and professionals. In C.A. Peck, S.L. Odom, & D.D. Bricker (Eds.), *Integrating young children with disabilities into community programs: Ecological perspectives on research and implementation* (pp. 133–146). Baltimore: Paul H. Brookes Publishing Co.

Hohmann, M., & Weikert, D.P. (1994). *Active learning practices for preschool and child care programs: Educating young children.* Ypsilanti, MI: High/Scope Press.

Jenson, R. (1994). *Video-based media as a method of illustrating child engagement.* Unpublished master's thesis, University of Kansas, Lawrence.

Kaiser, A., Hendrickson, J., & Albert, C. (1991). Milieu language teaching: A second look. In R. Gable (Ed.), *Advances in mental retardation and developmental disabilities* (Vol. IV, pp. 63–92). London: Jessica Kingsley Publishers.

Kimura, L. (1991). *Reliability analyses for environmental variables of the CEVIT (coding environmental variables and interactions on tape): A tool for observing young children with severe multiple disabilities in an integrated Montessori school.* Unpublished master's thesis, University of Kansas, Lawrence.

Klein, N., & Sheehan, R. (1987). Staff development: A key issue in meeting the needs of young handicapped children in day care settings. *Topics in Early Childhood Special Education, 7*(1), 13–27.

Krogh, S.L. (1982). Affective and social development: Some ideas from Montessori's prepared environment. *Topics in Early Childhood Special Education, 2*(1), 55–62.

Kuhn, T.S. (1970). *The structure of scientific revolutions* (2nd ed.). Chicago: University of Chicago Press.

Leon, D. (1992). *Reliability analysis for interaction variables of the CEVIT (coding environmental variables and interactions on tape): A tool for observing young children with severe multiple disabilities in an integrated Montessori school.* Unpublished master's thesis, University of Kansas, Lawrence.

Lillard, P.P. (1973). *Montessori: A modern approach.* New York: Schocken Books.

Lit, T.L. (1993). *A comparison of integration facilitators of young children with severe disabilities in an inclusive preschool setting.* Unpublished master's thesis, University of Kansas, Lawrence.

Loeffler, M. (Ed.). (1992). *Montessori in contemporary American culture.* Portsmouth, NH: Heinemann Educational Books, Inc.

Mense, J. (1990). *Service assessment of child care and preschool program availability for children with special needs: A descriptive analysis of a Kansas statewide survey.* Unpublished master's thesis, University of Kansas, Lawrence.

Noonan, M.J., & McCormick, L. (1993). *Early intervention in natural environments: Methods and procedures.* Pacific Grove, CA: Brooks/Cole Publishing Co.

Perez, M. (1992). *Parental attitudes and perceptions about integrating children with disabilities.* Unpublished master's thesis, University of Kansas, Lawrence.

Peterson, N.L. (1987). *Early intervention for handicapped and at-risk children: An introduction to early-childhood special education.* Denver: Love Publishing.

Rainforth, B., York, J., & Macdonald, C. (1992). *Collaborative teams for students with severe disabilities: Integrating therapy and educational services.* Baltimore: Paul H. Brookes Publishing Co.

Raver, S.A. (1991). *Strategies for teaching at-risk and handicapped infants and toddlers: A transdisciplinary approach.* New York: Merrill.

Safford, P.L. (1989). *Integrated teaching in early childhood: Starting in the mainstream.* White Plains, NY: Longman, Inc.

Shanks, P. (1990). *Rediscovering the potential in a children's house: A handbook for persons facilitating the integration of young children with severe disabilities in a Montessori environment.* Unpublished master's thesis, University of Kansas, Lawrence.

Stargardter, S. (1988). *Staff and parents perceptions about the integration of children with severe and multiple disabilities into a community preschool program.* Unpublished master's thesis, University of Kansas, Lawrence.

Stegemann, A. (1993). *A re-analysis of videotaped segments of three young children with severe disabilities in two preschool environments.* Unpublished master's thesis, University of Kansas, Lawrence.

Swan, W.W., & Morgan, J.L. (1993). *Collaborating for comprehensive services for young children and their families: The local interagency coordinating council.* Baltimore: Paul H. Brookes Publishing Co.

Thompson, B. (1994, October). *Inclusive programs for young children with significant disabilities: Reflections.* Paper presented at the annual meeting of the Kansas Association for the Education of Young Children, Manhattan, KS.

Thompson, B., & Guess, D. (1989). Students with the most profound multiply handicapping conditions: Teacher perceptions. In F. Brown & D. Lehr (Eds.), *Persons with profound disabilities: Issues and practices* (pp. 3–43). Baltimore: Paul H. Brookes Publishing Co.

Thompson, B., & Wegner, J. (1993, December). Project 2.2: Transitioning young children with severe disabilities from a special education program into inclusive community preschool and child care centers. In M. Rice & M. O'Brien (Co-Principal Investigators), *Kansas Early Childhood Research Institute on Transition, Final Report* (pp. 1–77). Washington, DC: U.S. Department of Education, Office of Special Education Programs.

Thompson, B., Wegner, J., Wickham, D., Shanks, P., Reinertson, B., & Ault, M. (1991). An investigation of the transition and integration of preschoolers with severe and profound multiple disabilities into a Montessori community preschool program: Program history, features, and research activities in progress, Circle of Inclusion Project. *Kansas Early Childhood Research Institute on Transition, Project 2.2. Working Paper No. 1.* Lawrence: Schiefelbusch Life Span Institute, University of Kansas.

Thompson, B., Wickham, D., Ault, M.M., Shanks, P., Reinertson, B., Wegner, J., & Guess, D. (1991). Expanding the circle of inclusion: Integrating young children with severe multiple disabilities. *Montessori Life, 1,* 11–15.

Thompson, B., Wickham, D., & Wegner, J. (1991). A qualitative research approach for investigating and evaluating an emergent early childhood inclusion model for children with severe disabilities in a Montessori preschool. *Kansas Early Childhood Research Institute on Transition, Project 2.2, Working Paper No. 2.* Lawrence: Schiefelbusch Life Span Institute, University of Kansas.

Thompson, B., Wickham, D., Wegner, J., Ault, M.M., Shanks, P., & Reinertson, B. (1993). *Handbook for the inclusion of young children with severe disabilities: Strategies for implementing exemplary full inclusion programs.* Lawrence, KS: Learner Managed Designs.

Vandercook, T., York, J., & Forest, M. (1989). The McGill action planning system (MAPS): A strategy for building the vision. *Journal of The Association for Persons with Severe Handicaps, 14*(3), 205–215.

Wegner, J. (1989). *Opportunities for communication intervention with preschool children with severe disabilities.* Unpublished manuscript, Department of Speech, Language and Hearing, University of Kansas, Lawrence.

Wegner, J. (1991). *From classroom to classroom: New ways to interact.* Unpublished doctoral dissertation, University of Kansas, Lawrence.

Whitehead, L., Deiner, P., & Toccafondi, S. (1990). Family assessment: Parent and professional evaluation. *Topics in Early Childhood Special Education, 10*(1), 63–77.

Wickham, D. (1993). *An investigation of video based individualized training for paraprofessionals in inclusive classrooms.* Unpublished doctoral dissertation, University of Kansas, Lawrence.

York, J., Vandercook, T., Caughey, E., & Helse-Neff, C. (1988). *Does the "Integration Facilitator" facilitate integration?* Minneapolis: University of Minnesota, Institute on Community Integration.

II

CHALLENGES AT SCHOOL

3

The Challenge of Educating Students with Special Health Care Needs

DONNA H. LEHR

SCHOOL SYSTEMS HAVE had a long history of providing basic health care to students, but school officials are now facing requests to provide education and health care to students whose needs are much more challenging than those previously encountered. Often, these are children who use such supportive technology as feeding tubes, tracheostomy tubes, or catheters. Some of these children are infected with the HIV virus.

The provision of specialized health care services themselves is not new. What is new is that the individuals requiring these specialized health care services are children living long enough to become students and that they are not automatically provided with education in institutions, hospitals, or homes (Lehr & Noonan, 1989). What is also new is that HIV is affecting children who are benefiting from medications that prolong their lives long enough for them to become students in schools in urban, suburban, and rural school systems. The challenges these children present do not stem from the complexity of the children's needs themselves; they stem from the need to provide these students with education and necessary health care in schools, not in hospitals or institutions. Simply put, to many this situation is new and challenging. This chapter discusses the scope and nature of the challenges and the practices that have been developed to meet these challenges.

INCIDENCE

The data on the numbers of children with special health care needs or AIDS are, at best, estimates. There has been no systematic collection of data to determine the actual number of children throughout the country who have special health care needs such as tube feeding, suctioning, and so on. However, estimates range from 20,000 to 100,000 (Palfrey et al., 1992). The number of children with special health care needs who attend public schools is also not known; however, some published studies provide data from specific states that serve to illustrate service provision within those states. Bradford, Heald, and Petrie (1994) report that at the time of their study, 25 students in Pennsylvania schools required tracheostomy care, 33 required tube feedings, 213 required catheterization, 29 required oxygen, and 12 required ventilators. Palfrey et al. (1992) reported that they provided consultation to school personnel in Massachusetts on methods for providing health care services for 17 students who receive tracheostomy care and 20 students who receive gastronomy tube feeding. However, the numbers cited in both studies greatly underrepresent actual numbers of students with these particular special health care needs. Bradford et al. (1994) used a survey and received only a 50% response rate; the Palfrey (1992) study reported on only those students for whom training was requested from the project discussed in the article. The authors of both studies point out that the trend is toward an increase in the numbers of students with special health care needs.

The number of school-age children with HIV is also growing (Centers for Disease Control and Prevention, 1994). The Centers for Disease Control and Prevention (CDC) reported a cumulative total in 1994 of 5,734 children who have been tested positive for HIV. The actual number of infected children is considered likely to be higher (CDC, 1994). It is estimated that there may actually be as many as 20,000 children infected with HIV (Palfrey et al., 1994). Of that number, it is possible that approximately 50% of the children who are infected with HIV will live long enough to become students (Annunziato & Frenkel, 1993) and thus become the educational responsibility of school officials.

CHALLENGES

Administrators with requests to provide education for students with special health care needs face situations that often challenge their understanding of the scope of school systems' responsibility. Some students' health care needs are so extensive that school administrators question whether the "education" provided is really education or if it should more appropriately be considered related services. Some students cause school administrators to be concerned about the individual's safety, particularly when the student is considered to be "medically fragile." Other students cause school administrators to be concerned about individual and public safety, most notably when the student is known to be HIV positive. Some district administrators question schools' responsibilities in terms of the costs of providing health care services, the need for school personnel to perform necessary services, and the fiscal obligations of the school.

These and other challenges are responded to in different ways. Practices vary for individual children, but not always based on those students' individual needs (Lehr & Noonan, 1989). The differences can be based on professional and legal interpretations of the responsibilities of schools and school personnel.

Medical Care versus Education

A major issue in the delivery of school services to students with special health care needs is the distinction between medicine and education. Martin (1991) highlights this issue by discussing a common reaction: "We shouldn't have to serve that child; their needs aren't really educational" (p. 1). The statement accurately reflects the sentiment of many people faced with providing education to students with complex health care needs. Consider Jimmy Alvarez:

> Jimmy Alvarez is an eight-year-old boy who has a rare neuromuscular degenerative condition caused by a genetically based metabolic disorder. His muscles are severely atrophic and his tone is flaccid. He requires assistance for all activities of daily living including careful feeding of a pureed diet, lifting out of his wheelchair for transfers, and changing his incontinence garments. He is prone to respiratory problems due to difficulty mobilizing secretions, so he receives mist treatments during the day and he must be closely observed for signs of infection or wheezing. His condition has also resulted in pancreatic failure so he needs to have his blood sugar checked on a glucose monitor four times each day. He then receives insulin injections after each test. The dosage is based on a sliding scale protocol. (Schwab, 1993, n.p.)

When children like Jimmy attend school, many observers question the school's priorities. They ask whether the services that are provided are educational or actually medical. They ask whether the student should be in school, given the amount of time that must be devoted to the provision of health care. Some people believe that the attention that needs to be given to the health care needs of a child like Jimmy is so extensive that little time is left for education; therefore, participation in an education program makes little sense.

Martin (1991) quickly dismisses the question of whether education should be provided to students with significant needs by discussing the decision in the case of *Timothy W. v. Rochester, New Hampshire, School District* (1989). The school district administrators considered Timothy W. too disabled to benefit from an education. They asserted that his needs were for related services such as physical and occupational therapy, not for educational services. The federal district court that heard the case affirmed the basic right to an education afforded all students with disabilities through the Education for All Handicapped Children Act of 1975 (PL 94-142), now called the Individuals with Disabilities Education Act (IDEA) (PL 101-476). The decision stated that "all means all," regardless of the severity of the student's disability. Although Jimmy does need extensive health care services, he is entitled to an education as are all other children.

Health and Safety Concerns

Many valid concerns regarding safety are raised when students with specialized health care needs enroll in schools. All children are entitled to receive quality care that promotes their well-being and health. For some children, however, such care is more difficult to provide and quality is more critical to achieve. Even the common childhood diseases (e.g., measles, chickenpox, colds) can have a greater impact on some students with special health care needs due to their increased susceptibility to these diseases (Lehr & Macurdy, 1994; Sobsey & Cox, 1991). Other diseases, such as HIV, cytomegalovirus, and hepatitis, require greater attention due to their unique relationship to children with developmental disabilities (i.e., potential increased prevalence and/or concerns regarding transmission).

Strong concerns are often expressed about a student who is HIV positive. In some very popularized cases in the 1980s, school officials excluded HIV-infected students from schools. These early decisions were based on fears of transmission. However, the courts ruled in favor of the students' inclusion in schools and relied on guidelines from the CDC and the American Academy of Pediatrics regarding known methods of transmission of the virus (Smith, 1990).

The definitive case on this issue is that of *Martinez v. School Board of Hillsborough County, Florida* (1988) (Martin, 1991). The initial complaint was filed on behalf of a child in response to the proposed plan for homebound instruction for the child, who was HIV positive, classified as mentally disabled, and lacked control of body secretions. (She was incontinent, drooled, and sucked her fingers.) The court determined that school-based instruction was appropriate only if the child was educated in a separate glassed-in room within a classroom. A higher court did not agree with that decision, particularly because of newly available information on methods of transmission of the HIV virus and newly established policies recommended by the American Academy of Pediatrics supporting school attendance of students who are infected with HIV, including those who lack control of body functions.

In this case and others, "the courts have relied on then-current medical knowledge" (Smith, 1990, p. 176) about methods of transmission. Courts since the *Martinez* case have found that placement in school is appropriate for students with HIV but must be based on the opinion of members of a placement team who "have the benefit of the latest reliable public health information with regard to the risks that the disease entails. This information would be considered along with information on the child's medical condition, behavior, and so forth" (Smith, 1990, p. 176).

In 1987 the American Academy of Pediatrics published its revised guidelines reflecting current understanding that transmission did not occur through casual contact. Also in that year, the National Association of State Boards of Education issued a guide to districts on policies regarding children and staff with AIDS. By 1992, a published survey of state departments of education revealed that 89% of the states had established attendance policies for HIV-infected students (Katsiyannis, 1992).

Individual safety must also be considered when children with special health care needs attend school because they are extremely vulnerable to disease and infection. The concern is for possible exposure of students with special health care needs to other students with communicable diseases. For students with chronic respiratory problems, it may be appropriate that the child spend some time out of school until an epidemic of colds by his or her classmates subsides. It may be appropriate for a student with a compromised immune system to be kept home from school when there is an outbreak of a common childhood disease such as chickenpox. In all cases, the decisions about attendance should be made with the involvement of all team members in consultation with the child's physician.

Defining Roles and Responsibilities

A frequent question regards responsibility for provision of critical health care services. Of particular concern is who can and should provide the services, and who should pay for them (Lehr & Macurdy, 1994; Lehr & Noonan, 1989). Answers to these questions come through the process of educational program planning, interpretations of laws and regulations, and definitions of professional practice.

Educational Program Planning In many cases, decisions about who should provide health care services to students are made by committee. The student's educational team, including school professionals, family members, and medical personnel, identifies the individual student's specific health care needs and determines who should assume implementation and fiscal responsibility. The decision is jointly determined and mutually agreed upon. This practice has resulted in different outcomes for individual students. In some cases, care has been provided by the following individuals:

- Teacher
- Nurse assigned to school
- Nurse assigned to student
- Health care aide
- Student

Fiscal responsibility is also assumed variously. Responsibility may be assumed by the school district, parent, the parent's private insurance, or by public insurance (Medicaid).

Legal Interpretations When agreements have not been secured through the team planning process, the disagreements have been resolved through due process procedures. A review of the decisions that have been made reveals differences in interpretation of special education laws, particularly the provision regarding related services within IDEA. How this act is interpreted will determine who is responsible for implementing procedures and paying for associated costs.

The Individuals with Disabilities Education Act defines *related services* as "transportation, and such developmental, corrective, and other supportive services . . . as may be required to assist a child with a disability to benefit from special education. . . ." (34 CFR Sec. 300.12[a]). This act defines *medical services* as those "provided by a licensed physician to define a child's medically related [disability] which results in a child's need for special education and related services" (34 CFR Sec. 300.13[b][4]).

One of the first cases in this area, *Department of Education, State of Hawaii v. Katherine D.* (1983), served to clarify that tracheotomy care was within the realm of school health as a related service and should be provided in school. The U.S. Supreme Court ruled similarly in *Irving Independent School District v. Tatro* (1984) when it determined that the provision of clean, intermittent catheterization was necessary during the school day for a child requiring special education, and this catheterization could be provided by someone other than a licensed physician.

Since these two cases were ruled on, questions have been raised about the responsibility of the school when the procedures required by the students are considered to be more complex than those needed by Amber Tatro and Katherine D. Tatro could be scheduled for catheterization, meaning that it could be delivered at a predictable time. Katherine D. required suctioning on an infrequent, intermittent basis, but just two or three times a day. However, some special health care needs are seen as being considerably more difficult to manage. Some students must have their vital signs monitored constantly; some must be suctioned very frequently. Some students require the provision of care that is not just based on time, but also on judgment of when the care is necessary. Does this change the intensity of need? Are these still related service needs? That is, are they services needed to enable a student to benefit from special education, or are they more complex and therefore medical in nature?

In the cases of *Detsel v. Board of Education of Auburn* (1986; 1987), *Bevin H. v. Wright* (1987), and *Granite School District v. Shannon* (1992), it was determined that each student required a level of health care that was more extensive than that addressed in *Tatro* and *Katherine D.* The courts determined that the students required constant monitoring and nursing care more intensive than that which was intended to be provided by school districts under IDEA. Each court decided the care needed to fall somewhere between a related service and a medical service as defined by the law. The services could be provided by someone other than a licensed physician; however, the required services were more extensive than typical school nursing services. In all three cases, the costs for providing the health care services were discussed and were a factor in making the distinction between a related service and a medical service.

When asked to clarify the distinction between related and medical services, Schrag (1993), the current Director of the Office of Special Education Programs, responded by restating the definitions of related services and medical services as well as reiterating the bases of the decision given in *Tatro.* As previously mentioned, in *Tatro,* the health care service of clean, intermittent catheterization was considered a related service since it was necessary for a child identified as having a disability who required the service during the school day, and it could be provided by a school health nurse or other trained school personnel, not just by a licensed physician. It should be noted that the frequency of the care, the level of expertise, and the cost associated with the provision of the service were not addressed in Schrag's response.

Despite decisions made in *Detsel, Bevin H.,* and *Shannon,* there is considerable evidence of school districts providing health care services that are needed by students (Palfrey et al., 1992). There are no known studies summarizing data on the fiscal responsibility for health care services for students; however, this author is aware of considerable variation throughout the United States. Melissa Detsel, who was authorized under Medicaid funding to receive 24 hours of home nursing care, was granted permission (after an appeal) to take a private duty nurse to school with her who would be paid by Medicaid (*Detsel v. Sullivan,* 1990). Some other children's health care needs are met in school by private duty nurses paid for by parents' private insurance policies. Still other children are provided with extensive health care services by registered nurses, licensed practical nurses, health care aides, or teachers or paraprofessionals who are employees of the school district.

Neither *Tatro* nor any of the other cases can be clearly pointed to as being the basis of practice for the provision of all health care services for students with special health care needs. It is only for the specific health care procedure of clean, intermittent catheterization that we have clear Supreme Court precedent. For students with the need for the provision of other health care procedures there is less clarity and, consequently, variable interpretations regarding whether the services they need are related services and therefore the responsibility of school district officials, or medical services and not the district's responsibility.

Professional Interpretations   Some of the variability may be accounted for by individual, district, state, or nationwide perspectives on professional responsibility. That is, decisions regarding who is responsible for providing specialized health care services are in part based on perceptions of who should be responsible.

Teachers in a study by Mulligan, Ault, Guess, Struth, and Thompson (1988) indicated that while they did implement a number of specialized health care procedures, they did not always believe that it should be their responsibility. They provided the services since no one else was available to do so. Thompson and Guess (1989) found that many teachers of students who are "medically fragile" considered it their responsibility to do whatever the parents would do. By contrast, the *Katherine D.* case came about as a result of staff members' objections to the request to perform the function of tracheostomy care. (That objection was also the basis of the original decision to exclude the student from a school-based education program.)

It is not only professionals' willingness to implement specific health care procedures that can affect their decisions on whether to do so; it is also individuals' perceptions of their own competence. An assumption cannot be made that because someone is a registered nurse, she or he has had sufficient experience with implementing specific health care procedures (Lehr & Noonan, 1989). Even nurses who have received extensive medical training have expressed concerns about implementing health care procedures that they have not been specifically trained to perform or have not implemented in many years (Hester, Goodwin, & Igoe, 1980).

State regulations of professional practice also play a significant role in determining who implements health care procedures. Each state has a nurse practice act that specifies roles and responsibilities for licensed nurses in the delivery of health care services and the delegation of responsibility. In effect, these laws specify which procedures nurses, including school nurses, can or must implement themselves and which procedures they can train others to implement under their supervision. Licensed nurses must comply with these regulations or risk losing their license to practice.

The nurse practice acts are at times very restrictive and come in conflict with service delivery to students with special education needs in least restrictive environments. As a consequence of unavailable school nurses, students are often clustered in settings where school nursing services are available, that is, in special schools (Lehr & Macurdy, 1994; Lehr & McDaid, 1993; Lehr & Noonan, 1989; Sobsey & Cox, 1991). Even in schools where there are nurses present, there remains the possibility that a particular nurse is not confident of his or her own skills in implementing the health care procedure. Furthermore, the nurse may not be confident in delegating the health care responsibility to another person with less specialized medical training, since the nurse retains ultimate responsibility for monitoring the delivery of the care. In response to these issues, some states have reviewed their laws and have made changes to them (Sobsey & Cox, 1991). For example, Kansas makes exceptions for nursing practices in schools to provide for greater flexibility (Sobsey & Cox, 1991).

Since the mid-1980s, there have been a number of states that have developed guidelines to assist school districts in delineating roles and responsibilities and in developing procedures for providing education and health care services to students with special health care needs. For example, the California Department of Education developed *Guidelines and Procedures for Meeting the Specialized Physical Health Care Needs of Pupils* (1990). Typical of many other states' manuals, this one includes background information on issues related to the provision of specialized health care in schools, a description of specialized health care procedures, a discussion of roles and responsibilities for the provision of care, a description of the procedure for preventing the spread of infectious diseases, and sample forms to guide school personnel in developing comprehensive plans to provide specialized procedures.

There have also been attempts at a national level to provide professionals with guidance on roles and responsibilities related to the provision of health care services in the schools. In a document developed by four professional organizations—the American Federation of Teachers, the Council for Exceptional Children, the National Association for School Nurses, and the National Education Association—roles and responsibilities were delineated (Joint Task Force for the Management of Children with Special Health Care Needs, 1990). The document lists 10 categories of health care procedures and, for each type of procedure within the categories, recommends which school personnel should assume implementation responsibility. Included are registered nurses, licensed practical nurses, certified teachers, related service personnel, paraprofessionals, and health care aides. Recommendations are based on the authors' perspectives of acceptable professional practices. However, some professionals have expressed concern about the perspectives presented in the guidelines (Lehr & Macurdy, 1994; Sobsey & Cox, 1991). The recommendations are based on the names of the health care procedures and the names of the roles of the individuals implementing the procedures. To ensure the safety of the students, decisions may be more appropriately based on the complexity of implementation of the procedure for individual students and the competence of the individuals implementing the procedures, regardless of their titles.

In general, professional responses to the prospect of implementing special health care procedures can be summarized by three questions: "Must I?" "Can I?" and "Should I?" Some professionals react to the prospect of providing specialized health care procedures in a manner similar to that of the prospect of toilet training. The procedures are not viewed as "pleasant"; in fact, some professionals ask, "Do I really have to implement this procedure?"

Some professionals have discussed their concerns about their competence to implement the procedure. Even school nurses, with extensive medical training, point to their lack of specialized training or practice in implementing particular health care procedures that they are not used to implementing in school. Some teachers question whether even with extensive training they have sufficient medical training to implement the procedures. Others question whether their implementation of procedures fits within the law. Some point to their perception of their roles as a teacher and question the appropriateness of a "teacher" providing care. ("My job is to teach, not provide this care, or to be a nurse.") Their concerns stem from questions regarding the role of a teacher. ("Is this what I should be doing with my time? I should be teaching.") Even some nurses raise the same question. They point to traditional roles of nurses and question whether they should be providing the more specialized health care required by some students.

EFFECTIVE PRACTICES

Despite the challenges often expressed, many school officials have worked very hard to develop solutions to the challenges of including students with special health care needs in schools. To accomplish this end, school personnel have had to extend current practice and incorporate new practices into their program planning and implementation. Schools have focused on the areas of individualized education programs (IEPs), confidentiality, hygienic care practices, and staff training.

Individualized Education Programs

For many students with special health care needs, changes have occurred in both the process involved in the developing of IEPs and the content of these plans. In many cases the membership of the planning team has necessarily expanded to include medical personnel such as the school nurse, the physician, and in some cases the home health care providers who have become a part of the children's extended family.

The addition of a comprehensive health care plan to the IEP is an increasing practice for students with special health care needs. Several model plans have been developed and are often included in manuals developed by state departments of education. Palfrey et al. (1992) recommend a health care plan as a good way to both document the student's routine and emergency needs and to delineate procedures for training and monitoring. They further recommend that the plan be reviewed by the student's physician, parent, educational administrator, and health care coordinator. It is critical that plans be reviewed frequently and that necessary changes be made to accurately reflect the current status and needs of the student. A sample plan is shown in Figure 1.

Lehr and Macurdy (1994) have pointed to the need to include objectives in a student's IEP that relate to the instruction of the student on the implementation of health care procedures, when appropriate. They emphasize the concern that all too often procedures are done to students without giving consideration to the possibility that the stu-

---

Name *Kristin Smith*   Date *9/5/92*

Health Care Need *gastrostomy tube feeding*

Protocol *attached*

Plan developed by *mother, teacher, school nurse, in consultation with physician*

Frequency *daily, during scheduled lunch*

Responsible Staff *teacher, teacher aide, school nurse as backup*

Training

  Dates *8/25* Trainer *public health nurse*

       Trainees *teacher, aide, school nurse* Topics *general first aid*

  Dates *8/26* Trainer *public health nurse*

       Trainees *teacher, aide, school nurse* Topics *CPR*

  Dates *8/27* Trainer *public health nurse*

       Trainees *teacher, aide, school nurse* Topics *tube feeding*

Monitoring

  Dates *9/4* Trainer *public health nurse*

       Trainees *teacher, aide, school nurse*

  Dates *10/2* Trainer *public health nurse*

       Trainees *teacher, aide, school nurse*

  Dates *1/8* Trainer *public health nurse*

       Trainees *teacher, aide, school nurse*

Emergency Indicators: color changes
                              breathing difficulties
                              g-tube comes out

Emergency Procedures: see emergency form

Figure 1. Sample health care plan. (From Lehr, D.H., & Macurdy, S. [1994]. Meeting special health care needs of students. In M. Agran, N.E. Marchand-Martella, & R.C. Martella [Eds.], *Promoting health and safety: Skills for independent living* [p. 80]. Baltimore: Paul H. Brookes Publishing Co.)

dents could learn to implement the procedures themselves or at least participate to some extent. Examples of such IEP objectives are shown in Table 1.

    Smith and Leatherby (1993) point out that an error that is sometimes made is that of including "objectives" on the IEP that are not

Table 1. Sample IEP objectives related to health care procedures

Tube Feeding

Student will explain (orally, in writing, given several options, etc.) reasons for alternative eating method.

Student will describe steps necessary in implementing the procedure.

Student will indicate desire to eat.

Student will measure feeding liquid to be placed in feeding bag or syringe.

Student will pour food in feeding bag or syringe.

Student will direct cleaning of feeding equipment.

Student will clean equipment.

Student will feed self.

Tracheostomy Suctioning

Student will indicate need to be suctioned.

Student will turn on suction machine.

Student will hold suction tube while procedure is being implemented.

Student will describe steps necessary to suction.

Student will explain to others the indicators of need for suctioning.

Catheterization

Student will indicate time to be catheterized.

Student will self-catheterize.

Student will describe steps in implementing the process.

Student will wash necessary materials.

Student will assemble necessary materials.

Student will hold catheter steady during procedure.

Student will describe indicators of problems related to catheterization.

From Lehr, D.H., & Macurdy, S. (1994). Meeting special health care needs of students. In M. Agran, N.E. Marchand-Martella, & R.C. Martella (Eds.), *Promoting health and safety: Skills for independent living* (p. 82). Baltimore: Paul H. Brookes Publishing Co.; reprinted by permission.

objectives at all, but actually "staff directives" (p. 81). For example, it is common to find objectives similar to "The student will be fed three times a day with a gastro-intestinal feeding tube" (Smith & Leatherby, 1993, p. 81). Directives such as this should be described in the section of the IEP that specifies related services or health care plans, not in the section on student outcomes.

Confidentiality

Confidentiality of information becomes a crucial issue when HIV-infected children are in school settings. According to Harvey (1994), "The underlying principle of confidentiality involves the right of privacy, based in both legal and ethical considerations" (p. 18). On the basis of these considerations, "information in a patient's record generally may not be disclosed to anyone other than the patient or authorized representative (often parents and legal guardians in the case of minors) without the informed consent of patients" (p. 18). The concern about protecting the privacy of individuals is due to the discrimination that often occurs toward individuals identified as having AIDS (Harvey, 1994). As Harvey points out, however, many of the existing laws regarding confidentiality predate HIV and/or relate to health care facilities, not schools, and cause confusion when applied to HIV-infected students in school settings. Increasingly, however, statutes are being revised to address these issues. In some states, new statutes require medical personnel to inform school personnel of the HIV-positive students, while other states permit it only when authorized by a parent or legal guardian (Harvey, 1994). In the case of minors, parents can give permission for medical personnel to provide confidential information to school personnel or can provide the information themselves.

The decision regarding who is informed about a student who tests positive for HIV and the potential impact on individuals in various roles within the school having knowledge of this identity require careful consideration. The "need to know" issues can be reduced to two critical questions: 1) who must know to effectively treat the child, and 2) who should know because they are at significant risk for being infected by the disease? It is obvious that physicians must know who is infected so that appropriate medical interventions can be prescribed. But it is considered not necessary for people in the school to know since they do not prescribe medical treatments for students (American Academy of Pediatrics, 1987; Harvey, 1994). It is generally agreed that the risks associated with transmission of the virus in school settings are minimal; consequently, the American Academy of Pediatrics (1987) recommends that it is not necessary for school personnel to be informed of the HIV status of specific students. The academy also points out that the need to know can be lessened through the use of universal precautions when providing care for *any* student.

Unfortunately, it is not the knowledge of the presence of the infection in a child in and of itself that is the problem. Even those who know that the risks associated with transmission are minimal continue to be fearful. Clark and Schwoyer (1994) provide an interesting analogy between some people's reaction to HIV-infected individuals and some people's reaction to a rattlesnake in a glass jar: "Although the person knows the snake cannot bite through the glass, one still flinches when the snake coils and strikes" (p. 267). It is the emotional reaction to a dreadful disease that results in discriminatory practice that can negatively affect a student who is HIV positive.

Hygienic Care Practices

The presence of a student with special health care needs requires increased attention to hygienic care providing procedures designed to reduce the risks of the spread of infectious diseases. While HIV has served as the impetus for attention to this area, the need extends beyond concern for transmission of just this disease, which actually is not easily spread in day-care and school settings. The transmission of hepatitis B and even just the common cold should be causes for concern for teachers working with students with special health care needs, for these students are more likely to be susceptible to and more extremely affected by infections (Lehr & Macurdy, 1994; Sobsey & Cox, 1991). The practical way to minimize the risks of transmission is relatively simple and has two components: 1) the use of good hygienic care providing practices, and 2) the use of these procedures with all students.

Effective practice includes a focus on 1) personal, student, and classroom cleanliness, with particular attention to hand-washing techniques; 2) toileting and diapering; 3) clean-up of body secretions; and 4) disposal of materials soiled by or used to clean body secretions. Specific guidelines are available from state departments of education and public health. Many guidelines for providing school-based services for students with special health care needs have included sections on hygienic care providing practices. The California Department of Education's *Guidelines and Procedures for Meeting the Specialized Physical Health Care Needs of Pupils* (1990) is one such example. The reader is referred to materials from these sources for specific guidelines.

The second component of effective practice for minimizing risk of transmission is the use of universal precautions—the application of practices of hygienic care when handling body secretions from all students, not just those known to have infectious diseases. There are two primary reasons for this approach. First, school personnel will not always know who has what diseases. Symptoms do not always accompany infectious diseases. Furthermore, even when the health status is known by some, with the current laws related to confidentiality of information and ethics regarding the reporting of the health status of students in schools, school personnel are not likely to know which students are infected by a disease such as AIDS. A second reason for the use of universal precautions is that even in the event that school personnel have knowledge of students' specific diseases, use of precautions for only those students serves as a red flag, pointing out the infected students to all. Using the same practices for all students serves to minimize risks of transmission and to maintain confidentiality of information regarding individual students' health statuses.

Lavin et al. (1994) point out that although school districts may have established policies regarding the use of universal precautions, use of the procedures is not consistent. Reasons included lack of equipment (e.g., running water, gloves) and a lack of a perception of real concern since the risk of transmission of HIV has been conveyed as being very minimal.

Staff Training

With the entrance of students with special health care needs into schools comes the need for new knowledge and skills on the part of school personnel. For many personnel, these students will be the first they have met who obtain nourishment through a tube or who require suctioning to remove secretions. To ensure not only the safety of such students in school but also their acceptance, it is critical that careful attention be provided to the training of school personnel. Lehr (1990a) has characterized effective training as having several key components. First, training must be provided for many individuals in various roles in the schools. It is certainly not necessary, or even appropriate, that everyone become competent in implementing specific health care procedures, but it is critical that many have a basic understanding of the student's needs for procedures and how to provide or secure assistance in the case of an emergency.

Second, Lehr characterizes effective training as carefully matching methods to outcomes. Many materials have recently been developed that explain the purposes and processes related to providing specific health care procedures. Such materials are beneficial in providing background information; however, they are insufficient to ensure competent implementation of procedures. Competence can be ensured only through demonstration and training by professionals who are adept at providing training to others. Another critical aspect of the training relates to its timeliness and systematic approach. It should be obvious that training must occur before a staff member is to implement a procedure; however, as Lehr (1990a) has pointed out, this is not always the case. Implementing procedures without appropriate training puts both the student and the care provider at risk. Training must also be ongoing to ensure continued accuracy of the implementation of procedures. Finally, Lehr stresses the need for training that is sensitive to the individual needs of the student. In some cases, the student may want to participate in presenting information to others, while in other cases it may be his or her preference not to be present while peers learn about the student's special health care needs.

While the debate may continue regarding who should implement specific health care procedures for students, there is no debate over the issue that whoever implements the procedures must be competent (Lehr & Macurdy, 1994). Similarly, it is recognized that training is critical not only for the individuals responsible for primary care, but also for other school personnel and peers. They must have the sensitivity, knowledge, and skills to support the students' education in school.

SUMMARY

Students with special health care needs can present considerable challenges to school officials. The complexity of their needs and the newness of their presence in schools understandably cause administrators and other school personnel to be concerned about how to meet their health care and educational needs. Lehr (1990b) has used the term *complex* to describe the health care needs of the students discussed in this chapter. She has also discussed her hope that the term is a temporary one, that the term *complex* is related to the newness of the situation, and that, in time, service provision will become more routine. Students with special health care needs do and will continue to challenge the school officials who are responsible for educating them; they need more carefully planned and implemented care and education than do many of their classmates. With careful attention to their care and educational needs, school officials can meet the challenges that these students present.

REFERENCES

American Academy of Pediatrics. (1987). Committee on Infectious Diseases: Health guidelines for the attendance in day-care and foster care settings of children infected with human immunodeficiency virus. *Pediatrics, 79,* 466–471.

Annunziato, P.W., & Frenkel, L.M. (1993). The epidemiology of pediatric HIV-1 infection. *Pediatrics Annals, 22,* 401–405.

Ault, M., Guess, D., Struth, L., & Thompson, B. (1988). Implementation of health-related procedures in classrooms for students with severe multiple impairments. *Journal of The Association for Persons with Severe Handicaps, 13*(2), 100–109.

Bevin H. v. Wright, 666 F. Supp. 71 (W.D. Penn. 1987).

Bradford, B.J., Heald, P., & Petrie, S. (1994). Health services for special needs children in Pennsylvania schools. *Journal of School Health, 64*(6), 258–260.

California Department of Education. (1990). *Guidelines and procedures for meeting the specialized physical health care needs of pupils.* Sacramento, CA: Author.

Centers for Disease Control and Prevention (CDC). (1994). *HIV/AIDS Surveillance Report, 6*(1), 4.

Clark, J.K., & Schwoyer, C.C. (1994). Lessons from controversy in applying universal precautions from HIV/AIDS. *Journal of School Health, 64*(6), 266–267.

Department of Education, State of Hawaii v. Katherine D., 727 F.2d. 809 (9th Cir. 1983).

Detsel v. Board of Education of Auburn, 637 F. Supp. 1022 (NDNY 1986).

Detsel v. Board of Education of Auburn, 820 F.2d. 587 (2d Cir. 1987).

Detsel v. Sullivan, 895 F.2d 58 (2d Cir. 1990).

Education for All Handicapped Children Act of 1975, PL 94-142. (August 23, 1975). Title 20, U.S.C. 1401 et seq: *U.S. Statutes at Large, 89,* 773–796.

Granite School District v. Shannon, 787 F. Supp. 1020 (D. Utah 1992).

Harvey, D. (1994). Confidentiality and public policy regarding children with HIV infection. *Journal of School Health, 64*(1), 18–20.

Hester, H.K., Goodwin, L.D., & Igoe, J.B. (1980). *The SNAP school nurse survey: Summary of procedures and results.* Project #1846002587A1. Washington, DC: U.S. Department of Maternal and Child Health.

Individuals with Disabilities Education Act Amendments of 1991, PL 102-119. (October 7, 1991). Title 20, U.S.C. 1400 et seq: *U.S. Statutes at Large, 105,* 587–608.

Irving Independent School District v. Tatro, 468 U.S. 883, 82 L.Ed. 2nd 664, 104 S. CT. 3371 (1984).

Joint Task Force for the Management of Children with Special Health Care Needs. (1990). *Guidelines for the delineation of roles and responsibilities for the safe delivery of specialized health care in the educational setting.* Reston, VA: Council for Exceptional Children.

Katsiyannis, A. (1992). Policy issues in school attendance of children with AIDS: A national survey. *Journal of Special Education, 26,* 219–226.

Lavin, A.T., Porter, S.M., Shaw, D.M., Weill, K.S., Crocker, A.C., & Palfrey, J.S. (1994). School health services in the age of AIDS. *Journal of School Health, 64*(1), 27–34.

Lehr, D. (1990a). Personal preparation to serve children with special health care needs. In A. Kaiser & C. McWhorter (Eds.), *Critical issues in preparing personnel to work with persons who are severely handicapped* (pp. 135–151). Baltimore: Paul H. Brookes Publishing Co.

Lehr, D. (1990b). Providing education to students with complex health care needs. *Focus on Exceptional Children, 25*(6), 1–8.

Lehr, D., & Noonan, M.J. (1989). Issues in the education of students with complex health care needs. In F. Brown & D.H. Lehr (Eds.), *Persons with profound disabilities: Issues and practices* (pp. 139–158). Baltimore: Paul H. Brookes Publishing Co.

Lehr, D.H., & Macurdy, S. (1994). Meeting special health care needs of students. In M. Agran, N.E. Marchand-Martella, & R.C. Martella (Eds.), *Promoting health and safety: Skills for independent living* (pp. 71–84). Baltimore: Paul H. Brookes Publishing Co.

Lehr, D.H., & McDaid, P. (1993). Opening the door further: Integrating students with complex health care needs. *Focus on Exceptional Children, 25*(6), 1–8.

Martin, R. (1991). *Medically fragile/technology dependent students: Drawing the line between education and medicine.* Unpublished manuscript, Carle Center for Health, Law and Ethics, Urbana, Illinois.

Martinez v. School Board of Hillsborough County, Florida, 692 F. Supp. 1293 (MD Fla. 1988).

Martinez v. School Board of Hillsborough County, Florida, 861 F.2d 1502 (11th Cir. 1988).

Palfrey, J.S., Fenton, T., Lavon, A., Porter, S., Shaw, D.M., Weill, K.S., & Crocker, A.C. (1994). School children with HIV infection: A survey of the nation's largest school districts. *Journal of School Health, 64,* 22–26.

Palfrey, J.S., Haynie, M., Porter, S., Bierle, T., Cooperman, P., & Lowcock, J. (1992). Project School Care: Integrating children assisted by medical technology into educational settings. *Journal of School Health, 62*(2), 50–54.

Schrag, J. (1993). Response to inquiry: Medical v. School Health Services Distinguished. *Individuals with Disabilities Education Law Report, 19*(6), 348–350.

Schwab, W. (1993). *Assuring competent health care provision in school: Case studies.* Paper presented at TASH TECH, Conference of the Association for Persons with Severe Handicaps, Chicago, IL.

Smith, P., & Leatherby, J. (1993). *Services for students with special health care needs: Guidelines for local school districts.* Louisville: Kentucky Department of Education.

Smith, W.L. (1990). OCR staff memorandum. *Education for the Handicapped Law Report, 16*(27), 712–718.

Sobsey, D., & Cox, A.W. (1991). Integrating health care and educational programs. In F.P. Orelove & D. Sobsey, *Educating children with multiple disabilities* (pp. 187–231). Baltimore: Paul H. Brookes Publishing Co.

Thompson, B., & Guess, D. (1989). Students who experience the most profound disabilities: Teacher perspectives. In F. Brown & D.H. Lehr (Eds.), *Persons with profound disabilities: Issues and practices* (pp. 3–42). Baltimore: Paul H. Brookes Publishing Co.

Timothy W. v. Rochester, New Hampshire, School District, 875 F.2d 954 (1st Cir. 1989).

4

Key Lessons Learned About Inclusion

DIANE BAUMGART AND MICHAEL F. GIANGRECO

It was late October, and the air was cool. An unexpected change in the daily schedule meant a shortened recess for that day. Noting the time limitation, the classroom assistant suggested that she stay inside with Mark, a student with multiple disabilities. The recess time allotted for the day would be consumed by the tasks of getting him out of his wheelchair, putting his coat on, and positioning him back into his wheelchair. This seemed like a logical suggestion to the teacher until Mark's classmate Amy said, "Why don't we just leave Mark in his wheelchair, put his coat on backwards, and tuck it in around the sides. That should keep him warm enough: it's not that cold out! Then he can be with us." Overhearing the conversation, another classmate, Bryan, raised a good point, "What will the kids in the other classes say? Won't it make Mark look weird if he goes to recess with his coat on backwards?" Amy replied, "It won't look weird if everyone does it."

That recess Ms. Lopez's fourth-grade class all went to recess with their coats on backwards.

THIS STORY RECOUNTS one of the numerous examples occurring with increasing frequency in classrooms where students with a wide range of characteristics are welcomed and included. When we hear such stories, we tend to focus on the new opportunities such situations present for students like Mark, who typically have been provided with edu-

Support for the preparation of this chapter was provided in part by the U.S. Department of Education, Office of Special Education and Rehabilitative Services, Personnel Preparation CFDA 84.029A (H029A00039), awarded to the University of Idaho, Department of Counseling and Special Education, and by Innovations for Educating Children with Deaf-Blindness in General Education Settings, CFDA 84.025F (H025F10008), awarded to the Center for Developmental Disabilities, the University Affiliated Program of Vermont, at the University of Vermont. The chapter represents the ideas and opinions of the authors, and no official endorsement by the U.S. Department of Education should be inferred.

cational services in settings apart from their peers without disabilities. But this story also gives us a glimpse of new opportunities available to teachers and students without disabilities. Students have real opportunities to experience and celebrate human diversity, use their creative powers to solve real challenges, and exert a positive influence on the community known as their classroom community. Similarly, teachers have new opportunities to teach a wide range of important social, affective, and problem-solving skills; model constructive ways to cope with change and new situations; and demonstrate that they are learners too!

In class after class, school after school, observations of successful inclusion reveal teachers and students creating ways of making it work (Baumgart, 1992; Giangreco, Dennis, Cloninger, Edelman, & Schattman, 1993; Helmstetter, Peck, & Giangreco (1994); Meyer, Ferguson, & Baumgart, 1992; Salisbury, Palombaro, & Hollowood, 1993; Schattman & Benay, 1992; Stainback & Stainback, 1992; Thousand, Villa, & Nevin, 1994; Villa, Thousand, Stainback, & Stainback, 1992). These many positive examples of inclusion in classrooms of the 1990s have been made possible by two decades of advocacy, policy making, and curricular/instructional efforts of people working to achieve a common goal—that the lives of children in our public schools will be better as a result of our schooling practices. These efforts have also been advanced through litigation that continues to affirm that the basic civil rights and tenets of our society must be extended to all people, including those with the most severe disabilities.

This chapter discusses two key legal cases and their legal precedents in the movement toward greater inclusion of students with the most severe disabilities. Following this, the chapter introduces the "socio-relations" perspective and its relation to policies and practices to guide educators in the inclusion movement. The chapter concludes with the presentation of seven key lessons learned as we explore the move toward inclusion-oriented education and related school reform. Each of these three areas serves as a reminder that previous assumptions have changed and that much remains to be learned as the school improvement process continues and expands.

LEGAL PRECEDENTS FOR
INCLUSION AND THE RIGHT TO EDUCATION

Although numerous legal cases have addressed the rights of students with disabilities, we have selected two for discussion here. The first case, *Timothy W. v. Rochester, New Hampshire, School District* (1989), reaffirmed the rights of students with the most severe disabilities to a free and appropriate education. The second case, *Oberti v. Board of Education of the Borough of Clementon School District* (1993), set legal precedents for inclusion of students with severe disabilities and addressed numerous arguments that were previously viewed as barriers to inclusion for students with severe disabilities. The discussion is based, in part, on the work of Laski, Gran, and Boyd (1993) on *Timothy W.* and that of Martin (1993) on the *Oberti* case.

The case of *Timothy W.* arose when, in 1980, a school district in New Hampshire refused to provide educational services to Timothy W. based on its assessment that his disabilities would prevent him from receiving any benefit from educational services. Timothy, a 13-year-old with multiple disabilities, including what was labeled as profound mental retardation, was refused educational services and other services by the Rochester school district. The district concluded that Timothy was not capable of benefiting from an education because he was too severely disabled to learn. Eventually, the district placed him in a 3-hour-per-day "diagnostic/prescriptive" program, but continued to deny Timothy any "educational" placement.

Family and experts continued to assert Timothy's ability to learn and his right to benefit from an educational program under the Education for All Handicapped Children Act of 1975 (PL 94-142), the corresponding New Hampshire state law, and Section 504 of the Rehabilitation Act of 1973 (PL 93-112). In May 1984 a complaint was filed, and in 1989 a court ruled that Timothy had been wrongly denied his right to appropriate public educational services, thus reaffirming the "zero student rejection" concept. School districts cannot determine eligibility criteria for services based on the severity of the disability or assumptions about the child's ability to benefit. Indeed, the court concluded that education for those with severe or profound disabilities is broadly defined, not limited to academic services, and may include basic functional life skills. The court further asserted that the school district has a responsibility to avail itself of new educational approaches in providing an education program geared to each child's individual needs (*Timothy W. v. Rochester,* 1989).

More than a decade after Timothy's initial exclusion, the focus of legal arguments has shifted to issues of where and how education is provided. In New Jersey, 5-year-old Raphael Oberti, a student with Down syndrome, was initially placed within a school exclusively for students with disabilities, but the school was located 45 minutes from his home. His family refused this placement, and an alternative was agreed upon. Raphael was placed in a kindergarten in his neighborhood school in the morning and a special education class for the afternoon. His special needs were addressed in the afternoon class, but few individualized education program (IEP) goals, curricular modifications, or supplemental supports were provided in the kindergarten program.

Raphael had difficulty in the kindergarten class and was considered disruptive. At the end of the school year, school district personnel proposed placement in a special education class for students with mental retardation—a placement that would require Raphael to be bused beyond the boundaries of his local school district. His parents requested a placement within a regular classroom in their neighborhood school.

In May 1993, the U.S. Court of Appeals for the Third District unanimously affirmed a federal district court ruling that Raphael be provided with special education services in a regular class in his local school. The court noted that the Individuals with Disabilities Education Act of 1990 (IDEA) (PL 101-476) has a presumption in favor of inclusion and outlined two reasons why. First, the court found that the benefits and opportunities for social and communication development and enhancement cannot be achieved in a setting where typical peers are not present. The second issue addresses the rights of students without disabilities to the reciprocal benefits of inclusion, including learning to work and communicate with their peers with disabilities. In addition, the court responded to other issues raised during the proceedings and outlined some obligations of the district, including making curricular modifications for Raphael.

The court maintained that IDEA requires schools, whenever possible, to provide supplementary aids and services to enable a student with disabilities to be educated in the regular classroom with peers who do not have disabilities. Conditions prior to placement in the classroom, such as the existing curriculum and/or instructional strategies not meeting the needs of a student with disabilities, are not legitimate reasons for exclusion.

The *Oberti* case reaffirms the right of students with disabilities to be educated with peers who do not have disabilities as a first placement option and requires schools to make necessary accommodations. The court reiterated the obligation of the district to provide support to teachers so that they can accommodate each child and the requirement to provide preparation to regular educators to facilitate the education of students with disabilities in the least restrictive environment. The court also confirmed that dumping children into the mainstream without such required special educational services as curricular modifications and supplemental aids and services is not likely to work and is not the intent of the law.

SOCIO-RELATIONS PERSPECTIVE

In these legal cases, the focus was on the rights of students with disabilities to a free and appropriate education in the least restrictive environment. In both cases the logic that excluded students from educational and/or regular class settings was the notion that these students were "inherently different" and therefore were not covered by equal protection under the law. The courts have exposed this logic as faulty. The rationale that included students was based on students with disabilities having the same rights as other children. Although the logic of "same rights" has supported innovative changes, Minnow (1990) notes that this logic eventually focuses on differences (i.e., the same rights do not mean the same interventions are appropriate). Minnow notes that reliance on a "same" or "different" perspective can have undesired outcomes and stigmas. This section of the chapter reviews a discussion of inclusion in which teachers focusing on "same rights/different needs" experienced problems in the placement of a student named Adam. The discussion of the teachers and their resolution is provided in the following paragraphs to highlight what Minnow describes as the "dilemma of differences" and the need for an alternative perspective to resolve the dilemma.

Perspectives on Difference

The issue of differences and their place within the discussion of disability has a long legacy. Numerous authors have described the integral role that attitudes and values play in defining disability (Blatt, Bogdan, Biklen, & Taylor, 1977; Cuban, 1989; Eisner, 1991; Gould, 1981; National Center for Research on Teacher Learning, 1992; Sarason, 1982; Sarason & Doris, 1979).

These issues on the nature of disability, differences, and values were discussed during a recent professional development course as teachers talked about the general subject of inclusion and about a student with severe disabilities, Adam, returning to his neighborhood school. General education teachers, special educators, and related service providers from a variety of schools were attending a district-sponsored professional development class on inclusion of students with disabilities. Typically, the class facilitator (assistant director of special education) introduced a topic, and then class members discussed readings and issues that had arisen during the week. A spirited discussion on "same rights/different needs" occurred.

The discussion centered around teachers' concerns with placing students with severe disabilities in classes that matched the students' chronological age, fearing teachers would "just be writing an IEP that fit the classroom rather than the student." The perspectives of the special education teachers are summarized as follows:

> I can see how inclusion can work for my students in one class at Grade 3 and one class at Grade 4, but the other classrooms . . . I don't know. It seems like [I will] make the *kid* fit the classroom and [fit] into those other classes. Is this what inclusion really is going to end up being? What if the kid doesn't fit? What do they do when the students [without disabilities] are just working on worksheet after worksheet? It seems like she would learn more if I pulled her out and really fit the curriculum to her needs.

The group struggled with the need to write IEPs based on a student's individual needs and with the difficulties they encountered in doing so within general class settings. The needs of a particular student, Adam, were mentioned as an example of the seemingly impossible task of writing an appropriate IEP and placing Adam in fourth grade. In Adam's school there was one fourth grade and one fourth grade teacher. The special education teacher working with Adam expressed her concern about Adam's not fitting in well in this classroom. She explained that his social and communication needs would not be met there, and placement in this classroom would detract from his present abilities. She predicted that Adam would become a "behavior problem."

Adam's teacher described this fourth grade: The students spend considerable time at their desks listening to the teacher and/or working on worksheets. This classroom is described in more detail under Traditional Approaches in Table 1.

After 30 more minutes of discussing Adam's needs, one elementary teacher asked, "Is this the *only* student who needs something different from what is offered and available in this classroom?" The answer from the group was a resounding "No!" They went on to discuss how many students, not just Adam, were *really* not learning in this and similar classes, and why. The facilitator used the example of Adam to refocus inclusion on the connection of Adam and other fourth graders as students. These associated needs of Adam's and the other students' catapulted the discussion in a new direction. For the first time, the discussion of inclusion went beyond the special needs of students with severe disabilities and focused on the learning needs of the student.

The scenario of Adam and "the problem with fourth grade as a placement" was helpful for a number of reasons. In this scenario, the age-appropriate placement was the only option since another less traditional or more flexible fourth grade teacher was not available. Initially, there appeared to be two choices. Adam could be placed into

Table 1.   Approaches to educating students with diverse characteristics

Traditional approaches	Inclusion-oriented alternatives
1. The teacher is the instructional leader.	1. Collaborative teams share leadership.
2. Students learn from teachers, and teachers solve the problem.	2. Students and teachers learn from each other and solve problems together.
3. Students are purposely grouped by similar ability.	3. Students are purposely grouped by differing abilities.
4. Instruction is geared toward middle achieving students.	4. Instruction is geared to match students at all levels of achievement.
5. Grade-level placement is considered synonymous with curricular content.	5. Grade-level placement and individual curricular content are independent of each other.
6. Instruction is often passive, competitive, didactic, and/or teacher-directed.	6. Instruction is active, creative, and collaborative among members of the classroom community.
7. People who provide instructional supports are located outside of, or come *primarily* from sources external to, the classroom.	7. People who provide instructional supports are located in, or come *primarily* from sources internal to, the classroom.
8. Some students do not "fit" in general education classes.	8. All students "fit" in general education classes.
9. Students who do not "fit in" are excluded from general classes and/or activities.	9. All students are included in general class activities.
10. Students are evaluated by common standards.	10. Students are evaluated by individually appropriate standards, including outcome performance measures.
11. Students' success is achieved by meeting common standards.	11. The system of education is considered successful when it strives to meet each student's needs.

Adapted from Giangreco, M.F., Cloninger, C.J., Dennis, R.E., & Edelman, S.W. (1994). Problem-solving methods to facilitate inclusive education. In J. Thousand, R. Villa, & A. Nevin (Eds.), *Creativity and collaborative learning: A practical guide to empowering students and teachers* (p. 323). Paul H. Brookes Publishing Co.; reprinted by permission of Paul H. Brookes Publishing Co.

the existing fourth grade, a learning environment in which his disability would "stand out" and his learning and social interactions would likely decrease. An alternative was placement in a separate "self-contained" classroom for academics and related services, using recess and school lunch (and maybe art and music as well) for social integration opportunities. A third option—revising the curriculum and instruction to meet the needs of Adam and many other fourth grade students—was "discovered" as teachers realized that the fourth grade classroom was not meeting the needs of other students.

The question about the unmet needs of other children in that classroom was the beginning of the realization that inclusion must go beyond disability issues if it is to work. It was Adam's disability label, a focus on differences and his right to have the same placement as his fourth grade peers, that made his placement seem problematic. The perplexity was confounded by the assumption that this fourth grade class should remain the same and that only Adam had unmet needs in this traditional classroom.

The group came to an understanding that inclusion was not, as earlier envisioned, "fitting Adam into this classroom" or teaching him elsewhere. As educators began to restructure the fourth grade classroom, they began to see how Adam's needs for active participation with objects and functional learning were needs he had in common with other students.

A New Perspective on Differences

The socio-relations perspective designs policies and programs by focusing on the needs people have in common as members of the same social category rather than differences between people. In the case of Adam, it was used to design a placement, curriculum, and instruction based on the associated needs of fourth graders. It is remarkably distinct from the differences/same rights perspective as a way of designing policies and services. Scholars in the area of policy reform (Gartner & Lipsky, 1987; Minnow, 1990; Sarason, 1982, 1990; Skrtic, 1991) discuss the conflicts and stigmas that result when programs, services, policies, and laws are designed around differences and existing social arrangements/structures. Minnow labels these conflicts the "dilemma of difference." The dilemma is either the struggle to treat people differently (by noting their inherent differences) without stigmatizing them or the struggle to treat them the same (noting their rights to have the same treatment) without denying them assistance.

Each side of the "dilemma of difference" struggle raises serious questions regarding "same" and "different" services, and both perspectives imply that a norm (often unstated or disguised as neutral) exists. One is "different" or "same" only in comparison to someone else or to some other group. In the case of Adam, the fourth grade classroom was the norm, and his inclusion was seen as a need to fit him into this existing place.

An example from another discipline may help to clarify the socio-relations perspective and highlight how its assumptions are evident and applicable to educational issues. Following is an example of gender discrimination in employment and the resolution using the socio-relations perspective (Minnow, 1988) to indicate the assumptions that the perspective challenges.

In 1987 the Supreme Court ruled on an issue of maternity leave for women employees in *California Federal Savings and Loan Asso-*

ciation v. Guerra (1987). At issue in the case was whether the federal ban against discrimination on the basis of gender allows treating pregnant women like other workers or whether it allows special treatment. Granting maternity leave on the basis of gender differences would result in a special privilege and possible stigmas (women may be considered "too different" for the job). Denying maternity leave and maintaining the same policies for all employees could result in equating workers and satisfactory performance with norms established historically by males (women must work under the same rules as men).

The court granted the leave, but not on the basis of gender *difference* or as a special privilege. Instead, the court associated men and women as members of the category of employees and within this category considered their associated needs to work, maintain, and care for their family. These associated needs were used to grant not "maternity" but "parental leave," based on the associated parental needs of men and women employees. Women's experiences were used as the benchmark and guarded against discrimination and stigma by improving the lot of women *and* men. A focus away from inherent differences (gender) and the attending social consequences assisted in the resolution of this case. The focus became the associated needs of women and men to work and maintain families, and resisted reaffirming social arrangements that make gender *difference* an issue.

The connection of the *Guerra* case to Adam's situation is enlightening. The dilemma of differences arose in discussing Adam and inclusion by focusing on his disability (difference) and his right to the same placement, while accepting the existing classroom and social arrangements as a standard to be maintained. Initially, the teachers mentioned only Adam's differences and what was needed, outside of this fourth grade class, to meet his needs and to write an appropriate IEP. What was not expressed, until one teacher questioned the appropriateness of the classroom for many students, were the associated needs of Adam and other fourth graders.

In the discussion of *associated needs* of these fourth grade students, the teachers eventually described the "inclusion-oriented" classroom depicted in Table 1. The curriculum, instructional strategies, climate, staffing, and physical structure were reconceptualized. The group realized that Adam's need for hands-on, activity-based, individualized curricula and learning; heterogenous and cooperative grouping strategies; physical movement; and integration of special education/related services into the classroom could actually become a benchmark to enhance not only his social relationships and learning needs, but also those of other fourth graders. Adam, and at least 15 other fourth graders with different labels (e.g., Chapter 1, gifted and talented, mildly educationally disabled, at risk, homeless, unmotivated), did not have to leave the room and get "different stuff" to learn and connect with school and classmates. Adam still has disabilities, but their social significance in terms of "different" was diminished when the associated needs of all students were considered.

Social arrangements, traditional approaches, and accompanying assumptions and norms often emphasize differences and make these differences matter. Reconceptualizing beyond the "one size fits all" approach can reduce the social significance of differences. These teachers learned that two questions—"What does Adam need?" and "Is this a need for any other student?"—refocused the problem toward the need for classroom change, school reform, and collaboration.

Those who work in schools, prepare teachers, and/or engage in school reform realize that reconceptualizing and collaborating can be challenging. What this section has tried to make more salient is that meeting the challenge requires an understanding of inclusion as more than a special education or disability issue. The work of school reform remains demanding, but options are unnecessarily limited when efforts and directions are set within old paradigms and assumptions (Brandt, 1993; Cuban, 1989; Goodlad, 1984; Harding, 1987; Schlechty, 1990; Skrtic, 1991).

Some directions to guide inclusive classroom reform efforts are offered in the next section. Each is based on lessons learned when traditional approaches to schooling are challenged and replaced with more inclusion-oriented practices.

INCLUSIVE EDUCATION: KEY LESSONS LEARNED

Within schools across the United States, educators are rethinking basic assumptions of what, why, and how to teach. The process of questioning and trying "new" things has opened up possibilities for teachers, students, and their families. Here are some of the things we have learned from school stakeholders—teachers, students, families, administrators, and other school personnel:

> **Lesson 1: In order to provide quality inclusive education for students, we must have an ever-developing vision of how students' lives will improve because the students attend our schools.**

Selection of curricular content and other school experiences should be related to individually determined and valued life outcomes, reflecting a healthy balance between the academic/functional and social/personal aspects of schooling (Giangreco, Cloninger, & Iverson, 1993). In special education, this means involving families and students in the selection of goals and their outcomes. Current elementary and secondary education reforms refer to essentially these same parameters as "authentic learning," "performance-based outcomes," and "school–parent partnerships." Numerous school changes in which partnerships and an enlarged curricular basis have enhanced learning and preparedness for the future are discussed in the literature and documented for students, including those with severe or profound disabilities, within the federal and district reform agendas (Lightfoot, 1978; Smith, Hunter, & Schrag, 1991). Reconceptualizing what, how, and why we teach is a large part of improving schools and the process of implementing inclusive classrooms.

Lesson 2: Although inclusive education may be promoted by the needs of students with disabilities, inclusive education is not a "disability" issue.

Although school inclusion is promoted and works well for many students with severe disabilities, school inclusion is not a disability issue. Inclusive education is a part of school improvement that seeks to provide meaningful education to the range of students in the classroom community. Students formerly enrolled in separate programs *have* enlarged the curriculum. Some elementary classrooms now have foreign language as a curricular component because former separate bilingual/bicultural programs were restructured to focus on the needs of all children to learn a foreign language (Baumgart, 1992). Some high school students have an engineering design project, a health practicum, and/or a challenging experience in drama class (Ferguson, Meyer, Jeanchild, Juniper, & Zingo, 1992) because their needs and those of their classmates with severe disabilities or complex health and medical needs are viewed as associated. Diversity, when viewed as a strength and joined to the socio-relations perspective, has been a creative and empowering force in schools. People who work with children in schools must be advocates for all children, not just those with specific labels (e.g., disabled, gifted, bilingual). It is critical that we empower school reform efforts by advocating more than "just" inclusion for students with disability labels (Giangreco, 1989).

Lesson 3: Educational equity is unlikely to occur if individuals are the gatekeepers to inclusive classrooms.

Inclusive education, as a part of school reform, must involve administrative support. Support must include articulated policies and procedures that ensure equal access for all students. We cannot have groups of teachers in the same or different buildings who "do inclusion" or "do not do inclusion" based on individual biases or fears of situations to which they are unaccustomed. Giving individual teachers the choice to exclude a student from the public classroom based on any range of personal characteristics (race, ethnicity, gender, religious affiliation) would not be tolerated—yet, unfortunately, it remains the norm when the personal characteristic is identified by a disability label. Eligibility criteria that initially led to exclusion, as in the *Oberti* and *Timothy W.* cases, prompted legal action and will likely continue to do so. Eligibility criteria for school inclusion have no place in current reform efforts and are indicators that *all* students are not considered in the reform agenda and that diversity is still not seen as a strength.

Lesson 4: Teamwork is essential to quality education. A key feature of teams is the pursuit of the same goals rather than agreement to pursue different goals.

Typically, no single individual possesses the range of knowledge and skills necessary to meet the diverse and complex needs of students with disabilities. Thus, people who possess a range of skills must organize themselves to take full advantage of each person's strengths, both professional and personal. A key factor that distinguishes a "team" from a mere "group" is that a team pursues a set of common or shared goals. The roles/functions that they engage in and the manner in which they make decisions are tied to these common goals. Membership on the team is established by asking a simple question: Who will be affected by decisions that the team makes? This question means that, although the team may have core members, membership is likely to change as situations and needs change.

Group consensus decision making and the needs of students have received attention in the literature as critical elements for implementing the array of services required to meet student needs (Baumgart & Ferguson, 1991; Giangreco, 1990; Giangreco, York, & Rainforth, 1989). Yet many professionals are still inexperienced in working within a collaborative team structure. Many are inexperienced in working with families and students as equal partners. Most received preservice preparation within a program that was discipline specific and based on autocratic decision making or "majority rules," rather than focused on cross-discipline collaboration and consensus decision making. The notion of educators as the "experts" must be replaced with an understanding that abilities and perspectives are combined within teams to enable consensus and to meet identified outcomes. This idea is distinctly different from roles and functions being delegated and based primarily on professional disciplines and students' disability labels.

Lesson 5: Teacher ownership of the education of all students placed in the classroom, including those with disabilities, is crucial to success.

Language is a powerful indicator of the ownership that general education teachers and administrators have of the education of various students (Giangreco, Dennis, et al., 1993). Implementing inclusion requires an increased understanding that past assignments of expertise related to abilities and deficits of students (e.g., different teachers for gifted students or for those with severe disabilities) was in part an attitude, in part a lack of exposure and experience, and in part practices and assumptions resulting from resource allocation and school structuring at the turn of the century (Ferguson, 1991; Schlechtly, 1990; Skrtic, 1991). When students were assigned labels and corresponding specialists, we often inadvertently encouraged classroom teachers to think of these students as someone else's responsibility (Baumgart, 1992). Within inclusive classrooms, ownership and the responsibility to teach students become a barrier to success if students remain "yours" or "mine" and do not eventually become "ours." It is advisable to establish an expectation of shared ownership and responsibility from the outset. Teachers with the expertise required to meet student needs must continue to be available to students within schools, but role changes and revised understandings of ownership and teaching responsibilities must also be expected.

A common mistake made when initiating the placement of a child with severe disabilities in a general education classroom is to establish the expectation that the teacher is merely a "host," that the responsibility for educating the child is not the teacher's but lies with support personnel, such as the special educator, the speech and language teacher, the physical therapist, or a paraprofessional. Sometimes this situation occurs in an effort to avoid subjecting teachers to situations to which they are unaccustomed. Our efforts to be sensitive to the change this represents for teachers has frequently backfired when special education staff later attempt to encourage greater responsibility on the part of the classroom teacher.

Lesson 6: Inclusive education thrives in settings where instruction is active and participatory.

Instruction that is active, participatory, and child directed produces innumerable learning opportunities for both teachers and students. Much of the literature on active, participatory, child-directed learning focuses on elementary and secondary classrooms in which students' questions and responses are used to extend and broaden curriculum and focus instruction on understanding in addition to factual recitation (Duckworth, 1987; Fosnot, 1989; Henderson, 1992). One parallel of child-directed learning within the disability literature, typically described as "behavior as communication," has also had a positive impact on instruction of students with severe or profound disabilities. Teachers using child-directed learning with students who have disabilities are seeking to understand the communicative intent behind "behaviors" (Baumgart, Johnson, & Helmstetter, 1990; Durand & Crimmins, 1988) and/or using behavioral state indicators (Ferguson, 1991; Siegel-Causey & Guess, 1990) to identify student intentions that alter previous perceptions of students' abilities. Communication signals have been discovered where previously it was assumed there were none. Using a child-directed approach and looking at "behavior as communication," teachers realized that a whine or cry may be a signal of loneliness or protest, hitting may indicate that a task is too difficult or boring, and humming and rapid eye movements may signal excitement/recognition (Evans & Meyer, 1985; Mallette et al., 1992).

In spite of these parallel developments across education, a common concern arises regarding school inclusion for students with severe or profound disabilities. The difficulty arises when classroom instruction is mainly passive and/or teacher directed (e.g., primarily lecture, worksheets, teacher recitation to the whole class). In these classes, behaviors like humming, loud teeth grinding, sleeping, or wheelchair banging are often viewed as inappropriate and as indicators that the student is not "ready for" inclusion. We propose that the first response to this concern should be to enhance the curriculum and instruction, based on the associated needs of all students. Active, participatory, cooperative, and "authentic" instruction, coordinated with didactic teaching and skill development, typically optimizes learning and minimizes "disruptive" responses for many students, including those with severe disabilities as well as those without disability labels. Including students in less than adequate general education experiences is not the goal of inclusive education. A second response should be to enhance the communicative interaction. This typically involves reflecting on "behavior as communication," identifying and listening to the intent of the behaviors, enlarging the audience of listeners, and teaching communication partners new ways to communicate. A third response should be to formulate appropriate learning goals for students within the shared activities. Multilevel instruction and curriculum overlapping are keys to successful learning within shared activities (Collicott, 1991; Giangreco & Putnam, 1991).

Multilevel instruction—targeting different learning goals within the same curricular area (e.g., individualized goals within math or communication)—can readily encompass the learning needs of a diverse group of students. It is not uncommon for teachers to address a wide range of learning goals within active, participatory, instructional activities. For example, curriculum overlapping—selecting individually appropriate objectives from different curricular areas during a shared activity—is another option for appropriately meeting the needs of students during certain activities. Teachers can address a fine motor or communication skill during shared activities (e.g., reaching for and grasping an object during a science activity, facilitating eye contact with peers as materials are shared in a math activity). For many teachers, curriculum overlapping and the principle of partial participation (Ferguson & Baumgart, 1991) are necessary components to enhancing students' participation in the richness of shared activities while ensuring each student's appropriate education.

Lesson 7: Teachers who are willing to learn from their students and create classroom communities that encourage student participation in the design of their educational experiences report success.

Again and again, teachers who allow diversity in their classrooms to fuel creative problem solving report success with inclusion. For many adults in schools, the range of diversity possible in their current classrooms exceeds their experience both as former students and as educators. At first, responding to the diversity in students' abilities and needs may occasion an overwhelming desire to "know" all the answers and solutions to what may arise. Teachers who join with their students in creative problem solving (Giangreco, 1993; Thousand et al., 1994), resisting the urge to "know *all* the answers" beforehand, find new vistas of understanding both for themselves and for the students they support within this process.

SUMMARY

This chapter reviewed two important legal cases, described and proposed using the socio-relations perspective to guide inclusion and school reform efforts in the future, and offered key lessons learned from those who have implemented inclusion of students with severe or profound disabilities in their schools. Because of the scope of this chapter, many issues have not been addressed, including the details of curriculum, staffing, and evaluation and the importance of personnel preparation and related higher education reform. We acknowledge the importance of these issues and concur with many that future efforts must address these areas in depth.

Reflection on the socio-relations perspective (rather than differences or same rights perspectives) can guide us in our inclusion and school reform efforts and policies. It is hoped that a visible indicator of future changes at many levels will include collaborative efforts to enhance education based on the relatedness of students' learning characteristics rather than the differences between students, resulting both in teachers with differing expertise working together as a team and in an absence of placements based only on a continuum of differences. It also is hoped that future references to students with disabilities will not consist of labels viewed as deficits and categories rooted in differences. We envision descriptors for students being required, given the range of diversity that exists among learners, but the descriptors must focus on students' strengths and related needs for services.

Finally, this chapter described inclusion within the context of school reform. As evidenced by the plethora of published material on school reform, schools have engaged in this process repeatedly. It is hoped that future efforts of school reform and systems change will be embraced as being the continuing work of schools and the creative people who work in them. Thus, change and reform will not be viewed as movement toward a desired end but rather will be embraced within the concept that "one good idea will always lead to another." Although current reform needs to be both broad and deep, change is also a result of an ever-developing vision of how the lives of students will be better because they attend our schools.

REFERENCES

Baumgart, D. (1992). Philosophy, differences and education. In T. Bunsen, D. Baumgart, & A.M. Huang (Eds.), *Forum on emerging trends in special education: Implications for personnel preparation* (pp. 115–128). Fourth Annual Forum. Greeley, CO: University of Northern Colorado, Division of Special Education.

Baumgart, D., & Ferguson, D. (1991). Personal preparation: Directions for the next decade. In L.H. Meyer, C.A. Peck, & L. Brown (Eds.), *Critical issues in the lives of people with severe disabilities* (pp. 313–353). Baltimore: Paul H. Brookes Publishing Co.

Baumgart, D., Johnson, J., & Helmstetter, E. (1990). *Augmentative and alternative communication systems for persons with moderate and severe handicaps.* Baltimore: Paul H. Brookes Publishing Co.

Blatt, B., Bogdan, R., Biklen, D., & Taylor, D.J. (1977). From institution to community: A conversion model. In E. Sontag, J. Smith, & N. Certo (Eds.), *Educational programming for the severely and profoundly handicapped* (pp. 40–52). Washington, DC: Council for Exceptional Children.

Brandt, P. (1993). On restructuring roles and relationships: A conversation with Phil Schlechty. *Educational Leadership, 51*(2), 8–11.

California Federal Savings and Loan Association v. Guerra, 107 S. Ct. 683 (1987).

Collicott, J. (1991). Implementing multi-level instruction: Strategies for classroom teachers. In G. Porter & D. Richler (Eds.), *Changing Canadian schools: Perspectives on disability and inclusion* (pp. 111–118). North York, Ontario: The Roeher Institute.

Cuban, L. (1989). Reforming again, again and again. *Educational Researcher,* *19*(1), 3–13.

Duckworth, E. (1987). *"The having of wonderful ideas" and other essays on teaching and learning.* New York: Teachers College Press.

Durand, V.M., & Crimmins, D.B. (1988). Identifying the variables maintaining self-injurious behavior. *Journal of Autism and Developmental Disorders, 18,* 99–117.

Education for All Handicapped Children Act of 1975, PL 94-142. (August 23, 1977). Title 20, U.S.C. 1401 et seq: *U.S. Statutes at Large, 89,* 773–796.

Eisner, E.W. (1991). What really counts in schools. *Educational Leadership,* *48*(5), 10–17.

Evans, I.M., & Meyer, L.H. (1985). *An educational approach to behavior problems: A practical decision model for interventions with severely handicapped learners.* Baltimore: Paul H. Brookes Publishing Co.

Ferguson, D.L. (1991). *Including exceptions: A system for education students with dual sensory impairments and other extreme disabilities in general education settings.* Funded project of the U.S. Department of Education, Office of Special Education and Rehabilitative Services, CFDA 84.025F to the Specialized Training Program, University of Oregon, Eugene.

Ferguson, D.L., & Baumgart, D. (1991). Partial participation revisited. *Journal of The Association for Persons with Severe Handicaps, 16*(4), 218–228.

Ferguson, D.L., Meyer, G., Jeanchild, J., Juniper, L., & Zingo, J. (1992). Figuring out what to do with the grown-ups: How teachers make inclusion "work" for students with disabilities. *Journal of The Association for Persons with Severe Handicaps, 17*(4), 218–226.

Fosnot, C.T. (1989). *Enquiring teachers, enquiring learners: A constructivist approach to teaching.* New York: Teachers College Press.

Gartner, A., & Lipsky, D.K. (1987). Beyond special education: Toward a quality system for all students. *Harvard Educational Review, 57*(4), 367–395.

Giangreco, M.F. (1989). Facilitating integration of students with severe disabilities: Implications of the principle of "planned change" for teacher preparation of programs. *Teacher Education and Special Education, 12*(3), 139–147.

Giangreco, M.F. (1990). Making related services decisions for students with severe disabilities: Roles, criteria, and authority. *Journal of The Association for Persons with Severe Handicaps, 15*(1), 22–32.

Giangreco, M.F. (1993). Using creative problem-solving methods to include students with severe disabilities in general classroom activities. *Journal of Educational and Psychological Consultation, 4*(2), 113–135.

Giangreco, M.F., Cloninger, C.J., Dennis, R.E., & Edelman, S.W. (1994). Problem-solving methods to facilitate inclusive education. In J. Thousand, R. Villa, & A. Nevin (Eds.), *Creativity and collaborative learning: A practical guide to empowering students and teachers* (pp. 321–346). Baltimore: Paul H. Brookes Publishing Co.

Giangreco, M.F., Cloninger, C.J., & Iverson, V.S. (1993). *Choosing options and accommodations for children: A guide to planning inclusive education.* Baltimore: Paul H. Brookes Publishing Co.

Giangreco, M.F., Dennis, R., Cloninger, C., Edelman, S., & Schattman, R. (1993). I've counted Jon: Transformational experiences of teachers educating students with disabilities. *Exceptional Children, 59*(4), 359–372.

Giangreco, M.F., & Putnam, J. (1991). Supporting the education of students with severe disabilities in regular education environments. In L.H. Meyer, C. Peck, & L. Brown (Eds.), *Critical issues in the lives of people with severe disabilities* (pp. 245–270). Baltimore: Paul H. Brookes Publishing Co.

Giangreco, M.F., York, J., & Rainforth, B. (1989). Providing related services to learners with severe handicaps in educational settings: Pursuing the least restrictive option. *Pediatric Physical Therapy, 1*(2), 55–63.

Goodlad, J.I. (1984). *A place called school: Prospects for the future.* New York: McGraw-Hill.

Gould, S.J. (1981). *The mismeasure of man.* New York: Norton.

Harding, S. (1987). Introduction: Is there a feminist method? In S. Harding (Ed.), *Feminism and methodology* (pp. 1–14). Bloomington: Indiana University Press.

Helmstetter, E., Peck, C.A., & Giangreco, M.F. (1994). Outcomes of interaction with peers with moderate and severe disabilities: A statewide survey of high school students. *Journal of The Association for Persons with Severe Handicaps, 19*(4), 263–276.

Henderson, J.G. (1992). *Reflective teaching: Becoming an inquiring educator.* New York: Macmillan.

Individuals with Disabilities Education Act of 1990 (IDEA), PL 101-476. (October 30, 1990). Title 20, U.S.C. 1400 et seq: *U.S. Statutes at Large, 104,* 1103–1151.

Laski, F., Gran, J., & Boyd, P. (1993, June). Right to inclusion and services in regular class affirmed by federal appeals court: Memo. (Available from Public Interest Law Center of Philadelphia, 125 S. 9th St., Suite 700, Philadelphia, PA 19107.)

Lightfoot, S. (1978). Black dreams and closed doors. In S. Lightfoot (Ed.), *Worlds apart: Relationships between families and schools* (pp. 125–175). New York: Basic Books.

Mallette, P., Miranda, P., Kandborg, T., Jones, P., Bunz, T., & Rogow, S. (1992). Application of a lifestyle development process for persons with severe intellectual disabilities: A case study report. *Journal of The Association for Persons with Severe Handicaps, 17*(3), 179–191.

Martin, R. (1993). In this issue: Inclusion. *Special Education Update, 3*(1), 1–8.

Meyer, G., Ferguson, D.L., & Baumgart, D. (1992). Mine? Yours? Ours? Whose kids are these anyway? Fieldnotes for regular class participation systems. Funded project by the U.S. Department of Education, Office of Special Education and Rehabilitative Services to the Specialized Training Project, University of Oregon, Eugene, OR 97403.

Minnow, M. (1988). Feminist reason: Getting it and losing it. *Journal of Legal Education, 38*(1 & 2), 47–60.

Minnow, M. (1990). *Making all the difference: Inclusion, exclusion, and American law.* Ithaca, NY: Cornell University Press.

National Center for Research on Teacher Learning. (1992). *Findings on learning to teach.* East Lansing, MI: Author.

Oberti v. Board of Education of the Borough of Clementon School District, 995 F.2d 1204 (3d Cir. 1993).

Rehabilitation Act of 1974, PL 93-112. (September 26, 1973). Title 29, U.S.C. 701 et seq: *U.S. Statutes at Large, 87,* 355–394.

Salisbury, C.L., Palombaro, M.M., & Hollowood, T.M. (1993). On the nature and change of an inclusive elementary school. *Journal of The Association for Persons with Severe Handicaps, 18*(2), 75–85.

Sarason, S.B. (1982). *The culture of the school and the problem of change* (2nd ed.). Boston: Allyn and Bacon.

Sarason, S.B. (1990). *The predictable failure of educational reform.* San Francisco: Jossey-Bass.

Sarason, S.B., & Doris, J. (1979). *Educational handicap, public policy, and social history: A broadened perspective on mental retardation.* New York: Free Press.

Schattman, R., & Benay, J. (1992). Inclusive schools: How are they different? *School Administrator, 49*(2), 8–12.

Schlechty, P. (1990). *Schools for the 21st century.* San Francisco: Jossey-Bass.

Siegel-Causey, E., & Guess, D. (Eds.). (1990). *Enhancing nonsymbolic communication interactions among learners with severe disabilities.* Baltimore: Paul H. Brookes Publishing Co.

Skrtic, T.M. (1991). *Behind special education. A cirtical analysis of professional culture of school organization.* Denver: Love Publishing.

Smith, A., Hunter, D., & Schrag, J. (1991). America 2000: A revolution in American education. *Impact Newsletter, 4*(3), 4–5.

Stainback, S., & Stainback, W. (Eds.). (1992). *Curriculum considerations in inclusive classrooms: Facilitating learning for all students.* Baltimore: Paul H. Brookes Publishing Co.

Thousand, J., Villa, R., & Nevin, A. (Eds.). (1994). *Creativity and collaborative learning: A practical guide to empowering students and teachers.* Baltimore: Paul H. Brookes Publishing Co.

Timothy W. v. Rochester, New Hampshire, School District, 875 F.2d 954 (1st Cir. 1989).

Villa, R., Thousand, J., Stainback, W., & Stainback, S. (1992). *Restructuring for caring and effective education: An administrative guide to creating heterogeneous schools.* Baltimore: Paul H. Brookes Publishing Co.

5

Widening the Stream

Ways to Think About Including "Exceptions" in Schools

DIANNE L. FERGUSON,
CHRISTOPHER WILLIS, AND GWEN MEYER

DESPITE LEGAL INCLUSION (Dussault, 1989), students with disabilities force us to face the limits of our teaching abilities. Teachers, whether "general" or "special," find that these students do not respond well to their current practices, and they are challenged to produce meaningful educational outcomes (Evans & Scotti, 1989; Ferguson, 1987; Guess & Thompson, 1991; Izen & Brown, 1991). Challenges posed by these students only multiply in our current climate of broad school reform and improvement.

As schools restructure and reform, where do these students fit? In many schools, students with disabilities are not even included in discussions about, or planning for, inclusive teaching. In other schools, where they are considered, many teachers, administrators, students, and family members, despite a commitment to the values of our emerging school improvement reforms, wonder if these changes apply to all

The demonstration project from which this chapter emerged, Including Exceptions: A System for Educating Students with Dual Sensory Impairments and Other Extreme Disabilities in General Education Settings, was funded by the U.S. Office of Special Education and Rehabilitative Services and conducted by the University of Oregon's Specialized Training Program. However, the opinions expressed therein do not necessarily reflect the position or policy of the U.S. Department of Education, and no official endorsement by the department should be inferred.

The authors wish to acknowledge the contributions of the Including Exceptions System staff, our consultants, and collaborators Myrna Zitek, Mary Dalmau, Michael Young, Lysa Jeanchild, Anne Todd, Eileen Rivers, and Diane Baumgart.

students except these few extremely disabled. As we strive to include *all students* in the life and experiences of general public education, how will these students succeed? What does learning mean for them? How will they meet school achievement standards? Who will see to their care and safety? What should schools expect them to accomplish? Many educators think there are limits to what we can accomplish, or should be expected to accomplish, for these students. Perhaps *all* really means *all except for* the very few students with disabilities whom we educators are not yet clever enough to incorporate into school communities in ways that foster for them ordinary identities as unique learners and confer on them true membership.

These sentiments may be all too familiar. They certainly represent a familiar response of many people in schools who encounter students with extreme multiple, medical, and sensory disabilities. This chapter offers a way to resolve the dilemma of "all, except" by exploring the current practice context and offering an alternative approach that emerged from a demonstration project titled Including Exceptions: A System for Educating Students with Dual Sensory Impairments and Other Extreme Disabilities in General Education Settings. Along the way, examples from this project illustrate topics.

THE PRACTICE CONTEXT

Who Are These Students?

It is important to be clear about the reasons that these students are perceived by teachers as complicated and difficult. Their impairments are serious and dramatic, and they may include significant or total sensory impairment in addition to very severe cognitive impairments, severe physical disabilities, chronic health impairments, and sometimes terminal illness. Regardless of the exact details of their impairments, however, teachers find that students with disabilities possess several important similarities.

Small Response Repertoires What most frequently singles these students out for teachers is that they seem to have few abilities and few behaviors. Some students may have only a handful of identifiable movements or sounds upon which teachers try to build more effective participatory behaviors. Others may engage in a small number of more complex, or larger, behavior patterns but still possess too few consistent behaviors for teachers to accommodate easily in their teaching practices.

Narrow Windows of Learning Opportunity Perhaps more challenging than small response repertoires is that these students seem only sometimes "available" for learning interactions. Students may frequently be asleep or drowsy, agitated or crying, or even awake and seemingly alert, but not "connecting" to the environment in any recognizable way. It is as if there were simply no content to their alertness, as is sometimes reported for individuals who experience coma or other altered states of consciousness as a result of brain injury (Eames & Wood, 1984; Plum & Posner, 1972). Recent investigations of the relationship between these variations in openness to learning and biobehavioral states may prove helpful (Guess et al., 1993; Guy, Guess, & Ault, 1993). However, the connection between biobehavioral-state information and intervention is not yet clear. It is also not clear that these "not available for learning" occasions are entirely negative. In some cases, perhaps, agitation, resistance, or self-stimulatory behavior may function as needed precursors to periods of more openness to learning and higher quality performance (Evans & Scotti, 1989; Ferguson, Meyer, & Willis, 1990).

Poor Instructional Control Openness to learning and small response repertoires might be manageable for teachers if students reliably responded to instructional efforts. However, these students often fail to respond consistently to stimuli. Even when these students are "available" for learning, teachers often report that they are "not reinforced by anything" that might be used to build more consistent response patterns. When some event, object, or experience does become identified as reinforcing, its power tends to dissipate quickly.

Too Little Time In addition to their learning challenges, this small group of students often requires a substantial amount of personal support—physical management, mealtime assistance, health monitoring, and frequent medications. In the face of substantial care needs and given the challenges of few abilities, narrow windows of learning opportunity, and poor instructional control, it is not surprising that the educational experiences of students with profound disabilities often become dominated by "caring for" activities.

Where Are These Students?

Despite efforts to include more students with disabilities in the rhythms and activities of general education, students with extreme multiple disabilities are more frequently assigned to separate schools or, at best, self-contained classrooms in public school buildings (Davis, 1992). We think this pattern of separation continues for some of these students because they are less likely to make demands, sitting quietly and passively wherever placed. In the busy, sometimes even chaotic, school environment, quiet, passive students risk being ignored, even forgotten, especially by teachers who struggle to manage the demands of other, less passive students.

Some students with disabilities are not exactly "quiet." While having few abilities, the few they have may be noisy in the extreme, challenging the tolerance of everyone by screaming, yelling, or making other loud noise. These students often find themselves placed in self-contained settings with a teacher who is always willing and able to take on yet another challenge. Their classrooms become disproportionately populated with "exceptions"—students who, for one reason or another, are too "something" for other, even special education, classrooms.

In sum, students with very severe multiple disabilities all too often find themselves in self-contained classroom situations with teachers who are not able to invest a lot of time in their programs. Sometimes, this teacher limitation is an unfortunate reality of having too many needy students for any one person to support. Other times, it is more a limitation of teacher ability, creativity, and energy. Regardless, the result is the same: students with very severe multiple disabilities and complex medical needs tend to pose not just personal challenges but also resource, time, and logistical challenges that are hard for schools and teachers to meet. As a consequence, both teachers and students suffer.

People's Perceptions of These Students

"He doesn't do anything." "Her brain is full." "She has reached her learning potential." "I cannot teach her anymore." "They are too fragile to try much with them." "They don't really learn." "They will likely never have a future that will contribute anything." These are all sentiments we have heard from teachers. Indeed, taken together they represent a prevailing perspective that influences how school "works" for these students. Even when teachers try to be innovative and creative, the challenges can be so great that the various assumptions of this prevailing perspective dominate, sometimes in interesting ways. Let us illustrate with some brief characterizations of how many people think about students with profound disabilities.

An Orchid Among the Dandelions As an exotic orchid stands out among dandelions, so does 15-year-old Cate stand out among her middle school classmates. It is not her stylish outfits or her large deep brown eyes that proclaim her rarity; neither is it her love of loud music, shopping, or being at the center of classmates' activities. In these ways she is a typical adolescent. Nor is it the fact that Cate uses a wheelchair and relies on others to speak for her, to interpret the look in her eyes and her tiny subtle movements. It is not even that she needs help eating, has seizures that need to be counted, and takes medications throughout the day. It is instead how her district, teachers, and other people in school define her.

Cate is 1 of 10 students in a "special skills classroom." She and her classmates do not know what grade they are in. Their teacher is not a district teacher but one provided by a county agency that contracts with the district to provide special services for students with severe disabilities. The students in Cate's class come from all over the area, standing out as a band of "outsiders" in this school. As a group, they are the dandelions in the school flower garden, except for Cate. She is separately tended to by nurses, hired by her mother, who accompany her to school. From the privacy of the home economics room, the nurses keep a constant eye: watching her respirations, skin color, temperature, and nutrient intake; administering medications; caring for her hygiene; changing her position; and wiping her mouth. Like an exotic orchid, she is braced so that she grows straight. A nurse is never far from her side, creating a mythology about her fragility, tending to her as a gardener with a hothouse flower, creating a barrier for both students and staff.

This year Cate ventured out of the hothouse a few times to band and art classes. In art, the nurse sat at the back of the class, letting the seventh-grade students support Cate as she painted a Christmas mural, drew a landscape, and made a ceramic plate. These other students began to see Cate through the cellophane of protection the nurses had helped to create. Polly Michaels, Cate's teacher, admits that the presence of the nurses provides great relief; she lets them take the lead. The nurses are the master gardeners for this rare species of flower, the ones with the special knowledge that keeps her alive and well. They seem to possess a magic that others cannot share. Polly Michaels, bound by rules established outside her domain, and busy elsewhere, does not actively challenge them.

She Is Everyone's Barbie Doll "The hothouse flower" is one metaphor for how school people come to see students with multiple disabilities, but there are many more. Sometimes, students like Nancy become everyone's Barbie doll. Nancy is dressed in coordinated clothes. She's quiet and pleasing to be around—cute, with pretty hair. Her days are filled with going along with the crowd: to physical education (PE) class, field trips, the dance, the wave pool, and art class. She is "plugged in" to groups where she seems to fit. Other kids in her high school get to know her through the peer tutoring program, choir class, and woodworking class. Some of her classmates are aloof: "No one wants to hang out with someone who doesn't do anything!" But many other classmates take Nancy along everywhere they go and help her do whatever they are doing. However, they think of her as someone who is interesting to have around, but not really someone who has a role, an opinion, a social place, or the same reason for being in school.

The Pickup Game Peter's experiences in school are more like being in a pickup game. In a pickup game of basketball at the local park or court, the players generally do not know each other. Everyone just shows up to play, and after a while you get to know not so much the people as their ball-playing talents: that person is a good outside jumper; she can really "jam" a basketball; or he is an awesome ball handler. No one plays like a team, and everyone has a different idea about how to get the ball into the hoop. Lots of good things can happen in a pickup game, as in Peter's life at his rural middle school. Peter is doing more things in more places in school with more people than last year, if you look across his whole experience. Day to day, however, he is "passed off" from one teacher or specialist to the next. These professionals execute their own plays, each having a different idea about what Peter should be doing in the game of school. No one knows very much about the others' plans, and they almost never coordinate the play, but Peter has a bunch of teachers and specialists working hard doing what they each know best, making the best moves they can. Peter ends up experiencing all kinds of things he has never encountered before with all kinds of classmates who come to see him as a real player.

The Perpetual Tourist Slim is one of Tammy Crenshaw's students. A quiet young man with unruly light brown hair, dark brown eyes, and an unhurried air, this is his first year at Western High. He attended special classes at Eastern High last year, but his parents were not happy with the program and requested that he be moved to Western High. Few of the students at Western know Slim. Not only is he new to the school, but he does little to call attention to himself, and because many of the general education classes are not considered appropriate for him, he spends a lot of time in Room 28. Sometimes he attends a weight-training class. He has a school job recycling paper and another picking up and delivering messages from the office. Twice a week he goes to the grocery story nearby to return aluminum cans or to make small purchases. However, most of his activities do not involve students outside Room 28.

Slim is also older than most of the students at Western High. He does not have a group of friends, and he never meets students who participate in sports or attend after-school activities. It's not that he wouldn't enjoy being more a part of the school community. It just never occurs to anyone to include him. Tammy Crenshaw and her staff do what they can to increase his visibility and membership, as well as that of the other students in Room 28, but sometimes they grow tired of what they believe is a losing battle. There are few in the school who understand their efforts, and most question the rationale for including Slim and "other kids like him." When Slim walks down the hall, he is generally ignored by the students and faculty except for the custodian, who, now and then, pats him on the back and slips him a piece of candy.

Ms. Crenshaw knows that Slim's participation in the life and classes of Western takes time for thought and planning—planning that is all too easy to let slide, given all the other students, all equally challenging, for whom she is responsible. In past years, in other schools, Slim spent a lot of time sitting in a chair with no teaching and little interaction from either adults or students, probably because he quietly tolerated the inattention.

Unpredictable arrivals and departures are characteristic in Slim's life. During the past 2 years he has attended two different high schools. This spring, because of a medical complication, he moved from the group home where he had been living to a new group home in a different town. So he is about to move to yet another high school in a different school district, his third in 3 years. Of course, it is easy to make these sudden and unsettling changes for Slim. He does not protest, and in the short run, any move can seem like it is in Slim's best interest. Rarely does the conversation consider changing the current situation; moving always appeals more. Because of his frequent moves, people never get to know Slim very well. Everyone changes with each move—at school, at home, and in the community. No matter where his travels take him, he seems a foreigner in a culture that never really understands him. There is never time taken to learn from the lessons his visits offer, to try to accommodate him by sharing the culture, or to assimilate him by starting new traditions that incorporate him.

The Prevailing Perspective in Sum

It is an unfortunate perception when students with multiple disabilities are seen 1) as requiring mostly care, not education or teaching; 2) as needing to be "stimulated" to respond so that maybe learning can occur sometime in the future; and 3) as their *disability* rather than as a person. These perceptions are rooted in a long and checkered cultural history of perceptions and assumptions about people with dramatic differences, as well as a substantial professional history of treatment and practice. Nevertheless, more often than not Slim, Nancy, Peter, Cate, and many others experience school on the fringe: barely tolerated and barely understood except by a tiny minority who rarely succeed in making their interpretations dominant.

A NEW APPROACH TO PRACTICE

Limited understanding about how best to help these students learn (Brown & Lehr, 1989), coupled with the prevailing perspective, tends to result in two patterns of response: Teachers and families focus on social rather than learning outcomes (Hamre-Nietupski, Nietupski, & Strathe, 1992) or try to elicit isolated skills that might later combine with other skills to achieve some functional outcome.

Not seeing students as *learners* of competence and ability can result in the kind of passive "participation" and presence characterized in "the perpetual tourist" or "everyone's Barbie Doll" (Downing, 1988). However, efforts to build the critical mass of skills that might later become combined into functional abilities can leave students with both limited membership and incoherent learning, such as with Peter and the pickup game. We are not at all suggesting that increasing students' behavioral repertoires is not a good idea, but we do agree with Meyer (1991) that to "set that goal as the *only* thing to do is problematic" (p. 633).

Rather than trying to teach tiny isolated skills (in the hopes of eventually building them into a functional repertoire) or passive presence (in the hopes of building social inclusion), we encourage teachers to think less about adding to students' behavioral repertoires and more about increasing their opportunities to practice their admittedly small and tenuous current behaviors in real school and community activities that are peopled by a diverse range of others. Using a "practice abilities" rather than an "add behaviors" logic is primarily a shift in how teachers frame their efforts: Beginning with practicing abilities is more likely to result in building skills, if skills are to be built at all. Practicing abilities has two further benefits. First, a student's health and physical condition might be maintained more easily as a result of increased supported active participation and involvement in activities (Rainforth & York, 1993). Second, well-supported active participation is more likely to enhance the image of the students in others' eyes, helping these students create the interpretations and understandings that might lead to a social place and role within the group (Ferguson, 1994).

We do not yet have the medical and educational knowledge to overcome dramatic performance differences between students with profound disabilities and their peers. At the same time, what little information is available to us suggests that carefully orchestrated and active practice of familiar behaviors in a predictable routine can indeed result in improving the consistency and quality of these behaviors (Smith & Ylvisaker, 1985; Szekeres, Ylvisaker, & Holland, 1985). Indeed, the routines may be the critical feature of the teaching context that will allow some students to initiate responses and reveal awareness and involvement (Gee, Graham, Goetz, Oshima, & Yoshioka, 1991). Organizing curriculum and teaching so that practicing abilities becomes the focus offers a way to marry learning and social outcomes so that both can be addressed in the day-to-day life of school. In the rest of this section we offer and illustrate strategies for employing a practice abilities logic in the design and management of curriculum, teaching, and membership.

Curriculum Strategies: Creating Age-Appropriate Activity Routines

Strategy 1: Creating a Student-Referenced Curriculum In order to design a curriculum that relies on a practicing abilities logic, a teacher needs to generate three sets of information about the student and the school situation. The first involves identifying potentially stimulating and apparently preferred activities within school and peer routines. There are a variety of resources for identifying activities and routines that might promote learning (e.g., Baumgart, Johnson, & Helmstetter, 1990; Falvey, 1989; Ferguson, Ralph, Meyer, Willis, & Young, 1993; Ford et al., 1989; Sailor et al., 1989). However, we prefer an approach that compares a student's interest in and capacity for engaging in activities typical of peers without disabilities. For example, the Home Activities Interview/Discussion (Ferguson et al., 1993; Wilcox & Bellamy, 1987) provides lists of activities organized into 3-year age groupings that any child or young adult might do in the areas of 1) personal management, 2) leisure, and 3) jobs and chores. Educators and family members discuss each group of activities to determine 1) how the student currently participates, even if only occasionally or partially; 2) if the student seems to enjoy or prefer the participation; and 3) if the student and family want to change the student's capacity for participation. A summary of this interview/discussion can guide the selection of school activities and routines in which students can practice their current abilities and also enjoy and encounter in their lives outside of school. Table 1 illustrates things we learned from completing this kind of activity-based assessment with Peter.

Strategy 2: Analyzing Physical, Medical, and Contextual Barriers The second critical piece of curriculum design information is an analysis of all the possible physical, medical, and contextual barriers to active participation that might be affecting any particular student. As we noted earlier, some students are "not available" for learning or practicing their abilities for significant portions of the school day. Sometimes students' unconnectedness, agitation, sleepiness, or seizures—four common ways students might be "unavailable"—are related to other environmental and physiological factors. For example, a student may be very sensitive to noise, light, or activity levels. Such sensitivity may elicit either agitation or sleepiness in a possible effort to close out the overstimulation. Teachers, parents, and other school personnel are often all too aware of these idiosyncratic

Table 1. Activity-based assessment summary for Peter

Overall, the picture we get of this student's abilities, interests, and participation in:	Ideas, priorities, preferences, cautions, and tasks

Personal Management

Vocalizes when he is hungry.

Favorite time of the day is lunch because he gets to eat and sit with his classmates. He grabs onto a spoon with little difficulty.

Orients head toward speaker.

Gives recorded sixth grade spelling tests by activating the tape recorder with a switch.

Uses a wheelchair. He is getting too heavy to lift. He needs to bear more weight on his legs. His new braces should help.

Needs to be positioned throughout the day. He uses a stander 1–2 times per day.

Tends to be passive during personal care routines.

Personal care routine
  Encourage Peter to bear more weight on his legs during transfers.
  Encourage Peter to grasp his toothbrush, washcloth, and so on, during personal care routines.
Use the school cafeteria
  Can hold spoon during lunch to feed himself.
  Eats lunch with peer buddy.
Carry materials or items on his tray during cooperative learning exercises and science experiments.
Assist Peter with developing a scrapbook that friends can use to get to know him better.
Doing homework
  Peter should have his own Student Activity Book. The teacher should write down what he has done and what his assignments are. Peter will stamp his name where other students sign their name.
Listen to radio, CD, or cassette player.

Leisure

Likes listening to "church" music.

Is very animated around his sixth-grade classmates. Enjoys being the center of attention.

Enjoys feeling smooth, wet textures.

Enjoys listening to his friend Jack reading him a story.

Likes to be outside where there is a breeze and enjoys "hanging out" with friends.

Enjoys going to the store.

Has his head up when he is moving around and where there is lots of noise (e.g., walks, PE, transitions in the hallway).

Attending events
  Participate in sixth grade field days.
  Participate in sixth grade field trips.
Participate in sixth grade science activities and experiments by handing out materials, grasping onto equipment, and verbalizing during small group discussions.
Using public library
  Listen to books read by peers during SSR.
  Push sixth grade books into book drop.
Just hang out with classmates during A.M. break in the hallway.
Participate in PE activities (e.g., floor hockey, basketball).
Creating art projects
Give Peter an allowance to go to the store across the street from school with friends.
Help with sixth grade class newsletter.

Jobs and Chores

Has not had much of an opportunity to do any class jobs except to carry materials on his tray from one part of the classroom to another.

Has delivered messages and picked up attendance slips.

Clean up personal area like his classmates.
Run school errands and make deliveries.
Take books back to the library.
Help with school recycling.
Try to have each of these activities done with his classmates instead of with adults.

responses, but they may never have taken the time to systematically share and analyze their information as part of the curriculum planning process. The Brainstorming Interview Guide, illustrated in Figure 1, was developed to organize just such a discussion.

The guide, a blank piece of paper, and a half hour or so with the people who know the student best are all that is needed. The group should include at least the student's teacher, classroom support staff, and family members. It might also include other related service per-

---

Question 1: What are all the things that might be having an impact on this student's learning, performance, moods, and behavior? Consider the following possibilities:

Home Events and Conditions
Medications
Interactions with parents and family
Interactions with neighbors and visitors
Food intake/diet changes
Sleep—amount, interruptions
Sickness—colds, flu, infections, etc.
Changes in schedule and routine
Changes in equipment and devices
Changes in weather and seasons
Other

School Events and Conditions
Interactions with teachers and staff
Interactions with peers
Interactions with other people
Food intake/diet changes
Sleep in school
Sickness
Reaction to visitors/strangers
Changes in schedule and routine
Room/school temperature
Reaction to environmental noises
Reaction to people noise and activity
    levels
Changes in equipment and materials
Other

Moods and Behavior

General mood
Alertness
Muscle tone
Posture
Active/inactive

"Agitation"
Sounds/noises
Random movements
Eyes open/contact/focus
Responsiveness to sounds
Responsiveness to sights

Crying/moaning/whimpering
Self-stimulation
Self-injury
Seizures
Breathing rhythm and quality

Question 2: What explanations or "hunches" do we have about how these conditions, moods, events, and activities relate to one another?

Question 3: What 2–3 (or 4–5) behaviors are we most energetically trying to focus on this student being able to use more frequently and consistently?

Question 4: What are our current teaching efforts, and how might we consider changing them? Consider:

Schedule of activities
Groupings
Teaching prompts
Communication strategies
Things tried at home
Current information
    systems

Amount of time and balance of
    teaching efforts across the
    day and week
Range and features of
    environments used for
    teaching
Things tried at school

Figure 1.   Brainstorming Interview Guide.

sonnel and peers who have a particular interest in and sensitivity to the student. The guide prompts and focuses discussion around a diverse set of topics that one member of the group records. The purpose of the discussion is to take full advantage of all the intimate bits of information and hunches about the student's feelings, moods, reactions, and preferences that everyone has but may not be using to design and manage the student's environment and learning activities.

For example, using this tool with Cate helped to get her teacher, Polly Michaels, more involved in her daily routines instead of letting the nurses be her only contacts. Talking together, they realized that most of them thought her frequent colds and ear infections affected not only her moods (making her agitated and crabby) but might also be related to her falling asleep so much. They also learned that at home, a very quiet environment, her sleep pattern did not seem to relate to having a cold. She spent a lot of time by herself, often lying on the floor in front of the TV, and tended to sleep a lot whether she was sick or not. The discussion also reveals that the nurses tended to leave her prone in a quiet corner of the room (possibly encouraging sleep) when she was congested, making it even less clear whether the cold or the prone position and relative lack of stimulation contributed more to the sleep patterns. Her mother reported an apparent attentiveness to men, which led Ms. Michaels to think that she might be more alert and interested in groups with boys or when assisted by male teachers.

Everyone had some experience with Cate being animated and laughing, but all seemed to relate these moods to when she was sitting up, either in her chair or on the floor, or at mealtimes. Since such times also tended to involve other peers and adults, the group speculated that she might be animated more often if grouped with others who were likely to provide a wide variety of stimulation. Her interest in activity around her promoted speculation that she might enjoy an art class. Her positive reaction to noise and activity might be encouraged by something even noisier, such as band class. Everyone in the group had also experienced times when Cate was especially agitated, moaning and even screaming for large blocks of time, but no one could really relate these moods to anything in particular. Her medication was minimal and had been stable, and the agitated times did not always seem to happen when she had a cold or when the weather was changing or in response to any other contextual variable the group could think up. They decided they needed more systematic information on such periods of agitation.

Based on this information, as well as the information generated from the Home Activities Interview/Discussion, Polly Michaels included Cate in two mixed-ability learning groups that included peers without disabilities (including boys), enrolled her in a band class, and devised a schoolwide job that involved collecting and delivering all the attendance slips. An information system (discussed later) was also developed that focused on how much Cate practiced such abilities as grasp and release, eye gazing toward a speaker, and push-passing materials across tables in all these activities. The system also collected information about the amount of noise and activity in the environments; whether Cate was animated, sleepy, laughing, or agitated; and if she seemed congested from a cold. The group hoped that the more systematic collection of information might reveal patterns that would answer some of their continuing questions about when and how Cate responded.

With Slim, the interview focused on the amount of time he spent sleeping, which was unpredictable and frequently long. Several members of his planning team attributed his sleeping to an unstimulating daily schedule or to medication he took to control his many seizures. The discussion also revealed that an unstable home routine might be contributing to Slim's unpredictable sleep patterns. Slim was also susceptible to respiratory infections that easily turned into pneumonia, and his teacher, Tammy Crenshaw, wondered if being in school all day was tiring him and contributing to the frequency of his illnesses. The group decided that they needed information about Slim's awake and asleep times, his seizures, and when he was ill. A data system (discussed later) was developed to be used at home as well as at school to try to gather around-the-clock information on how these factors might be affecting Slim's participation in school and what things might be changed to get Slim more actively involved. Ms. Crenshaw also began to develop a different schedule that included activities and locations in the school that might be more stimulating and interesting to Slim. Since Slim was new to the group home, the Home Activities Interview had not generated very much information about activities that Slim might like or do frequently.

Strategy 3: Analyzing the School and Classroom Context The last important piece of curriculum design information is an analysis of school and classroom activities, climate, environmental conditions, teaching formats, and other features of the day-to-day life of schools that represent both opportunities and challenges for students with profound disabilities. Since most of these students are likely to be in self-contained settings, their teachers may not be involved enough in the life of the school to have a quick command of all the opportunities and locations that might offer opportunities for the students to practice their abilities. The School Context Analysis form helps teachers gather this information. Table 2 summarizes the information included. The form is organized so that the teacher, an assistant, or anyone associated with the classroom can collect information by simply watching and noticing. The form also guides discussion with other teachers to generate other helpful information. Once completed, the form becomes a strategy for identifying possible learning contexts as well as resources or changes that may be needed for a particular student in that context. Again, various formats are available (e.g., Giangreco, Cloninger, & Iverson, 1992). Regardless of what format is used, the goal is to collect and consider information about the school and individual classrooms and teachers, together with information about the student's abilities, lifestyle, and challenges, in order to plan a schedule of familiar and interesting activities and routines that offer opportunities for students to practice their abilities.

Teaching Strategies

Strategy 1: Using Peer Groups   The natural tendency of many teachers is to work individually with very complicated and very disabled students. As Peter's experience illustrates, however, we encourage grouping students as much as possible for two reasons. First, groups offer many different activities and general stimulation to capture students' interest and alertness. A common lament of teachers of students with profound disabilities is that the teacher cannot seem to get any response from these students. Teachers and students can quickly become bored and frustrated. However, groups of peers naturally offer a variety of stimulation. Using the natural activity of peer groups can leave the teacher free to both orchestrate the participation of the more disabled students and generate information on the appropriateness of the group's activity for awakening and sustaining each student's attention and interest. In our experience with 19 students over 3 years, our most consistent finding is that many students do respond by being more awake and alert for longer and longer periods of time. However, other students can find some activities overly stimulating and may respond with less alertness or attention. These differing kinds of responses require teachers to collect information on not only students' responses in activities, but also on the qualities of the activity itself in order to identify potential patterns that might guide changes in either schedules or activities.

A second reason for teaching students with very severe disabilities in the context of groups is that group activities tend to offer many more opportunities for students to overlap practice of their abilities with the ongoing activities of others in the groups. For example, in many routine classroom activities, Peter practices orienting to multiple speakers

Table 2. School context analysis information

School	Overall layout	
	Possible places to teach	Classrooms, office, cafeteria, hall areas, auditorium, and so on.
	Types of classes/courses	Age/grade, cross age/grade, computer, art, events, school jobs, music/choir/band, school/community partnership activities, school/grade field trips, and so on.
	Reform/restructuring status	Number of new things being tried, degree of common vision/commitment of faculty, leadership involvement, family/community involvement, level of energy/enthusiasm/frustration, and so on.
	School schedule	Periods/classes, lunch, recess, homeroom; schedule for "specials"; block schedules, and so on.
	Physical layout	Size of rooms, availability of small teaching spaces, places for privacy, storage spaces, stairs/elevators/ramps, amount of light, variations in heat, overall noise level, and so on.
Personnel	School resources	Counselor, physical and occupational therapists, speech therapist, classroom assistants, peer teaching programs, nurse, psychologist, vice principal, talented and gifted teacher, Chapter 1 assistants, and so on.
	Classroom resources	Class size, available assistants, team teaching/planning patterns, and so on.
Curriculum and teaching	Approach and formats	Lecture, demonstration, large/small group, cooperative learning groups, experiment/activity-based, mixed/same ability groups, outcome-based, and so on.
	Materials and resources	Published curriculum texts, teacher-created materials, home/community materials, computers, audiovisuals, student-created materials, use of community members/families as experts, use of other spaces/places in school and community, and so on.
	Student evaluation approaches	Memory tests, demonstrations, exhibitions, portfolios, self-assessment, cooperative group assessment, single criterion grading systems, individualized criterion grading system, rubrics, and so on.

or choosing the next person, grasping and passing a wide variety of materials throughout the lesson, and keeping his head up during class activities. The "practice" of orienting, of choosing, or grasping can easily be maximized in many group activities if these behaviors are developed as antecedents to the activities of all others in the group. For example, a student may grasp and pass materials needed for a task to others in the group or may orient toward an object or person to make choices for the group during an activity. Thus, the student is able to maximize the practice of his or her abilities, but this kind of active participation can also encourage others in the group to see the student as a valued member with a specific role and place (Giangreco et al., 1992).

Strategy 2: Using Information Systems Many teachers report a great deal of difficulty collecting useful data on the learning performance of very complicated students. Too often, conventional data systems used in either special or general education tell people what they already know—that the student cannot perform the behavior or task independently and that the level of performance is inconsistent over time (see, for example, Farlow & Snell, 1989). As recommended by Meyer and Janney (1989), teachers need new data collection strategies that are more user friendly and reflective of the multiple outcomes sought by teachers.

The new approach encouraged here—helping students practice their current abilities in the context of natural activity routines—certainly requires a new approach to data collection. In order to maximize ability practice, teachers need information not only on what they are trying to help their students achieve (are students practicing abilities?) but also on features of the natural context and various responses of the students that might be affecting the goal to maximize opportunities for practice.

Teachers should shift their focus from collecting "data" to creating ongoing, flexible information systems. Information systems are needed because within schools, and especially with regard to students with disabilities, *data* has come to mean measurement, usually in terms of counts, frequencies, or duration, of some behavior. By contrast, *information* might include any of these as well as a range of other variables, including narrative notes on hunches, ratings, quality of responses, opportunities for practice, direct observations, or assessment of different persons' perspectives. Teachers need a broad set of information to take into account when making decisions about curriculum design, teaching design, and learning outcomes for these students.

For example, in Nancy's situation the teacher developed a system that focused on whether Nancy practiced her abilities "a lot" or "a little" during the entire school day. Although this estimation is not as precise as counting responses, it can be collected with more ease in most instances. The same information sheet also collected information on Nancy's "awake" and "sleeping" times, and whether or not she smiled or seemed especially rigid. Her teacher wanted to know if there were any patterns to her waking and sleeping in comparison to the activity schedule. Finally, she also collected information on the size of the group she was in and the amount of noise and activity generated by the group to see if any patterns emerged that might suggest a relationship among her interest, the qualities of the group, the time of day, and her capacity to engage in a lot of practice of her abilities.

Figure 2 illustrates Nancy's information system. Notice that on this particular day she participated "Lots" during the morning, especially during laundry, computer time, and lunch. She was prone only during one period and smiled but was very rigid "Lots" during swimming. She slept very little. She seemed happy in her stander after swimming and in her wheelchair near the end of the day. The general noise level fluctuated throughout the day and did not seem to relate to either her mood or responses in any clear way.

By contrast, Slim's teachers tracked his waking and sleeping, his seizures, and his illnesses at school and at home. Was he awake or asleep, and during what parts of the day and night? How many seizures was he having, and when did they occur? Did he seem to be sick before, after, or during extended periods of sleeping and wakefulness? And how did nutrition enter into the equation? His teacher, Tammy Crenshaw, and the others who spent time with Slim wanted to know which of these factors influenced the way in which he participated in the activities where he was practicing his abilities of "walking," "reaching and touching," "grasping and push passing," and "holding objects." Were there any trends or patterns? Did they influence each other?

Flexible information systems allow teachers and other school personnel to tailor information to each student's unique situation. The information systems are designed to collect information throughout the school day using whatever time period fits the classroom and school routine. Information can be tailored to each student, but systems generally include information about 1) the approximate number of opportunities students get to practice abilities; 2) the quality with which they perform in different activities and settings, and at different times of the day and week; and 3) the events occurring both with the students and the environment that might be affecting the students' responses.

Typically, the data systems require the collector to "estimate" or otherwise make judgments, rather than count things. This estimating

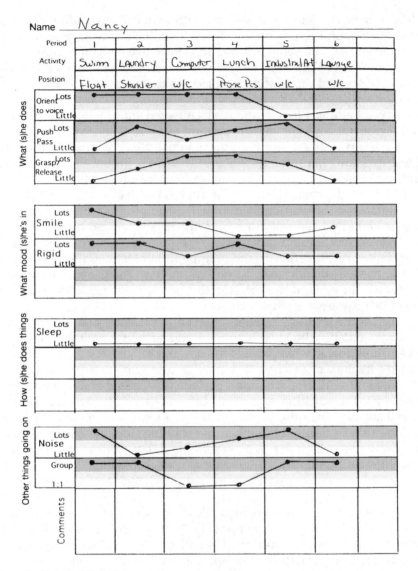

Figure 2. Nancy's data system.

is easier, faster, and less intrusive than careful counting. Even though individuals might interpret some of the estimations differently ("Lots" might mean various things to different people), the point is to notice broad patterns that might relate the student's opportunities to practice abilities in comparison with other things that might have an impact on or affect that practice. Discrepancies in interpretation show up and become clarified as teachers and assistants use the information to make more sense out of what is happening for each student. Indeed, some teachers reported that this kind of discussion helped them get to know the students better. Instead of tending to think of the students as having a "good" or "bad" day, they now had more information that allowed them to understand each student's complexity a bit more completely as it related to the day-to-day life of school.

Teachers use these information systems to make a variety of adjustments. For example, Peter presented several challenges at the beginning. He often sat with his head down on his tray and tended to spend a lot of time sleeping. He had frequent seizures that seemed to make him less available for learning and participation, but his activity level, energy, and interest also seemed to vary according to where he was in the school and who was with him. His information system, illustrated in Figure 3, required collecting information at the end of each period of the day (eight periods in all) about 1) how much he had practiced using his hands, keeping his head up, and vocalizing; 2) if he was having seizures and if he was alert; and 3) if he was engaged with other students or an adult instructor.

In just a week, the information system revealed that during the morning (the first four periods), Peter was more active in the periods he spent in English and PE than during the periods in the self-contained special education classroom. His head was more consistently up in the general education classes, and he was judged more alert and more involved with peers by the classroom assistant who recorded the information. He also seemed to have "Lots" of seizures. Since he had small seizures quite frequently, the teacher questioned even recording the information.

Figure 4 summarizes data collected by Peter's teacher. Simply scanning several sheets of data (each sheet contained information for several days) helped teachers identify a pattern: Peter seemed to vocalize, use his hands, keep his head up, and remain alert when he was involved in general education settings with peers without disabilities. Some of his least alert times were in the special education classroom. This pattern encouraged Peter's teachers to pair Peter with a peer during silent reading so that the peer might read to him and to arrange for Peter to be involved in more special activities with one of the sixth grade classes (parties, field days, etc.). By March the pattern in Peter's seizures seemed stable enough, despite some continued increase in more active settings, and he began to attend lunch and science class with peers.

Other students' information systems are not always as revealing. Sometimes the patterns emerge only slowly and over time. For exam-

Name Peter   Date October 3, 1995

PRACTICE ABILITY	Monday								Tuesday							
	English	Special Education	Physical Education	Special Education	Special Education	Sustained Silent Reading	Special Education	Physical Education	English	Special Education	Physical Education	Special Education	Special Education	Sustained Silent Reading	Special Education	Physical Education
Vocalization	✓	✓							✓			✓	✓			
Use hands	✓								✓		✓	✓		✓		
Head up	✓	✓	✓		✓			✓	✓		✓	✓	✓	✓	✓	✓
How is Peter?																
Seizures	✓	✓	✓	✓				✓	✓			✓	✓			
Alertness	✓		✓		✓			✓	✓		✓	✓	✓	✓		
Other Stuff Going On																
With kids/noise	✓		✓	✓	✓			✓	✓		✓	✓	✓	✓		
With instructor	✓		✓	✓				✓	✓		✓	✓		✓		

PRACTICE ABILITY	Wednesday								Thursday								Friday							
	English	Special Education	Physical Education	Special Education	Special Education	Sustained Silent Reading	Special Education	Physical Education	English	Special Education	Physical Education	Special Education	Special Education	Sustained Silent Reading	Special Education	Physical Education	English	Special Education	Physical Education	Special Education	Special Education	Sustained Silent Reading	Special Education	Physical Education
Vocalization	✓		✓	✓	✓	✓			✓	✓	✓	✓	✓	✓	✓	✓	✓	✓	✓	✓		Absent		
Use hands	✓		✓	✓	✓	✓		✓	✓		✓	✓	✓	✓	✓	✓	✓		✓			Absent		
Head up	✓		✓	✓	✓	✓		✓	✓	✓	✓	✓	✓	✓	✓	✓	✓		✓	✓		Absent		
How is Peter?																								
Seizures	✓	✓	✓	✓	✓	✓		✓	✓	✓	✓	✓	✓	✓	✓	✓	✓	✓	✓	✓		Absent		
Alertness	✓	✓	✓	✓	✓	✓		✓	✓	✓	✓	✓	✓	✓	✓	✓	✓	✓	✓	✓		Absent		
Other Stuff Going On																								
With kids/noise	✓		✓	✓	✓				✓		✓	✓		✓	✓	✓	✓		✓			Absent		
With instructor	✓		✓	✓	✓			✓	✓		✓	✓		✓		✓	✓		✓			Absent		

✓ = Participated
Blank = No Participation

Figure 3. Peter's data system.

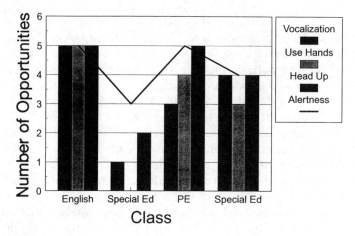

Figure 4.   One-week summary of Peter's data.

ple, it took months to get any ideas about Slim's sleeping and waking. He slept so much that it was a major barrier to even trying to build an activity routine, and his times of sleeping were rarely predictable. His teachers wondered if he slept because he was bored or sick, or because he did not sleep at home. They thought maybe his sleeping was his way of avoiding demands. They wondered if they should make him do things to keep him awake or if they should let him sleep because "he needed his rest."

While the teachers wrestled with their questions, they recorded daily information about Slim's sleeping and wakefulness. Patterns began emerging after a 4-month period of time. The daily data showed clearly that if he came to school asleep, he usually slept all day, and if he came to school awake, he usually remained awake for most of the day. But still the staff could not predict the periods of sleep or wakefulness. He might sleep at school for several days in a row and then come to school awake and alert the next day, but they didn't know why. When he was sleeping, he would sleep so soundly that no one was able to rouse him. If the staff managed to rouse him from sleep enough to involve him in an activity, he would occasionally fall asleep in the middle of the activity, no matter what he was doing. He could fall asleep walking to the lunchroom or even during a noisy PE class. They decided that his sleeping was not due to either avoidance or boredom. His sleep patterns were erratic at home as well. When the school staff and the home staff compared notes, they discovered that he could be awake for 24 or 36 hours at a time without sleeping and then sleep for the same amount of time. Or he might sleep for only a few hours before he was awake again.

Another pattern was that Slim slept more at home and at school when he was sick or having frequent seizures. Intuitively the staff had known this, but the data made it very clear that their hunches were correct. Yet another pattern was that Slim had more seizures when he was sick, and he was sick more during the winter months of January and February. The data for these months showed Slim sick and out of school for 13 of the 40 school days, sleeping 15 out of the 22 days he was in school, and having 8 days of seizures. He was awake for only 12 days. By comparison, during the month of December when Slim was sick for only 2 out of 15 school days, he was awake for 8 days, asleep for only 2, and had seizures 3 days. Figure 5 illustrates the 6 months of data. The staff theorized from this information that perhaps when Slim was sick and his resistance was low, any activity sapped what energy he had and made it more likely that he would be sick again. Once that cycle started, it was hard to break. They also realized that when Slim's seizures increased, his medication doses were raised, probably contributing to his sleepiness.

It was when Slim was not sick and not having seizures that he was awake for the long periods of time. No one had any good reasons for this phenomenon, but they explained his subsequent "crashes" as making up for lost sleep during those long wakeful periods. The teacher thought maybe the group home just was not good about setting up a regular bedtime schedule for Slim, but the group home said they did indeed have a schedule but that "he just didn't follow it." Based on their interpretations of the information, the school staff decided that they needed to be more vigilant about Slim's health, and they decided to work together with the group to design criteria to determine when he should return to school following any illness. They also decided to develop better communication regarding medication changes. They felt strongly about trying to make the most of the times Slim was at school, and they continued to involve him in school activities, whether or not he was awake and participating.

We share this example about Slim because it illustrates the complexity that teachers can face with some students and the home–school collaboration that is necessary. We cannot say that we have been able to adjust Slim's daily routines in ways that are resulting in a lot more active participation. However, the continued focus on collecting information that might give other explanations about his sleep patterns helped everyone focus on the most important outcome: trying to find ways to increase Slim's active practice of his abilities in natural activity routines and contexts. The process led to action, not just to letting things be.

October

S	M	T	W	Th	F	S
				1	2	3
4	5	6	7	8	9	10
			No Data			
11	12	13	14	15	16	17
			No Data			
18	19	20	21	22 ✓	23	24
25	26 ✓	27 ▓	28	29	30 ✓	31

November

S	M	T	W	Th	F	S
1	2	3 ✓	4	5	6	7
8	9 ▓	10 ✓	11	12	13	14
15	16 ▓	17 ✓	18	19 ✓	20 ✓	21
22	23 Sick	24 ▓✓	25	26	27	28
29	30 ✓					

December

S	M	T	W	Th	F	S
	1 ✓	2	3	4	5	
6	7 ▓	8	9 ▓	10	11	12
13	14 Sick	15	16 ▓✓	17 Sick	18	19
20	21	22	23	24	25	26
			Vacation			
27	28	29	30	31		
			Vacation			

January

S	M	T	W	Th	F	S
			Vacation		1	2
3	4 ▓	5 ✓	6 ✓	7 ✓	8	9
10	11 ✓	12 Sick	13 Sick	14 Sick	15 Sick	16
17	18	19 Sick	20 ▓	21 Sick	22	23
24 / 31	25 ✓	26 ✓	27 ✓	28 ✓	29	30

February

S	M	T	W	Th	F	S
	1 ▓	2 ✓	3	4	5 ▓✓	6
7	8 ▓✓	9 ▓✓	10 ✓	11 ✓	12 ✓	13
14	15 Sick	16 Sick	17 Sick	18 Sick	19 Sick	20
21	22 Sick	23 Sick	24 ▓	25 ▓	26	27
28						

March

S	M	T	W	Th	F	S
	1	2 ✓	3	4	5	6
7	8	9	10	11	12	13
			No Data			
14	15	16	17	18	19	20
			No Data			
21	22	23	24	25	26	27
			No Data			
28	29	30	31			

Note: ▓ Seizures
 ✓ Sleep all day

Figure 5.   Illustration of Slim's data in a 6-month period.

Inclusion in School Life: Achieving Membership as a Learner

Membership in any group is a complicated social phenomenon. Any of us becomes a member of a group only when that group creates a shared definition that includes us—as in the following description of Peter's experiences learning to make waves in science class. This scene occurred during observations and visits and is derived from field notes.

> Peter's friend Jon is pushing him into the classroom along with the rest of the class as they all return from the library. There is some confusion about what is going to happen next. There are three wave tanks along the window. Some kids walk over to look at the wave tanks, other kids are talking with each other, and some doodle in their notebooks or just sit quietly at their desks. Jeffry tries to get Peter to grab and throw a ball. I found out later that Jeffry had been practicing this with Peter in preparation for next week's sixth-grade field days.
>
> Ms. Green asks the class to settle down and sit at their seats, but nothing happens until she repeats the direction for the third time. Jon pushes Peter next to his desk and sits down while Ms. Green begins to introduce the oceanography lesson. She explains that there will be two activities. Half the class will work individually drawing underwater animals that will later make up a mural in the hallway. The other half of the class will form groups of four and answer questions about the movement of waves and currents in the wave tank. Throughout this explanation, Peter's head rests on his tray. Leah shook him several times to get him to pay attention and told Jon, "I guess he doesn't like science."
>
> Ms. Green points to the left side of the class and tells students to start drawing sea creatures. Students begin moving around in search of large pieces of paper, markers, and pencils. Ms. Green pointed to the right side of the class where Peter sat and tells them to gather around the wave tanks. Jon shakes Peter and says, "It's time to work now, we're going to the wave tanks." Ms. Green gives each wave tank group a worksheet. One student in the group takes responsibility for moving the water with a block of wood, another for writing down what happens as prompted by the questions on the worksheet. Still another student moves the jetty in the water to different locations, while the fourth student keeps time and serves as the group "encourager." The first couple of minutes in each group involves the parceling out of these different roles and tasks.
>
> In Peter's group, Jon says he'd like to move the jetty. Paul offers to be the scribe, and Jennifer asks to move the piece of wood. Paul counters that maybe Peter can move the wood, and a little debate results until Jennifer agrees to be timekeeper. After a moment or two of thought, Jennifer suggests, "I'll help Peter make the waves." Peter raises his head.
>
> Jon moves the jetty on a small sandbar in the wave tank while Paul reads the first question: "Describe what the sand does under the jetty after the waves hit it a few times." Jennifer helps Peter grab onto a piece of wood and helps him move his arm in slow, sweeping movements. "The sand is coming out from under the jetty," Paul exclaims. Peter looks at Paul and smiles.

Peter is not just physically present in science class; he has both valued social and learning roles defined and facilitated by his classmates and teacher. The group has created membership for Peter as a friend and as a learner.

How Membership as a Learner Can Be Inclusive

Students with very severe multiple disabilities have a more difficult time becoming members of our classrooms and communities, perhaps because they offer us so little assistance in understanding their role in our social groups. Another problem is that schools, unlike many other group settings, are defined as learning places. An important part of school membership is being viewed as a learner. Other researchers have documented that students with very severe disabilities can become socially embedded in classroom groups (e.g., Giangreco et al., 1992), but becoming a learner as well as a peer is even more of a challenge. One high school PE teacher describes this challenge regarding one of his students, Brad (Rivers, 1993):

> I think he's more active in class. He's more alert. I think it's obvious when they wheel him into the gym or towards that area that they realized where he's going and that he sort of gets excited about it. Days are different. But he's more alert it seems like. . . . He was sort of, I'm not gonna say subdued at first, but it looks like he's more social, you know—more socially adapted to the class. I mean you can tell he likes it and he enjoys going to it. I think he has a feel for, like he has a reason for being there, I think. That's what I see. I think PE is doing a lot for him. . . . I know he's alert and awake the hour that we're in PE. And I can honestly say he doesn't like to be rolled out of the class. He knows he likes it and I think it is doing him good for that hour. . . . The [teacher assistant] has him acknowledge baskets scored, runs scored, keeping score on paper by his acknowledgment. I think he's come to have a lot of verbalizations as far as trying to get stuff out. . . . He's trying to get something across or, or explaining himself somehow or whatever. . . . There is something there. However we decipher it. But we may never, we may never know what's there, okay? But the bottom line is he is interacting and his reactions I think are good. There's some, there's some moments of meaningfulness I think when he's there. And I think that's important. I believe he sees that there's a meaning for him.

SUMMARY

We believe that membership as a learner is what Brad is achieving and is the challenge of school for any student, but especially those with severe multiple disabilities. For any student the purpose of schooling ought to be "to enable all students to actively participate in their communities so that others care enough about what happens to them to look for ways to incorporate them as members of that community" (Ferguson, 1994). Since schools are fundamentally learning environments, membership in the school community involves not just fitting in, or being accepted, but having a role as a learner.

Vocalizing more, moving an arm in a wide sweeping movement, "choosing" the next event or person with a turn of the head, holding onto things that need to be delivered, slightly raising a hand to indicate "yes," and being alert, interested, and smiling are all learning outcomes that both teachers and students are beginning to see as evidence that these students are members of the school's community of learners. Elsewhere (Ferguson, 1994), we have described ways of thinking through this more challenging kind of membership. More important, we believe, is the fundamental shift in emphasis described earlier, to first think differently about learning. Becoming a learning member of public schools rather than "an orchid among the dandelions," "the center of the pickup game," "the perpetual tourist," or "everyone's Barbie Doll" requires a shift from trying to stimulate senses and responses or adding responses to an already very small repertoire to maximizing the opportunities for students to practice their existing abilities. Eventually, even when few in number, others will come to see these as having an important learning role and social place in school activities.

REFERENCES

Baumgart, D., Johnson, J., & Helmstetter, E. (1990). *Augmentative and alternative communication systems for persons with moderate and severe disabilities.* Baltimore: Paul H. Brookes Publishing Co.

Brown, F., & Lehr, D.H. (Eds.). (1989). *Persons with profound disabilities: Issues and practices.* Baltimore: Paul H. Brookes Publishing Co.

Davis, S. (1992). *Report card to the nation on inclusion in education of students with mental retardation.* Arlington, TX: Arc.

Downing, J. (1988). Active versus passive programming: A critique of IEP objectives for students with the most severe disabilities. *Journal of The Association for Persons with Severe Handicaps, 13,* 197–201.

Dussault, W.L.E. (1989). Is a policy of exclusion based upon severity of disability legally defensible? In F. Brown & D.H. Lehr (Eds.), *Persons with profound disabilities: Issues and practices* (pp. 43–59). Baltimore: Paul H. Brookes Publishing Co.

Eames, P., & Wood, R. (1984). Consciousness in the brain-damaged adult. In R. Stevens (Ed.), *Aspects of consciousness: Vol. 4. Clinical issues* (pp. 1–39). London: Academic Press.

Evans, I.M., & Scotti, J.R. (1989). Defining meaningful outcomes for persons with profound disabilities. In F. Brown & D.H. Lehr (Eds.), *Persons with profound disabilities: Issues and practices* (pp. 83–107). Baltimore: Paul H. Brookes Publishing Co.

Falvey, M.A. (1989). *Community-based curriculum: Instructional strategies for students with severe handicaps* (2nd ed.). Baltimore: Paul H. Brookes Publishing Co.

Farlow, L.S., & Snell, M.E. (1989). Teacher use of student performance data to make instructional decisions: Practices in programs for students with moderate to profound disabilities. *Journal of The Association for Persons with Severe Handicaps, 14*(1), pp. 13–22.

Ferguson, D.L. (1987). *Curriculum decision-making for students with severe handicaps: Policy and practice.* New York: Teachers College Press.

Ferguson, D.L. (1994). Is communication really the point? Some thoughts on intervention and membership. *Mental Retardation, 32*(1), 7–18.

Ferguson, D.L., Meyer, G., & Willis, C. (1990). *The elementary/secondary system: Supportive education for students with severe handicaps. Module 4a: Regular class participation system.* Eugene: Specialized Training Program, University of Oregon.

Ferguson, D.L., Ralph, G., Meyer, G., Willis, C., & Young, M. (1993). *The elementary/secondary system: Supportive education for students with severe handicaps. Module 1d: Individually tailored learning: Strategies for designing inclusive curriculum.* Eugene: Specialized Training Program, University of Oregon.

Ford, A., Schnorr, R., Meyer, L., Davern, L., Black, J., & Dempsey, P. (1989). *The Syracuse community-referenced curriculum guide for students with moderate and severe disabilities.* Baltimore: Paul H. Brookes Publishing Co.

Gee, K., Graham, N., Goetz, L., Oshima, G., & Yoshioka, K. (1991). Teaching students to request the continuation of routine activities by using time delay and decreasing physical assistance in the context of chain interruption. *Journal of The Association for Persons with Severe Handicaps, 16*(3), 154–167.

Giangreco, M.F., Cloninger, C., & Iverson, V. (1992). *Choosing options and accommodations for children: A guide to planning inclusive educators.* Baltimore: Paul H. Brookes Publishing Co.

Guess, D., Siegel-Causey, E., Roberts, S., Guy, B., Ault, M.M., & Rues, J. (1993). Analysis of state organizational patterns among students with profound disabilities. *Journal of The Association for Persons with Severe Handicaps, 18,* 93–108.

Guess, D., & Thompson, B. (1991). Preparation of personnel to educate students with severe and multiple disabilities: A time for change? In L. Meyer, C. Peck, & L. Brown (Eds.), *Critical issues in the lives of people with severe disabilities* (pp. 391–398). Baltimore: Paul H. Brookes Publishing Co.

Guy, B., Guess, D., & Ault, M. (1993). Classroom procedures for the measurement of behavior states among students with profound disabilities. *Journal of The Association for Persons with Severe Handicaps, 18*(1), 52–60.

Hamre-Nietupski, S., Nietupski, J., & Strathe, M. (1992). Functional life skills, academic skills, and friendship/social relationship development: What do parents of students with moderate/severe/profound disabilities value? *Journal of The Association for Persons with Severe Handicaps, 17*(1), 53–58.

Izen, D.L., & Brown, F. (1991). Education and treatment needs of students with profound, multiply handicapped and medically fragile conditions: A survey of teachers' perceptions. *Journal of The Association for Persons with Severe Handicaps, 14*(1), 13–22.

Meyer, L., & Janney, R. (1989). User-friendly measures of meaningful outcomes: Evaluating behavioral interventions. *Journal of The Association for Persons with Severe Handicaps, 14,* 263–270.

Meyer, L.H. (1991). Advocacy, research and typical practices: A call for the reduction of discrepancies between what is and what ought to be and how to get there. In L.H. Meyer, C.A. Peck, & L. Brown (Eds.), *Critical issues in the levels of people with severe disabilities* (pp. 629–649). Baltimore: Paul H. Brookes Publishing Co.

Plum, F., & Posner, J.B. (1972). *The diagnosis of stupor and coma* (2nd ed.). Philadelphia: E.A. Davis Company.

Rainforth, B., & York, J. (1993). Handling and positioning. In F.P. Orelove & D. Sobsey, *Educating children with multiple disabilities: A transdisciplinary approach* (2nd ed., pp. 79–118). Baltimore: Paul H. Brookes Publishing Co.

Rivers, E.S. (1993). *Moments of meaningfulness: A case study of student membership.* Unpublished doctoral dissertation, University of New Orleans, LA.

Sailor, W., Anderson, J., Halvorsen, A., Doering, K., Filler, J., & Goetz, L. (1989). *The comprehensive local school: Regular education for all children with disabilities.* Baltimore: Paul H. Brookes Publishing Co.

Smith, G.J., & Ylvisaker, M. (1985). Cognitive rehabilitation therapy: Early stages of recovery. In M. Ylvisaker (Ed.), *Head injury rehabilitation: Children and adolescents* (pp. 275–286). San Diego: College-Hill Press.

Szekeres, S.F., Ylvisaker, M., & Holland, A.L. (1985). Cognitive rehabilitation therapy: A framework for intervention. In M. Ylvisaker (Ed.), *Head injury rehabilitation: Children and adolescents* (pp. 219–246). San Diego: College-Hill Press.

Wilcox, B., & Bellamy, G.T. (1987). *The activities catalog: An alternative curriculum for youth and adults with severe disabilities.* Baltimore: Paul H. Brookes Publishing Co.

6

Quality Inclusive Schooling for Students with Severe Behavioral Challenges

DEBORAH L. HEDEEN, BARBARA J. AYRES,
LUANNA H. MEYER, AND JACQUELYN WAITE

THE LITERATURE ON problem behavior in children and adults is extensive. This literature is diverse in theory and approach, ranging from psychodynamic to operant behavioral frameworks and including reports on individual therapy of various kinds; group therapies from different theoretical perspectives; behavioral consultation with multidisciplinary personnel and/or families; social and psychological support for families and the children themselves; medication and even surgical procedures; and various kinds of specific habilitative, educational, and therapeutic programs, packages, and places. Yet demonstrations of successful outcomes are relatively rare. In their comprehensive meta-analysis of 12 years of intervention research with challenging behaviors reported in 18 professional journals, Scotti, Evans, Meyer, and Walker (1991) found only 44 out of more than 400 published studies that could be regarded as effective interventions. Even more disappointing is the evidence available that what we know about intervening with serious challenging behaviors in children and youth can be applied and will be successful in inclusive educational environments.

The interventions reported in this chapter were carried out while the first three authors were affiliated with Syracuse University. This work was supported in part by the New York Partnership for Statewide Systems Change, Grant H0086J0007, and by the Consortium for Collaborative Research on Social Relationships, Cooperative Agreement H086A20003, awarded by the Office of Special Education Programs, U.S. Department of Education. However, the opinions expressed herein are not necessarily those of the U.S. Department of Education, and no official endorsement should be inferred.

We do not yet have a database demonstrating the effectiveness of individually appropriate services and support needed to intervene with serious challenging behavior in general education classrooms.

There appear to be two possible reasons for this state of affairs: first, the presence of such serious challenging behaviors as aggression, self-injury, and severely disruptive behaviors effectively preempts enrollment of students with disabilities in inclusive programs. Thus, the literature almost exclusively reports interventions carried out in wholly or partially segregated (e.g., "integrated") classrooms rather than in inclusive classrooms. Second, the literature reporting successful interventions with significant behavior problems describes extraordinary intervention resources and personnel—including the researchers themselves—that are simply not available in typical settings. In most instances, the reader can only infer the level of researcher involvement in the intervention effort. It is rare to locate any intervention report that emphasizes typical resources as a precondition of validating a most promising practice recommended for adoption in typical schools and classrooms. Each of these two issues is briefly discussed in the following section in order to introduce the two case studies in this chapter.

THE PREEMPTIVE NATURE OF CHALLENGING BEHAVIOR

We now have considerable evidence that one of the ultimate challenges to inclusion in any environment is behavior. The U.S. Department of Education's Office of Special Education Programs has for over a decade now overseen 5-year awards to states and agencies for Statewide Systems Change efforts designed to increase access to the general education school and classroom for children with the most severe disabilities. Each year at the Annual Project Directors' Meeting, presentations and various discussions continue to highlight the student who seems to present the most significant challenge to inclusion—the student with serious behavior problems (Consortium on Inclusive Schooling Practices, 1994). Currently, the New York Partnership for Statewide Systems Change Project is conducting an extensive evaluation of its technical assistance to 35 school districts throughout the state for the three school years from 1991 to 1994. Initial interviews with various school district personnel and constituents consistently mention the student who exhibits dangerous or highly disruptive behaviors as the most serious challenge to inclusion. For example, of the 33 students whose challenging behaviors resulted in referral to our Child-Centered Inservice Project during the 1986–1989 school years, none were in an inclusive setting (although all were attending a self-contained class in a general education school, some were specifically placed in that setting from segregated schools in order to qualify for our assistance), and only 4 were integrated into general education classes for any portion of the school day (Meyer & Janney, 1992).

In our view, if a student exhibits behavior that is dangerous, there must be sufficient guarantees that others will not be exposed to the potential for injury. But in most instances, behavior described as "dangerous" at first referral may in reality represent little to no risk of injury to anyone—including other children—if reasonable precautions are taken. In the two examples presented in this chapter, the students' acting-out behaviors could raise safety concerns. However, in both cases, relatively straightforward precautions could be designed to protect others, and rigorous standards were enforced to ensure that those precautions were in place at all times. The behavior itself does not determine whether or not inclusion is possible—an assessment of risk to others should be the deciding factor.

THE USABILITY OF VALIDATED INTERVENTIONS

Many of the guidelines for the most promising practices for intervening with serious behavioral challenges actually continue to be developed and validated in either highly specialized settings or typical settings augmented with resources as part of the study that would not otherwise be available. Dunlap and Kern (1993) introduce a detailed case study that entailed extensive additional resources as well as a lengthy assessment period with the following caveat:

> As we present the model, we provide examples from our experiences. . . . The first and most detailed example was an especially intransigent case that required great efforts in both the assessment and intervention phases. However, we urge the reader to recognize that most cases are relatively straightforward and do not demand the time or personnel that were needed in this instance. (p. 179)

These authors were candid in prefacing their first success story with an acknowledgment that the process was not likely to be practical for typical schools and situations. We also agree with their argument that where serious behavioral challenges are longstanding and serious, the intervention may need to be similarly intensive.

However, a continuing concern of our own is whether the validated interventions carried out with the advice and assistance of researchers regarded as experts in the field will be usable to the teachers, parents, and other practitioners seeking strategies needed for homes, schools, and other community settings. We have some evidence that even specialized teachers do not continue to use data collection procedures known to inform various kinds of intervention decisions after these teachers complete their graduate training programs (Burney & Shores, 1979; Haring, Liberty, & White, 1980). Studies of teachers' use of data collection systems revealed that they tended to discount the validity of the kinds of objective and graphic representations of student performance they had been taught, often arguing that the techniques were, in their view, inaccurate and unreliable as well as being demanding and difficult to manage in a real classroom (Fisher & Lindsey-Walters, 1987; Grigg, Snell, & Lloyd, 1989). Ayres, Meyer, Erevelles, and Park-Lee (1994) also found that even special education teachers selected as exemplary by their supervisors reported difficulty in implementing "most promising practices" as these were described in the literature—even though they reported familiarity with the practices.

Meyer and Evans (1993) express concern that the problem goes beyond the issue of whether or not practitioners can replicate the application of extraordinary resources, including additional personnel in real settings. Another factor could be the extent to which those expected to carry out an intervention can be motivated to do so and are committed to the approach. In continuing to describe interventions with challenging behaviors as a highly technical endeavor rich with professional terminology and constructs and supplemented by "expensive" data collection requirements, we may be virtually guaranteeing that those interventions will have limited appeal to the very people who need them (Evans & Meyer, 1993; Meyer & Evans, 1993).

We have been intrigued by the broad and almost instant appeal of some procedures, even in situations where empirical evidence regarding their effectiveness has not been forthcoming. Although one answer might be that people want to believe in sweeping claims regardless of contrary arguments, another answer might be that some procedures more readily "tap into" the natural capabilities and ordinary knowledge that each of us has in our repertoires, regardless of technical training or professional educational level. The widespread and thoroughly human notion of "common sense" might be one such set of principles that few would argue requires empirical validation. Similar constructs that seem to have universal appeal are "common decency" or "do unto others as you would have them do unto you." Appeals to our human side and to principles of being kind to others—as firmly rooted in many cultural traditions as the opposing principle of "an eye for an eye" (revenge)—may simply make us feel better about ourselves than a highly technical and professional practice. This may explain why an approach such as "Gentle Teaching" (McGee, Menousek, & Hobbs, 1987) has had the impact it has even though its proponents did not emphasize empirical demonstrations of effectiveness. People like the idea of "gentle teaching"; it may match reasons for entering the teaching profession in the first place. Thus, approaches to team problem solving such as Lifestyles Futures Planning (O'Brien, 1987) or Circle of Friends (Forest & Lusthaus, 1989; Vandercook, York, & Forest, 1989) seem to have intuitive appeal to family members and professionals alike.

It may be that empirical guidance for interventions with challenging behavior will be most compelling when the research involved has not only demonstrated effective behavior change, but also has done so while attending to two critical issues: 1) the validated intervention is one that care providers approve of and therefore are comfortable implementing, and 2) the approach must be one that can be realistically implemented in actual settings and situations, without extraordinary resources, expertise, or personnel. For this situation to occur, researchers may need to shift from scientist to scientist-practitioner in more fundamental ways than have thus far been the case (Evans & Meyer, 1993; Meyer & Evans, 1993).

COMPONENTS OF EFFECTIVE INTERVENTIONS

In this chapter, we describe successful interventions with two different students who have severe developmental disabilities and severe behavioral challenges. In both instances, the services and supports we describe were implemented in age-appropriate general education classrooms, where the students followed the same routines and attended school with their peers without disabilities. In one case, the student was attending a segregated school at referral, and the program described here began with 6-year-old Shawn's move to an inclusive kindergarten class in his neighborhood school. In 11-year-old Becky's case, our intervention began at the start of her second year in an inclusive program, initiated by a request for help from the building principal and school staff, whose experiences with Becky formed the basis for their belief that she would be better served at another school in a self-contained program.

The model that was used in these cases involved multiple components, incorporating principles and practices described in our own earlier work (Evans & Meyer, 1985; Meyer & Evans, 1989; Meyer & Janney, 1992), as well as in closely related work by many colleagues (Carr et al., 1994; Dunlap, Robbins, & Kern, 1994; Durand, 1990; Horner et al., 1990; LaVigna & Donnellan, 1986; Lovett, 1985; McGee, Menolascino, Hobbs, & Menousek, 1987). Each of these studies has emphasized a team problem-solving approach whereby educators, parents, and other care providers can be successful in designing an educative approach that incorporates positive supports. Important factors to consider in such a plan include relationships between the child and others, ecological and setting variables, social-communicative interactions and skills, activity and lifestyle preferences, meaningful curricula and daily activities, choice and self-determination, and user-friendly evaluation procedures to guide the intervention effort.

Relationships with Others

Meyer and Evans (1989) emphasized that team planning to address challenging behavior should begin by looking closely at the person's lifestyle rather than by immediately planning a program to address single behaviors. They described a team planning process building on O'Brien's (1987) Lifestyles Futures Planning that they have utilized clinically with agency personnel as a first step for analyzing complex situations. More recently, Berryman and Evans (1994) describe "naturalistic interventions" designed to enhance adaptive lifestyles that were systematically compared to positive behavior management programs designed for a sample of adults with challenging behaviors (see also Berryman, Evans, & Kalbag, 1994). Results were fairly similar for the two groups, with one exception—the naturalistic intervention group overall showed more positive interactions between the person with a disability and staff, and greater improvements in certain indices of quality of life. What was even more evident was the change in attitude reported by the naturalistic group, shifting from a focus on "problems" to an emphasis on continuously looking at whether or not the person involved had a reasonable lifestyle, including increased self-determination (Berryman & Evans, in press). Although it may be difficult to measure the impact of friendships and normalized social relationships on someone's behavior, common sense dictates that we acknowledge the importance of these critical aspects of life and begin the effort (Forest & Pearpoint, 1990).

Ecological Factors and Setting Variables

Events, situations, and environments can be strong predictors of when problem behavior does and does not typically occur (Berkman & Meyer, 1988; Brown, 1991; Dunlap & Kern, 1993; Evans & Meyer, 1985; Meyer & Evans, 1989). For example, Brown (1991) showed that teaching individuals how to use and understand a daily schedule was associated with decreases in problem behavior that had been associated with transitions and changes in the program. The hypothesis that would explain this pattern is that, unless the student can understand and predict (or even feel some control over) what are otherwise confusing disruptions in his or her day, it is natural for an individual to react with negative behavior, which may be the only strategy he or she has to express unhappiness or confusion. Other environmental variables can be particularly distressing to some students, such as a crowded classroom (McAfee, 1987) or being expected to work for extended periods of time (Dunlap & Kern, 1993). Yet it may not be enough to simply change these variables and assume that, for example, the student knows that an activity time has been shortened.

Communication and Understanding

Communication has been increasingly emphasized as not only important to the development of skills for life but also as an explanation for the occurrence of challenging behavior (Donnellan, Mirenda, Mesaros, & Fassbender, 1984; Durand, 1990). If a child does not have a communication system, he or she must communicate with behaviors, and sometimes these nonverbal behaviors are challenging behaviors. Similarly, if a child does not share comprehension of the communication system used in the environment, he or she may react negatively to ongoing events that he or she does not understand. Dunlap and Kern (1993) describe a student for whom manipulations of setting events such as the length of work would not prevent behavior problems unless staff communicated effectively with the student that the length was shorter before the work began. The student they describe, Jill, reacted negatively to even a short period of work when only verbal cues were used to introduce the task: "Jill was also provided with visual cues by presenting her a worksheet containing only the problems she was required to complete. . . . [We added] the caveat that Jill would need to clearly comprehend (e.g., with the assistance of visual as well as verbal cues) that the session would be relatively brief in duration" (p. 192).

Activity Preferences

The nature of the activity for the child can have a dramatic impact on behavior. Weeks and Gaylord-Ross (1981) demonstrated that severe behavior problems in children with severe disabilities were reliably associated with difficult tasks, and self-injury, aggression, and crying were substantially reduced through errorless learning and by ensuring that the task was not too difficult for the child. Evans and Voeltz (1982) replicated these findings with several children who had multiple and severe challenging behaviors, and they significantly reduced the occurrence of those behaviors through activity and task changes. There is also evidence that children show reliable decreases in challenging behavior when engaged in activities they enjoy and prefer. Kern-Dunlap, Clarke, and Dunlap (1990) demonstrated a decrease in problem behavior associated with the incorporation of a favorite hobby into a 13-year-old girl's daily assignments. Meyer, Evans, Wuerch, and Brennan (1985) demonstrated clear patterns of excess behavior in several students with multiple disabilities and mental retardation as a function of engagement in preferred versus nonpreferred leisure activities.

Meaningful Curriculum

The educational literature increasingly acknowledges the role that curricular content plays in student motivation, learning, and behavior. In general education, issues around meaningful standards, curricular content that relates concepts learned to daily life and future career choices, natural language approaches to early reading and mathematics, thematic instruction, and authentic assessment are all examples of most promising practices that acknowledge difficulties in motivating students academically unless they can appreciate the value of what they are learning. In special education, individualized goals and objectives might be team priorities, but the activities designed to achieve them might not be meaningful to the student. Dunlap, Kern-Dunlap, Clarke, and Robbins (1991) showed how shifting from traditional tasks completed through worksheets and textbook exercises to activities focused on the same academic skills but using socially and personally motivating activities and exercises resulted in the complete elimination of disruptive classroom behavior in a 13-year-old girl with multiple disabilities. A major intervention component in a case study by Berkman and Meyer (1988) of an adult man was the substitution of a personally meaningful daily program that enabled him to see how his participation had an immediate and clear impact on his world. In this report, after nearly four decades of severe challenging behaviors, the individual's self-injury and aggression were virtually eliminated through an intervention that emphasized major lifestyle changes, including moving to an apartment in the community, finding friends and roommates of his choosing, and getting a job.

Choice and Self-Determination

Shevin and Klein (1984) discussed the critical issue of choice for persons with disabilities, and there has been increased focus on this topic since the first approaches to teaching and enabling choice making described by Lovett (1985) and Wuerch and Voeltz (1982). Most recently, Seybert, Dunlap, and Ferro (1994) describe the positive effects of introducing choices for three students with intellectual disabilities into their daily activities carried out in the regular school environment. (See Chapters 13, 14, and 15 for further discussion of choice and self-determination.)

User-Friendly Evaluation Strategies

Finally, creating positive behavioral support for students with challenging behaviors involves the integral use of data to make important decisions. At each stage of an intervention plan, information on the child's behavior in various contexts should guide decision making by the team. Meyer and Janney (1989) described a user-friendly set of assessment and evaluation techniques that were validated in a variety of school and community settings for children with severe behavioral needs (see also Meyer & Evans, 1989). This approach and several of these measures were adapted in the case studies described in this chapter.

We believed that it was important to reflect this "user-friendly" attitude in the materials that team members were expected to use in our efforts. A module by Janney, Black, and Ferlo (1989) was designed for parents, teachers, and other care providers and included the basic principles and practices of an educative approach to children's behavioral needs (Evans & Meyer, 1985; Meyer & Evans, 1989). We also supplemented these still "technical" readings and resources with a more personalized account about someone with autism to encourage team members in understanding the child's perspective and imagining how the child might feel (Grandin, 1986). What follows are two "stories" that document the process that supported positive behavioral change for two young people with autism and severe learning needs.

SHAWN'S STORY

In June 1992, Shawn's school district in central New York applied for technical assistance from the New York Partnership for Statewide Systems Change Project to increase quality inclusive schooling options for students with severe disabilities. Their application was precipitated, in part, by Shawn's mother. Shawn was then 6 years old, and he had been educated with the label of autism in a regional, segregated school for students with severe disabilities. Shawn's mother decided that, in the fall, his school year would be different: He would go to kindergarten in his neighborhood school. She mentioned a lawyer in her discussions with the district, so Shawn was chosen as the focus of one requirement for participation in the Systems Change Project—getting started with at least one student during the first year of planning. One of the authors of this chapter was selected as the district's consultant with experience in inclusive schooling; participation in the New York project required committee planning by the district to work toward its own goals with regularly scheduled, on-site support from a consultant, along with the focus on a specific student, as part of the learning process.

In preparation for Shawn's transition to kindergarten, it was important for team members to meet him and learn about his strengths and needs. One way that this information was gathered was through visits to his classroom at the segregated school. The following is a description of the consultant's first meeting with Shawn:

> I first met Shawn in October when we started planning for his transition from the special school to Lakeview Elementary School. I'll never forget the day when the director of special education, the building principal, and I drove the hour-long trip from his neighborhood school to the regional program. I had heard that Shawn often became sick in the mornings on the bus, and now I knew why. We were driving along winding roads and up and down hills, and by the time we arrived I was feeling a little carsick myself! We walked into the building and located the classroom. As we entered the room, our attention was immediately drawn to one side of the room where a boy was sitting with an adult at a computer. The boy was confined to a wooden chair that had a leg abductor and a waist strap. He was covered with a blanket that he held tightly around his head and back. The woman working with him was trying to pull one of his hands away from the blanket, and as she struggled with him, he began to make loud noises. At one point she did get his hand unhooked from the blanket, but he immediately grabbed her hair. It took the assistance of another adult to get his long thin fingers untangled from her hair. When his hand was free and the blanket had been removed, the boy started to hit his head relentlessly. It was at this point that I noticed the many bald spots that covered his head and the scratch marks on his face and arms.
>
> The woman wasn't successful in getting him to interact with the computer and finally gave him back the blanket, released him from the chair, turned in our direction and said loudly, "Well, that's Shawn." She added that all he wanted was to be left alone or to play in the swing or jump on the trampoline, that he was very aggressive and self-abusive, and that she had tried everything. By now, Shawn was standing in front of a large window wrapped up in the blanket, rocking back and forth and flicking his fingers rapidly in front of his face as he stared out the window.
>
> I had met and worked with students like Shawn before—some within inclusive settings—so I could envision his inclusion, but when I looked at the director of special education and the principal they were barely managing to conceal their apprehension and nervousness. I was sure I knew what they were thinking: Here is a boy who won't sit without restraints, hides under a blanket, won't interact with people, hits his head and screams, pulls his hair out along with the hair of others, and we are going to put him in a kindergarten class?
>
> After spending some time in the classroom we left for our trip back to town. In the car we discussed our observations, and the director of special education and principal shared some of their concerns about Shawn's inclusion in kindergarten. At some point, I asked them a very direct ques-

tion: "Are you committed to welcoming Shawn into the elementary school?" To my delight, they both said, "Yes." They had not been impressed with what they had observed in the special education classroom, especially what seemed like a lack of respect shown to the students and the lack of activity in the classroom. From then on we never questioned *if* or *why* we were bringing Shawn back—we took the next step and began asking *how* we would include him in kindergarten.

The kindergarten teacher wrote this about her introduction to Shawn:

Having been employed in my school district for 7 years, including 4 as the teacher-coordinator of the gifted and talented program, 1 in a sixth-grade English position to fill a year's leave of absence, and 1 in second grade, I looked forward to filling a permanent kindergarten position which had opened during the summer. While preparing my new classroom for the opening of the school year, I began to hear rumors from my colleagues regarding a child I would have in my room. I was informed that my predecessor had agreed to take a child with a severe disability into his, which had since become my, classroom during this school year. Apparently, since I had inherited the room, so came the child. I dismissed the rumors as beginning-of-the-year gossip. However, once the year began, the rumors persisted. I was even being approached by fellow faculty members inquiring as to when the student would be arriving.

Eventually, at a faculty meeting, we were all told that a child with a disability would be entering our district in January and would be placed in a kindergarten classroom. We were told that the child was autistic and would require extra support. We were also told that the child's name was Shawn.

As the school year progressed, I began to think more and more of what had been said. I was intrigued by Shawn's diagnosis and was curious to learn more, even though he obviously was not going to be in my classroom. I read articles, books, periodicals, anything I could get my hands on about autism, and it was about that time that I became "hooked." I went to my principal and said, "I would like to have Shawn in my classroom." Her response was an enthusiastic hug and expression of delight in my welcoming reaction to Shawn.

To prepare for the transition which was to happen in my classroom, I first visited Shawn in the school he was currently attending and had been attending for over 3 years. My only objective for the visit was to observe Shawn and his interactions with others. I was depressed with what I observed. The day I visited, Shawn was in a classroom with one teacher, two teaching assistants, and three other children with disabilities, none of whom were able to communicate verbally. I wondered how this child would ever learn to communicate verbally without role models his own age. I also pondered how he would be able to form any significant friendships when he was constantly confined by adults. Then I began to look at Shawn.

I saw a child whose entire head was covered with a blanket. He rocked back and forth, both standing and sitting, and showed no reaction to anyone or anything, except when the blanket was taken away, at which point he screamed until it was given back.

I saw a child being led to a chair that had a bar up the center so the occupant could not slide out or get out without standing up. Shawn was placed into the chair and remained there while the rest of his class participated in a group activity. No one attempted to assist him so that he could participate, nor did anyone ask if he wanted to join the others.

During my visit, his teacher told me that she was not sure what Shawn was capable of academically. He was now 6 years old and as far as she knew, could identify colors and shapes and could put together a six-piece puzzle. Other than that, little was expected of him. His speech teacher did indicate that she thought he might be able to read by some of the things he had been doing on the computer for her, but after 3 and a half years, why didn't someone know?

I was also told that Shawn was such a challenging student to work with that the three adults in the classroom rotated "taking" him on a weekly basis. All these things were told to me within Shawn's range of hearing. Would they have been said in front of him had he been able to vocally state what he felt? I wondered.

Before I left that day, Shawn reached out and touched my leg with his hand. I had not spoken to him, touched him, or communicated with him in any way during the time I spent there. When he reached out and initiated contact with me, his fate was sealed—he would be in my classroom in January.

A major theme of the lifestyles planning approach advocated by O'Brien (1987) and incorporated into the design of behavioral interventions in Meyer and Evans (1989) is *perspective taking:* looking at the child not as a "disabled student" but as a child with many characteristics—one of which is having a disability. The director of special education, the building principal, and the kindergarten teacher seeing Shawn for the first time were as struck by the restrictiveness of his segregated program as they were by Shawn's disability or behavior. None of the other children were talking, so how would Shawn learn to communicate and with whom would he converse? Shawn exhibited self-injurious and disruptive behaviors when he was asked to work, but he was obviously allowed to be alone to "do his own thing" no matter how negative that might be, and when he was required to work the staff did not seem to be confident that they knew what his skills were or what he might like to do. And, again through the eyes of "ordinary people," Shawn's day did not look positive in comparison to what these observers knew about the typical school day of other young children—why then would he want to participate in the activities of this classroom?

Thus, two assumptions would be fundamental to the design of Shawn's kindergarten experience. First, rather than assume that he was incompetent, we would assume that he was competent and could hear and understand everything that was said to him or about him. Therefore, we needed to treat him like all the other kindergarten students and would not talk about him in his presence as if he were not there or listening. Second, rather than assume that because he had autism being a little boy was less important than his disability, we would assume that he might like the same kinds of activities and objects that other young children like. Each assumption affirmed that Shawn's status as a child was more important than his status as a person with a disability, and whatever he would do could not be allowed to sacrifice his status as a child in order to "meet his needs" as a child with a disability. In other words, we could not take away Shawn's childhood as the context for attempting to "cure" his autism. And we affirmed Shawn's need for teachers, support personnel, and peers who respected and cared about him as part of the necessary context for any meaningful attempt to teach Shawn.

What might we list as the theoretical and empirical bases for these affirmations? There are several, and, despite our hesitancy to turn these straightforward principles of human needs into technical terms, our supporting evidence includes the following:

- In their comprehensive meta-analysis of behavioral interventions, Scotti et al. (1991) found that both integration and active programming that addressed needs other than the behavior problems themselves were significantly related to positive outcomes. Segregated settings and lack of active programming were associated with less effective outcomes.
- There is a growing database on the positive impact of peers without disabilities through direct contact (e.g., reciprocal teaching or peer tutoring), peer modeling, and increased access to a variety of play and related opportunities because of friendships and other social support relationships (Forest & Pearpoint, 1990; Haring, 1991; Strain & Odom, 1986; Walter & Vincent, 1982).
- Having friends and other meaningful social relationships with peers (and with adults) is related to self-esteem and self-fulfillment (Haring, 1991; Kishi & Meyer, 1994; McKinney, Fitzgerald, & Strommen, 1982). We also believe that people are motivated by personal social relationships—pleasing others who matter to them—at least as much as they might be motivated by such material reinforcers as food, money, and possessions.
- Disability becomes a social barrier not because of the personal characteristics of the individual with a disability but as a result of the obstacles created by our treatment of the person with a disability—such as attending a segregated school apart from one's family, peers, and neighborhood (Gartner & Lipsky, 1987; Haring, 1991).

Thus, we would design a program within the context of Shawn's childhood and contact with his peers, family, and neighborhood. The components of that program are described next.

Team Planning to Design Shawn's Program

One of the first steps in planning for Shawn's transition was to develop a building inclusion committee that would work together to create and implement a plan. Shawn would be the initial focus of this committee, but later we would discuss the inclusion of other students within the building and the district. The committee met monthly starting in October and included the consultant, the director of special education, the building principal, the kindergarten teacher, the speech therapist, the school psychologist, a resource teacher, a fourth grade teacher, the physical education teacher, and, when possible, Shawn's mother. In an early team meeting, we discussed the basic assumptions that would guide our efforts to include Shawn. We agreed that Shawn was an intelligent, thoughtful human being, that he understood others, and that we needed to treat him with the respect afforded to all other kindergarten students. We also accepted that his behaviors served a purpose and that, most likely, those behaviors were social-communicative in nature. That is, as he had no better way to communicate, his behaviors, including screaming, hitting, and pulling hair, were efforts by him to let others know about his needs, feelings, and desires. We recognized that he needed to learn new, more appropriate ways to communicate with others.

Soon after, we agreed on certain basic principles in the design of his specific classroom program and individualized education program (IEP). We would not force Shawn to sit in a chair or participate unwillingly in activities through the use of physical or mechanical restraints. We decided to interpret Shawn's need for the blanket as a support need, so it would become our task to provide the necessary emotional and physical support to enable Shawn to be comfortable within the classroom so that the blanket would no longer be needed. In addition, if Shawn was to be treated as a full-time member of the kindergarten classroom, our challenge would be to address his individual instructional goals and objectives through the flow of ongoing kindergarten classroom activities whenever possible—and not use pull-out activities unless absolutely unavoidable. Related services such as speech therapy would also be provided in the classroom, using an integrated therapy approach (Campbell, 1987; Dunn, 1991).

A team approach would be used so that Shawn's education was not the responsibility of any one person. The team developed an action plan, including those things that needed to be done prior to the actual transition to the kindergarten class, as well as some time lines that would follow. Because the adults believed they were not fully prepared for an entire school day, the initial arrangement would be for Shawn to attend kindergarten for 3 hours daily during his first two weeks. To prepare those team members who would be working directly with Shawn, visits were arranged for them to observe his classroom at the regional program and for Shawn to visit the kindergarten classroom in his neighborhood school. Finally, a teaching assistant (TA) who would work alongside the kindergarten teacher to support Shawn was hired during this preparation period. Because the TA was to be a classroom assistant rather than Shawn's personal assistant—and to ensure that all the children in the classroom felt they had two adults to depend on and go to in times of need—the TA was hired in time to become familiar with the other children, the teacher's style, and the classroom routines prior to Shawn's arrival.

Meshing Shawn's Goals and Objectives with Kindergarten Activities

By our next meeting a few weeks later, we were ready to talk more specifically about Shawn and his individual goals and objectives. We looked over his IEP, and we rephrased goals and objectives into priorities by using everyday language. These were then written out as a one-page document that everyone could use as a reminder of Shawn's needs and to ensure that his IEP was established as a working document. Our next step was to use a matrix format that allowed us to mesh his goals and objectives with the kindergarten activities. These kindergarten activities were to be the vehicle through which we would address Shawn's specific needs. We covered the walls of our meeting room with chart paper to complete the matrix in Figure 1. Shawn's goals and objectives were listed down the left side of the paper, and the kindergarten activities were listed across the top of the paper. We started with the first activities and routines of the day, describing what took place during this time and then discussing how Shawn's objectives could be addressed during that specific activity, and we continued this process as we went through the school day. This step in the planning process helped the team members envision Shawn's participation and understand that he would be addressing his own individualized goals and objectives within the classroom through shared activities with his classmates; it also helped in the process of planning adaptations. The kindergarten teacher describes the process as she remembers it:

> With the consultant's help, we looked at Shawn's IEP and my daily schedule and set up ways in which his goals could be incorporated into my kindergarten program. Our speech teacher included Shawn's goals

DAILY SCHEDULE OF ACTIVITIES

Activity: IEP Objectives:	Morning Arrival	Gym	Lunch Count (math)	Calendar	Story	Centers	Lunch
Increase participation in routines, manipulate objects, recognize name	✓ Put things away	✓ Participate in games, exercise	✓ Follow along with number line	✓ Use personal calendar	✓ Has copy of story and turns pages	✓ Use of materials	✓ Carry tray, get utensils
Increase self-care skills (eating, dressing, toileting)	✓ Coat, restroom						✓ Eating, grooming
Increase social interactions – initiate and join peers	✓ Students meet at bus and greet	✓ Partner activities	✓	✓		✓ Peers at centers	✓
Increase communication skills-yes/no and making choices from objects/words	✓ What does he want to do first, where does he want to play	✓ Choice of activity	✓ Choose sticker, walk with partner to board	✓ Indicate choices on personal calendar	✓ Locate pictures in story by pointing	✓ Choose center, choose materials	✓ Choose food, milk

CODE: ✓ = Opportunity to Address Objective

Figure 1. Meeting IEP objectives in the inclusive classroom.

into the work she would be doing with him as well. This process helped us to see that not only would Shawn be meeting his IEP goals, but he would also be in the position of having appropriate role models for developing social skills and, eventually, friendships.

Shawn's Transition to Kindergarten

The kindergarten teacher understood that Shawn's inclusion was not simply a matter of professional planning by the team—he was going to be part of a classroom with 21 peers who needed to understand him and interact with him in a positive way. The teacher describes the next steps for Shawn's transition:

At the end of November, I presented the idea of having a new student in our classroom to my existing class. At first, I just let them know we would have a new student named Shawn in our class after winter break. The children knew that Shawn was in another school and that it would be hard for him to start in a new school. We discussed ways in which we could make the transition easier for him and decided that we would send him pictures we made and books we had written. We set up a "Shawn Box" for all the treasures we wanted to send him so he would feel comfortable in our school. I had pictures of all the students, and we wrote a class letter to him. All the students told Shawn something about themselves, and I glued their pictures next to what they had said. We sent the letter to Shawn in the middle of December. Then, just before winter vacation, I began to talk about things that are alike and things that are different within my class. Then we talked about people and discussed their similarities and differences. I read the students stories of children with disabilities, and we discussed how their lives are the same and different because of the disability. Finally, I told them about Shawn's disability and what it meant.

Before Shawn ever entered our building, my students knew that his voice didn't work for him and that we would all have to teach him ways in which to tell us things. They knew that in order to get our attention, Shawn would sometimes hold on to our hair or our clothes. We practiced what we would say or do if Shawn needed us. My basic assumption was that Shawn was a thinking, feeling, intelligent human being who, through an accident of nature, was born without the capacity to speak in the conventional manner. Because of this disability, he had worked for 6 years trying to perfect a way in which he could let others know what he thought and how he felt. My objective was to help him perfect a system which would be functionally usable for him and socially acceptable to others. I felt that once he could release the thoughts that had imprisoned him for so long, he would be able to develop positive social skills that would allow him to begin some lasting friendships.

Shawn was scheduled to be with us for 3 hours in the morning for a 2-week period, and he arrived just after winter break. When the 3 hours were up, he was bused back to his special school. After spending 1 day with us, there was no way my class was ever going to let him go! In fact, we wanted him with us all day, every day, before the 2 weeks were up. He had been a member of our class in our hearts since November.

Outcomes of Shawn's Kindergarten Experience

Shawn arrived at his neighborhood school the Monday morning after winter break and was greeted enthusiastically by 21 new classmates who all walked and talked! The first activity of the day was gym class, in which the physical education (PE) teacher had planned activities that she thought Shawn might like. She determined these activities by thinking about favorite activities of the other kindergarten students. The consultant remembers the transition that first day from the classroom to the gym and the activities that followed:

> It was time for gym, and the kindergarten students were asked to line up with a partner. One of the girls asked if she could be Shawn's partner. While Shawn was visibly shaken in his new surroundings, we knew it was important to connect him with his peers as much as possible that first day. Shawn needed considerable support from an adult to prevent him from hitting his head and pulling his hair; we came up with a way for the adult to provide enough support so that his classmate could hold his hand on the way to class. As they walked down the hall together, the girl pointed out different rooms and brought Shawn's attention to the artwork on the walls.

When the students reached the gym, the gym teacher provided Shawn with his first choice-making opportunity. A multicolored parachute was the day's activity, and all of the students, including Shawn, chose a color of the parachute to hold during the games. Shawn seemed fascinated by the activity, and, for the most part, the TA was able to support him without difficulties. At one point during PE class, Shawn did pull a classmate's hair. The teacher told the girl to remain calm and not pull away; the girl sat quietly, and the adults helped Shawn remove his fingers from her hair. The activity then continued. The students had been prepared with the knowledge that Shawn was unable to use his voice to talk, so they understood that he had probably done this to try to tell them something. Later that day, the kindergarten teacher asked the students if they had any questions about their new classmate; one asked why Shawn made noises and pulled hair. The teacher asked the children what they thought, and many ideas were generated about how he was probably nervous and afraid his first day and how he was excited about PE class and the parachute. They were able to interpret his behavior as his reaction to events and what he was trying to say—in other words, as communication.

Other behaviors changed and were allowed to change gradually. For example, Shawn had been in a restraint chair in his old school and at first refused to sit in a chair. He was allowed to stand for activities, and after some time he was more interested in sitting for comfort. The adults identified activities that Shawn enjoyed most, and they provided opportunities for him to sit for those activities first. Shawn was also allowed to get up from his chair whenever he felt it was necessary; he was never made to sit unwillingly. Within a few weeks, he was sitting through most of the classroom activities. His style of walking also changed naturally over time. When he first came, he used a gallop-type gait, lunging forward with his body and the same foot for each step. As he participated in the many transitions within the classroom and building, walking alongside his peers, his gait became like that of his peers—no therapy or instruction was provided, and, apparently, he learned incidentally from watching his classmates.

Initially, Shawn required considerable adult support to prevent him from hurting himself and others. In the beginning, when Shawn attempted to hit his head or pull his hair, the adult would gently hold his hand and redirect him to the ongoing activity. Over time, his head hitting and hair pulling decreased as his interest and participation in activities increased. Within a month, Shawn no longer needed constant physical support from an adult. With regard to pulling someone else's hair, adults and students learned when Shawn was most likely to engage in these behaviors and how to recognize and respond to the noises and body movements that indicated he was becoming excited, anxious, or nervous. When this occurred, the students were encouraged to increase the space between themselves and Shawn. If that did not work, Shawn was assisted to move away and to get involved in another activity. As these behaviors were prevented, classmates became more active in engaging Shawn in activities and could even succeed in getting him involved when a similar request from an adult had been met with refusal. We also believe that the kinds of socially acceptable hand-holding that are common in kindergarten classrooms provided Shawn with a far more natural alternative to the blanket that he had used in his previous school as a self-restraint strategy.

Finally, Shawn's teachers and parents believed that as he began to communicate more effectively he was less likely to hit himself or pull hair. Even during the remainder of that first year, Shawn learned to respond to choices by pointing to objects or pictures (e.g., what milk to drink, what color to paint, what center to play at, what student to walk with). He began using a yes/no card and pointing to letters of the alphabet. Shawn's classmates had similar communication cards, so they could ask him questions throughout the day, giving him many opportunities to use his emerging communication skills.

Shawn's kindergarten teacher wrote about Shawn's progress throughout the year and what she believes his inclusion taught her and the other students:

> From January to June was an unbelievable experience for all of us. Shawn learned that there were people he could trust and value. He developed a continuing friendship with a number of students in my classroom, but particularly David. To David, Shawn was his "best bud." David would not go anywhere, except the bathroom, unless he could literally drag Shawn too. There seemed to be no activity they couldn't conquer as a team. When Shawn grabbed for David, David would tell him to let go and then show him how friends let friends know they care by giving a hug or giving each other five. Soon, the general school population would pass Shawn in the hall with their hands out, whispering, "Hey, Shawn, give me five!"
>
> The other students in my classroom benefited by having Shawn in our classroom in ways they will carry for a lifetime. They experienced that different is neither good nor bad, just different. This became very evident one day as we were doing a circle activity where three students were in a line and we, the audience, had to recognize ways in which the three were alike and different. After the usual "Shawn's a boy, Susie and Amy are girls" response, this little hand shot up in the air and the voice said, "They're different because they talk in different ways: Susie and Amy use their voice and Shawn uses his communication card." This is a lesson adults have been trying to learn for years!
>
> My students learned acceptance of others based on who you are, not what you do or don't do, can or can't do, will or won't do. They learned

to take issue with real problems, not irrelevant situations. We discussed how we could safely get Shawn out of our building during a fire drill if he had taken his shoes off, making his safety the problem to solve, not the shoes that he continually took off. We brainstormed ways in which we could teach Shawn how to get our attention if he needed us rather than focus on the times he would grab us. They learned to face all problems in the same way, whether it was a friend cutting in line in front of them, or a valued treasure which disappeared in the classroom. My students became problem solvers of very real problems and now have the capacity to apply the same process in all areas of their lives.

Perhaps the person who benefited most from having accepted Shawn into a regular classroom was me, his very regular classroom teacher. From the first day he stepped foot into my room, the self-doubt and inhibitions regarding whether I could teach "special" children completely disappeared. The only priority was Shawn and how I could help him become the best person he was capable of becoming.

Reflecting on the time I spent with Shawn, the thing I think he helped me most to see was that there really is no difference in working with a child with a severe disability than there is in working with any child. Shawn taught me that the needs of my students consistently fall upon a continuum—some requiring little more of me than a smile and an encouraging word, and others requiring daily one-to-one work in all areas of development. If I were to place Shawn on the continuum, he probably would fall somewhere near the low end of the need for academic development but near the high end for social development, exactly the opposite of students I work with year in and year out. Yet all along the continuum are students with a variety of needs, all waiting to be met. Shawn helped me to meet them.

The time I shared with Shawn enabled me to solidify my philosophy, not only in education, but in life as well. I had heard Dr. Jim Fitzpatrick, an educational speaker from Vermont, a number of times over the past few years. His message had always been "Assume that a child is giving you the very best she or he can at any particular moment." Out of the hours I had heard him speak, that one line never left my subconscious. Shawn allowed me to concretely practice what Dr. Fitzpatrick had said. Not only did I accept everything Shawn did as the best he could do at that moment, but I began to realize that I was also assuming the same of all children. I am not saying that I appreciated "unacceptable" behavior from Shawn or the other children, or that I did not deal with it if it did occur. What I am saying is that by accepting behavior as the best anyone could give me at the time, I was able to change my reaction and began to look at situations proactively, using situations as learning experiences. This form of absolute appreciation and acceptance has allowed me to be a person who genuinely enjoys all students for just being themselves.

A final lesson I learned from this experience that I will take with me always is the strength derived from teamwork and cooperation. First, our consultant was absolutely invaluable. Her experience in autism, facilitated communication, inclusive education, and group process really made this program work for us. Her unique ability to "coerce" me into problem-solving situations for myself without me even realizing it, left me with the feeling that I could trust myself to do what needed to be done. . . .

The speech therapist in my district has also been an extremely valuable part of this process. Her availability made my job so much easier. Her expertise at weekly team meetings guided my compliance with Shawn's educational goals. Her insightfulness was the key to many of the discoveries we made at team meetings. . . .

My school psychologist, whose dream of an inclusive school was put to the test with the inclusion of Shawn, made all of this happen for all of us. Her dream and the inclusion of Shawn has made a change in our entire building. A number of teachers have voluntarily left the security of tenured classroom positions to accept positions in blended classrooms at different grade levels. Our special education department has been totally revamped as our classified children are included with all other students. Our special education teachers have begun to join in classrooms rather than pull students out for remediation. Parents are welcomed and encouraged to take part in the decision-making process regarding the education of their children. . . . We need to use the experiences like the one with Shawn to create a change that is not just unique for "special" students, but is relevant and meaningful for *all* students.

In addition to changes described by the kindergarten teacher, Shawn's mother also talked about how his experience affected him at home and in the community:

On Changes in Shawn's Skills and Behavior: He seems more interested in things. . . . Like if you want him to draw with a piece of chalk and hand it to him, he does not automatically put it in his mouth as much as he did before. . . . He will listen to his sister when she explains all about how something works or what you do with it. He lets you read to him more. He'll sit with his sister and let her read to him.

He does have times when you take him out and he's a little difficult, but everybody has bad days. But mostly he'll walk along with you like he's supposed to and if he knocks something off a shelf, sometimes he will pick it up without me telling him to—and he'll arrange it just right so that it is facing the right direction.

On Expectations: I'd like to see him of course not have autism in the first place, but that's probably impossible. But I'd like to see him have as much of a chance as he can to do what he can instead of being held back. . . . Don't assume [he] can't do something—at least find out if [he] can do it. I have a friend with an autistic son and she came down to observe Shawn, and she was quite impressed that—how can I explain it—you don't seem to be going out of your way. I don't know how to say this so it sounds right—I mean, you're treating Shawn like a normal kid. You are accepting his differences and just trying to teach him the best way you can. You have taught the kids how to accept him. Instead of getting all upset because he has a certain behavior, you just sort of work with it.

When he was at a special school they had all kinds of impressive equipment. What I meant by this [neighborhood] school not doing anything special, I meant they don't have all kinds of special rooms and equipment—and yet they are doing a lot more for Shawn than was ever done before. With an autistic kid it seems like the more normal you treat them, the more normal they act. [In the special school], he wasn't really being treated too normal, and he didn't have any role models. He still has his autistic behaviors, but it seems like he is beginning to realize what isn't acceptable and what is.

On Shawn's Relationships with Others: You're doing a good job with him compared to how he was treated before. He's just being treated like a regular kid. We go out and kids who know him will say, "Hi, Shawn" and they'll talk to him.

She [the kindergarten teacher] helped kids to understand how he was and the kids I think are probably the most important part. The kids were really good with him—I couldn't believe it. They treated him almost like they would any other kid. They accept his different behaviors and they're friends with him, and they try to play with him and try to help him and understand him.

I think he's not as afraid of different people. Like if we are out at the store and he sees another kid that says something, he seems more interested in what they are doing.

Shawn's story reveals how many of the basic features of the typical kindergarten classroom are actually well suited to the accommodations discussed earlier to address severe behavioral challenges in young children. For example, kindergarten classrooms are characterized by regular routines, frequent movement, and short time periods when children are expected to be "on task." Activities are designed to be highly motivating, to incorporate hands-on materials and familiar games and routines, and to highlight relationships with daily activities and needs. Furthermore, the teacher communicated activities in advance and gave the children explicit instructions and clear guidelines. Shawn had the benefit of following his peers whenever he was confused about what was expected. In many ways, Shawn's kindergarten classroom was the ideal environment for his needs as a child with autism, as well as for his needs as a young child.

Shawn's story illustrates how an educational plan was created through a team approach to assist in his transition from a segregated school to his neighborhood school. Careful consideration was given to the kindergarten classroom, to preparing students for Shawn's arrival, and to problem solving for situations that might occur during school. Shawn's kindergarten classroom, however, did not provide the context for formal data collection—which might be essential in some cases, particularly for older students whose behavior problems might be long-standing and more resistant to incidental programming. Shawn's team kept anecdotal records regarding his behavior and videotaped him in typical daily school and classroom routines across time (a 3-hour sample approximately every 5–6 weeks). The records were informal notes, but they were viewed by the team as ample evidence of behavioral improvement, and the videotaped segments created a compelling chronicle of those changes over time. In addition, his IEP goals were monitored through informal teacher assessment as well and checked off as they were mastered. Shawn's team felt that more formal data collection was not needed and that they would not be able to collect such data in the context of a typical school program. This is a reality of many school situations.

The needs represented by the student in our next example seemed to demand more formal data collection, and the team agreed. Becky provides us with an opportunity to describe a monitoring process that was user friendly for her school and it gave the team the information needed for her educational program. Becky was older, and she was already attending her neighborhood school. Over time, her behaviors had become destructive and disruptive, and the school no longer knew how to meet her needs. Again, through a team approach, data were collected regarding the child's challenging behaviors, and an intervention plan was designed to best accommodate Becky in her fourth grade classroom.

BECKY'S STORY

Becky had just begun her second school year in an inclusive educational program. Becky was 11 and was labeled as having autism. Her difficulties in school were long-standing. The behaviors listed in her record over the years included hitting, kicking, yelling, swearing, and running away from the classroom. Within a month of the beginning of the school year, the principal at Cooper Elementary School called the special education coordinator to request assistance with Becky, who was enrolled in a regular fourth grade class with special education services and supports; she had 24 fourth grade classmates. Becky's district was moderate in size (11,000 students in a city of 50,000), and this was the district's second year of inclusion. The principal felt that it would be better if Becky was sent to another school that could meet her educational needs. In reply, the special education coordinator noted that the district no longer had any self-contained classrooms and that if Becky was unable to remain at his school, then she would be sent to another elementary school in the district. One of the authors of this chapter was a teacher on special assignment in the district, and she agreed to serve as consultant to the team to solve problems and create an educational plan that would be successful for Becky. The consultant's notes state the following:

> I began my work at Cooper near the end of October. The special educator, classroom teacher, teaching assistant, and speech therapist were overwhelmed and frustrated in working with Becky. When Becky was

upset, she would hit, kick, and yell simultaneously. The first time I observed her getting upset, it lasted for at least 45 minutes. At the end she would cry and then want a hug from the adult. The first time that I worked through one of these difficult times with Becky, I was physically and emotionally exhausted and sweating by the end. Becky was in the same condition.

When I arrived, the staff handed me a key to the time-out room that they were using for Becky. The approach with Becky seemed to be "You'll behave." During the first day I was there, Becky's behavior escalated to the point where she began hitting, kicking, and talking extremely loudly in the classroom. The teaching assistant told me that when this happens, they take Becky to the time-out room. While I question the use of time-out, I was curious to see what Becky would do in the room. So the TA and I assisted Becky to the room by holding her arms and walking with her. The room that was used for the time-out room was the art supply room.

As soon as she entered the room, she began throwing paint bottles and construction paper off the shelves. She also ripped paper off big rolls of paper on a cart. Becky is very quick, and once she is holding onto something it is very difficult to get it out of her grasp. I was attempting to be one step ahead of her, but since I had never been in the room, I was not prepared for such a chaotic mess. Once I realized that this room only encouraged her behaviors and provided no structure to assist her in calming down so that she could reenter her classroom, I asked Becky if she would like to go for a walk and get a drink of water. Leaving the time-out room was the best decision, and we never used the room again.

School personnel seemed to have already given up on Becky, and her reputation in the building was widespread. When the consultant met teachers during break or lunch and explained her work with Becky, many stated that Becky was out of control and should not be in "their" school. The overall staff impression of Becky was that she was too loud in the hallways and in her classroom. The other fourth-grade teachers were glad that Becky was not in their classroom. Becky's classroom teacher, Mrs. Henderson, felt that Becky should be removed from the classroom when she was loud and interfering with others' learning. The log continues:

She [Mrs. Henderson] stated that she had worked very hard to include Becky, and she had already rearranged the classroom three times to accommodate Becky's needs. She was also concerned about some of the other students in her classroom. There were four students who received Chapter services, and the teacher regarded four students as having Attention Deficit Hyperactive Disorder and another eight as gifted—although these students were not formally labeled. During the first week of data collection, I noted that she had few direct interactions with Becky—she let the teaching assistant work with her. Becky also received scheduled direct services from the special education teacher responsible for her program, sometimes in the classroom and sometimes on a pull-out basis.

Even this pattern took its toll on staff, as evidenced by these consultant notes:

> During the fall, we trained four different teaching assistants to work with Becky. The last TA that was hired continued through the year, but three had quit after a few weeks because, they said, it was too hard for them to work with her. I think they had a difficult time separating what Becky said when she was upset from who she was when she was pleasant to be with. When Becky was upset, she would call you an "ugly witch" and tell you over and over, "I hate you!" For most people, those are difficult words to hear repeatedly. Even with training, some people had a hard time knowing how to anticipate her actions, prevent possible problems, and position themselves so that they wouldn't get hit or kicked.

Becky's needs were clearly complex, and she was strong enough that her behaviors threatened staff both physically and psychologically. Our planning and intervention for Becky was in some ways more explicit than for Shawn, because, in Becky's case, the behaviors were long-standing and far more enduring. Thus, while many of the components of planning for Becky were quite similar to the process, principles, and strategies described for Shawn, we focus specifically on several components that were critical to meeting Becky's needs.

Assessing Needs

Becky did have behavior problems, but she also had preferences. One of our earlier goals was to gather information on these preferences. Becky loved stories about kittens and ballerinas, drawing with colored markers and pencils, jumping rope, using the tape recorder and listening to music, and being outside and climbing and swinging from the jungle gym at recess. This information could also help us motivate her to engage in classroom and other appropriate activities—this is a bit different than thinking about reinforcers, since our emphasis is on finding preferences that could easily be incorporated into learning tasks as content rather than as consequences. We did not collect this information because we wanted to use her preferences as reinforcers, but rather because knowing what these were might help us understand patterns of behavior at different times and, in at least one instance, might actually explain a behavior. For example, Becky's brother and sister also went to Cooper Elementary School, and she enjoyed eating breakfast with them at school and watching them from her class window when they were at recess. (Note: One of Becky's problem behaviors was running from her seat to stare out the window; staff had assumed she was *getting away* from work. It appeared instead that she was trying to do something she preferred: watching a sister or brother at play!) Becky also liked the attention of her classroom teacher and being with her friends.

Next, in order to gain a better understanding of her problem behaviors and develop hypotheses about their functions, the consultant used a scatterplot procedure to record eight behaviors to try to identify patterns across the day. The scatterplot data sheet adapted from procedures used by Touchette, Macdonald, and Langer (1985) involved a matrix with 15-minute time periods marked off for the entire day on the vertical axis and the 5 days of the week across the horizontal axis at the top of the paper. Codes used for the behaviors included R = running in the hallways; N = making noise in hallway; H/K = hitting/kicking staff (these behaviors happened together); H = hitting students; L = loud at desk; F = full assistance to remove her from activity because of behaviors that interfered with others' learning; T = loud at table (in the back of the classroom); and V = volume of her voice high. After collecting data on the scatterplot for a week, it was clear that every day from 11:00 to 11:30 and 1:30 to 2:00 (students went home at 2:15) were times when Becky had the most difficulty with her behaviors. Because so many different people worked with Becky, it had seemed impossible to have a clear understanding of how the days and weeks actually looked. Having someone simply record the frequency of her different behaviors across these time periods enabled us to have a better understanding of Becky's behaviors and specific times during the day when Becky needed additional support or a change in routine.

Other assessment procedures that were helpful included the daily log and incident record described in Meyer and Janney (1989). At the end of each day, staff working with Becky completed the daily log form to help team members understand her interests and describe activities that were difficult for Becky. The incident record (see also Meyer & Evans, 1989) documented her difficulties during transition from her school desk to the bus at the end of the day. Becky would insist that she needed to put everything from her desk into her backpack to take home. The adults did not initially have a consistent approach to this issue—on some days, she was allowed to take home a library book or a subject book from her desk, while on other days she could not. Similarly, there were days when the worksheets went home and other times when worksheets had to stay at school because they would be needed again the next day. Her classmates could tolerate this ambiguity, but Becky needed more guidance. We created a folder that was labeled "Becky's papers to take home." Whenever a paper was finished that could go home, it was placed in the folder. We decided that all books would remain in school because it was too difficult for Becky to make this discrimination. After about a week of explanation and practice, Becky adjusted to taking home only those materials in her folder.

Another tool that was used was the Motivation Assessment Scale (MAS) (Durand, 1988). The scale indicated that many of Becky's needs were sensory and tangible—she seldom displayed negative behavior in order to escape or get attention. The scale suggested that her motivation was often to hold, manipulate, and use objects (markers, pencils, books, papers); once Becky would get these objects, she would not allow them to be taken away from her. We addressed this issue by identifying specific materials that would be used for different activities. For example, Becky used a calculator during math, colored pencils during reading, and a glue stick during art. After a time, she associated the specific materials with the activity, making participation and transitions easier for her to understand.

Changes in the Ecology/Social Setting for Becky

Becky sat in the back row in her classroom next to a large heat register. The classroom was arranged in four rows. This seating arrangement provided little opportunity for Becky to work with her peers—she couldn't even see what they were doing because she could see only their backs. We asked her classroom teacher if she could place Becky closer to the "front" of the room and near some students who liked spending time with her. Mrs. Henderson rearranged the desks so that there were two rows on the left side of the classroom and two rows on the right. Instead of the rows facing to the front of the class, the rows faced the center of the room (see Figure 2). This arrangement worked exceptionally well because now Becky could look across the room and see students working. When an adult was assisting Becky, that person's seating position did not interfere with any other student's view of the chalkboard or the teacher. This seating arrangement also made it easy for Becky and the teaching assistant (TA) to leave the room without disturbing others while they were working. Finally, Becky had five girls around her that liked her. These students had little difficulty finishing their own work, and they were eager to help Becky with hers.

We also needed to find another place for Becky to go when she was too loud to be in her classroom. This was to be part of her crisis intervention plan until Becky mastered new behaviors that would allow her to remain in the classroom. We first found another small room that was used for testing; there was a desk and chair in the room. The next day when she started getting loud and throwing her crayons, we walked with her to the new room. We brought a book with us that we planned to read to her while she calmed down, and then we would return to the classroom. Becky flipped the chair over and tried to stand on the desk. She then turned the two light switches in the room on and off, over and over again. The entire time she was in the room, she

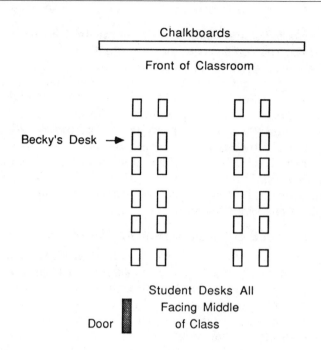

Figure 2.   Becky's fourth grade classroom revised seating arrangement.

continued to be loud and active. Clearly, Becky did not like this room, and it would not function as a "calming down" location.

We looked for an alternative. Outside the special education resource room, a smaller room served as an entryway for students to get to the resource room. We (the special educator, the TA, and the consultant) decided that Becky might like working in this little room because other students came into these rooms to work each day. Because Becky also liked music and books about kittens and ballerinas, we placed these items in the room. Whenever Becky left the classroom, it was not viewed as punishment, but as a way for Becky to "take a break" and then return when she was ready. The next day when Becky became loud, we walked her to the room that we called "Becky's room." She sat down at the desk, and we read books and listened to some music. Becky seemed to like this place, and she was able to relax and then return to her classroom without protest.

Traditional learning theory assumptions might lead us to interpret what we had done as a reward for Becky's negative behavior, and we might have expected Becky's "loud-in-the-classroom" behavior to escalate in order to obtain this reward. We might have also expected her to refuse to leave "Becky's room." Neither of these things happened. We believed that, to borrow a phrase repeated from Shawn's kindergarten teacher, Becky had "given us the best behavior she could" under the present circumstances—she wasn't trying to manipulate us directly, although she was telling us that she needed a break. When we responded to her needs by giving her a break rather than a punishment, she was apparently able to recoup and return to work. It seemed to us that this is the same kind of strategy that many of us follow when we are frustrated with something and cannot take another minute! When we treated Becky as we would want to be treated, her behavior improved. In addition, we made many other changes that also helped Becky to do her share in the process.

Rearranging Becky's Schedule

Becky had the most difficulty during times when she was expected to engage in fine motor activities and the least amount of difficulty when she was involved in gross motor activities. We changed her schedule so that she could be more active. On Mondays and Wednesdays, at times when classmates were engaged in seatwork or other fine motor activities, she joined another fourth grade class for music; because she really liked music, the music teacher felt comfortable with her and she did not need any additional adult support during this time. Becky also had many friends in this additional class—students she knew from lunch, from recess, and from her neighborhood. On Tuesdays, she went to the resource room to use the computer rather than remaining with her class during lectures and seatwork. Similarly, on Thursdays, she went with the TA to a nearby store to purchase a snack. She was also given a break from classroom activities she found most difficult. On Fridays, when the gym was available, she was able to jump rope and run laps. Although we planned for these various times when Becky might be out of her fourth grade classroom for different activities and even other classes, an important goal was to increase her participation in her classroom and decrease the time she was out of the classroom. Our reasoning was that the more her teacher and the other students saw Becky being successful in the classroom, the more comfortable they would be and the more encouragement they would give her.

Transitions were difficult for Becky, and our scatterplot data had also revealed peaks in difficult behavior when she was asked to change activities. We created a picture activity schedule for her and began using this schedule so that she would eventually be able to predict changes. Photos were taken of Becky participating in all activities that were part of her typical day at school. A hand-size photo book was used so that the pictures could be easily inserted or removed, depending upon the daily schedule. We showed Becky the photo of her next activity prior to transitions, and we worked toward the goal of making the world more comprehensible to her. The photo album was also helpful when Becky exhibited resistant behaviors. For example, one morning she went to her locker and then lay down on the floor rather than moving on to her classroom. The consultant was with her and said that her friends were in the classroom getting ready for school to start. She said, "No, uh-uh." The consultant then showed her a picture of herself and her friends working at their desks and said, "I wonder what book Marcy is reading at her desk. Let's go ask Marcy." Becky looked at the picture, and a big smile appeared on her face. She stood up, placed her coat in her locker, and walked to her classroom.

On another occasion when she was in the bathroom, she started pulling toilet paper off the roll. She was shown her picture book and told that her friend, Jenny, was having snack time. Becky looked at the picture of Jenny and herself at snack, and she walked back to the classroom with no protest.

Working with Becky's Peers

At first, it was difficult to persuade Becky to sit at her desk and complete work assignments. Her teacher said it was okay for Becky to move her chair to another student's desk so they could work together; the team felt that having other students as role models would assist her in acquiring good work habits and behaviors. She seemed unsure of how to do things and having a peer nearby to watch made it easier for her to do what was expected. Thus, rather than us telling Becky what to do, we cued her to select a peer as a model for the task. Becky would pick a student to work with and then move her own chair to that student's desk.

Several meetings were also held with Becky's classmates so that we could help them understand why she did some of the things she did and how to view her interactions with them. For example, at one point Becky began swearing in class. At first, students found this amusing, and Becky continued swearing as she observed their reactions. We talked with her classmates and explained that their laughter was telling Becky that what she was doing was funny and appropriate. We asked them to pretend that they did not hear her when she swore and to continue whatever they were doing without reacting. Within a few weeks, Becky had stopped swearing in class.

One day students were drawing maps of a city—one of their tasks was to name all the stores. Tanya told students sitting near her that she had named a store "Becky's Candy Store." Becky heard her name and said, "Shut up, Tanya!" Tanya replied, "Becky, I was telling kids that I named a store after you." Becky seemed upset, saying "No, uh, uh!" The adult who was nearby said, "Becky, it's a good thing that Tanya said." Tanya smiled, shook her head and said, "Yes, Becky, it's a good idea to have a store called Becky's Candy Store." Becky then smiled and said, "Yes, a candy store." All of us learned that it was important to smile when talking with Becky. We reasoned that she had a hard time interpreting voice quality: Whenever someone's face looked too serious or upset, she would immediately start saying things like "no," "shut up," and "go away." We selected photos for Becky's book showing her and her friends smiling, and we talked with her about how her friends were happy that she was at school and what a good worker she was.

There were other situations that needed to be explained to students. Becky was intrigued with the hair ribbons and hair clips her classmates wore in their hair. Sometimes she would reach up and grab the clip or ribbon in a girl's hair, yanking it back or to the side. Some of the girls cried because it hurt. When this happened, Becky would act embarrassed and hide under or behind something, and she would also sometimes cry. Becky wore rubber bands in her own hair and could easily remove them. We explained to her friends that she might think their clips and ribbons would come out of their hair as easily as her rubber bands. We explained to Becky that touching the clip or ribbon was acceptable, but pulling on it would hurt her friend. We also cautioned her friends to think about their location to Becky whenever they were wearing an attractive hair item or hooped earrings.

Team Planning and Becky's Relationships with Adults

We all decided that it was important to work together, and we knew that we needed to be open with one another and willing to learn. At weekly meetings, we focused on how things were going and what we needed to do next. Because many of the team members had never worked with a child who had autism, we agreed to read *Emergence: Labeled Autistic* by Grandin (1986). The team believed that this book helped them to understand why Becky did some of the things she did. We also read a chapter in *Gentle Teaching* by McGee, Menousek, and Hobbs (1987). The consultant created a framework that illustrated the four postures developed by McGee et al. (1987). Table 1 provides definitions and examples of these postures. We had discussions about our "posture" in relation to how we were interacting with Becky. The original posture of staff was authoritarian, and our goal was to move to a posture of solidarity.

Table 1. Interactive postures

Interactive posture[a]	Definition	Example
Solidarity	Values the student's perspective and creates many opportunities for interdependency. The adult respects the student and provides growth-directed experiences for the student. Student success is important, and the adult will assist the student in a positive and supportive manner. The relationship between the adult and student is one of working together for positive outcomes. The adult is interested in what the student has to say and uses that information to create appropriate educational goals for the student.	During a cooking activity, the adult asks the student to select a job: a) reading the recipe, b) measuring the milk and pouring it into the bowl, or c) stirring the pudding. The student participates in making the pudding with the adult.
Authoritarian	Values that the adult is in charge and has all the answers. The adult uses "I" messages, such as "I like it when you're all quiet" when talking with students. There is usually only one way to do something, and the adult's way is the right way. If the student does something that the adult doesn't like, the adult works to eliminate the behavior with little consideration for the purpose of the behavior or replacing the behavior with a more appropriate response.	During a cooking activity, the adult tells the student what his or her role will be during the activity and how to participate.
Overprotective	Values taking care of and protecting the student. The adult working with the student is unsure of the student's abilities; thus, the adult does most things for the student. The posture fosters dependency in safe and predictable routines. The adult feels sorry for the student and views the disability as the focal point of the student. Student is not accountable for participating; the adult takes total responsibility during activities.	During the cooking activity, the adult makes the pudding while the student watches, and then the student enjoys eating the pudding.
Cold-mechanistic	Values completion of task/activity as the primary goal of teaching. The adult is very robot-like when responding to student during activities. Quite often the adult will use tangible or edible rewards as the method of getting the student to participate in the activity. The reward becomes more important to the student than the interactions with the adult. The adult knows little about the student because the focus of the adult–student relationship is to complete tasks.	During a cooking activity, the adult rewards the student with a raisin for each successful step of the task that the student completes.

[a]These postures were described in McGee, Menolascino, et al. (1987). The definitions and examples were developed for Becky's team.

To help with the process of changing our group posture, each of us completed the handout on "our interactive style with students" (see Figure 3), a self-assessment created by the consultant using the Gentle Teaching framework (McGee, Menolascino, et al., 1987) in a format modeled on Durand's Motivation Assessment Scale (MAS) (Durand, 1988). Teaching assistants reported that the form helped them to think more critically about what kinds of interactions they had with a student. Based on one's score, the staff member is to set a personal goal to improve in two areas when interacting with the student. Becky's team members reviewed personal progress frequently. As the consultant noted in her own log,

> When I completed this handout on Becky, I found that I was in the authoritarian role/posture. I went back through the handout in order to understand what I was doing that caused this to happen, since my goal was to work *with* Becky instead of forcing Becky to participate. I found that if we let Becky create her own plan for the day, there were no behavior problems. She always had a variety of things that she wanted to do, but the problem occurred when I would ask Becky to do something that all the other students were doing.
>
> For example, if she had her math book open on her desk and the teacher said, "Okay, students, it's now time to take out your spelling books," Becky would resist taking out her spelling book if she had not completed her math. Even when I explained the steps and showed pictures, she still resisted the transition to the next lesson. If I forced the issue of putting the math book away and taking out the spelling book, she would throw pencils and books and get extremely loud. Indeed, forcing the issue was not a successful way to interact with Becky, and quite often only caused new problems. I found that if I let her continue looking at her math book while I took out the spelling book and prepared her paper, it was easier for her to make the transition. Sometimes, I would start reading the spelling words from her book and then say, "Let's think of a sentence with the word *fast*." This lead-in would attract her interest in what other students were doing, and soon she would put the math book away in her desk.

A variety of people worked with Becky daily. As a collaborative team, we decided to support Becky in her classroom whenever possible. One TA was scheduled to work with Becky in the morning and another in the afternoon. Both TAs worked full-time at the school with different responsibilities during the times they were not assigned to Becky. Natural supports were used during music (the music teacher), snack (she was with her peers), and lunch/recess (lunch aides). The special educator provided support during reading each day, and the morning TA covered math time. The afternoon TA assisted with social studies and science. The speech therapist helped with Becky's class projects. When Becky was having successful experiences, we gave her a great deal of positive feedback and encouragement. We knew that it

Instructions: Think about one particular student when completing this form. Read each statement and circle the number that most closely describes your interactive style.

	Never	Almost never	Seldom	Half the time	Usually	Almost always	Always
1. I have been doing the same routines with the student for a long period of time.	0	1	2	3	4	5	6
2. I am viewed by the student as the person who is always in charge.	0	1	2	3	4	5	6
3. I am more concerned with the student being successful than with the student's independence.	0	1	2	3	4	5	6
4. I believe that a "reward system" with tangibles is the best way to ensure interactions with the student.	0	1	2	3	4	5	6
5. I help the student because I am unsure of his or her capabilities.	0	1	2	3	4	5	6
6. I demand that the student follow rules that I view as important.	0	1	2	3	4	5	6
7. I create interactions that are dignifying for the student.	0	1	2	3	4	5	6
8. I know little about the student because my main focus is to accomplish work.	0	1	2	3	4	5	6
9. I create opportunities for the student that are safe and predictable versus risk taking.	0	1	2	3	4	5	6
10. If the student is doing something that is not appropriate, I work to eliminate the behavior.	0	1	2	3	4	5	6
11. I am interested in the student's point of view.	0	1	2	3	4	5	6
12. I ignore the student when she or he acts inappropriately.	0	1	2	3	4	5	6

13. I feel sorry for the student and therefore protect the student from others.

    0   1   2   3   4   5   6

14. I design steps of a task in a specific order for the student that are based on how I would do the activity.

    0   1   2   3   4   5   6

15. If the student is having a difficult time with the task or behavior, I assist the student through the situation.

    0   1   2   3   4   5   6

16. The working environment I create is focused on the task without considering the quality of interactions with the student.

    0   1   2   3   4   5   6

Write in the numbers that you circled for the 16 statements, and total each column. (These four concepts are from McGee, Menolascino, Hobbs, and Menousek [1987].)

OVERPROTECTIVE	AUTHORITARIAN	SOLIDARITY	COLD-MECHANISTIC
1. _____	2. _____	3. _____	4. _____
5. _____	6. _____	7. _____	8. _____
9. _____	10. _____	11. _____	12. _____
13. _____	14. _____	15. _____	16. _____
_____	_____	_____	_____

Figure 3. Our interactive style with students.

was important to build a trusting relationship with her, so whenever we explained something to her, she needed to be certain we would follow through with the plan. For example, if she wanted to jump rope, we might tell her that first she needed to finish her math and then she could jump rope. It was critical for us to follow through—after math, she would be allowed to jump rope so that she would trust our words.

We used an index card with a sequence to help Becky achieve a better balance between doing what she preferred and what her classwork demanded. Becky's preference, of course, was to follow her own idea and not the teacher's. Before the activity began, the adult read the first part of the index card (teacher's turn), which asked Becky to participate in the class activity. When the activity was completed, the adult read the second part of the index card (Becky's turn), which gave Becky a chance to initiate an activity. We explained this as turn taking: Her index card read, "It's a good idea to take turns."

> Teacher's turn: Please listen and wait. It's time to _____.
> Becky says: I will listen and wait. I will be a good helper.
> Becky's turn: Teacher, listen and wait. I have a good idea. Let's _____.
> Teacher says: I will listen and wait.

Finally, the team worked together to create a *Prevent, Teach, Respond* plan for Becky (see Figure 4). Figure 4 provides an overall one-page display of the guidelines Becky's team wrote to ensure that our interactions would be consistent (see Meyer & Evans, 1989; Meyer & Janney, 1989). We started with only a few ideas for each area, and as we continued working together and problem solving our list grew and even changed over time. The one-page display helped us to use a common language when talking about behaviors, interactions, and interventions.

Personal and Therapy Needs

The occupational therapist (OT) designed several activities and materials to give Becky the sensory input that her MAS score suggested she needed (Durand, 1988). A beanbag chair was placed under one of the tables in the classroom, and any child could use it during free time or story time. Sometimes when Becky was overwhelmed or overstimulated, she would go to the beanbag chair. This enabled her to remain in the classroom, in a place that was calming and secure for her. The OT explained that the pressure of the beanbag around a person's body can assist in relaxation. The OT also recommended a weighted vest for Becky: Her vest was blue, with sand weights inserted around the bottom edge. Becky decorated the vest with fabric markers, and it was placed on the back of her desk chair so she could put it on whenever she wanted. At times, Becky seemed to be anxious or uncertain about

Name: _____ Becky   Date: _____

Prevent	Teach	Respond
1. Hold Becky's hand in hallway or in large rooms (gym) to prevent running through hallway.	1. Practice skills that will teach Becky "turn taking" with peers and adults.	1. When Becky begins to kick/hit adult, reach out hand and hold Becky's hand in a supportive manner to assist her in calming down while redirecting to activity.
2. If Becky is tired of sitting at desk, use table in back of room or beanbag chair.	2. Teach the value of peer interactions and working with peers on class lessons by providing opportunities for Becky in the classroom.	2. Redirect to lesson as often as necessary when Becky becomes distracted by other materials (stickers, markers, books).
3. Use picture schedule to talk about upcoming activities and to assist with transitions.	3. Model for peers ways in which they can have positive interactions with Becky. Provide language and materials for students to use.	3. If Becky's voice becomes loud during lesson, state what she needs to do before ending activity so that there is closure to lesson before leaving classroom for a break or cool-down time.
4. Have Becky work with peers at their desks.	4. Establish routines and responsibilities for each activity: a) getting materials out, b) using materials, and c) cleaning up and putting materials away.	4. Reassure Becky that you understand that she is trying to tell you something and how frustrating that must be. Provide Becky with words to pick from so that she may communicate her needs.
5. Have students tell Becky what they are working on so she will be encouraged to do the same.	5. Teach Becky that as a fourth grade learner she is accountable. She turns in assignments and takes quizzes when other students do.	
6. Stand near classroom door or close the door in order to redirect Becky to classroom activity.		
7. When ideas are abstract, write steps on paper in order to sequence the event for Becky.		

(continued)

Figure 4. Becky's program summary.

Figure 4. *(continued)*

Name: _____ Becky   Date: _____

Prevent	Teach	Respond
8. Avoid "power struggles" with Becky because they only make the situation worse. Acknowledge Becky's message and state clear expectations of plan. Direct your attention to materials.	6. Teach Becky to use words that tell peers and adults that she needs a "break," "stop," or "done" instead of using a loud voice or running out of the classroom.	5. Focus your attention on activity instead of creating a power struggle.
9. Use class materials to redirect Becky to task.	7. Teach Becky that she can be successful with academic materials by dividing activities into small steps with "breaks" in between working.	6. Use a confident voice with Becky that will give her the stability and structure that she needs during frustrating times.
10. If Becky begins to move around room without purpose, possibly throwing things on floor and saying, "No, I don't want to," have Becky sit on floor (assist her to a sitting position if necessary). Sitting on floor helps Becky to refocus and relax. Use materials to gain Becky's attention.	8. Teach Becky that she can trust our words and actions by being consistent and predictable with our messages.	7. Set expectations of an activity that will make Becky successful during the task.
	9. Teach Becky that she can give positive feedback to peers and adults by smiling, saying nice words, handshaking, and sharing materials.	8. Always use positive words and facial expressions with Becky to build her self-confidence and self-esteem.
11. Ignore swearing while continuing to engage Becky in activity. Teach students to ignore swearing also (avoid smiling and giggling when Becky swears).	10. Whenever Becky uses new strategies that we have taught, explain to Becky how helpful it was for her to use the strategy. Explain the benefits of using the positive strategies.	9. When a situation escalates, remain confident without focusing on distracting behavior. Remain with Becky during difficult time, and begin as soon as possible on next activity.
12. Avoid using the library with Becky. Bring two books to her in classroom to read. The library is a very stimulating place for Becky.		10. Allow for a few minutes to transition from one activity to the next if needed.

164

an event. When an adult suggested that maybe she would want to wear her vest, she would put it on and become noticeably relaxed and interested in working once again. Other activities suggested by the OT included jumping rope, running, and hanging or swinging from bars. These activities were more age appropriate than traditional isolated therapy activities and they provided the same sensory feedback.

We also learned that Becky was temperature sensitive. She was hot when other students were comfortable in the room. There were times when she would run out of the classroom and down the hallway to a large window. She would lean against the window for a long time before she would be willing to return to the classroom. At first, we thought she liked the reflection of the window or looking outside at the park. We then realized that this was her way to cool down when she was too warm. If left alone, she would return to her work after a brief period. In sum, we became better at understanding her needs.

Outcomes for Becky

Team members continued using the various strategies listed in the previous section throughout the school year, even after the consultant was completely phased out at the end of March. Becky's difficult behaviors, which had once continued for 45 minutes, now occurred rarely and lasted for only a few minutes. She was now participating in inclusive schooling—the classroom teacher became as comfortable in giving Becky extra help as the special education teacher and TA became in working with all of the students. Her classroom teacher, in particular, had many positive things to say to Becky each day and enjoyed looking at Becky's work—and Becky loved taking her finished work to the teacher. Becky's friends continued to hang out with her and enjoyed helping her during lessons. In January, the classroom teacher announced to the team that she no longer wanted Becky taken out of the classroom. She said that if Becky was going to learn how to be a fourth-grade student, then she would have to be in the classroom to do it. She said she would ask the TA for help if things did get really loud; otherwise, she wanted Becky in the room with her classmates. Becky's peers also commented on her growth as a fourth grader. Table 2 presents the transcript of a meeting in March between the special education teacher and six of Becky's friends addressing the changes they had seen.

SUMMARY

Our descriptions of the events surrounding Shawn and Becky and their inclusion in the general education environment are not presented as a

Table 2. Transcript of a March meeting of Becky's special education teacher (SPE) and six of her friends

SPE: The reason I called you together is because we'd like to do some planning for Becky for next year, and you kids are super with her. You're her friends and you do things positively with her. You can help us, the teachers, so we know how to plan for Becky to make her life at Cooper a success. How has Becky grown this year? What changes have you seen her make this year?

Tanya: She settled down a lot this year, because last year if she got angry she'd go over to people's desks and just knock them over. She just wanted to be left alone.

Nikki: She needs to work on when she's doing work and she gets mad, she just can't get up and walk to the windows.

SPE: Do you have any ideas why she walks to the window?

Tanya: She thinks someone special is out there. When she gets angry, she just wants to leave everything.

Nikki: She likes to holler at her brother and sister out the window.

SPE: Do you think she gets distracted? Do you ever get distracted?

All students: Yeah.

SPE: Maybe she doesn't know how to control her body to stay sitting. She hears a noise on the playground and she wants to go look and see what it is. You all do a wonderful job by just saying, "Becky, come and sit down."

Tanya: Sometimes when Becky gets angry she runs around in the hall. She tried to run out the door, but if teachers block the door on Becky she still tries to go through them. When she does finally get out, she kind of settles down.

Nikki: All she wants is some free time.

Aaron: She likes to run around and get all her energy out.

Tanya: What I'm trying to figure out is why she never goes out the door by the lunchroom. She always runs down the hall and goes out the other door.

SPE: Oh, she does?

Tanya: She says things like she wants to go to the library, but she's pointing towards the gym.

SPE: So how do you know what she wants?

All students: She wants the gym.

Tanya: The gym is more like a place for Becky. She can run around; she can feel free.

SPE: Is her pointing or her words what she wants to do?

All students: Her pointing.

SPE: You've learned that what she says isn't always what she means.

Nikki: She says, "Stupid Steven, stupid Steven" and you know she doesn't mean to say that, and she says, "Shut up."

SPE: We're trying to give her different words to use for when she does say something that is not a good thing to say.

Tanya: Becky will say, "Fat Jason, fat Jason." She just keeps saying it. It's just like a tape going in her mind. It keeps rewinding, playing, rewind, play. And another thing, I've noticed during spelling . . . like lesson 27, the words are "done," "go," "jump," and then lesson 28, "library," "eat," "table." She don't remember that. It's kind of that lesson she forgets it, go to another [lesson]—she forgets it.

SPE: She can't connect the things?

Tanya: No. We should make little cards that say, "cat" or "dog" or "hat," and then spell them out and ask Becky if she knows what the word spells, and just work with her.

Nikki: We could teach her how to sound them out.

Table 2. *(continued)*

Aaron: We could put a picture on the top of the card.

SPE: What things did she do this year that surprised you?

Nikki: She goes across the monkey bars really good.

Leah: She really knows how to play instruments in music class.

Diana: She knows a lot more kids this year.

Nikki: Her coloring and her drawing have improved.

Diana: She gets embarrassed or cries when she hurts someone.

SPE: Yes, showing her feelings is a new thing for Becky. Think of one thing that you wish or hope for Becky. It could be something for today or for when she's an adult.

Diana: I hope that she can write better. She can write—it's just that she doesn't want to sit down and write. She needs to take the time to write.

SPE: That might just be something she is unable to get from her mind to her hand right now and hopefully that will come.

Leah: In the future before she's like 20, I think it would be nice for her to learn how to read and write.

SPE: That's a good goal.

Josh: I wish she wouldn't call people names and stuff.

Tanya: I hope when Becky grows up she can get the education that she needs.

SPE: I have a goal for Becky. My wish for Becky, because I know she has a lot of good ideas in her head, is that I hope she becomes a communicator so that she can allow other people to know all the neat things that she knows.

---

typical, behavioral "intervention package." Some—who prefer a technical list of what to do and what not to do—may regard this as a disadvantage. Others are still searching for the one critical intervention component that will, once and for all, remediate a student's challenging behavior—or the intervention package that can be used by any team with any student to meet needs as they arise. We do not believe that the research literature should be expected to provide clear and straightforward answers, nor do we believe that this literature can ever realistically isolate the key independent variable through a series of experiments that clearly establishes a relationship meaningful beyond the specifics of one situation. However, this is not a pessimistic point of view, nor is it antiscientific. Researchers working in this area increasingly acknowledge the complexity of the challenge:

> Because severe behavior problems are usually complex and may not be maintained by a single variable, successful interventions often require multiple concurrent manipulations. For example, it is possible that an intervention for one individual could simultaneously require changes in the schedule of reinforcement, additional staff training, curriculum changes in target functional skills, new options for augmentative communication, and an increase in the number of social contacts. Although the effects may be difficult to replicate experimentally because of the highly individualized nature of this type of intervention, a growing num-

ber of case descriptions are contributing relevant information to the design and implementation of such comprehensive interventions. (Dunlap et al., 1994, p. 236)

We present our two case studies *not* as attempts to validate an intervention, or even as a multiple component intervention package, which both clearly are. But we present them precisely because of their complexity and the complexity of the children's needs, we doubt that a traditional experimental sequence of documenting functional relationships will be practical for most situations now confronting practitioners and parents in inclusive settings. We believe that those responsible for programs for students such as Shawn and Becky need a process that guides team decision making, some basic information and consultation from someone with a background in effective interventions for individuals with similar needs, and support to implement and develop most promising practices in both general and special education. We also have confidence that given these basic resources and encouragement to apply both the "ordinary knowledge" that comes with being a teacher or a parent, good decisions can be made. Also, when decisions need to be modified based on their impact, the team will be comfortable moving on to the next step rather than solving the "problem" by referring the child elsewhere.

REFERENCES

Ayres, B., Meyer, L.H., Erevelles, N., & Park-Lee, S. (1994). Easy for you to say: Teacher perspectives on implementing most promising practices. *Journal of The Association for Persons with Severe Handicaps, 19,* 84–93.

Berkman, K.A., & Meyer, L.H. (1988). Alternative strategies and multiple outcomes in the remediation of severe self-injury: Going "all-out" nonaversively. *Journal of The Association for Persons with Severe Handicaps, 13,* 76–86.

Berryman, J., & Evans, I.M. (1994). *Supervising direct care staff in naturalistic behavioral intervention: Process and outcomes.* Manuscript submitted for publication.

Berryman, J., Evans, I.M., & Kalbag, A. (1994). The effects of training in nonaversive behavior management on the attitudes and understanding of direct care staff. *Journal of Behaviour Therapy and Experimental Psychiatry, 25,* 241–250.

Brown, F. (1991). Creative daily scheduling: A nonintrusive approach to challenging behaviors in community residences. *Journal of The Association for Persons with Severe Handicaps, 16,* 75–84.

Burney, J.P., & Shores, R.E. (1979). A study of relationships between instructional planning and pupil behavior. *Journal of Special Education Technology, 2*(3), 16–25.

Campbell, P.H. (1987). The integrated programming team: An approach for coordinating professionals of various disciplines in programs for students with severe and multiple handicaps. *Journal of The Association for Persons with Severe Handicaps, 12,* 107–116.

Carr, E.G., Levin, L., McConnachie, G., Carlson, J.I., Kemp, D.C., & Smith, C.E. (1994). *Communication-based intervention for problem behavior: A user's guide for producing positive change.* Baltimore: Paul H. Brookes Publishing Co.

Consortium on Inclusive Schooling Practices. (1994, November 7–9). *Executive summary: Meeting with statewide systems change representatives.* Washington, DC: Project Director's Meeting/State Networking Meeting, Severe Disabilities Branch.

Donnellan, A.M., Mirenda, P.L., Mesaros, R.A., & Fassbender, L.L. (1984). Analyzing the communicative functions of aberrant behavior. *Journal of The Association for Persons with Severe Handicaps, 9,* 201–212.

Dunlap, G., & Kern, L. (1993). Assessment and intervention for children within the instructional curriculum. In J. Reichle & D. Wacker (Eds.), *Communicative alternatives to challenging behavior: Integrating functional assessment and intervention strategies* (pp. 177–203). Baltimore: Paul H. Brookes Publishing Co.

Dunlap, G., Kern-Dunlap, L., Clarke, S., & Robbins, F.R. (1991). Functional assessment, curricular revision, and severe behavior problems. *Journal of Applied Behavior Analysis, 24,* 387–397.

Dunlap, G., Robbins, F.R., & Kern, L. (1994). Some characteristics of nonaversive intervention for severe behavior problems. In E. Schopler & G.B. Mesibov (Eds.), *Behavioral issues in autism* (pp. 227–245). New York: Plenum.

Dunn, W. (1991). Integrated related services. In L.H. Meyer, C.A. Peck, & L. Brown (Eds.), *Critical issues in the lives of people with severe disabilities* (pp. 353–377). Baltimore: Paul H. Brookes Publishing Co.

Durand, V.M. (1988). The Motivation Assessment Scale. In M. Hersen & A.S. Bellack (Eds.), *Dictionary of behavioral assessment techniques* (pp. 309–310). New York: Pergamon.

Durand, V.M. (1990). *Severe behavior problems: A functional communication training approach.* New York: Guilford Press.

Evans, I.M., & Meyer, L.H. (1985). *An educative approach to behavior problems: A practical decision model for interventions with severely handicapped learners.* Baltimore: Paul H. Brookes Publishing Co.

Evans, I.M., & Meyer, L.H. (1993). Once more with feeling: On the importance of moving ahead. *Journal of The Association for Persons with Severe Handicaps, 18,* 249–252.

Evans, I.M., & Voeltz, L.M. (1982). *The selection of intervention priorities in educational programming of severely handicapped preschool children with multiple behavior problems.* Final Report, Grant No. G00-790-1960. Honolulu: University of Hawaii, Departments of Special Education and Psychology.

Fisher, M., & Lindsey-Walters, S. (1987, October). *A survey report of various types of data collection procedures used by teachers and their strengths and weaknesses.* Paper presented at the annual conference of The Association for Persons with Severe Handicaps, Chicago.

Forest, M., & Lusthaus, E. (1989). Promoting educational equality for all students: Circles and maps. In S. Stainback, W. Stainback, & M. Forest (Eds.), *Educating all students in the mainstream of regular education* (pp. 43–57). Baltimore: Paul H. Brookes Publishing Co.

Forest, M., & Pearpoint, J. (1990). Supports for addressing severe maladaptive behaviors. In W. Stainback & S. Stainback (Eds.), *Support networks for inclusive schooling: Interdependent integrated schooling* (pp. 187–197). Baltimore: Paul H. Brookes Publishing Co.

Gartner, A., & Lipsky, D.K. (1987). Beyond special education: Toward a quality system for all students. *Harvard Educational Review, 57,* 367–395.

Grandin, T. (1986). *Emergence: Labeled autistic.* Novato, CA: Arena Press.

Grigg, N.C., Snell, M.E., & Lloyd, B. (1989). Visual analysis of student evaluation data: A qualitative analysis of teacher decision making. *Journal of The Association for Persons with Severe Handicaps, 14,* 23–32.

Haring, N.G., Liberty, K.A., & White, O.R. (1980). Rules for data-based strategy decisions in instructional programs. In W. Sailor, B. Wilcox, & L. Brown (Eds.), *Methods of instruction for severely handicapped learners* (pp. 159–192). Baltimore: Paul H. Brookes Publishing Co.

Haring, T.G. (1991). Social relationships. In L.H. Meyer, C.A. Peck, & L. Brown (Eds.), *Critical issues in the lives of people with severe disabilities* (pp. 195–217). Baltimore: Paul H. Brookes Publishing Co.

Horner, R.H., Dunlap, G., Koegel, R.I., Carr, E.G., Sailor, W., Anderson, J., Albin, R.W., & O'Neill, R.E. (1990). Toward a technology of "nonaversive" behavioral support. *Journal of The Association for Persons with Severe Handicaps, 15,* 125–132.

Janney, R.E., Black, J., & Ferlo, M. (1989). *A problem-solving approach to challenging behaviors.* Syracuse, NY: Syracuse University Division of Special Education.

Kern-Dunlap, L., Clarke, S., & Dunlap, G. (1990). *Increasing the "meaningfulness" in curriculum content to reduce problem behaviors in a severely emotionally disturbed student.* Paper presented at the tenth annual convention of the Florida Association for Behavior Analysis (FABA), Orlando.

Kishi, G.S., & Meyer, L.H. (1994). What children report and remember: A six year follow-up of the effects of social contact between peers with and without severe disabilities. *Journal of The Association for Persons with Severe Handicaps, 19,* 277–289.

LaVigna, G.W., & Donnellan, A.M. (1986). *Alternatives to punishment: Solving behavior problems with non-aversive strategies.* New York: Irvington.

Lovett, H. (1985). *Cognitive counseling and persons with special needs.* New York: Praeger.

McAfee, J.K. (1987). Classroom density and the aggressive behavior of handicapped children. *Education and Treatment of Children, 10,* 134–145.

McGee, J.J., Menolascino, F.J., Hobbs, D.C., & Menousek, P.E. (1987). *Gentle teaching: A nonaversive approach for helping persons with mental retardation.* New York: Human Science Press.

McGee, J.J., Menousek, P.E., & Hobbs, D. (1987). Gentle Teaching: An alternative to punishment for people with challenging behaviors: In S.J. Taylor, D. Biklen, & J. Knoll (Eds.), *Community integration for people with severe disabilities* (pp. 147–183). New York: Teachers College Press.

McKinney, J.P., Fitzgerald, H.E., & Strommen, E.A. (1982). *Developmental psychology: The adolescent and young adult.* Homewood, IL: Dorsey Press.

Meyer, L.H., & Evans, I.M. (1989). *Nonaversive intervention for behavior problems: A manual for home and community.* Baltimore: Paul H. Brookes Publishing Co.

Meyer, L.H., & Evans, I.M. (1993). Science and practice in behavioral intervention: Meaningful outcomes, research validity, and usable knowledge. *Journal of The Association for Persons with Severe Handicaps, 18,* 224–234.

Meyer, L.H., Evans, I.M., Wuerch, B.B., & Brennan, J. (1985). Monitoring the collateral effects of leisure skill instruction: A case study in multiple baseline methodology. *Behaviour Research and Therapy, 23,* 127–138.

Meyer, L.H., & Janney, R.E. (1989). User-friendly measures of meaningful outcomes: Evaluating behavioral interventions. *Journal of The Association for Persons with Severe Handicaps, 14,* 263–270.

Meyer, L.H., & Janney, R.E. (1992). School consultation to support students with behavior problems in integrated educational programs. In T.R. Kratochwill, S.N. Elliott, & M. Gettinger (Eds.), *Advances in school psychology: Vol. VIII* (pp. 153–193). Hillsdale, NJ: Lawrence Erlbaum Associates.

O'Brien, J. (1987). A guide to life-style planning: Using *The Activities Catalog* to integrate services and natural support systems. In B. Wilcox & G.T. Bellamy, *A comprehensive guide to* The Activities Catalog: *An alternative curriculum for youth and adults with severe disabilities* (pp. 175–189). Baltimore: Paul H. Brookes Publishing Co.

Scotti, J., Evans, I.M., Meyer, L.H., & Walker, P. (1991). A meta-analysis of intervention research with behavior problems in persons with developmental disabilities: Treatment validity and standards of practice. *American Journal on Mental Retardation, 96,* 233–256.

Seybert, S., Dunlap, G., & Ferro, J. (1994). The effects of choice-making in reducing the problem behaviors of students with intellectual disabilities. Unpublished paper. (Available from G. Dunlap, Florida Mental Health Institute, University of South Florida, Tampa, FL, 33612.)

Shevin, M., & Klein, N.K. (1984). The importance of choice-making skills for students with severe disabilities. *Journal of The Association for Persons with Severe Handicaps, 9,* 159–166.

Strain, P.S., & Odom, S.L. (1986). Peer social initiations: An effective intervention for social skills deficits of exceptional children. *Exceptional Children, 52,* 543–551.

Touchette, P.E., MacDonald, R.F., & Langer, S.M. (1985). A scatter plot for identifying stimulus control of problem behavior. *Journal of Applied Behavior Analysis, 18,* 343–351.

Vandercook, T., York, J., & Forest, M. (1989). The McGill Action Planning System (MAPS): A strategy for building the vision. *Journal of The Association for Persons with Severe Handicaps, 14,* 205–215.

Walter, G., & Vincent, L. (1982). The handicapped child in the regular kindergarten classroom. *Journal of The Division for Early Childhood, 6,* 84–95.

Weeks, M., & Gaylord-Ross, R. (1981). Task difficulty and aberrant behavior in severely handicapped students. *Journal of Applied Behavior Analysis, 14,* 19–36.

Wuerch, B.B., & Voeltz, L.M. (1982). *Longitudinal leisure skills for severely handicapped learners: The Ho'onanea curriculum component.* Baltimore: Paul H. Brookes Publishing Co.

III

CHALLENGES WITHIN THE COMMUNITY

7

Community Life for All Individuals

FREDDA BROWN AND CAROLE R. GOTHELF

THE GROWTH OF community services for individuals with disabilities has been dramatic since the 1970s. Accomplishments in these services are to a large degree an outcome of the change in our philosophies concerning people with disabilities. However, the chasm between philosophy and practice can be wide. The time it takes to change practices is frustrating for those seeking new alternatives. However, this gradual rate of change is perhaps necessary for a valid and permanent demonstration of those changes. Although it may be difficult to collaborate with service providers who are reluctant to change, we should remember that it is these individuals who must negotiate funding mazes, cautious boards, and the general inertia of society as they attempt to grow and develop beyond their current practices. All changes come with great challenge.

It is easy to forget that the practices today that are considered outdated are based on the best practices of time past. The efforts that were taken to instill these practices were no doubt considerable and likely met with resistance, as they are today. But they were done in the name of growth and respect for individuals with disabilities. The changes that occurred in the early 1990s were innovative for their time and set the groundwork for the current trends. The current development of philosophies and practices (e.g., natural supports and autonomy) is a natural outgrowth of these prior changes. It is our belief that the impetus for change and the value base in the 1970s were the same as they are now. For example, the values that motivated professionals to prove that an individual with severe disabilities could be "trained" to lift an arm (Fuller, 1949) was as important in 1949 as the current trend to provide natural supports is today. Twenty years from now our current paradigms may seem immature, naive, and out of date. It is hoped that these trends will not be dismissed as obstacles to progress but acknowledged as critical to the continued development of a framework based on respect and autonomy.

One outcome of having been in this field for many years is being a personal witness to change. The first author's initial experience with individuals with disabilities came in the form of a work-study scholarship that took place at a developmental center in metropolitan New York. A majority of the individuals served at this center had prior placements at Willowbrook State Hospital and, following the 1972 Geraldo Rivera exposé (Smith, 1982), were transferred to other facilities. The stories of these individuals were, as we may remember, tragic and lamentable. We encountered individuals whose bodies had atrophied from having been tied into chairs or in four-point restraint for years; individuals who had their teeth removed to reduce biting; and individuals whose major repertoires were aggression, self-injury, self-stimulation, and so on.

In their new residence, located on the 15th floor of a large building, we untied people; reinforced them for not biting or rocking; reinforced them for being in-seat and compliant; and reinforced them for putting pegs in a pegboard, stacking three cubes, or making eye contact. At times we delivered aversive consequences for inappropriate behavior. Successes were smiles, hugs, vocal imitations, or eye contact following a verbal cue. Although today these goals would be considered in conflict with best practice, the values and philosophies that drove our work at that time were no different than they are today. We wanted better lives for these individuals, and it was our mission to do everything we could to support each person to achieve a better life. Our vision of what constituted a "better life" was different from what it is today, but without our visions of years past, we could not have today's visions.

This chapter tries to capture some visions of community life as of the mid-1990s. The first section of this chapter describes current trends in community residential services and the expansion of residential alternatives, and the second section describes the continued maturation of a guiding philosophy.

CURRENT TRENDS IN RESIDENTIAL SERVICES

Current literature reveals three major trends in the delivery of residential services to individuals with severe intellectual disabilities, multiple disabilities, and problem behaviors. Following is a brief description of these trends. (Nisbet, Clark, and Covert [1991] provide an in-depth review of these and other developments in community residential services.)

From Institutions to Community and from Large to Small

Few people would debate the validity of the goal of deinstitutionalization. The advantages of movement from large institutions to smaller community settings have been extensively cited in the literature. For example, these advantages include increases in adaptive behavior (Bell, Schoenrock, & Bensburg, 1981; Conroy, Efthimiou, & Lemanowicz, 1982; Larson & Lakin, 1989; Thompson & Carey, 1980), decreases in problem behavior (Belcher, 1994), and decreases in cost of care (Heal & Daniels, 1978; Templeman, Gage, & Fredericks, 1982). Further, the advantages of community living seem to increase and improve as the residence becomes smaller and more intimate (Brown & Rosa, 1994; Horner et al., 1992).

The legal support for the movement is well established (e.g., *Halderman v. Pennhurst State School and Hospital,* 1977; *Wyatt v. Stickney,* 1972). Indeed, the closing of large state facilities for individuals with developmental disabilities is perhaps the most promising sign of society's commitment to community life for all individuals. As a sign of progress, it "is no longer national news when a mental retardation institution closes" (MacNamara, 1994, p. 239). In 1992, 14 years after the New Hampshire Association for Retarded Citizens initiated a suit against the state, New Hampshire's Lanconia State School and Training Center was closed down (Covert, MacIntosh, & Shumway, 1994). On April 24, 1993, after 6 years of legal battles, the Mansfield Training School (Connecticut) shut its doors (MacNamara, 1994). Lakin, Braddock, and Smith (1994) report that 25 state institutions were closed between 1988 and 1991.

The number of institutionalized individuals with disabilities is steadily declining. Between 1967 and 1987, there was a decrease of 100,000 (White, Lakin, Hill, Wright, & Bruininks, 1988). The characteristics of community residences are also changing. Lakin et al. (1994) found that the size of residences into which individuals with developmental disabilities are moving is growing smaller. From 1982 to 1992, they documented a decrease in the number of individuals in state and nonstate facilities serving 16 or more people (from 179,966 to 120,343) and a dramatic increase in the number of individuals in facilities serving 1–6 individuals (from 33,188 to 119,675).

Although empirical verification does not suggest the ideal number of individuals who should live together, there are certain trends in the research. It is likely that the number of individuals in a home is only one factor contributing to the appropriateness of the home. For example, Landesman-Dwyer (1981) suggested that social groupings were more important than the actual size of the residence in determining quality of life. However, current thought is that the smaller the number of individuals sharing one home, the better the quality of life and the more normalizing the experience (Bradley, 1994; Brown & Rosa, 1994; Rotegard, Hill, & Bruininks, 1983). Horner et al. (1992) present a model that provides support in settings where one, two, or three people live together. They suggest that the greater the support needs of the individual, the more critical the need for a smaller living arrangement. In a survey of group homes in New York, Brown and Rosa (1994) found that autonomy decreased as the size of the home increased and that homes rated as less autonomous generally used more intrusive procedures to encourage activity participation.

From a Residential Continuum to Supported Living

In 1988, Taylor described the many problems with relying on a continuum of services. In addition to identifying critical flaws in a continuum approach (e.g., justifying restrictive environments, reliance on a "readiness" model), he described how the trend to more fully integrate individuals with disabilities was beginning to be effective in erasing the more restrictive side of the continuum. That is, more restrictive options were beginning to be replaced with smaller, community-based settings. However, Taylor cautioned that the same flaws in the more restrictive continuum are also apparent in the new community-based and less restrictive continuum. As long as there is a continuum, there will always be a "more restrictive" side, with disability labels determining placement within the context of the continuum.

The concept of a continuum offers little guidance. A continuum implies movement along a defined path of options according to certain criteria or combination of criteria (e.g., level and type of disability, age, support needs). The options that make up the continuum are predetermined. Even though we may have successfully curtailed the restrictive side of the continuum and will continue to do so as the years pass and trends continue to evolve, we are still left with static options based on an arbitrary set of criteria. Taylor (1988) suggests that we consider a variety of options, free from the confines of a continuum, that might meet an individual's needs. This concept is clearly superior to the continuum model as it seeks to move from "the development of facilities and programs into which people must fit to the provision of services and support necessary for people with severe disabilities to participate fully in community life" (p. 51).

Supported living is a concept that guides us away from the confines of a continuum and that urges us to look instead at the support that each individual needs to fully participate in a personally determined lifestyle. The types of supports that are needed to assist the person to achieve the preferred lifestyle guide the development of the person's home, rather than expecting the individual to fit within current "agency options" or numbers of "beds." According to O'Brien and O'Brien (1994), "Supported living entails providing people with disabilities the individualized help they need to live successfully in homes of their choice. It contrasts with residential service, which groups people with disabilities in residential facilities for the purpose of training, treating, or caring for them" (p. 110).

Bellamy and Horner (1987) delineate three characteristics of supported living. First, "lifestyle accountability" promotes attention to and measurement of the impact of support on critical lifestyle variables. This is an important feature as it focuses on the individualized outcomes of support rather than on a narrow measure of procedural accountability (e.g., numbers of goals and objectives, involvement of appropriate team members). Second, "individually determined support" is the most critical feature: It returns the power and control of the individual's life to the individual and his or her family. Finally, "broadened technology of residential support" expands the available range of supports for an individual. That is, supported living goes beyond health, safety, and training of new skills, broadening its focus to include any type of support that will assist the individual to achieve a self-determined lifestyle (Bellamy & Horner, 1987).

The concept of supported living is based on a person-centered model. According to Smull and Smith (1994),

> Real supported living requires that we learn how people want to live and then support them in the lives that they want (within the constraints of available resources and any issues of health and safety). It requires efforts that help people be supported by their communities and have opportunities to contribute to their communities. Real supported living requires that people with disabilities and the people providing the direct supports be empowered. It requires that agencies move from tidy organizational structures where people with disabilities "fit" into program vacancies to a fluid structure that changes with the desires of the individuals supported. It requires that control be shared rather than flowing from the top of a hierarchical arrangement. (p. 4)

The idea is elusively simple: serve the individual regardless of his or her disability, label, or past history; find a home; and build in the staff supports necessary for the individual to live successfully in the community (Taylor, 1991). All people, regardless of labels, have the right to live in their own homes as participating and sanctioned members of their community with whatever support they need (Klein, 1992; O'Brien & O'Brien, 1994). The requirements of supported living are unambiguous; each individual served receives an entirely different combination of types and amounts of services. These services are flexible and change over time along with the individual's needs and preferences.

As a result of the continued development toward individually determined supported living options, two important philosophies are clearly evolving. First, personal needs, rather than a label, are increasingly used to determine appropriate living environments. We have begun to leave behind the notion that all individuals with a particular label belong in a standardized setting. A second philosophy that continues to grow concerns the changing needs of an individual. As an individual's needs change over time, so must the supports he or she receives, and these supports should be provided within the individual's home setting rather than having the individual move to a different setting. The practice of supported living is enabled when our values are clear and focused. Once we commit to this mission, we begin the practice of supporting people with disabilities to reclaim their communities (STARHAWK, 1991).

From Agency-Owned Homes to Personal Home Ownership

Increasingly, agencies supporting individuals with disabilities are meeting many of the new challenges facing the delivery of individualized supports and continued improvement of each person's quality of life. However, some professionals, families, and consumers believe that an agency's ability to help achieve a self-determined quality of life for an individual is prohibited by the very fact that it is an "agency" (e.g., Bradley, 1994; Klein, 1992; O'Brien, 1994; O'Brien & O'Brien, 1994; Smull & Smith, 1994). Inherent in the very nature of an "agency" is the control that the agency has over numerous aspects of an individual's life. Ultimately, an agency is legally responsible for the individual. This legal responsibility will naturally shape certain decisions. For example, discussions on such topics as the dignity of risk are relegated to discussions on liability. Practically speaking, an agency must address the conveniently empty room at one of the "sites" when a new person is to be served, dismissing such issues as the person's preferences in housing, lifestyle, and roommates.

Nisbet et al. (1991) point out that group homes are no longer considered the housing model of choice for persons with severe disabilities. Rather, alternative models such as supported apartments, home ownership and cooperatives, family support and care, and shared living are now being developed (Nisbet et al., 1991). O'Brien and O'Brien (1994) state that "a small and slowly growing number of people with severe disabilities do not rely on agencies to provide the support they need, nor do they depend completely on the help of family members. They, or their families and friends, raise and manage necessary funds and organize a support system for themselves. They resolve the question of structure without agency intervention" (p. 119).

The trend toward home ownership is growing. However, at the core of this trend is not the actual financial ownership of the home but rather a psychological and emotional ownership of the place where one lives. O'Brien (1994) describes a home as having three dimensions: a sense of place (e.g., personalizing one's home to make it your own), control (e.g., choosing where and with whom one lives), and security of place (e.g., permanency and protection of one's tenancy). As Klein (1992) states, home ownership "does not mean that people actually own their homes in all cases. In fact, in most cases people have not yet been able to hold their own mortgages. People are beginning, however, to sign their own leases, co-sign with a friend or family member, or in some cases, hold mortgages. Under these arrangements, the home clearly belongs to the person, rather than the agency" (p. 300).

Reclaiming the Community

Individuals with disabilities are sons and daughters, brothers and sisters, and cousins and neighbors. They are born to the community. Up until the Industrial Revolution, they were part of the community in which they were born. However, as society became more developed and more specialized, individuals were required to become "productive" in order to be considered full members of the community. Those who could not assume a productive role in the community were typically consigned to segregated communities. As the general population grew, so did the numbers of individuals with disabilities; these segregated communities became larger and more isolated until they ceased to resemble the community and became custodial institutional facilities.

Now the pendulum has swung back. People with disabilities are reclaiming their place in the communities in which they were born. Society's collective consciousness is changing (STARHAWK, 1981). We are slowly moving from a consciousness of providing care within a paternalistic hierarchy to a position of inclusion and participation within a diverse community (Knoll & Racino, 1994). As a result, the practices of the field of disabilities are also moving. We are slowly shifting from a system-centered model in which an agency maintains fixed format programs (serving individuals who more or less fit into the program's capacity) to a person-centered model in which direction comes from the individual (through learning to identify his or her own capacities, needs, and desires). In full alliance with individuals with disabilities, we are shaping the supports necessary for them to lead a satisfying life in the community (Mount, 1992). Our challenge is to ensure that this change is not merely a function of the ebb and flow of social mores but is truly reflective of a shift in society's values.

Human services organizations are shaped by the assumptions that they make about the people they serve (Peter, 1991). These values are expressed through the organization's mission (and its mission statement, if explicitly stated), as well as its operational practices. When an organization is person centered and values choices, meaningful relationships, and community participation, we will see actions and services that encourage supported living and valued social roles (Helen Keller National Center/Technical Assistance Project, 1993).

The shift in values and assumptions that we are seeing in community services represents a profound level of change (Kiracofe, 1994). This shift will eventually result in renewed operations and practices. One cannot talk about people with disabilities as citizens in the community and at the same time have practices that amount to responding to them as commodities in a program (Klein, 1992). This shift in values forces us to refocus our mission. We are challenged to accept the fact that there is no one "right answer" in enabling people with disabilities to reclaim their communities and develop a satisfying life. We can no longer see our role as the deliverers of packaged solutions to the individuals we serve. We must provide support for individuals, help them identify their needs and desires, and help them acquire for themselves whatever they need to obtain a valued and productive life (Knoll & Racino, 1994).

The status quo has begun to be chipped away. This shift in values is becoming increasingly evident in the mission statements of both state agencies and private agencies. The New York State Office of Mental Retardation and Developmental Disabilities (OMRDD) recently revised its mission statement. This revision provides a statutory framework for individual support services for the state of New York. In their new statement they "reflect a primary mission of promoting independence, inclusion, individuality and productivity for persons with mental retardation and developmental disabilities" (New York Office of Mental Retardation and Developmental Disabilities, 1994).

The Connecticut Department of Mental Retardation (DMR) (1986) has articulated as its mission that all people with mental retardation will experience the following:

- Presence and participation in Connecticut town life
- Opportunities to develop and exercise competence

- Opportunities to make choices in the pursuit of a personal future
- Good relationships with family members and friends
- Respect and dignity

MARC: Community Resources, Ltd., a small agency in Portland, Connecticut, states its mission in the following manner: "To facilitate the process of inclusion for individuals with developmental disabilities as valued participants within their community" (MARC: Community Resources, Ltd., 1994).

Practices at the Options for Community Living in Madison, Wisconsin, are based on the belief that "every person has the right to live in a home in the community as an active and accepted member" (Johnson, 1985, p. 2). Their mission is to

> provide support and coordinate services to enable adults with developmental disabilities to live on their own in small dispersed settings. The agency works with people to help them make their own choices and reach their own goals, with support available as often and for as long as it is needed. (Johnson, 1985, p. 2)

Johnson (1985) describes several critical values that echo through these examples of mission statements:

1. Every person has the right to live in a home of his or her choice.
2. Every person has the right to be a fully participating member of the community.
3. People learn most efficiently when they have the daily opportunity to face the conditions of the environment to which they must adjust.
4. Individuals with developmental disabilities share the same need as others to control their own lives, to manage their own affairs, and to make their own decisions.
5. People with developmental disabilities have the same need as others to be accepted by the community, valued for their contributions, and able to participate in relationships and activities with a variety of people in their community.

Although all of these organizations may have different levels of achievement, what they have in common is acknowledgment of the need to move toward their goal as reflected in their mission statement. Each mission statement reflects the values that will drive and shape future changes. These values have moved us to redefine our roles as service providers. Mission statements articulate a vision of the future, and the values secure a route by which we get there.

CURRENT TRENDS, COLLABORATION, AND INDIVIDUALS WHO CHALLENGE THE SYSTEM

Many of the current trends discussed in this chapter are becoming more routinely applied to individuals with mild, moderate, and even severe disabilities. It is unfortunate, however, that they have been less frequently demonstrated with those individuals who remain most vulnerable—that is, individuals with profound and multiple disabilities and those with severe problem behaviors. That individuals with mild and moderate levels of disabilities are successfully deinstitutionalized has been well documented. Today, however, the goals of deinstitutionalization are increasingly directed to all individuals, regardless of their levels of disability. Although progress concerning individuals with severe intellectual and multiple disabilities and problem behaviors has been somewhat slower (Best-Sigford, Bruininks, Lakin, Hill, & Heal, 1982; Scheerenberger, 1982), it *is* occurring (Best-Sigford et al., 1982; Bruininks, Hauber, & Kudla, 1980; Bruininks, Hill, & Thorsheim, 1982; Hauber et al., 1984).

Efforts at resolving the potential conflict between inherent characteristics of service delivery and a self-determined quality of life may be the foundation of the next paradigm leap of our field. It is critical, however, that these efforts include individuals who challenge the system. Often the desire to demonstrate new ideas and practices moves professionals to focus on individuals with fewer challenges. This emphasis does serve a purpose. It allows us to demonstrate success, and this success is necessary for the development of models that can evolve to include all individuals.

However, this approach is also dangerous. First, it does not meet the criteria of zero exclusion. Second, attention is not paid to the unique issues facing individuals who challenge the system, creating major gaps between theory and practice. Third, ignoring these unique issues creates skepticism on the part of supporters of the very concepts we are trying to promote. Finally, professionals who do conduct research or provide services to such individuals may be penalized, since their outcomes may not appear as laudable as efforts that exclude those with the most challenges. Including all individuals in the dramatic changes that are occurring is critical.

Controversy and competition within our field can create needless stresses and obstacles that slow the realization of our mission. Creating artificial lines of division and distinction among people who fundamentally share the same values can be destructive. For example, including "anti-professionalism" (Knoll & Racino, 1994) as part of a knowledge base for support personnel sets up a barrier between groups of individuals who might otherwise work together and be more powerful in advocating and establishing supports for individuals. An alternative strategy is to "braid together the voices of people with disabilities and their families, human service professionals, community members and university researchers in a way that is highly unique, and uniquely powerful" (Peck, 1993).

It seems at times that our field has developed "best practices" for the individuals we support (e.g., transdisciplinary model, collaborative teaming) and has failed to generalize these effective strategies to ourselves, as researchers, advocates, service providers, and monitoring agencies. Research must be driven by a strong values base, which must be developed by a meaningful collaboration of individuals with disabilities, their families, support personnel, and researchers. If we all share the same values base, there should be little conflict among practice, advocacy, and research. Research can contribute to advocacy, and advocacy strengthens the values base on which research must be grounded. And, most important, research, advocacy, and practice must include those individuals with disabilities who challenge the system.

SUMMARY

The vision of how to achieve a meaningful quality of life continues to evolve. In order for us to realize our mission, two things are critical. First, all parties must work together to improve the lives of individuals with disabilities. It takes many forms of contribution to achieve our mission. Second, we must apply our successes to individuals who are the most challenging and face the challenges with confidence, clarity, objectivity, and flexibility.

REFERENCES

Bell, N.J., Schoenrock, C., & Bensberg, G. (1981). Change over time in the community: Findings of a longitudinal study. In R.H. Bruininks, C.E. Meyers, B.B. Sigford, & K.C. Lakin (Eds.), *Deinstitutionalization and community adjustment of mentally retarded people* (pp. 195–202). Washington, DC: American Association on Mental Deficiency.

Bellamy, G.T., & Horner, R.H. (1987). Beyond high school: Residential and employment options after graduation. In M.E. Snell (Ed.), *Systematic instruction of persons with severe handicaps* (3rd ed., pp. 491–510). Columbus, OH: Charles E. Merrill.

Best-Sigford, B., Bruininks, R.H., Lakin, C., Hill, B.K., & Heal, L.W. (1982). Resident release patterns in a national sample of public residential facilities. *American Journal of Mental Deficiency, 87,* 130–140.

Bradley, V.J. (1994). Evolution of a new service paradigm. In V.J. Bradley, J.W. Ashbaugh, & B.C. Blaney (Eds.), *Creating individual support for people with developmental disabilities: A mandate for change at many levels* (pp. 3–9). Baltimore: Paul H. Brookes Publishing Co.

Brown, F., & Rosa, C.J. (1994). *Autonomy and group homes: A survey of New York State.* Manuscript submitted for publication.

Bruininks, R.H., Hauber, F.A., & Kudla, M.S. (1980). National survey of community residential facilities: A profile of facilities and residents in 1977. *American Journal of Mental Deficiency, 84,* 470–478.

Bruininks, R.H., Hill, B.K., & Thorsheim, M.S. (1982). Deinstitutionalization and foster care for mentally retarded people. *Social Work, 7,* 198–205.

Connecticut Department of Mental Retardation (DMR). (1986). *Mission statement.* East Hartford, CT: Author.

Conroy, J.W., Efthimiou, J., & Lemanowicz, J.A. (1982). A matched comparison of the developmental growth of institutionalized and deinstitutionalized mentally retarded clients. *American Journal of Mental Deficiency, 86,* 581–587.

Covert, S.B., MacIntosh, J.D., & Shumway, D.L. (1994). Closing the Laconia State School and Training Center. In V.J. Bradley, J.W. Ashbaugh, & B.C. Blaney (Eds.), *Creating individual supports for people with developmental disabilities: A mandate for change at many levels* (pp. 197–211). Baltimore: Paul H. Brookes Publishing Co.

Fuller, P.R. (1949). Operant conditioning of a vegetative human organism. *American Journal of Psychology, 62,* 587–599.

Halderman v. Pennhurst State School and Hospital, 446 F. Supp. 1295, 1314–1320 (E.D. Pa., 1977).

Hauber, F.A., Bruininks, R.H., Hill, B.K., Lakin, K.C., Scheerenberger, R.C., & White, C.C. (1984). National census of residential facilities: A profile of facilities and residents. *American Journal of Mental Deficiency, 89,* 236–245.

Heal, L.W., & Daniels, B.S. (1978). A cost effectiveness analysis of residential alternatives. *Mental Retardation, 3,* 35–49.

Helen Keller National Center/Technical Assistance Project. (1993). *An interagency approach to achieving person-centered outcomes: A state and local team partnership.* Sands Point, NY: Helen Keller National Center.

Horner, R.H., Close, D.W., Fredericks, H.D.B., O'Neill, R.E., Albin, R.W., Spragues, J.R., Kennedy, C., Flannery, K.B., & Heathfield, L.T. (1992, May). *Oregon community support: Providing support for people with severe problem behaviors.* Paper presented at the meeting of the Association for Behavior Analysis, San Francisco.

Johnson, T.Z. (1985). *Belonging to the community: A series of six papers describing options in community living.* Madison, WI: Options in Community Living.

Kiracofe, J. (1994). Helping agencies shift from services to supports. In V.J. Bradley, J.W. Ashbaugh, & B.C. Blaney (Eds.), *Creating individual supports for people with developmental disabilities: A mandate for change at many levels* (pp. 281–298). Baltimore: Paul H. Brookes Publishing Co.

Klein, J. (1992). Get me the hell out of here: Supporting people with disabilities to live in their own homes. In J. Nisbet (Ed.), *Natural supports in school, at work, and in the community for people with severe disabilities* (pp. 277–339). Baltimore: Paul H. Brookes Publishing Co.

Knoll, J.A., & Racino, J.A. (1994). Field in search of a home: The need for support. In V.J. Bradley, J.W. Ashbaugh, & B.C. Blaney (Eds.), *Creating individual supports for people with developmental disabilities: A mandate for change at many levels* (pp. 299–323). Baltimore: Paul H. Brookes Publishing Co.

Lakin, K.C., Braddock, D., & Smith, G. (1994). Trends and milestones. *Mental Retardation, 32,* 248.

Landesman-Dwyer, S. (1981). Living in the community. *American Journal of Mental Deficiency, 86,* 223–234.

Larson, S., & Lakin, C. (1989). Deinstitutionalization of persons with mental retardation: Behavioral outcomes. *Journal of The Association for Persons with Severe Handicaps, 13,* 324–332.

MacNamara, R.D. (1994). The Mansfield Training School is closed: The swamp has been finally drained. *Mental Retardation, 32,* 239–242.

MARC: Community Resources, Ltd. (1994). *Mission statement.* 12 Fairview St., Portland, CT.

Mount, B. (1992). Benefits and limitations of personal futures planning. In V.J. Bradley, J.W. Ashbaugh, & B.C. Blaney (Eds.), *Creating individual support for people with developmental disabilities* (pp. 97–108). Baltimore: Paul H. Brookes Publishing Co.

New York Office of Mental Retardation and Developmental Disabilities (OMMDD). (1994). *Governor's Program Bill,* #A.10885B\Sanders, Charted August 2, 1994.

Nisbet, J., Clark, M., & Covert, S. (1991). Living it up! An analysis of research on community living. In L.H. Meyer, C.A. Peck, & L. Brown (Eds.), *Critical issues in the lives of people with severe disabilities* (pp. 115–144). Baltimore: Paul H. Brookes Publishing Co.

O'Brien, J. (1994). Down stairs that are never your own: Supporting people with developmental disabilities in their own homes. *Mental Retardation, 32,* 1–6.

O'Brien, J., & O'Brien, C.L. (1994). More than just a new address: Images of organization for supported living agencies. In V.J. Bradley, J.W. Ashbaugh, & B.C. Blaney (Eds.), *Creating individual supports for people with developmental disabilities: A mandate for change at many levels* (pp. 109–140). Baltimore: Paul H. Brookes Publishing Co.

Peck, C. (1993, November). *Braiding research and advocacy together.* Paper presented at the meeting of The Association for Persons with Severe Handicaps, Chicago.

Peter, D. (1991). We began to listen. In S.J. Taylor, R. Bogdan, & J.A. Racino (Eds.), *Life in the community: Case studies of organizations supporting people with disabilities* (pp. 129–138). Baltimore: Paul H. Brookes Publishing Co.

Rotegard, L.L., Hill, B.K., & Bruininks, R.H. (1983). Environmental characteristics of residential facilities for mentally retarded people in the United States. *American Journal of Mental Deficiency, 83,* 49–56.

Scheerenberger, R.C. (1982). Public residential services, 1981: Status and trends. *Mental Retardation, 20*(5), 210–215.

Smith, K. (Producer). (1982, January 7). *20/20.* New York: ABC News.

Smull, M.W., & Smith, G. (1994). Moving to a system of support: Using support brokerage. *AAMR News and Notes, 7*(4), 4–6.

STARHAWK. (1981). *Rebirth of the goddess: A talk on witchcraft, feminism, and social change.* (Presented at the University of Wisconsin, Madison). Mt. Horeb, WI: CIRCLE.

STARHAWK. (1991). *Magic vision and action*. Tape #A151. Boulder, CO: Sounds True Productions.

Taylor, S.J. (1988). Caught in the continuum: A critical analysis of the principle of the least restrictive environment. *Journal of The Association for Persons with Severe Handicaps, 13,* 41–53.

Taylor, S.J. (1991). Toward individualized community living. In S.J. Taylor, R. Bogday, & J.A. Racino (Eds.), *Life in the community: Case studies of organizations supporting people with disabilities* (pp. 105–112). Baltimore: Paul H. Brookes Publishing Co.

Templeman, D., Gage, M.A., & Fredericks, H.D. (1982). Cost effectiveness of the group home. *Journal of The Association for the Severely Handicapped, 6*(4), 11–16.

Thompson, T., & Carey, A. (1980). Structured normalization: Intellectual and adaptive behavior changes in a residential setting. *Mental Retardation, 18,* 193–197.

White, C.C., Lakin, K.C., Hill, B.K., Wright, E.A., & Bruininks, R.H. (1988). *Persons with mental retardation in state operated residential facilities: Year ending June 30, 1987 with longitudinal trends from 1950 to 1987*. Minneapolis: University of Minnesota, Center for Residential and Community Services.

Wyatt v. Stickney, 344 F. Supp. 373, 387 (M.D. Ala. 1972), aff'd sub nom., Wyatt v. Aderholt, 503 F.2d 1305 (5th Cir. 1974).

8

Residential Living for Individuals with Profound Disabilities Who Are Deaf-Blind

H.D. Bud Fredericks

THIS CHAPTER IS concerned with community integration. In particular, it discusses residential living, an area that significantly affects the quality of life of any individual. As we shall see, quality of life is multidimensional. For individuals who are deaf-blind and/or have profound cognitive disabilities, it includes at the very least the degree to which they are able to exercise choice and thereby gain access to the same range of living and leisure options, including social relationships, that people without disabilities in the same economic strata are able to gain access to. Those who support individuals with disabilities must ensure that they not only are provided the means to communicate those choices but also are aware of the range of choices that are available. In addition, health and safety must be ensured, and a pleasant, supportive environment must be achieved. For the populations under consideration, those who are deaf-blind and profoundly cognitively impaired, the implementation of all of these factors requires special emphasis by staff members and, consequently, extensive staff training.

To include both populations in a chapter about community living almost certainly does a disservice to one or both of the populations, for both are highly heterogeneous. Those who are deaf-blind have a wide range of sensory deficits. A small percentage are totally deaf and totally blind. Most have some residual hearing or vision. In addition, the time of onset of vision or audiological loss may affect the manner and quality of the communicative function of the individual. Finally, within the deaf-blind population, we find the entire range of cognitive abilities from gifted to mentally retarded. In many cases, because of the sensory deficits, we do not have the ability to ascertain the cognitive functioning level of the individual.

Those who are profoundly cognitively impaired can also show a wide range of competencies. For example, they may also have physical defects that further limit their functioning. On occasion, these physical impairments mask a higher level of capability that becomes revealed over time only through extensive community interactions. This latter phenomenon has been observed by numerous community residential providers in individuals who had long histories of incarceration in large institutions before moving to community facilities.

Thus, as we speak of these two populations within community settings, we must continually keep in mind that each person's needs are idiosyncratic and that the options developed for them must be individualized. Although examples of individual residents are offered within the chapter, all options and opportunities must necessarily be presented as general principles.

The focus of this chapter is on residential living and includes leisure activities. We have chosen not to organize these in separate sections but to incorporate leisure activities within the discussion of residential living because of the interaction of these domains. Participation in leisure activities is a critical factor in residential living. In fact, it enhances the quality of each of our lives.

This chapter explores the different types of residential options, citing the advantages and disadvantages of each. In addition, it provides guidelines for the selection of any residential option in terms of the philosophy of the service provider and the staff, the characteristics of the physical setting, the training and the competencies of the staff, the individual's preferences and opportunity for growth, and safety considerations.

RESIDENTIAL OPTIONS

In this chapter we include only those residential options that are generally recognized as state of the art. Therefore, any congregate facility that houses more than six individuals is not discussed, since it is not considered an environment that is appropriate for the population under consideration. Six or fewer persons in a group home characterizes the residence as a small group home. This number is generally recognized by leading researchers (Felce & Repp, 1992; Hull & Thompson, 1981; Rotegard, Hill, & Bruininks, 1983).

However, many states have adopted the five-person group home as a definition of "small group home." The primary reason for this definition lies in a preponderance of zoning laws that indicate that five unrelated individuals can live in a home in a residential area zoned as a "single dwelling." Thus, the establishment of a small group home in such a residential environment does not require seeking a variance from zoning laws.

The following are four types of living arrangements that are considered to be the state of the art.

Group Home

Reluctantly, we consider a group home a dwelling that houses five individuals. We do so because this configuration is currently the preferred option in many states. However, we believe that it should be obsolete and that congregate facilities that house more than three people should be critically questioned. If possible, alternatives should be developed. This recommendation is based on the principle that people with disabilities should live in facilities similar to those occupied by the general population. With the exception of some college students, one seldom finds more than three unrelated individuals living together. To achieve inclusion in the community, hallmarks that tend to highlight differences between people with disabilities and others should be eliminated. Five-person group homes and homes that accommodate larger groups are such hallmarks.

Given these criteria, a small group home that houses three individuals would be acceptable. One of the advantages of this number of residents is that most three-bedroom homes, if adapted as discussed in this section, can comfortably accommodate three persons who have disabilities. Thus, a wide range of neighborhoods and a much broader range of homes become suitable for consideration.

One alternative to consider in congregate living is the purchase of a home in lieu of renting. The purchase of a home for many constitutes the epitome of the "American Dream." Purchases can be arranged in a number of ways. For example, all potential residents can join together in the purchase and develop a contract among them that specifies what will happen when one moves. In another alternative, one person can purchase and the others can pay rent toward the monthly mortgage payment. Ownership will generally not threaten Supplemental Security Income (SSI) payments and does provide for the individuals' greater security than that afforded by government-owned facilities or facilities owned by a private corporation. Private corporations have been known to develop financial difficulties. Certainly anyone knowledgeable about residential programs in any state can identify corporations that have declared bankruptcy or given up management of a home because of changes in policy or management within the corporation. In addition, government-owned homes are subject to the whims of legislation and taxation. Although most have demonstrated long-range stability, the threat of closure is ever present in states that are going through financial difficulties. For instance, the state of Oregon, because of tax limitation legislation, currently faces the prospect of closing down all its vocational programs for adults with developmental disabilities and perhaps closing a small number of residential facilities.

However, the individual who owns his or her own home has a continuing investment that is gathering equity. Although financial difficulties within a state or a corporation may cause cutbacks in staff support, the home is still there. The person is not forced to find another place to live. Staff support can be obtained either from government sources or paid for privately.

Apartment Living

Apartments are becoming one of the more preferred living arrangements for individuals who have disabilities. The size of the apartment is determined by the number of people who will live in it. A two-bedroom apartment for two individuals has become the most common option. There is a paucity of published information about the effects of apartment living on individuals who are deaf-blind and profoundly disabled. Certainly the tenant support program conducted by the University of Oregon Neighborhood Living Project in Seattle, Washington, is a prime example of the effectiveness of apartment living for this population (Parker & Boles, 1990; Romer & Horner, 1987). Apartment living may be the preferred residential lifestyle was supported by Burchard, Hasazi, Gordon, and Yoe (1991). They found that persons in supervised apartments achieved the most normative lifestyles, with greater personal independence and community integration.

Foster Care

Many states use a system of adult foster care in which an individual with disabilities lives with a family and, in essence, becomes a member of that family. The family members provide support for the individual. Although this model does provide a natural system of supports, it should be recognized as one that is not usual among the population without disabilities. Yet in some cases where the individual wants to live in a family environment, it may be preferred.

Supported Living

Supported living can occur in a variety of formats. A person may live in a residence of his or her choice and be provided with whatever support is necessary to achieve that choice. This support can include individual attendants, periodic staff checks, live-in housemates who are not disabled, or neighbors who agree to provide support. Variations on the model are limited only by one's ingenuity. Supported living can be used in any type of residence and can be altered as the needs of the individual change. Because it is based on choice and is not a bureaucracy-imposed model, it is becoming the preferred residential option (Parker & Boles, 1990).

RESIDENTIAL CHARACTERISTICS

The selection of a residential option for an individual who is deaf-blind or who is profoundly disabled requires the careful consideration of a number of factors. To consider these factors, several checklists have been developed. An excellent one developed by the Helen Keller National Center/Technical Assistance Project (HKNC-TAP) in conjunction with the Hilton Perkins Advisory Committee and the National Parent Network for Persons Who Are Deaf Blind (1991) is available from the HKNC/TAP. Another checklist that provides detailed descriptions of high-quality features in residences as specified by parents has been developed in Oregon under the sponsorship of ARC-Oregon (Wilson & Brodsky, 1989). It is this checklist that shall provide the framework for the remainder of the chapter since it includes considerations of leisure time and recreation. In discussions of residential living and leisure activities, six domains or aspects are considered: 1) philosophy, 2) physical setting, 3) staff, 4) regard for the individual, 5) personal growth, and 6) safety. These domains serve a number of purposes. They provide a set of standards against which advocates, professionals, and clients can measure the quality of residential programs, both during their establishment and during their operation. In other words, they are a vehicle through which the programs can be evaluated.

Philosophy

In any residential setting where there is staff support, a statement of philosophy should be crafted so that both residents and staff clearly understand their relationship. Such a statement must address at least two distinct but related variables: first, the health and safety of the residents must be identified as a major outcome; second, the provision of resident rights and choices, which should mirror the rights and choices of the general population, must be ensured. Staff within the residence are there for support; they ensure that residents are safe and that every precaution is taken to maintain their health. At the same time, staff assist residents in achieving their preferences.

These two concepts, residents' rights and choices and their health and safety, should provide clear guidelines for the development of a staff philosophy. However, clear guidelines are not always possible because there is always the probability of tension between the two. Anyone who has been in a staff residential position has faced such tension. A few examples will suffice to illustrate the dilemma. It is the right of an adult resident to drink alcoholic beverages, but if the drinking becomes excessive and if the resident is in danger of becoming an alcoholic, does the staff have the obligation to intercede in order to preserve the health of the resident? If the resident eats excessively and is gaining weight, is there a point at which the staff should intervene? Should this be when the resident has become 10 pounds overweight? Twenty, 30, or 50 pounds? Similar conflicts arise in such things as unprotected sex, illegal use of drugs, and obsession with pornography.

Certainly staff can counsel the resident and try to encourage moderation. However, if the resident refuses to accept the advice, what is the legal responsibility of the staff to protect the resident from some sort of self-destruction? We have seen litigation brought against large residential facilities for failure to change a resident's self-abuse. Might not staff also be held legally liable for failure to protect a resident's health in community-based facilities? Although we know of no legal action taken to date, discussions with protection and advocacy lawyers indicate that such legal responses to failure to protect health and safety are clearly possible.

There is no easy answer to these situations, which cause tension between the concepts of health and safety and resident rights. Each situation must be dealt with individually so that decisions can be reached by the resident, staff, funding authorities, case managers, family, and significant others. Only by addressing the situation directly, discussing possibilities, and deciding on a course of action agreed upon by all the principal participants can the staff be given comfortable guidelines for intercession (Bannerman, Sheldon, Sherman, & Harchik, 1990).

One of the ways in which tension between health and choice may be reduced is through the development of written policies and procedures. Whenever living situations require staff to support residents, such policies and procedures should be crafted. At the very least, there should be a written set of policies and procedures for the dispensing of medication and the handling of residential money. If conflicts or potential conflicts can arise because of a resident's excessive use of alcohol or drugs, overeating, or unprotected sexual activities, specific and detailed procedures should be written and agreed upon by all those who have a legal, familial, or advocacy relationship with the resident or the program.

If residential services are funded by a governmental agency, a much more elaborate set of policies and procedures will usually be required. However, additional detailed procedures that relate to a specific resident may also be necessary for the situations described previously. If a philosophy statement and an accompanying set of policies and procedures are not developed and made operational within a program, there are three distinct dangers: 1) the right of the resident to make and implement choices may be denied or restricted; 2) staff may not have clear guidelines as to how to respond to resident preferences, and the resulting ambiguity may cause staff frustration and lessen morale and competence; and 3) the agency exposes itself to liability from two perspectives: violation of resident rights and failure to provide for resident health and safety.

Physical Setting

Any home or apartment should be in a residential neighborhood that is generally recognized as being safe. This means that residents are likely to be safe when they are by themselves in the surrounding streets. In addition, the residence and the surrounding area should be clean, and homes should be in good repair.

When choosing homes, transportation to stores, recreational facilities, churches or temples, and restaurants becomes a major consideration. The ideal location is one in which some of these facilities are within walking distance and where nearby public transportation will permit access to others. Neighborhood stores, as opposed to stores at the other end of a bus line, are preferable so that the individuals can be taught to become familiar with those stores. Familiarity of location of items in an environment is important for a person with sensory deficits. Therefore, continued use of the same store creates a knowledge of it. Frequenting the same neighborhood store allows a resident to become known by the store clerks. Very often these store clerks become part of the individual's support system and develop into friendly acquaintances who provide additional people with whom to interact. In addition, when necessary, these people may provide assistance.

The home or apartment must meet the varied needs of the individuals who will reside there. Each person should have his or her own bedroom, there should be adequate storage space for personal belongings, there should be at least one bathroom for each group of three people who reside there, and the common living spaces should comfortably accommodate all the residents at one time.

The residential environment will almost certainly require physical adaptations to ensure not only safety but also comfort for the person who is deaf-blind. Unnecessary obstacles should be removed, and furniture and appliances should also be consistently placed in the same location. Touch cues may be added to various walls to help the person identify which part of the home he or she is in. An alarm system must be installed that is appropriate for the sensory competencies of the individual. A bed that vibrates in response to an alarm might be considered. Phones with teletypewriter (TTY) capability will need to be installed.

For the person who is profoundly disabled and also ambulatory, few physical adaptations will be necessary. However, if any of the individuals are in wheelchairs, the environment will have to accommodate the chairs. Corridors and entryways will have to be wide enough. The bathroom and kitchen may have to be modified to provide access for the wheelchair. It is suggested that light switches be installed at wheelchair height. In our experience, the padding of protruding wall corners helps reduce damage from wheelchairs. If the individuals are inexperienced wheelchair drivers, wood panels at wheelchair height along hall walls will also reduce damage to the walls.

Doors and windows must be able to be locked, and window shades, blinds, or drapes must be able to be closed. Residents should be taught to administer these security measures, and if they are unable to do so, staff must be trained to ensure that the residence is secure for those living there.

Finally, the furniture should be well crafted and functional for all who live there. The home should be decorated with pictures and wall hangings, and it should have adequate lighting in addition to wall or ceiling lights. Every effort should be made to involve the residents in choosing their own furniture and decorations.

Staff and Support Personnel

Within any residential option there must be enough staff to ensure that the person with disabilities will have the degree of support he or she requires. Around-the-clock support may have to be scheduled. The number of staff for any facility is determined by two factors: the number of residents and the capabilities of the residents. If individuals use wheelchairs, the number of persons required to transfer the person unable to transfer himself or herself will have to be determined. If a person with disabilities requires a two-person transfer, then there must be provision for two people at all times. It is unfair to the individual with disabilities not to be allowed to transfer when the need arises due to an insufficient number of staff.

Another consideration that dictates staff numbers is the capability of the resident to gain access to community activities independently. Certainly the resident who can independently walk or take public transportation to a desired location in the community does not need staff assistance. However, the person with profound cognitive disabilities and the person who is deaf-blind may need staff accompaniment. If so, there must be an adequate number of staff not only to accompany people into the community but also to remain in the home to provide support for those remaining there. To determine staffing patterns, one must also consider the peak hours of need. For example, staffing needs are obviously minimal when residents are at work or during sleeping hours. The mix of considerations includes the care and safety of residents, community access, and such necessary activities as food preparation, shopping, and medical visits.

Unfortunately, in many locations the state, regional, or county funding agencies will develop some generic formulae for staffing patterns that are then prescribed for various sizes of residential facilities. In lieu of such formulae, staffing patterns should be determined individually, based on the persons residing in a residence and considering their capabilities for independence, their health and safety needs, and their need to gain access to the community for necessary shopping, appointments, and recreational activities.

Not enough can be said about training support personnel. In this author's estimation, training is the most important element in providing quality support. In setting up training programs, four areas are more important than any others: philosophy, health and safety, communication, and positive environments.

A structured period of training before the new staff starts working is essential. This training should include, at the very least, the philosophy of the program, procedures regarding medication, information about each of the residents, instruction on behavioral programs, safety considerations, and the importance of quality of interactions with residents. Table 1 contains an outline of training necessary for new staff. Staff should then be monitored closely during their first few days on the job, with feedback being given by the manager or skill trainer or by more experienced staff who have been given training responsibilities. Modeling by experienced staff followed by "hands-on" efforts by the new staff (with feedback) is considered an excellent method to conduct training during the first few weeks on the job.

Table 1. List of subject areas in which direct care staff are trained

Subject areas of initial direct care staff training

The following are taught over a period of 2–3 days prior to the new staff working with residents:
Philosophical overview
  Rights of resident
  Overview of staff duties
Activities catalog/individual assessment
Individualized support plan (ISP)
Choice/preferences of resident
Safety in the home
Fire drills
Food/nutrition/menus
Individual care considerations
Medications, administration, and record keeping
Formal and informal teaching of residents
Communication
Vehicle safety
Professionalism

In addition to the above subjects, all new staff participate in 1- to 3-day workshops on each of the following subjects during their first 60 days of employment:
First aid
CPR

Restraints and holds (to be used only for the protection of the individual or others, and only in emergency situations or those prescribed by the IHP/ISP team)

IHP, individualized habilitation plan.

Philosophy As a foundation for any personnel training program, a strong philosophical basis must recognize the rights of the individual with disabilities, especially in terms of making choices. Staff and support personnel must facilitate and support the implementation of those choices. Our experience indicates that this basic philosophical position needs continual reiteration. As previously discussed, staff and supervisors should realize that there will be continual tension between ensuring the rights of the person with disabilities and ensuring that the person is kept safe and healthy. For instance, we discussed the resident's right to drink alcoholic beverages or to eat excessively. Both of these could cause significant health problems. This subject is worth hours of discussion with staff to help clarify their roles yet ensure the preservation of the rights of the individual who has disabilities.

Another source of tension with staff is the conflict between their personal values and the behavior and values of some of the residents. For example, some staff members may not condone extramarital sex or drinking of alcoholic beverages. If a resident chooses to engage in those activities, some staff may be unable to support the resident at these times. Every accommodation should be made to be sensitive to the staff's reluctance to support these activities. Movement to another facility, change in scheduled working hours, and designating other staff on the shift to support the resident may be necessary. If such accommodations cannot be made, the staff member may have to seek employment elsewhere. The primary consideration must be that the resident's autonomy cannot be compromised because of staff values or beliefs.

Health and Safety As indicated previously, the health and safety of the individual with disabilities are paramount. Staff must be trained to respond to all situations in which the health and safety of the person are in jeopardy and must assist in preventive practices that will help maintain health. All staff should be proficient in dispensing medication and in keeping medical records.

Communication Finally, staff must be trained to communicate with the residents. To communicate with a person who is deaf-blind, a variety of communication methods may be used, depending on the communication abilities of the resident. These include touch cues, signing in the hand, using amplification systems, or any combination of these. Probably the most comprehensive description of communication with persons who are deaf-blind can be found in the works in preparation by the American Foundation for the Blind. The document will be available in fall 1995. Another document that provides a good overview of communication needs and techniques for the person who is deaf-blind can be found in Sauerburger (1993).

To communicate with people who are profoundly cognitively disabled and who are nonverbal, a communication system must be established that will allow the individual to communicate with support personnel, especially to express needs and desires. Communication boards and symbolic systems are widely used, as are concrete box systems. A concrete box is a container with objects that represent the needs or desires of an individual. For instance, a small ball might represent going outdoors. Concrete boxes are also used to provide a daily schedule. The object representing the first event of the day is placed in the first partition of the box; the second partition contains the object for the second event, and so on. Staff must be thoroughly familiar with the system in use and not only respond to the communication efforts of the resident but also encourage the resident to use the system to communicate. In addition, support personnel must learn to read the body language of the individuals, interpret the meaning of sounds, and thereby help to establish communication with the resident.

An example will illustrate these points. Susan, who is totally deaf and totally blind, resides in a home with three other people who are not deaf-blind but who are profoundly cognitively disabled. There are two staff members on duty during waking hours. The group home man-ager (the person in charge of the home) and the skill trainer (the person responsible for staff and resident training) are also available to assist with residents as needed. Susan, now 28 years old, had been in a large institution since age 3, and for the past 2 years has been residing in the group home. Susan responds to about 10 basic signs that are given to her by way of her hands. She has a concrete box communication system whereby she is able to indicate her needs and desires. That system is continually undergoing expansion as staff add to Susan's activities and thereby increase her interests. As new staff come into the facility, they must undergo an intensive training program to be able to communicate with Susan. Susan has learned to make a sound to get staff attention. Staff then lead Susan to the communication box to de-termine her needs. On occasion, Susan will move to the box indepen-dently, guiding herself along the wall to get there. On the wall have been taped different-shaped pieces of wood that are cues to Susan as to what part of the home she is in. These wooden shapes correspond to some items in the communication box, such as restroom (triangle) and kitchen (circle).

In this home, staff have to be very alert to objects that may be left in unusual places by the other residents so as to ensure Susan's ability to move about the home safely and with little confusion. When other residents are in the home, one staff member checks every hour in the rooms where Susan may wander to ensure that all furniture is in the correct location and that no loose objects are on the floor.

Susan will tend to sit on the couch, be quiet, and not ask for attention for long periods of time. Staff during these times attempt to interact with her, engaging her in activities in which she has an inter-est. Staff have learned to recognize a low guttural sound that she makes to indicate when she does not want anymore of their attention. Like most of us, Susan has periods of time when she prefers to be alone and has learned to make the sound that indicates that need.

In the previous example, Susan had few signs that she understood. Therefore, it was feasible to train all staff in the use of those signs. As Susan has learned additional signs, staff have learned them also. All staff also learned the communication systems used by each of the other residents. However, with other individuals who are deaf-blind, the same arrangement might not be possible.

Let us take the example of Jeff, who is totally blind in one eye and has some residual vision in the other eye. He is significantly deaf and is believed to be moderately mentally retarded, although there are staff members who do not believe that he is retarded. Jeff lives in a three-bedroom apartment with two apartment mates, both of whom are disabled but highly verbal. Staff members are available as needed, but there are not always staff present in this apartment because they cover two other similar apartments. Jeff is well educated and has lived at home most of his life. He has acquired a significant signing vocabulary and can sign quite rapidly. He is capable of self-care, but he needs someone to prepare his food and help with his money. Since staff are not always present and since his apartment mates cannot sign as well as Jeff (although they are learning), interpreters have been hired to be with Jeff during most of his waking hours so that he can communicate with others, especially with his apartment mates, whom he really likes and with whom he wants to live.

Two interpreters work with Jeff during the week. Because an interpreter is with Jeff during most of his waking hours, Jeff has excellent opportunities to gain access to community activities and has developed a rich agenda of sports events that he likes to attend. A small college is located in the same community, and Jeff attends most of the athletic events there as well as attending the football, basketball, and baseball games of the local high school. The interpreter acts as his announcer, and Jeff asks questions about players whose names he has learned. Jeff has an ideal situation for gaining access to recreational activities in the community.

Susan is not quite as fortunate because of the staffing pattern in her group home—two staff members for five residents, each of whom requires considerable support during community-based activities. Thus, Susan does not go to the community as often as Jeff, nor does she have as rich a recreational schedule. She does participate in the community about three times a week. One of her favorite activities is to go to the local YWCA to swim. On occasion, she also likes to take long walks but frequently indicates that she does not want to participate.

She has developed a sorting activity with metal shapes that she likes to engage in at home, and as of this writing staff are trying to determine some utility for this activity. The shapes are metal pyramids, cubes, balls, and tetrahedrons. Staff believe that Susan came to the home with the shapes from the state institution. She keeps them in a large shoe box that she stores under her bed. When she chooses to engage them, she removes the box from under the bed, sits at a table, fingers each shape, and places it around the box, congregating each shape at a specific location around the box. The task is done very slowly and deliberately. Staff, because they have been trained to try to engage the residents in age-appropriate activities, have tried to substitute other sedentary tasks, but all have been rejected by Susan, who prefers to sort her shapes.

A word should probably be inserted here about age-appropriate activities and their place in one's home. There is no philosophical quarrel with the concept of exposing individuals with developmental disabilities to age-appropriate activities, and certainly we want to teach and encourage individuals to be age appropriate when in a public situation. However, this author, who supervises a number of homes for persons with developmental disabilities, believes that in the privacy of one's home, if an individual's favorite activity is not age appropriate, he or she should still be allowed to engage in that activity.

Positive Environments In addition to learning to communicate with the residents, it is important to create a positive environment within a home. Within the residences that Teaching Research operates in Oregon for individuals who are medically fragile or who exhibit significant challenging behaviors, a nonaversive behavior intervention prevails. Yet we recognize that during any 8-hour shift, staff cannot always be totally positive. At times, they must give correction; at times they disagree with a resident; and at times their humanness takes control and they may deliver a dirty look or raise their voice slightly. Anything more aversive is prohibited, and staff who frequently raise their voice or engage in "dirty looks" or "putdowns" should probably be seeking employment elsewhere. There is a requirement that each staff member maintain at least a 4:1 positive/negative interaction rate with each resident. By insisting on such a ratio and by employing managers who ensure its maintenance, the homes are pleasant places in which to live. In addition, we have found in some cases that such a ratio reduces the socially unacceptable behaviors of some residents.

Figure 1 shows an observation form that has been developed for use within residential environments to measure the positive/negative interactions between staff and residents. The form can be used in two ways. First, observations can be taken of one staff member, recording that staff member's interactions with each resident. When a staff member is first hired and begins work with the residents, observations are taken daily by the manager or the skill trainer. These observations will be taken during times when there are a number of residents present and when the work situation is more stressful for the staff member. Observation is taken continuously during a half-hour period. Soon after completion of the observation, the observer points out to the staff member the positive aspects of what was observed and then the areas that need improvement. This process of daily observation occurs for a period of 2 weeks. Thereafter, observations occur weekly for the next 6 weeks. After that period, observations are done randomly across all staff about once a month.

The second way in which the form shown in Figure 1 can be used is in cases in which we are dealing with a resident who is exhibiting

POSITIVE/NEGATIVE OBSERVATION SHEET
Teaching   Research

Name _____   Observer _____
Area _____   Time _____

INDIVIDUALS	+	−	RATIO	COMMENTS

PERCENTAGE = Total # Positive / Total # Positive and Negative = _____ %

Figure 1.   Positive/negative observation form. (From Fredericks, B., & Staff of the Teaching Research Infant and Child Center. [1982]. *A data-based classroom for the moderately and severely handicapped* [rev. ed.] [p. 189]. Monmouth, OR: Teaching Research Publications; reprinted by permission.)

challenging behaviors. That resident's name is placed at the top of the form, and each staff member's name is placed under the "Individuals" heading. We always suspect poor staff interactions with the resident. In those cases each staff member's interactions with that one resident are recorded. A tally mark is made for each positive and negative interaction. No tallies are made for neutral comments. Table 2 shows the

Table 2.   Positive and negative interactions

Positive interactions
Compliment—tell a person how well he or she did
Praise—tell a person how pleased or proud you are of him or her
Smile—facial expression denoting pleasure or approval
Affection—touches that communicate support

Negative interactions
Corrections—verbalizations that correct a person in any manner
Putdowns—any form of implied or stated criticism
Demands/directives—telling a person what to do
Angry voice tone—any words delivered in raised or irritated tone of voice indicating displeasure with the other person
Dirty looks—scowl or frown

interactions that are considered positive and those that are negative. A 4:1 positive/negative interaction ratio is desirable during the training of staff members. A 3:1 ratio is acceptable on a continuing basis.

Regard for the Individual

We hope that we have emphasized sufficiently that the residence is "the home" of the person with disabilities and must be respected as such. In addition, the resident's choices and preferences should be also honored and supported. Regard for the individual can be manifested in other ways. Many of the individuals about whom we are writing will need assistance in three areas: personal appearance, food preparation, and the cultivation and maintenance of social relationships.

There is no reason for anyone who is disabled to appear in public with ill-fitting or mismatched clothes or to be disheveled. Staff should help the person maintain a clean, neat appearance that will not draw negative attention. Good habits of personal hygiene must also be encouraged. None of this should be construed to mean that residents must conform to some standard dress code decided by the staff, but it does mean that within their lifestyle choices, they should be encouraged to be neat and clean.

The quality of the meals one eats is often an important factor in measuring the quality of one's life. Individual meals should be nutritious and appetizing. Menus should have variation but, once again, should be amenable to the individual preferences of the resident.

Perhaps one of the more difficult areas for staff and advocates is assisting residents to develop and maintain social relationships with family and friends. Staff members need to provide frequent opportunities for residents to be in the company of others. In the case of those who are deaf-blind, the staff should help others to communicate with the person who is deaf-blind. Since people who are not used to communicating with someone who has a sensory deficit will often be reluctant to attempt to communicate, encouragement and modeling will often help.

The telephone has become an important instrument in our social lives. Homes with individuals who are deaf-blind should have telephones adapted to be used by those who are deaf-blind or, at the very least, should have staff who can act as interpreters during a phone conversation.

Personal Growth

Personal growth includes many of the areas that we have been analyzing: an effective means of communication, necessary adaptive equipment to move about the community, the ability to make daily choices, and an interesting and pleasant place in which to live. It also includes the opportunity to learn and to develop new skills. Many of these skills should focus on running the household. All residents should be involved in helping to care for their own needs and also should assist in the overall functioning of the home. An individual can learn to assist in such activities as cleaning the home, preparing meals, and helping with the shopping.

Hundreds of skills are required in order to manage one's own apartment. Most of these skills are learned by most of us through an incidental learning paradigm. In a few cases we may take a course or study a manual. When purchasing a microwave oven to put in our apartments, we learn a little about it at the store, but we really do not solve all its intricacies until we study the manual and do some trial cooking. To manage an apartment, we learn how to shop, store food, cook, clean, and manage a budget. Each of these skills contains a large number of subskills. For a person with significant cognitive disabilities, learning these tasks can be formidable. Petersen, Trecker, Egan, Fredericks, and Bunse (1983) have developed an assessment instrument that helps service providers and parents inventory and prioritize those skills that need to be taught to an adolescent or adult with severe or profound disabilities.

The issue is frequently raised by some staff and professionals that since they do not have to learn skills in their homes, why should people with disabilities be required to learn skills in their homes? Therefore, why this emphasis on training? There are probably a number of answers to this question. First, many people without disabilities do engage in training to improve their domestic skills. Microwave cooking courses, auto repair, and home repair courses are found in most community college catalogues. Individuals spend hours studying the manual for the new home computer or teach themselves the intricacies of microwave cooking and programming the taping of a television program. Second, many people with disabilities want to learn certain skills and want people to stop doing things for them. Very frequently, people with disabilities perceive those who support them as controlling their lives; they want to be more independent. However, people with disabilities should not have to participate in any training program if they choose not to.

Individual participation in training programs must be determined through a planning process that results in an individualized support plan (ISP) that is developed by a team consisting of the individual and the individual's guardians, advocates, residential and vocational staff, and case managers. (This plan goes by a variety of names, depending on the state in which you live.) Most often it is called the individualized habilitation plan (IHP) or the ISP. Through this team process the individual may determine whether he or she wishes to be taught any specific skill. It is also through this process that plans can be made to assist the individual in gaining access to social relationship opportunities, community activities, and other personal growth situations.

Susan and Jeff have an annual IHP. Susan's parents are both deceased, and she has lost contact with any siblings. However, she does have a community advocate who attends each IHP meeting. The case manager for Susan coordinates the meeting, and in attendance are the manager of the residence, one of her favorite staff members, her work trainer, and the community advocate. Jeff's IHP has similar representation except that his mother, father, and younger sister attend. Jeff can communicate his desires and his willingness to engage in training through his interpreter and through his parents, both of whom can communicate with Jeff using sign language in his hands. However, Susan has limited communication ability. She can sign yes or no. Therefore, questions are carefully asked of her during the IHP process. If Susan could not communicate at all, the staff, the case manager, and the community advocate would attempt to speak for her. Many nonverbal persons communicate their needs very well through their behaviors.

Safety

The final domain to consider in residential living is safety. This subject has been mentioned a number of times previously, but it should be emphasized. All aspects of safety must be considered. For example, proper medical care and treatment must be monitored. Assistance should be available to ensure regular dental check-ups, an emergency exit plan from the home in case of fire or other emergency, adequate safeguards to ensure protection against abuse by staff, and the teaching of home and community safety.

SUMMARY

Residential living for people with disabilities constitutes, as it does for all of us, the most important part of these individuals' lives. Our home is where we spend most of our time, where we relax, and where we build relationships. Singer (1987), in talking about residential living, said, "In the most general sense we want to provide a positive quality of life for the people that we serve" (p. 27). He went on to describe the ways in which various people measured quality of life. Close (1977) emphasized skill development. Wolfensberger and Glenn (1975) focused on the home being as normal as other people's homes. Romer

(1987) cited the frequency of community activities and social relationships. Singer (1987) opted for the answers to two questions that would indicate a good quality of life: 1) how do the people who spend the most time with the residents treat them? and 2) are the residents happy? He admitted that these questions are difficult to measure but that we should make every effort to do so.

In this chapter, we did not attempt to specify which of these characteristics are most important to ensure a good quality of life. Instead, we provided an overall system to evaluate the quality of a residence. We believe that the Singer (1987) question of happiness is probably the bottom line to measure quality of life. Because of its elusive nature, however, we suggest that happiness or something approximating happiness can be achieved by a person who feels safe, who can make choices, who can develop and maintain valued social relationships, who has the opportunity to engage in recreational activities, and who has the opportunity to learn those things that he or she desires to learn. Finally, those who achieve happiness live in an environment that is pleasant because it is comfortable and the people who share that environment treat them in a respectful and friendly manner.

REFERENCES

Bannerman, D.J., Sheldon, J.B., Sherman, J.A., & Harchik, A.E. (1990). Balancing the right to habilitation with the right to personal liberties: The rights of people with developmental disabilities to eat too many doughnuts and take a nap. *Journal of Applied Behavior Analysis, 23,* 79–83.

Burchard, S.N., Hasazi, J.S., Gordon, L.R., & Yoe, J. (1991). An examination of lifestyle and adjustment in three community residential alternatives. *Research in Developmental Disabilities, 12*(2), 127–142.

Close, D.W. (1977). Community living for severely and profoundly retarded adults: A group home study. *Education and Training of the Mentally Retarded, 12,* 256–262.

Felce, D., & Repp, A. (1992). The behavioral and social ecology of community houses. *Research in Developmental Disabilities, 13*(1), 27–42.

Fredericks, B., & Staff of the Teaching Research Infant and Child Center. (1982). *A data-based classroom for the moderately and severely handicapped* (rev. ed.). Monmouth, OR: Teaching Research Publications.

HKNC-TAC/Hilton Perkins Project. (1991). *An assessment instrument for families: Evaluating community based residential programs for individuals with deaf-blindness.* New York: Helen Keller Center.

Hull, J.T., & Thompson, J.C. (1981). Factors contributing to normalization in residential facilities for mental retardation persons. *Mental Retardation, 19*(2), 69–73.

Parker, R., & Boles, S. (1990). Integration opportunities for residents with developmental disabilities: Differences among supported living sites and residents. *Education and Training in Mental Retardation, 25*(1), 76–82.

Petersen, J., Trecker, N., Egan, I., Fredericks, B., & Bunse, C. (1983). *The Teaching Research curriculum for handicapped adolescents and adults: Assessment procedures.* Monmouth, OR: Teaching Research Publications.

Romer, L.T. (1987). Community-based residential options for persons with severe/multiple disabilities: Impact of services on people's lifestyles. In A.M. Covert & B. Fredericks (Eds.), *Transition for persons with deafblindness and other profound handicaps* (pp. 11–24). Monmouth, OR: Teaching Research Publications.

Romer, L.T., & Horner, R.H. (1987). *Final report: Transitions to integrated services.* U.S. Office of Special Education. Grant #008430096 awarded to Specialized Training Program, University of Oregon, Eugene, OR.

Rotegard, L.L., Hill, B.K., & Bruininks, R.H. (1983). Environmental characteristics of residential facilities for mentally retarded persons in the United States. *American Journal of Mental Deficiency, 99*(1), 49–56.

Sauerburger, D. (1993). *Independence without sight or sound.* New York: American Foundation for the Blind.

Singer, G.H.S. (1987). A systems approach to quality residential services for those who are profoundly handicapped with deafness and blindness. In A.M. Covert & B. Fredericks (Eds.), *Transition for persons with deafblindness and other profound handicaps* (pp. 25–38). Monmouth, OR: Teaching Research Publications.

Wilson, D., & Brodsky, M. (1989). *Aim for excellence handbook.* Salem, OR: Northwest Instructional Design.

Wolfensberger, W., & Glenn, L. (1975). *PASS 3, a method for quantitative evaluation of human services.* Toronto: National Institute on Mental Retardation.

9

Supported Living for People with Profound Disabilities and Severe Problem Behaviors

ROBERT H. HORNER, DANIEL W. CLOSE,
H.D. BUD FREDERICKS, ROBERT E. O'NEILL,
RICHARD W. ALBIN, JEFFREY R. SPRAGUE,
CRAIG H. KENNEDY, K. BRIGID FLANNERY,
AND LORA TUESDAY HEATHFIELD

THIS CHAPTER DESCRIBES the support of 12 individuals with severe developmental disabilities and severe problem behaviors. The chapter is organized around two emerging themes in the field of developmental disabilities: the concept of supported living (Lakin, Hayden, & Abery, 1994) and the developing technology of positive behavioral support (Carr et al., 1994; Durand, 1990; Horner et al., 1990; Reichle & Wacker, 1993). Supported living is a policy built around a vision of people with disabilities living active, rich lives in regular communities. Supported living means that people are supported as active participants in their communities regardless of the type and severity of their disability. Supported living "is living where you want, with whom you want, for as long as you want, with whatever support is needed" (H.D. Freder-

---

The activity that is the subject of this chapter was supported in whole or in part by the U.S. Department of Education, Grant No. H133B2004. However, the opinions expressed herein do not necessarily reflect the position or policy of the U.S. Department of Education, and no official endorsement by the department should be inferred.

icks, personal communication, March 1983). The concept of supported living is built on respect for the preferences of people with disabilities and on a belief that people with disabilities have both the right and the responsibility to be an active part of our society. The intensity, cost, and effectiveness of our support for people with disabilities will be most acceptable if that support allows people to live reasonable lives in regular places. Supported living is more than a policy about *where* people live; it is a recognition that *how* a person lives (the richness of life) is tied to many factors, including 1) the physical environment, 2) regular patterns of activities, 3) the availability of community opportunities for work and leisure activities, 4) the network of social support available, and 5) the quality of training and support available (Bradley, 1994).

Supported living is being defined and implemented today both as an approach to support and as an approach to policy (Smull & Danehey, 1994). A growing number of demonstrations of successful supported living are being reported across the United States (Bradley, Ashbaugh, & Blaney, 1994; Hayden & Abery, 1994). One important issue, however, is the extent to which this powerful, flexible approach to support will be applied to people with problem behaviors. This chapter is written, in part, to describe an effort to provide supported living for individuals who have long histories of severe problem behaviors. A major goal of the chapter is to ensure that people with problem behavior continue to be viewed as part of the supported living agenda.

The second theme that prompts this chapter is the growing focus on the use of positive behavioral support. Problem behaviors are the single most common reason why individuals with disabilities are excluded from school, work, and community settings (Larson & Lakin, 1989; Scheerenberger, 1990; White, Lakin, Bruininks, & Li, 1991). As a field, we have been struggling for many years to provide clinical support to people with extreme problem behaviors without resorting to the delivery of painful and humiliating interventions (Donnellan, LaVigna, Negri-Shoultz, & Fassbender, 1988; Meyer & Evans, 1989; Repp & Singh, 1990). These efforts have led to a growing recognition that an effective technology of support will be more than a behavior-reduction technology. Effective behavioral support often involves attending to many features, including communication options, activity patterns, physiological variables, features of the physical setting, social interaction patterns, and personal skills available to an individual (Carr & Carlson, 1993; Carr et al., 1994; Dunlap, Kern-Dunlap, Clarke, & Robbins, 1991; Durand, 1990; Horner et al., 1990). As we have learned more about effective behavioral support, we have learned that long-term reduction of problem behaviors often involves long-term

change in fundamental features of a person's living and learning environments (Emerson, McGill, & Mansell, 1994; Lucyshyn, Olson, &
Horner, 1995). It no longer seems logical to expect that a single, simple
change in the reinforcers or punishers experienced by a person will
be sufficient to produce the kinds of changes that we deem truly valuable (Meyer & Evans, 1993). Those who are describing their efforts to
provide positive behavioral support are calling for demonstrations and
descriptions where systematic assessment has been used to build comprehensive plans of support that result in reductions in problem behaviors and in valued changes in the lifestyle of people with disabilities (Kearney, Durand, & Mindell, 1995). Few examples exist,
however, that describe comprehensive efforts to support people with
serious histories of problem behavior (Allison, Volosov, & Axelrod, in
press; Lowe, DePaiva, & Felce, 1993; Mansell & Beasley, 1993), and
those that do exist typically focus on single individuals (Berkman &
Meyer, 1988; Foxx, Zukotynski, & Williams, 1994; Lucyshyn et
al., 1995).

This chapter describes the procedures and outcomes of a longitudinal effort to support a group of adults with histories of very severe
problem behavior. We present this demonstration as an example of
applying the principles of supported living to the challenges presented
by people who have limited experience directing their own lives and
who have long histories of destructive behavior. The chapter also presents an example of providing people with positive behavioral procedures that are the least restrictive—yet still effective—options available (Van Houten et al., 1988). We describe the people who have
received support, how we measured the impact of support, the process
of assessment and support delivery, and the outcomes we have observed during a 4-year period from 1989 to 1993.

THE PEOPLE

Twelve individuals with moderate to severe intellectual disabilities
and serious problem behaviors participated in this effort. These individuals were among a group of 25 people who were selected by the
psychology and direct service staff of an 1,100-person institution as
the residents displaying the most dangerous and difficult behaviors in
the institution. Over a 4-year period, 24 of these individuals moved
from the institution to supported living options in the community.
This chapter describes the experiences of the first 12 people who
moved. Demographic information about each person is provided in
Table 1. In 1989, they were between the ages of 18 and 44 and had
lived in the institution an average of 19.7 years (range 5 to 31). All

Table 1. Participant demographic information

Name	Age in 1990	Gender	IQ	Diagnosis	AAMR classification	Years in institution	Major problem behavior
Person AK	32	F	18-Leiter International Performance Scale	Mental retardation due to unknown prenatal influence, craniofacial anomaly, Cornelia de Lange Syndrome	Profound mental retardation	23	Pica SIB
Person BR	37	M	Profoundly retarded <20	Mental retardation due to other conditions	Profound mental retardation	31	Pica Tantrums Aggression
Person CG	44	M	Vineland, not testable	Mental retardation due to other conditions	Profound mental retardation	12	Pica
Person DJ	34	M	Estimated <20—profound	Mental retardation due to unknown prenatal influence	Profound mental retardation	27	SIB
Person ET	29	M	Vineland, estimated <20—profound	Mental retardation following prenatal hypoxia	Profound mental retardation	19	Aggression SIB
Person FS	25	F	IQ—46 VABS—20—moderate/ severe	Mental retardation following psychiatric disorder, autism	Profound mental retardation	13	SIB Aggression
Person GC	38	F	Vineland, profound	Mental retardation due to other conditions	Profound mental retardation	27	Aggression SIB
Person HA	42	F	Vineland, profound	Autism with behavior manifestation of anxiety, hyperactivity, and biting	Profound mental retardation	24	Aggression SIB
Person IS	31	F	Various IQ tests between 1969 and 1984 Ranging IQ 27—43	Mental retardation due to other conditions unspecified	Severe mental retardation	20	Aggression Property destruction SIB
Person JL	23	F	Leiter IQ 47	Severe mental retardation due to other conditions unspecified	Severe mental retardation	14	Aggression SIB
Person KK	18	M	Vineland, profound <20	Mental retardation due to other conditions	Profound mental retardation	5	Aggression Property destruction Tantrums
Person LD	28	M	Vineland, severe, estimated at 35	Mental retardation due to encephaly	Severe mental retardation	21	Pica SIB

SIB, self-injurious behavior.

participants had hospitalized themselves or someone else on multiple occasions as a result of their problem behaviors. Each person had received intensive behavioral interventions in the institution that included extended periods of four-point restraints, electroconvulsive therapy, aversive mists, psychotropic medication, and repeated mechanical restraint. In addition, serious efforts had been made to employ such positive behavioral procedures as differential reinforcement, increased activity options, increased choice, Gentle Teaching (McGee, Menolascino, Hobbs, & Menousek, 1987), and structured instruction. While clinical data from the institution suggested that there were periods with reduced levels of problem behavior, the overall pattern for each person was of ongoing, intense problem behaviors. Eight of the 12 people exhibited problem behaviors with sufficient intensity and frequency to require 1:1 staff support in the institution during waking hours.

The 12 individuals described in this chapter were selected as the first to move, based on nominations from state officials and family connections that made it logical for them to live in the two communities where support structures were available.

MEASURING IMPACT

Among the most complex questions facing our field is how to determine whether the support we provide is having a positive impact on the life of a person (Meyer & Evans, 1993). Research efforts typically involve intense collection of very specific measures for a short period of time. These results provide valuable and reliable indices of the effects of specific support strategies on specific behaviors. However, it is more difficult to demonstrate substantive, longitudinal change in the lives of individuals by using conventional experimental measures. The exciting feature of current efforts toward positive behavioral support is the emphasis not just on reducing problem behaviors, but on reducing problem behaviors in a manner that results in real changes in what people do, where they go, who they see, and the control they exert over choices in their lives. There is growing consensus that these "lifestyle" outcomes are desirable but little consensus on how they should be measured or defined. For the purposes of this demonstration, we selected five major evaluation questions to determine if the support being provided was resulting in substantive, lifestyle changes:

1. Is supported living associated with adequate health and safety?
2. Is supported living associated with reduction in the frequency or intensity of major problem behaviors?

3. Is supported living associated with physical and social inclusion?
4. Is supported living associated with an overall lifestyle that is perceived as positive?
5. Is supported living for people with severe problem behaviors cost effective?

These questions provide a balance between the practical constraints that medical and fiscal realities require and the more personal goals of each individual. Our objective was to obtain a range of measures that provide a picture of the feasibility and impact of supporting people in their local communities. Measures for each major evaluation question are summarized in Table 2 and described in more detail as follows.

Health and Safety Measures

Health and safety are outcomes we typically measure through their absence (e.g., poor health, injury). We consider health and safety to be extremely important indices of successful support. People with severe problem behaviors often face major limitations in their lives due to our

Table 2.   Evaluation questions and measures

Evaluation questions	Measures
1. Is supported living associated with appropriate health and safety?	a) Annual medical examinations b) Injury reported in incident reports
2. Is supported living associated with reduction in the frequency and/or intensity of major problem behaviors?	a) Functional Analysis Observation form —Frequency of events with aggression, SIB, pica, or property destruction b) Time sampled direct observation of problem behaviors
3. Is supported living associated with physical and social inclusion?	a) Valued Outcomes Information System —Frequency of physically integrated activities —Frequency of socially integrated activities b) Resident lifestyle inventory —Frequency of physically integrated activities c) Social Network Analysis Form —Number of people in social network —Frequency of socially integrated activities
4. Is supported living associated with an overall lifestyle that is perceived as positive?	a) Social validation questionnaire b) Time sampled direct observation of engaged time
5. Is supported living cost effective?	Dollars spent compared with benefit obtained

SIB, self-injurious behavior.

efforts to provide environments that are healthy and safe for them and for those around them. We used two measures of health and safety: annual medical evaluations and injuries reported in incident reports.

Annual Medical Evaluations Each of the 12 participants received a medical examination at least annually. These evaluations included review of all major health systems and status checks on specific medical conditions (e.g., scoliosis).

Incident Reports The direct service staff completed an incident report anytime an event occurred that resulted in restraint of a person, a need for additional staff support, injury to staff, injury to a participant, or unplanned medical care. The incident report defined the time, place, and content of the event; who was involved; and the resolution of the event. The incident reports and the medical reports associated with an injury served as one index of the extent to which the support resulted in reasonable levels of safety.

Measures of Problem Behaviors

Four major classes of problem behaviors were identified for analysis: 1) aggression, 2) self-injury, 3) property destruction, and 4) pica. Aggression was defined as any instance of hitting, kicking, biting, or scratching others. Self-injurious behavior (SIB) included self-hits, self-kicks, self-bites, self-scratches, or the hitting of head (or other body parts) against hard objects. Property destruction was defined as the throwing, dismantling, or breaking of property. Pica was defined as the ingestion of inappropriate, nonfood objects. Direct observation of these behaviors occurred through clinical support in the community and through structured research observations in both the community and the institution.

Clinical Observations in the Community The frequency of events including one or more instances of a problem behavior was recorded 24 hours a day by direct support staff using the Functional Analysis Observation Form (O'Neill, Horner, Albin, Storey, & Sprague, 1990) or its equivalent. Each staff member received training in the collection of data. At any one time up to 70 staff participated in data collection. The data were summarized weekly into events per week by major problem behavior categories and presented at weekly staff meetings.

Research Observations in Institution and Community To gain an indication of change in problem behavior levels from the institution to the community, direct observation data were collected by trained observers using time sampling procedures and computerized data collection equipment and software (Repp, Harman, Felce, Van Acker, & Karsh, 1989). Data were collected on the problem behaviors previously listed plus stereotypy (the repeated performance of a nonproductive response—e.g., rocking, finger flicking). Observers also recorded if a participant was 1) engaged in instruction, 2) engaged in a noninstructional activity, or 3) not actively engaged. Data were collected across six 10-minute observations over 3 days. The six observations were combined to define rates of problem behaviors per hour and proportion of engaged time (engaged in instruction plus engaged in activity). The direct observation probes were collected once or twice before participants moved and three or four times after they moved. Two observers were present on 15% of the direct observation probes, allowing the calculation of occurrences only by interobserver agreement, which met or exceeded 85% for all codes across all participants.

Measures of Physical and Social Inclusion

Direct Observation in the Community The Valued Outcomes Information System (VOIS) (Newton et al., 1988) was used to collect information about the activities performed in typical community contexts and about activities that included companions who were not paid to provide support. Data were collected by the same staff who collected problem behavior data. Data collection involved the completing of an "activity tag" after each valued activity lasting at least 15 minutes. The tag provided an index of what activity occurred, if the activity occurred in the community, and if the activity occurred with people other than housemates and people paid to provide support. The VOIS generates a weekly count of the number of activities that are physically integrated and the number of activities that are socially integrated. VOIS data were presented at weekly staff meetings and served as a foundation for designing individualized plans and for assessing the impact of ongoing support. Validity and reliability assessments of the VOIS have been reported by Newton (1986).

Activity Pattern Interview A second index of activity patterns was obtained through Resident Lifestyle Inventory (RLI) interviews with the staff who knew each participant best. The RLI (Kennedy, Horner, Newton, & Kanda, 1990) is a 144-item list of activities that were rated simultaneously by the two staff working most closely with a participant. For each activity the staff rated 1) whether the activity occurred during the last 30 days, 2) the frequency of occurrence, and 3) whether the activity typically occurred in the community or in the home. An activity was defined as occurring in the community if it occurred outside the property boundary of the home. The RLI has congruent validity of .81, test-retest reliability of .83, and social validity confirmed by more than 70% of direct service staff reporting that the use of the RLI improved their effectiveness in delivering support (Kennedy et al., 1990). RLI data were collected in the institution prior to moving and following relocation to the community.

Social Network Interview To provide a second index of social inclusion, the Social Network Analysis Form (SNAF) (Kennedy, Horner, & Newton, 1989) was administered with the same interviewees and at the same time as the RLI. The SNAF provided a list of the people actively involved in a person's life and organized these individuals as family, friends, neighbors/others, or staff.

Social Validity Measurement

In addition to collecting specific counts of activities and problem behavior events, an effort was made to glean a summary assessment of the overall impact of support. This was done in two ways. The first was through two "advocate" surveys conducted in the first and second year of support. The case manager or family for each participant was asked to complete a brief survey in which they rated the impact of support on an individual's life using a 10-point Likert-type scale (1 = poor, 10 = excellent) with each of the following categories: 1) health/appearance, 2) community integration, 3) social relationships, 4) access to preferred activities, 5) problem behaviors, and 6) overall quality of life.

The second effort to assess the overall impact of support was through a longitudinal, qualitative analysis with one person. This analysis included a year of extensive personal interviews with staff, friends, and family of one participant and resulted in an in-depth report about the overall impact of support living for this one person (Lucyshyn et al., 1995).

Supported Living Procedures

Supported living involves the development of individualized living options that are rich and varied, and promote prosocial behavior. To achieve this individualization, an initial assessment was conducted with each participant to better understand 1) their problem behavior; 2) the perceptions of others about physical, social, and instructional features of positive environments for each person; and 3) the personal preferences of the individuals. The assessments from the institution were used to design the initial support. After each person moved, ongoing assessment and revision of support procedures continued.

Cost-Effectiveness Supported living must not only result in reasonable lifestyles for people but must also achieve this goal within a reasonable cost to society. Fiscal information on the cost of community support was collected following procedures prescribed by the Oregon Administrative Rules. The individualization of support resulted in very different costs for different people. The total costs for support of the 12 individuals was monitored monthly and has been summarized and compared with institutional costs in a more extensive cost-benefit analysis by Knobbe, Carey, Rhodes, and Horner (1995).

Assessment of Problem Behavior

Problem behavior was assessed in the institution following the recommendations of O'Neill et al. (1990). Interviews were conducted with the direct service staff in the institution, with the family of the person, and with the psychological staff. The interviews focused on identification of 1) problem behaviors, 2) antecedent events predicting problem behaviors, 3) presumed consequences maintaining problem behaviors, and 4) prosocial behaviors that the person performed that could serve the same behavioral function as the problem behaviors. The interviews led to the development of specific hypotheses about the existence of response classes and the antecedents and consequences controlling occurrence of behaviors in each response class.

Direct observation data were then collected by institution staff using the Functional Analysis Observation Form (O'Neill et al., 1990). These data were collected either across a single 8-hour shift for 3–5 days or 24 hours a day for 3–5 days. The observational data were then examined to determine consistency or inconsistency with the hypotheses developed through the interviews. In cases where the observational data were unclear or the hypothesis was not confirmed, brief, functional analysis manipulations were conducted (Iwata, Vollmer, & Zarcone, 1990; Mace, Lalli, & Shea, 1992; Wacker et al., 1990).

Assessment of Social and Physical Inclusion

The RLI and SNAF interviews were used with the direct service staff of the institution and family members to define the activity patterns and social contacts of each person. The RLI provided a description of the activity patterns for each person, and the SNAF interviews documented the social networks and social interaction patterns for each individual.

Assessment of Medical Needs

Interviews with nursing staff and review of medical records were conducted to identify the medical support needs of each individual (cf. Pyles & Bailey, 1990). General health, specific health problems, diet, sleep patterns, medications, and current medical supports were reviewed. From these interviews and reviews, specific recommendations were obtained about 1) the scope of medical services that would be needed in the community and 2) the specific health and safety skills needed by direct service staff in the community (e.g., preparation of meals, administration of medications, suctioning).

Assessment of Features "Critical" for Successful Inclusion

Two procedures were used to obtain additional information about the features of support deemed most important by family and direct service providers. One was to conduct a personal futures plan for each participant (Mount, 1994; O'Brien, 1987; Smull & Danehey, 1994). All the family, friends, and staff interested in a particular person were gathered together for 3–6 hours to talk about a vision for the future—the things that "work" for the person and the things that should be avoided.

The second procedure was to conduct personal interviews with the family members, the direct service staff of the institution, and the psychology staff of the institution to identify "critical features" of effective support. A critical features interview focused on 1) physical features of the living setting, 2) living alone or with others, 3) location of a new home in the state, 4) type and amount of staff support that would be needed, 5) activity routines, 6) sleeping and eating routines, 7) strong preferences and dislikes of the person, and 8) instructional and behavioral procedures that were likely to be effective.

Development of Support Plan Prior to Moving

A support plan was developed for each participant prior to his or her move. The plan included where the person would live, with whom the person would live, the level and type of medical support the person would receive, the staffing pattern to support the person, a detailed plan for initial response to problem behaviors, and procedures for addressing any other unique challenges identified in the futures planning or critical features interviews.

The support plans were transformed into specific proposals for participants to live in regular houses that they leased or rented. The plans called for participants to live alone, with one housemate, or with two housemates. Staffing patterns typically followed a shift format with 1:1 or 1:2 staff-to-participant ratios during the waking part of the day and a 1:1 or 1:3 ratio at night (with an awake staff). However, it is important to note that no consistent staffing pattern was adopted. For example, one person who had very high rates of aggression received a 2:1 staffing pattern (as he did in the institution) and one person who slept very little had a modified staffing schedule to accommodate increased time awake. In addition, one or two "on call" staff were available 24 hours a day, 365 days a year, to respond to difficult or uncomfortable situations. After the assessment had been completed and transformed into a plan of support, a budget was developed for projected costs related to that support.

Negotiations with state officials, family, and case management led to the finalization of plans of support and plans for transition to the community. Implementation of the plans involved renovation of environments to be leased or rented. In some cases windows needed to be replaced with hardened material, flooring needed to be replaced, or bathrooms needed to be remodeled. The plans also included training of new support staff, a time for new staff to meet the participants and meet the staff from the institution, time for participants and their advocates to decorate and visit their new homes, and finally the actual move. In four instances, the move to the new home included a time when the institution staff worked with a participant in his or her new home. This was done to soften the number of novel features each person experienced as part of the move.

Implementing Support Plans

Implementation of the new support plans in the community included 1) development of active daily routines that included frequent community events, 2) instruction on skills related to communication and personal health, 3) development of social contacts with nonpaid individuals, 4) development of job or school options, and 5) systematic strategies for preventing and responding to problem behaviors.

Behavior support plans were individually developed and included multiple components driven by the hypotheses from initial functional assessments (Carr et al., 1994; Dunlap et al., 1991; Repp, Felce, & Barton, 1988). However, it was necessary to continue assessment in the community for all individuals. Rather than developing and implementing a single behavior support plan, the 4 years were characterized by continual assessment and revision.

Lucyshyn et al. (1995) provide a detailed description of the development and modification of the behavior support plan for one individual (FS) across a 2-year period. In general, however, the behavior support plans each built from the functional assessment hypotheses and focused on strategies for 1) rearranging the physical setting, 2) rearranging schedules (Brown, 1991), 3) changing task or antecedent features, 4) teaching new skills (e.g., communication), 5) modifying consequences to ensure that positive behaviors were rewarded and undesirable behaviors were not rewarded, and 6) defining specific procedures for protecting health and safety in dangerous situations. The global themes in the support plans were to design the environments so the problem behaviors were irrelevant, ineffective, and inefficient (Horner et al., 1990; Horner, O'Neill, & Flannery, 1993).

The specific procedures associated with each support plan are beyond the scope of this chapter. However, some examples may help illustrate the breadth of support plans. Several plans focused on initial modifications of the physical features of a person's home. For example, JD had a long history of hitting his head and hands against windows. The windows in his home were replaced with nonbreakable plastic prior to his move. FS had a history of hitting her head on the water-control knobs in the shower. Her shower was modified so that she would be farther from the knobs. BR demonstrated sensitivity to grass allergies during the spring and summer. His home was equipped with a filtering system to reduce the pollen count during these times of the year (a strategy used by many allergy sufferers in the Pacific Northwest).

A central focus of most support plans was to increase the range, variety, and preference of daily activities. For example, CG regularly slept only 3–5 hours. Her daily schedule was modified to include early activities to avoid a long history of problem behaviors during the early morning when she typically had been required to wait.

Among the most consistent elements across the support plans was instruction of communication and other functional skills. TE was taught to signal when he wanted activities to stop and when he wanted activities to continue or to be repeated. These signals were selected specifically to replace functions of self-injury that were identified in the functional assessment.

AK and GC had long histories both of eating cigarette butts off the street and of using smokeless tobacco that they could obtain from staff. It was determined by their advocates and medical supporters that the chewing of tobacco and the eating of items off the street were problems. Over a period of several months, a program was implemented in which a signal was taught for requesting tobacco from staff. Any attempt to obtain items from the street was physically blocked, and the person was redirected to asking for tobacco. Once pica attempts in the community had decreased and the person was fluent at the use of tobacco requests, the content of the tobacco chew was systematically altered to gradually shift from tobacco to mint chew. This sequence of steps was repeated for AK on two occasions when pica attempts reemerged (typically in association with staff changes).

AK also received direct training in riding in a car. She had extensive experience with state vans but was resistant to sitting in an automobile. Initial opportunities to travel by car were associated with screaming and dramatic aggression toward staff. During her first week in the community, a desensitization program was implemented in which she sat by the car and listened to the radio (a presumed reinforcer). She later sat in the car and ate lunch (first with the car motor off and then with the car motor on). She then sat in the car for brief trips to obtain preferred items (e.g., coffee). She now rides in a variety of cars and uses the community bus system.

DL received training on drinking skills. He was taking Lithium at the time of his move. Lithium has the side effect for some individuals of making the mouth dry. This may have been related to DL's repeated efforts to drink from the shower, the toilet, and faucets. Instruction was provided on the use of a glass in both the kitchen and bathroom. Drinking from nontypical sources was physically interrupted, and DL was redirected to the use of a glass. This process was effective, and over time DL's physician chose to alter the medication.

The use of activity pictures was included in se⟨ ral support plans in an effort to 1) make daily activity sequences more predictable for the individual and 2) develop a formal system for choice making within the day. Vaughn and Horner (1995) report one such effort in which choices made in response to verbal choice options resulted in destructive behavior, while the same choice options made with pictures resulted in both different selection patterns and reductions in the problem behaviors. We have become more aware of the importance of not just making choices available but making them available in a manner that is uniquely functional for the individual.

Several individuals had long histories of aggression toward others through biting, hair pulling, hitting, and kicking. For these individuals, physical safety was critical. When physical redirection was ineffective in maintaining safety or when people were physically at risk, aggression (and SIB) resulted in physical restraint following procedures prescribed by the Physical Assault Response Training (PART) protocol as defined in Oregon Administrative Rules.

A single model or technique of support (e.g., Gentle Teaching, Over Correction) was not used across individuals. None of the support plans relied on a single strategy (e.g., only changing consequences). The general pattern most closely followed the approach described by Carr and Carlson (1993) in which support procedures were tailored to the person, problem, behavior, and setting.

An effort was made to organize support so that direct service staff were involved in continuous assessment and revision of support procedures. Staff met weekly and reviewed data on problem behaviors, physically integrated activities, socially integrated activities, and training. In addition, a monthly meeting was held with the advocates, supervisory staff, and direct service staff to review activity patterns, health, instructional gains, and behavioral progress. These meetings, in conjunction with semiannual individualized support plan (ISP) meetings, were used to assess and shape the effectiveness and quality of support. Two themes emphasized in this process were 1) that the preferences of the participant were consistently solicited and included as part of all decisions and 2) that those people closest to the participant had the greatest influence in contributing to programmatic changes.

DOES SUPPORTED LIVING MAKE A DIFFERENCE?

Supported living makes an impressive difference. For the 12 people participating in this analysis the results indicate that 1) major problem behaviors decreased, 2) access to physically inclusive activities increased, 3) social networks and social activities improved, 4) health and safety were as good or better than under institutional support, and 5) these outcomes occurred at a cost that was comparable to the costs of providing institutional support. When family and case managers evaluated the impact of support, they reported significant satisfaction with the lifestyle being led by their family member or participant. The major area of ongoing concern for family members and case managers was social inclusion.

A major challenge when describing the impact of support on a person's life is to strike a balance between detailed description of important indicators and a broad picture of the individual's life. Achieving this balance is especially difficult when describing many different people who present very different pictures. One of our goals in this chapter is to provide longitudinal descriptions of a group of people across five key lifestyle indicators.

The 12 people described in this report left the institution at three different times. In March 1989, the first three people moved to homes in the community (Group A). In June and July of 1989 six more people moved (Group B), and in September of 1989 the last three people moved (Group C). Nine of the people moved to one metropolitan area (population 175,000), and three people moved to a second community (population 50,000). We have summarized the data by the three groups (A, B, C) in some cases to allow examination of the multiple baseline framework created by the timing of the moves.

Health and Safety

Health and safety results are organized to indicate whether participants received adequate medical care and if there were injuries and emergencies suggesting that they were physically at risk. The 12 individuals each visited their physician at least annually (and most often several times each year). A systematic effort was made to enroll participants with their own personal physicians in each community. A review of the medical records across the 4-year period of analysis indicated 1) physicians reported that the overall health of the participants remained stable or improved, 2) the frequency of contact with physicians implied that each person was receiving regular contact with his or her doctor, and 3) medical concerns resulted in medically appropriate follow-up.

Incident report data provide a picture of the extent to which support in the community was safe. Table 3 provides a summary of the total number of incidents involving injuries. The results are organized per individual across 6-month periods. The first 18 months following each person's move are divided into three 6-month periods to demonstrate initial trends. These data are compared to results in the 6-month period ending March 1993 (when data collection for this report ended). Note that the different dates of moving to the community result in the initial 6-month periods being unique to each person. Complete data sets for two participants (AK and KK) are not reported due to the unavoidable absence of data.

The results indicate that on average the 10 participants with full data sets experienced 1.1 injuries during their first 6 months, 0.3 injuries during their second 6 months, 0.5 injuries during their third 6 months, and 0.1 injuries during the final 6 months of their 4-year report period. During the same 6-month periods, the staff and others experienced an average of 1.7, 0.1, 0.1, and 0.2 injurious events per participant. The results show that injuries were more common for both staff and participants during their first 6 months following their move and that, within a year, the likelihood of injuries was quite low. Those participants with histories of aggression were more likely to experience events in which staff and others required medical attention.

Problem Behaviors

The participants were individuals with long histories of severe problem behavior. Their problem behaviors had led to their exclusion from society and to repeated physical risk to themselves or others. Table 4 summarizes the average frequency per week of the most significant problem behaviors for each participant across the same 6-month periods as in Table 3. The data are organized by problem behavior "events." A problem behavior event could include many responses (self-hits, bites, etc.), but a period of 3 minutes without problem behaviors was required before a new event would be recorded. With three participants (LD, IS, HA), some serious problem behaviors reduced to negligible levels, and data collection for those behaviors was discontinued. With one participant (DJ), the system for data collection was altered to focus on probe sessions, and comparable data sets are not available. For KK and GC, there were 6-month periods where the data sets were incomplete and hence not comparable. The rightmost col-

Table 3. The total frequency per 6-month period of injuries requiring some level of medical attention

		1st 6 months after move	2nd 6 months after move	3rd 6 months after move	Last 6 months ending 3/93
Person AK		Missing data			
Person BR	Injury to self	1	0	0	0
	Injury to staff	0	0	0	0
Person CG	Injury to self	3	1	1	0
	Injury to staff	0	0	0	0
Person DJ	Injury to self	1	0	0	1
	Injury to staff	1	0	0	1
Person ET	Injury to self	1	0	1	0
	Injury to staff	1	0	0	0
Person FS	Injury to self	2	2	0	0
	Injury to staff	6	0	0	0
Person GC	injury to self	0	1	2	0
	Injury to staff	3	0	0	0
Person HA	Injury to self	0	0	0	0
	Injury to staff	1	0	0	0
Person IS	Injury to self	2	0	0	0
	Injury to staff	3	0	1	1
Person JL	Injury to self	0	0	1	0
	Injury to staff	3	0	0	0
Person KK		Missing data			
Person LD	Injury to self	1	0	0	0
	Injury to staff	0	0	0	0

Table 4. Average frequency of problem behavior events per week during 6-month periods

		1st 6 months after move	2nd 6 months after move	3rd 6 months after move	Last 6 months ending 3/93	% change from first to last 6 months
Person AK	Aggression	3.4	1.25	1.1	1.9	−44
	SIB	2.9	1.6	1.8	1.1	−62
	Pica	2.9	1.2	1.8	3.8	+31
	Property destruction	0.28	0	0	0.05	−82
Person BR	Aggression	2.5	2.4	1.04	0.08	−97
	SIB	6.5	3.8	1.9	0.56	−91
	Pica	0.11	0	0	0.04	−64
Person CG	SIB	4.28	0.43	1.27	0.7	−83
	Pica	0.86	0.28	0.36	0.37	−57
Person DJ	Aggression	1.6	1.8	New system	New system	N/A
	SIB	>1,000	>1,000	New system	New system	N/A
Person ET	SIB	65.4	84.7	54.65	26.1	−60
Person FS	Aggression	1.7	8	4.5	9.9	+482
	SIB	3.5	6.4	2.6	4.4	+25
Person GC	Aggression	89.7	20.2	N/A	1.6	−98
	SIB	12.3	45.7	N/A	7	−43
Person HA	Aggression	7.34	3.04	2.96	2.5	−66
	SIB	3.37	Discontinued	Discontinued	Discontinued	~100
	Property destruction	3.6	Discontinued	Discontinued	Discontinued	~100
Person IS	Aggression	12.5	12.45	5.2	2.4	−80
	SIB	6.8	<1	Discontinued	Discontinued	~100
Person JL	Aggression	8.33	2.5	2	1.5	−82
	SIB	4.8	1.8	1.1	0.42	−91
Person KK	Aggression	2.4	1.6	0.91	N/A	−62
	Property destruction	14.75	4.75	3.6	N/A	−75
Person LD	SIB	23.4	21.2	5.37	Discontinued	~100
	Pica	4.3	1.2	2.4	2.04	−44

SIB, self-injurious behavior.

umn in Table 4 indicates the percentage of change in average event frequency from the first 6-month period to the last 6-month period in the data set.

The results indicate several patterns. For all but one participant (FS), there are reductions in the frequency of some or all serious problem behavior events. In most cases the reductions indicate a gradual decline across the 6-month periods. With several individuals, however, the data suggest greater fluctuation. With FS, for example, periods of very low frequencies were punctuated by short periods with very high frequencies of problem behaviors. A more detailed description of FS's experience has been reported by Lucyshyn et al. (1995).

The results document important behavioral gains for all 12 participants. In every case, dangerous problem behaviors were reduced for extended periods of time. With the exception of FS's burst of problem behaviors in early 1993 (which have since reduced), all participants demonstrated at least a 60% reduction in one or more classes of severe problem behavior. In some cases the reduction in problem behavior was fast and dramatic, but in most cases reductions have been very gradual, associated with multiple support plan modifications and punctuated by brief relapses.

The results do *not* indicate that movement to the community with increased activity and structured support resulted in the immediate and durable termination of all problem behaviors. Nearly every problem behavior that had been reported in the institution was observed following movement to the community. Taken together, however, the data in Table 4 represent 264/person-months in which a general approach to support (functional assessment, small living options, increased choice, increased activity, structured training) was associated with reductions in long-standing dangerous responses. The net effect is that all 12 people are still living safely in their local communities in homes that they rent. For some individuals, their problem behaviors still pose a concern, but the frequency and intensity of these behaviors are not viewed as a threat that should force their removal from the community.

A second data source related to problem behaviors is available from the time sampled, direct observation data. The data are organized around three groups of participants based on the dates they moved (Group A: February–March, Group B: June–July, Group C: September). Figure 1 presents the average rates of stereotypic responses prior to and after moving. The results demonstrate a reduction in levels of stereotypy for each group following the move to the community. The individual data within each group indicate that even though no plans of support specifically targeted stereotypic responses, there were dra-

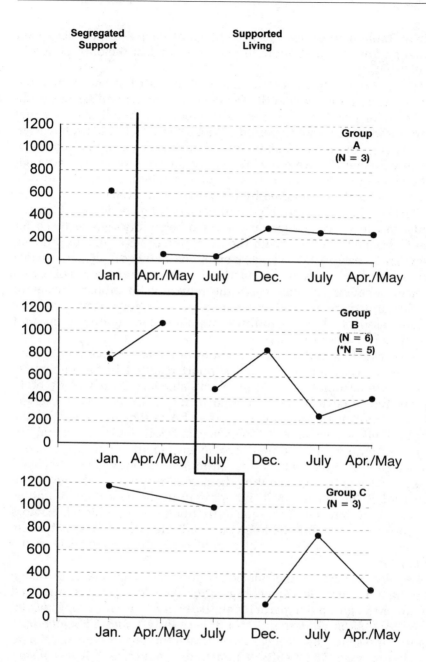

Figure 1. Average rate per hour of stereotypy before moving and after moving.

matic reductions in the levels of stereotypy for some individuals and negligible reductions for others. It is possible that increased patterns of activities provided alternative reinforcers that resulted in reduced stereotypy, but only for some participants. The different results across people are consistent with research patterns reported by Repp, Singh, Karsh, and Dietz (1991). Repp et al. also found that increased levels of activity were associated with reduced stereotypy for some but not all participants.

Physical and Social Inclusion

The level of activities that were physically and socially integrated was available through direct observation (VOIS) data after the move and from interview data (RLI and SNAF) before and after the move. These data sets indicate that the participants did more activities in the community following their move, engaged in more activities with nonpaid people, and had larger social networks.

Figure 2 presents the average frequency of physically integrated activities per month for each of the three groups of participants. The RLI interview data provide an indication that there was a substantial increase in the frequency of community activities associated with receiving support in the community. The VOIS direct observation results document a high level of physical inclusion (100–120 activities per month) after movement to the community.

Figure 3 presents the average frequency of socially integrated activities per month per group, along with the average size of social networks reported on the SNAF. These two different indices of social inclusion document increased social involvement of participants after their move to the community. The SNAF data indicate that the average number of people in a person's social network increased from 3–7 in the institution to 15–22 in the community. Each participant recorded more people in their social network, and each participant's social network included some individuals who were neither family nor persons paid to provide support.

In some cases personal friendships had developed with community members; in other cases, less well-defined relationships developed. For example, AK developed the skills and preference to visit a local coffee shop during the morning twice a week. This activity was always accompanied by a staff member, and the staff person noted that another customer also seemed to frequent the coffee shop on a similar schedule. After several weeks the other customer was invited to join AK and her staff. This resulted in a weekly social interchange that lasted for many months and ended only when this individual moved away. The social contact was perceived as something AK looked for-

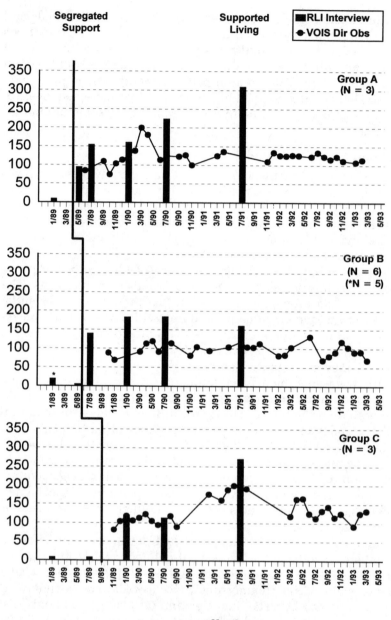

Figure 2. Average frequency of activities in the community per month.

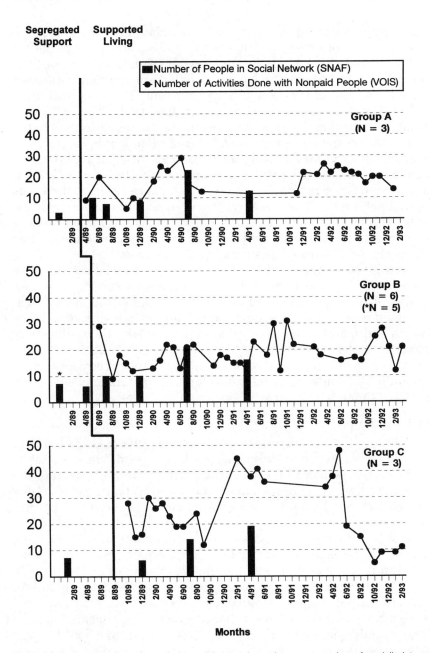

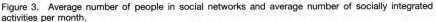

Figure 3. Average number of people in social networks and average number of socially integrated activities per month.

ward to and something the community member enjoyed. The social interaction did not extend to other activities or contacts, and the fact that AK did not speak made for a very gradual development of their relationship. The experience led us to reflect on the many different ways that social interactions can develop and influence our lives (Newton, Horner, Ard, LeBaron, & Sappington, 1994). The VOIS data indicate that participants were engaged in regular social contact in the community, but the patterns varied. For the nine people in groups A and B, social activities gradually increased over the first 18 months of community support and stabilized at approximately 20 socially integrated activities per month. For the three people in Group C there was an initial pattern of 20–30 socially integrated activities per month that rose to 40-plus per month for 18 months and then dropped precipitously in conjunction with staff changes at the home of these three individuals. This pattern has subsequently improved.

We want to emphasize that while measures of social activity have proven useful for modifying and developing social supports, we find this area of lifestyle support to be the most challenging. Social relationships are of tremendous importance and yet are very difficult to establish and maintain (Abery & Fahnestock, 1994). The development of effective social supports for people with problem behaviors is in its infancy. We have a great deal to learn about the role of social relationships and how best to foster their development and maintenance (Haring, 1991; Kennedy et al., 1989; Newton et al., 1994).

Social Validation

It is easier to report changes that have occurred in a person's life than it is to report on whether those changes were "good." In most cases, we rely on the person to tell us if the changes are positive from the person's perspective. However, the 12 people who participated in this effort have atypical ways of expressing their preferences and perceptions.

To obtain the next best assessment of the quality of support being provided, two groups (family/advocates of the participants and direct support staff) were asked to rate the impact of support on the lifestyle of each participant. Ratings were done after approximately 6 and 18 months of support. Raters completed a survey anonymously and used a rating scale (1 = poor, 10 = excellent) to assess the effects of support on the overall quality of life and on five specific lifestyle domains (health/appearance, community integration, opportunity to perform preferred activities, social relationships, problem behaviors).

The results are presented in Table 5. The family/advocates and staff rated overall lifestyle as 7.4 and 7.7, respectively, in 1989 and 8.0

Table 5. Average perception of impact support on quality of life (10 = excellent, 1 = poor)

		Health and appearance	Community integration	Preferred activities	Social relations	Problem behaviors	Overall quality of life
Family/advocates	Summer 1989 (n = 13)	8.4	7.9	7.8	5.6	7.1	7.4
	Winter 1990 (n = 14)	8.1	7.6	7.7	6.7	7.3	8.0
Direct support staff	Summer 1989 (n = 18)	7.6	7.3	6.9	5.4	6.3	7.7
	Winter 1990 (n = 22)	8.0	7.1	7.4	5.8	6.8	7.6

and 7.6 in 1990. In general, the family/advocates were impressed with the impact of support on the lifestyle of the individuals. All scores were 7.0 or greater except in the area of social relationships, where the family/advocates provided ratings of 5.6 in 1989 and 6.7 in 1990. The direct support staff provided average ratings that were slightly lower than the family/advocates, but the basic pattern with social relationships (5.4 in 1989 and 5.8 in 1990) as the dominant concern was consistent with the ratings of the family and advocates.

A related index of the overall impact of support on the lives of the participants is available from the time sampled, observation data collected before and after community support. One measure assessed in these observations was the proportion of time spent in instruction, active engagement, and no engagement. Figure 4 presents the proportion of time participants were observed to be in instruction or active engagement. Prior to their move, participants spent an impressively consistent 40% of their time actively engaged in activities. This low level of activity may have contributed to the high rates of stereotypy reported earlier. After moving to their communities, the participants' activity patterns changed substantially. Not only did the type of activities change, but also the base rate of activities performed changed. The participants now spent closer to 80% of their time actively engaged in activities, and a greater proportion of these activities were identified by their family/friends as activities they preferred. Given the documented value of enriched environments (Horner, 1980; McGee, Krantz, & McClannahan, 1985), this shift in activity levels may have been among the more important elements associated with improvements in problem behaviors and acquisition of independent skills.

Cost Effectiveness

The cost of providing segregated support to people with developmental disabilities is increasing at a dramatic pace (Braddock, Hemp, Fujiura, Bachelder, & Mitchell, 1990; Smith, 1994). Costs also are rising (though not as dramatically) for support in the community (Lewis & Bruininks, 1994). Policy makers are faced with complex demands to minimize costs yet improve both the quality and quantity of community supports. In this environment any demonstration of programmatic success also bears a responsibility to demonstrate financial feasibility. However, financial data must be reported with great care. Comparisons of costs in different locations require care to equate type and level of support provided and indexing of funds across years. A careful cost analysis of the present effort was conducted by Knobbe et al. (1995).

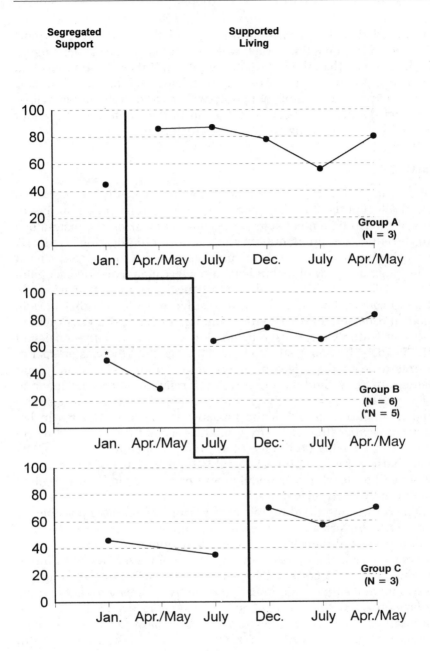

Figure 4. Average percentage of time engaged before moving and after moving.

They found that the average annual cost of the community support described in this chapter in 1990 was $111,000 per person. This figure was slightly less than the $117,000 per person if these individuals had remained in the institution. The basic message from the cost figures is that it is expensive to support people with severe problem behaviors, but higher quality of life can be achieved in the community for about the same level of funding spent in the institution.

SUMMARY

People who exhibit serious problem behaviors typically are described in research reports, book chapters, and professional presentations in terms of their problem behaviors. The reports focus on the technology used to reduce the problem behaviors, and the implications typically are precise but narrow. In this chapter we both acknowledge the need for thorough analyses of technology and suggest an expanded scope of outcomes. Effective behavioral support means support that not only reduces problem behaviors but also results in a lifestyle that is rich, varied, and personalized. The functional assessment and environmental design features of positive behavioral support are very consistent with the goals of supported living. In both cases the focus is on spending time to learn the preferences, communication systems, and competencies of an individual. From this information, efforts are made to design physical spaces, activity routines, learning opportunities, and social interactions in which the person will succeed. Change in behavior and expansion of lifestyle quality occur through building on success and focusing on the long-term impact of support (Brown, Davis, Richard, & Kelly, 1989). The goal is both to reduce dangerous behaviors and to develop sustainable patterns of behavior that will be of value to the person for decades.

The results described in this chapter indicate that it is possible for people with histories of very extreme problem behaviors to become active members of their local communities. Some serious problem behaviors were reduced to near-zero levels, some were reduced in intensity, and some have not yet changed. In every case, however, ongoing assessment and support modification have led to lifestyles that involve regular contact with typical people, places, and events in the local communities. Some of the advances have been slow to come, and some have been fragile (e.g., dramatic problem behavior escalations are still associated with staff turnover for FS). In general, however, the results demonstrate changes that go beyond behavior reduction. The overall quality of the lives of these 12 people has been improved dramatically.

As a demonstration, these 12 individuals signify that exclusionary support can no longer be defended on the grounds that problem behaviors cannot be addressed in the community. As an evaluation analysis, the results suggest a range of measurement and design considerations that must be addressed as we struggle to fit research procedures to the relevant issues of our time.

REFERENCES

Abery, B.H., & Fahnestock, M. (1994). Enhancing the social inclusion of persons with developmental disabilities. In M.F. Hayden & B.H. Abery (Eds.), *Challenges for a service system in transition* (pp. 83–119). Baltimore: Paul H. Brookes Publishing Co.

Allison, G., Volosov, P., & Axelrod, S. (in press). Moving people from more restrictive to less restrictive treatment programs. *Research in Developmental Disabilities.*

Berkman, K.A., & Meyer, L.H. (1988). Alternative strategies and multiple outcomes in the remediation of severe self-injury: Going "all out" nonaversively. *Journal of the Association for Persons with Severe Handicaps, 13,* 76–86.

Braddock, D., Hemp, R., Fujiura, G., Bachelder, L., & Mitchell, D. (1990). *Public expenditures for mental retardation and developmental disabilities in the United States: State profiles (3rd ed.: FY 1977–88. A working paper).* Chicago: Institute for the Study of Developmental Disabilities.

Bradley, V.J. (1994). Evolution of a new service paradigm. In V.J. Bradley, J.W. Ashbaugh, & B.C. Blaney (Eds.), *Creating individual supports for people with developmental disabilities: A mandate for change at many levels* (pp. 11–32). Baltimore: Paul H. Brookes Publishing Co.

Bradley, V.J., Ashbaugh, J.W., & Blaney, B.C. (Eds.). (1994). *Creating individual supports for people with developmental disabilities: A mandate for change at many levels.* Baltimore: Paul H. Brookes Publishing Co.

Brown, F. (1991). Creative daily scheduling: A nonintrusive approach to challenging behaviors in community residences. *Journal of The Association for Persons with Severe Handicaps, 16,* 75–84.

Brown, F., Davis, R., Richard, M., & Kelly, K. (1989). Residential services for adults with profound disabilities. In F. Brown & D. Lehr (Eds.), *Persons with profound disabilities: Issues and practices* (pp. 295–332). Baltimore: Paul H. Brookes Publishing Co.

Carr, E.G., & Carlson, J.I. (1993). Reduction of severe behavior problems in the community using a multicomponent treatment approach. *Journal of Applied Behavior Analysis, 26,* 157–172.

Carr, E.G., Levin, L., McConnachie, G., Carlson, J.I., Kemp, D.C., & Smith, C.E. (1994). *Communication based intervention for problem behavior: A user's guide for producing positive change.* Baltimore: Paul H. Brookes Publishing Co.

Donnellan, A.M., LaVigna, G.W., Negri-Shoultz, N., & Fassbender, L.L. (1988). *Progress without punishment: Effective approaches for learners with behavior problems.* New York: Teachers College Press.

Dunlap, G., Kern-Dunlap, L., Clarke, S., & Robbins, F.R. (1991). Functional assessment, curricular revision, and severe behavior problems. *Journal of Applied Behavior Analysis, 24,* 387–397.

Durand, V.M. (1990). *Severe behavior problems: A functional communication training approach.* New York: Guilford Press.

Emerson, E., McGill, P., & Mansell, J. (1994). *Severe learning disabilities and challenging behaviors.* London: Chapman & Hall.

Foxx, R.M., Zukotynski, G., & Williams, D.E. (1994). Measurement and evaluation of treatment outcomes with extremely dangerous behavior. In T. Thompson & D. Gray (Eds.), *Destructive behavior in developmental disabilities: Diagnosis and treatment* (pp. 261–273). Thousand Oaks, CA: Sage Publications.

Haring, T. (1991). Social relationships. In L.H. Meyer, C.A. Peck, & L. Brown (Eds.), *Critical issues in the lives of people with severe disabilities* (pp. 195–217). Baltimore: Paul H. Brookes Publishing Co.

Hayden, M.F., & Abery, B.H. (1994). *Challenges for a service system in transition: Ensuring quality community experiences for persons with developmental disabilities.* Baltimore: Paul H. Brookes Publishing Co.

Horner, R.H. (1980). The effects of an environmental "enrichment" program on the behavior of institutionalized profoundly retarded children. *Journal of Applied Behavior Analysis, 13*(3), 473–492.

Horner, R.H., Dunlap, G., Koegel, R.L., Carr, E.G., Sailor, W., Anderson, J., Albin, R.W., & O'Neill, R.E. (1990). Toward a technology of "nonaversive" behavioral support. *Journal of The Association for Persons with Severe Handicaps, 15*(3), 125–132.

Horner, R.H., O'Neill, R.E., & Flannery, K.B. (1993). Building effective behavior support plans from functional assessment information. In M.E. Snell (Ed.), *Systematic instruction of persons with severe handicaps* (4th ed., pp. 184–214). Columbus, OH: Charles E. Merrill.

Iwata, B., Vollmer, T., & Zarcone, J. (1990). The experimental (functional) analysis of behavior disorders: Methodology, applications, and limitations. In A.C. Repp & N.N. Singh (Eds.), *Nonaversive and aversive interventions for persons with developmental disabilities* (pp. 301–330). Sycamore, IL: Sycamore.

Kearney, C., Durand, V.M., & Mindell, J. (1995). It's not where you live but how you live: Choice and adaptive/maladaptive behavior in persons with severe handicaps. *Journal of Developmental and Physical Disabilities, 7*(1), 11–24.

Kennedy, C.H., Horner, R.H., & Newton, J.S. (1989). The social networks and activity patterns of adults with severe disabilities: A correlational analysis. *Journal of The Association for Persons with Severe Handicaps, 15,* 86–90.

Kennedy, C.H., Horner, R.H., Newton, J.S., & Kanda, E. (1990). Measuring the activity patterns of adults with severe disabilities using the Resident Lifestyle Inventory. *Journal of The Association for Persons with Severe Handicaps, 15,* 79–85.

Knobbe, C.A., Carey, S.P., Rhodes, L., & Horner, R.H. (1995). A comparison of benefits and costs of community residential and institutional services for eleven adults with severe mental retardation who exhibit challenging behaviors. *American Journal on Mental Retardation, 99,* 533–541.

Lakin, K.C., Hayden, M.F., & Abery, B.H. (1994). An overview of the community living concept. In M.H. Hayden & B.H. Abery (Eds.), *Challenges for a* service system in transition: Ensuring quality community experiences for persons with developmental disabilities (pp. 3–22). Baltimore: Paul H. Brookes Publishing Co.

Larson, S.A., & Lakin, K.C. (1989). Deinstitutionalization of persons with mental retardation: Behavioral outcomes. *Journal of The Association for Persons with Severe Handicaps, 14,* 324–332.

Lewis, D.R., & Bruininks, R.H. (1994). *Costs of community-based residential and related services to individuals with mental retardation and other developmental disabilities.* Baltimore: Paul H. Brookes Publishing Co.

Lowe, K., DePaiva, S., & Felce, D. (1993). Effects of a community-based service on adaptive and maladaptive behaviors: A longitudinal study. *Journal of Intellectual Disability Research, 37,* 3–22.

Lucyshun, J.M., Olson, D., & Horner, R.H. (1995). Building an ecology of support: A case study of one young woman with severe problem behaviors in the community. *Journal of The Association for Persons with Severe Handicaps, 20*(1), 16–30.

Mace, F., Lalli, J.S., & Shea, M.C. (1992). Functional analysis and treatment of self-injury. In J.K. Luiselli, J.L. Matson, & N.N. Singh (Eds.), *Self-injurious behavior: Analysis, assessment, and treatment* (pp. 122–152). New York: Springer-Verlag.

Mansell, J., & Beasely, F. (1993). Small staffed houses for people with a severe learning disability and challenging behaviour. *British Journal of Social Work, 23,* 329–344.

McGee, G.G., Krantz, P.J., & McClannahan, L.E. (1985). The facilitative effects of incidental teaching on preposition use by autistic children. *Journal of Applied Behavior Analysis, 18*(1), 17–32.

McGee, J.J., Menolascino, F.J., Hobbs, D.C., & Menonsek, P.E. (1987). *Gentle teaching: A nonaversive approach to helping persons with mental retardation.* New York: Human Sciences Press.

Meyer, L.H., & Evans, I.M. (1989). *Nonaversive interventions for behavior problems: A manual for home and community.* Baltimore: Paul H. Brookes Publishing Co.

Meyer, L.H., & Evans, I.M. (1993). Evaluating positive approaches to the remediation of challenging behavior. In J. Reichle & D. Wacker (Eds.), *Communicative alternatives to challenging behavior: Vol. 3. Integrating functional assessment and intervention strategies* (pp. 407–428). Baltimore: Paul H. Brookes Publishing Co.

Mount, B. (1994). Benefits and limitations of personal futures planning. In V. Bradley, J. Ashbaugh, & B. Blaney (Eds.), *Creating individual supports for people with developmental disabilities* (pp. 97–108). Baltimore: Paul H. Brookes Publishing Co.

Newton, J.S. (1986). *Validation of a residential outcomes information system.* Unpublished master's thesis, University of Oregon, Eugene.

Newton, J.S., Horner, R.H., Ard, W.R., LeBaron, N., & Sappington, G. (1994). A conceptual model for improving the social life of individuals with intellectual disabilities. *Mental Retardation, 32*(6), 393–402.

Newton, J.S., Stoner, S.K., Bellamy, G.T., Boles, S.M., Horner, R.H., LeBaron, N., Moskowitz, D., Romer, L., Romer, M., & Schlesinger, D. (1988). *Valued Outcomes Information System (VOIS) operations manual.* Eugene: University of Oregon, Center on Human Development.

O'Brien, J. (1987). A guide to lifestyle planning: Using The Activities Catalog to integrate services and natural support systems. In B. Wilcox & G.T. Bellamy (Eds.), *A comprehensive guide to The Activities Catalog* (pp. 175–189). Baltimore: Paul H. Brookes Publishing Co.

O'Neill, R.E., Horner, R.H., Albin, R.W., Storey, K., & Sprague, J.R. (1990). *Functional analysis: A practical assessment guide.* Pacific Grove, CA: Brooks/Cole.

Pyles, D., & Bailey, J.S. (1990). Diagnosing severe behavior problems. In A. Repp & N. Singh (Eds.), *Perspectives on the use of nonaversive and aversive interventions for persons with developmental disabilities* (pp. 381–402). Sycamore, IL: Sycamore.

Reichle, J., & Wacker, D. (Eds.). (1993). *Communicative alternatives to challenging behavior: Integrating functional assessment and intervention strategies.* Baltimore: Paul H. Brookes Publishing Co.

Repp, A.C., Felce, D., & Barton, L.E. (1988). Basing the treatment of stereotypic and self-injurious behaviors on hypotheses of their causes. *Journal of Applied Behavior Analysis, 21,* 281–289.

Repp, A.C., Harman, M.L., Felce, D., Van Acker, R., & Karsh, K.G. (1989). Conducting behavioral assessments on computer-collected data. *Behavioral Assessment, 11,* 249–268.

Repp, A.C., & Singh, N.N. (1990). *Nonaversive and aversive interventions for persons with developmental disabilities.* Sycamore, IL: Sycamore.

Repp, A.C., Singh, N.N., Karsh, K., & Dietz, D. (1991). Ecobehavioral analysis of stereotypic and adaptive behaviors: Activities as setting events. *Journal of Mental Deficiency Research, 35,* 413–429.

Scheerenberger, R. (1990). *Public residential services for the mentally retarded: FY 1988–1989.* Fairfax, VA: National Association of Superintendents of Public Residential Facilities for the Mentally Retarded.

Smith, G. (1994). Paying for supports: Dollars, payments, and the new paradigm. In V. Bradley, J. Ashbaugh, & B. Blaney (Eds.), *Creating individual supports for people with developmental disabilities: A mandate for change at many levels* (pp. 481–490). Baltimore: Paul H. Brookes Publishing Co.

Smull, M., & Danehey, A.J. (1994). Increasing quality while reducing costs: The challenge of the 1990s. In V. Bradley, J. Ashbaugh, & B. Blaney (Eds.), *Creating individual supports for people with developmental disabilities: A mandate for change at many levels* (pp. 59–78). Baltimore: Paul H. Brookes Publishing Co.

Van Houten, R., Axelrod, S., Bailey, J.S., Favell, J.E., Foxx, R.M., Iwata, B., & Lovaas, O.I. (1988). Association for behavior analysis position statement on client's rights to effective behavioral treatment. *Journal of Applied Behavior Analysis, 21,* 381–384.

Vaughn, B.J., & Horner, R.H. (1995). The effects of concrete versus verbal choice systems on problem behavior: A case study. *Augmentative and Alternative Communication.* Manuscript submitted for publication.

Wacker, D., Steege, M.W., Northup, J., Sasso, G., Berg, W., Reimers, T., Cooper, L., Cigrand, K., & Donn, L. (1990). A component analysis of functional communication training across three topographies of severe behavior problems. *Journal of Applied Behavior Analysis, 23,* 417–429.

White, C., Lakin, K., Bruininks, R., & Li, X. (1991). *Persons with mental retardation and related conditions in state-operated residential facilities: Year ending June 30, 1989 with longitudinal trends from 1950–1989.* University of Minnesota, Center for Residential and Community Services, Institute on Community Integration, Minneapolis.

IV

CHALLENGES AT WORK

10

Access to Employment for All Individuals

Legislative, Systems, and Service Delivery Issues

JOHN BUTTERWORTH AND WILLIAM E. KIERNAN

SINCE THE MID-1980s, there has been increasing concern with providing access to employment for all individuals with disabilities. The introduction of supported employment in the 1980s as a service model based on individual supports that continued throughout employment and a philosophy of job placement without prerequisites has dramatically increased the opportunities for employment for persons with the most challenging disabilities (Powell, Pancsofar, Steere, Butterworth, Itzkowitz, & Rainforth, 1991; Wehman & Moon, 1988). Supported employment was first introduced into federal legislation as a model for employment services by the Developmental Disabilities Act Amendments of 1984 (PL 98-527) and then established as a funding stream within the Rehabilitation Act in 1986. The Rehabilitation Act Amendments of 1986 (PL 99-506) specified that supported employment was for "individuals with severe handicaps for whom competitive employment has not traditionally occurred or has been interrupted or intermittent as a result of severe handicaps." This legislation reflects the growing recognition of real work opportunities as a cornerstone in the process of social inclusion, economic self-sufficiency, and personal satisfaction for persons with disabilities. Changes in the technology of employment support have also increased employment opportunities, including the use of on-site supports, job modifications, assistive technology, and consumer-focused planning. Gaining access to employment and vocational training for individuals with disabilities has also been included as a key component of both disability-specific and generic federal legislative initiatives.

Despite these advances in strategies and legislation, supported employment remains a disappointment for individuals with the most challenging disabilities. Since the mid-1980s, the number of persons in supported employment has grown steadily, with recent data showing that an estimated 90,375 persons with disabilities receive supported employment services from the vocational rehabilitation system (Revell, West, Wehman, & Kregel, 1994). McGaughey, Kiernan, McNally, Gilmore, and Keith (1994) report that of the more than 1 million persons with disabilities estimated to be served by community rehabilitation providers, about 30% are in integrated (competitive, supported, and transitional) employment settings. Despite the significant increase in the number of persons with disabilities in real work settings, individuals with the most challenging disabilities largely remain in segregated day and employment settings (Mank, 1994; McGaughey, Kiernan, McNally, & Gilmore, 1993; Wehman & Kregel, 1994).

Addressing employment support for individuals with severe disabilities is dependent upon an understanding of the role and meaning of work to individuals and in our society. Bates (1989) addressed the meaning of work by defining this concept broadly, recognizing the importance of work to the individual and society: "Work should be valued for its contributions to an individual's self sufficiency and for its benefit to the individual's community, regardless of the pay level or the nature of the work itself. By placing greater value on work as a personal and social contribution, there is . . . a greater likelihood that a system that values the unique contributions of all citizens will be created" (pp. 266–267). Bates's point, that access to vocational opportunities cannot be based solely on standards of independence and productivity, also provides a focus for this chapter. The role of employment opportunity must be considered in the context of its contribution to the overall quality of life of the individual, as well as to the well-being of the community.

Access to employment for individuals with severe disabilities requires a creative approach to designing supports and recognizing the meaning of community in the workplace. It also requires respect for the role of employment in an individual's life. In the early years of the supported employment movement, there was a high expectation that employment would result in the development of friendships and inclusion in community life. It has become clear that these goals need to be addressed directly, both within and outside of the workplace. Success in employment must be looked at more broadly than in terms of wages and hours of work, just as employment is but one component that contributes to overall quality of life (Halpern, 1992).

This chapter reviews legislative and service delivery factors that influence access to employment for individuals with disabilities. It begins with a review of the current status and progress of employment for persons with disabilities. A summary of key legislation affecting employment support and training highlights both the legislation and the values behind the shift from a perspective of dependence to independence for persons with disabilities in the work setting. This section on legislative initiatives sets the stage for the third section, which addresses the development of innovative approaches to the provision of supports to individuals with severe disabilities. The final section offers thoughts on the individual and systemic issues that must be faced as the efforts to expand the opportunities for integrated employment for persons with challenging disabilities continue. Basic to this discussion is an assumption that employment in an individual job of a person's choice is both reasonable and the most appropriate goal for all individuals.

CURRENT STATUS OF EMPLOYMENT
FOR PERSONS WITH DISABILITIES

During the 1980s, the philosophy that provided the foundation for day and employment services for individuals with severe disabilities shifted from support of facility-based employment toward integrated, community-based employment with supports. Central to this shift was the realization that job training and support could continue after job entry. This approach, sometimes referred to as "place-train-support," implies that a worker can enter employment without meeting the prerequisites assumed by a more traditional "train-place-support" approach (Rusch & Hughes, 1990). Refinement of supported employment service technologies and changes in the distribution of jobs from a manufacturing to a service base stimulated the movement of individuals with disabilities into integrated jobs. The advantages of integrated employment over segregated day and employment programs for persons with disabilities, families, employers, and society have been well documented (Bellamy, Rhodes, Bourbeau, & Mank, 1986; Kiernan & Stark, 1986; McGaughey et al., 1994; Revell et al., 1994).

Since the mid-1980s, supported employment for persons with disabilities has grown (Revell et al., 1994). Much of this growth is a reflection of the considerable investment at the federal level by the Rehabilitation Services Administration through system change grants to states to establish supported employment service systems and demonstration programs at the local level (McGaughey et al., 1993; Shafer, Revell, & Isbister, 1991; West, Revell, & Wehman, 1992). Wehman, Kregel, and Shafer (1989), in their survey of state vocational rehabilitation agencies, reported a total of 32,342 supported employment participants nationally in fiscal year (FY) 1988. This reported figure jumped to more than 74,000 in FY 1991 from the data received from 42 states and an estimate of more than 90,000 had all states provided data (Revell et al., 1994). Of those served, about two thirds (62.8%) had a diagnosis of mental retardation and 22.2% had a diagnosis of mental illness.

Persons with significant developmental disabilities may more frequently receive services funded by the state mental retardation and developmental disabilities (MR/DD) systems. Studies of state MR/DD agencies reported a similar increase in the use of supported employment services. Of the approximately 312,000 persons served in day and employment programs by the 50 state MR/DD agencies in FY 1990, 16% were reportedly served in supported employment. This reflects a considerable increase from the 10% participation rate in supported employment reported by MR/DD agencies in FY 1988 (McGaughey et al., 1993).

Despite these encouraging statistics, two parallel trends affect access to employment for individuals with challenging disabilities. First, persons with severe disabilities have had limited access to supported employment services. In FY 1990, 72% of the individuals served in integrated employment by community rehabilitation programs (both competitive and supported) had either mild or moderate mental retardation. For those individuals receiving supported employment services through MR/DD agencies in FY 1990, 44% had mild retardation, 28% moderate retardation, and 13% severe or profound retardation (McGaughey et al., 1993). Similar findings were reported by Revell et al. (1994), with the vast majority of persons served in supported employment being individuals with less significant disabilities. The use of supported employment is particularly low for individuals with physical or multiple disabilities. For example, studies report that individuals with cerebral palsy represent only between 1.8% and 3.2% of those in supported or integrated employment (Kiernan, McGaughey, Schalock, & Rowland, 1988; Wehman et al., 1989).

A second disturbing finding is that despite the increase in the number and percentage of individuals in supported employment, there has been very little change in the network of segregated day activity, day treatment, and sheltered employment programs (Mank, 1994). A guiding assumption in the development of supported employment has been that integrated employment options would replace existing sheltered day and employment services. In fact, 82% of the day and employment services provided by MR/DD agencies in FY 1990 were segregated (McGaughey et al., 1993), and the actual number of new individuals entering segregated day and employment services in 1991 is greater than the number entering integrated employment (McGaughey et al., 1994). These data indicate that supported employment is being implemented as an add-on to the existing continuum of day and employment services, rather than as an alternative to segregated services.

A variety of explanations have been provided for the lack of change, including funding issues, lack of trained staff, the considerable investment in fixed assets by community rehabilitation providers, employer and co-worker apprehensions, and the economy. Although each of these may contribute, the challenge for those who advocate the use of supported employment and more broadly integrated employment for persons with disabilities is to seek more creative application of both paid and natural resources for support. This may include reengineering of traditional jobs, involvement of employers and co-workers in the training and support processes, and better incentives for consumers, family members, and service providers to enter integrated employment. Access to the labor market for persons with disabilities is driven, in part, by the effectiveness of disability-specific and civil rights legislation. The following section summarizes the major legislation that can aid the movement from segregated to integrated employment settings for persons with disabilities.

KEY LEGISLATIVE INITIATIVES IN EMPLOYMENT

Access to employment for individuals with disabilities is affected by federal, state, and local legislation and programs. This section offers some views on the values and principles relating to employment policies and practices as they have been articulated in disability rights, education, and rehabilitation legislation since 1990. Table 1 provides an overview of key disability-specific and generic legislation related to employment opportunities that are discussed, along with typical local resources for service delivery. Employment of persons with disabilities is increasingly affected by generic legislation that addresses job training and economic development. This discussion is followed by a presentation of promising practices in employment and then a review of some of the challenges and issues to be addressed from both a systemic and an individual perspective.

Table 1. Employment-related legislation and programs

	Federal legislation and programs	State resources[b]	Local resources[b]
Disability specific	Americans with Disabilities Act (1990)	State vocational rehabilitation agencies	Local schools
	Rehabilitation Act (1992[a])	State disability agencies (e.g., departments of mental retardation or developmental disabilities)	Local rehabilitation service providers
	Individuals with Disabilities Education Act (IDEA) (1990[a])	State antidiscrimination or disability rights legislation (38 states)	
	Technology-Related Assistance for Individuals with Disabilities Act (1988)		
Generic	Carl D. Perkins Vocational and Applied Technology Education Act (1990[a])	State department of employment services	Vocational-technical schools
	Job Training Partnership Act (1992[a])	State education agencies	Private industry councils/ regional employment boards
	School-to-Work Opportunities Act (1993)		Local employment agencies
	Fair Labor Standards Act (1966)		
Income maintenance and health care	Supplemental Security Income (SSI)	State departments of public health or public welfare	
	Social Security Disability Insurance (SSDI)		
	Medicaid		

[a]Most recent amendments
[b]Includes state or local contacts for federal programs

Americans with Disabilities Act of 1990 (PL 101-336)

The passage of the Americans with Disabilities Act (ADA) represents an extension of civil rights legislation to persons with disabilities. The ADA broadly defines *disability* and establishes that persons who have a physical or mental impairment that substantially limits the person in some major life activity cannot be discriminated against in seeking employment, gaining access to public services (e.g., transportation, municipal buildings, parks, and communications), and gaining access to public accommodations (e.g., hotels, restaurants, movies, and recreational resources) and telecommunications services. Although the ADA has been viewed from a compliance perspective, it provides a broad philosophical base for subsequent adult service and education legislation, including the 1990 amendments to the Rehabilitation Act (Cullen & Pappanikou, 1992; Wehman, 1993). The ADA is a statement of beliefs that persons with disabilities are to be accorded the same opportunities as persons who are not disabled, and its emphasis on choice, opportunity, and inclusion will influence the future delivery of supports and the development of services for persons with disabilities.

The essence of the ADA with respect to employment is simple yet elegant. People with disabilities who are qualified to do the essential parts of a job may not be discriminated against in employment solely on the basis of their disability. In this respect, the ADA extends the protections previously afforded since 1973 through Section 504 of the Rehabilitation Act to individuals who work for businesses or organizations that receive federal funding. The principal impact on employment opportunities in the ADA is the requirement that businesses with 15 or more employees make reasonable accommodations to the disabilities of qualified applicants or employees unless undue hardship would result. While the term *reasonable accommodations* has no hard and fast definition, examples may include providing an interpreter during a job interview, altering work schedules, exchanging duties with other workers, or making the workplace physically accessible. The definition of undue hardship will vary based on the size and resources of the company. The ADA encourages employers to consider job modification and job accommodation as well as technology to enhance the fit of the skills of the individual to the requirements of the job.

Summary and Challenges While the prohibition against discrimination in employment provides a powerful philosophical and moral mandate for all individuals with disabilities, the legal mandate for persons with severe disabilities is less clear. The ADA defines qualified applicants as individuals who, with or without reasonable accommodations, can perform the essential functions of a position. Many individuals with severe disabilities will not be able to perform the essential functions of an existing job description and will require a more creative approach that includes job restructuring and job creation.

Rehabilitation Act Amendments of 1992 (PL 102-569)

The Rehabilitation Act provides the largest source of funding and vocational services for individuals with disabilities. Locally, vocational rehabilitation (VR) services are provided through state VR agencies. In the past, access to VR services was limited by the requirement that support be provided to individuals for whom there was a "reasonable" expectation that they could work. The Rehabilitation Act Amendments of 1992 present broad changes for this service delivery system and reaffirm that persons with disabilities have a right to live independently, enjoy self-determination, make choices, contribute to society, pursue meaningful careers, and enjoy full inclusion (see Table 2).

The 1992 amendments to the Rehabilitation Act reconfirm that the focus of rehabilitation services remains the achievement of employment, defined "as entering or retaining full-time or if appropriate part time, competitive employment in the integrated labor market (including satisfying the vocational outcomes of supported employment)" (Section 7[6]). In order to support a personal employment goal, the VR system can provide or can fund a wide variety of assessment, counseling, training, and placement services. Table 3 lists some of the services explicitly authorized by the Rehabilitation Act, which also addresses interagency coordination to support the transition from school to adult life, adopts the definition of transition as noted in IDEA, and strongly encourages the vocational rehabilitation counselor to become involved while the student is still in school (National Transition Net-

Table 2. Rehabilitation Act Amendments of 1992 (PL 102-569): policy statement

It is the policy of the United States that all programs, projects, and activities receiving assistance under this Act shall be carried out in a manner consistent with the principles of:

(1) Respect for individual dignity, personal responsibility, self-determination, and pursuit of meaningful careers, based on informed choice, of individuals with disabilities;

(2) Respect for the privacy, rights, and equal access (including the use of accessible formats) of the individuals;

(3) Inclusion, integration, and full participation of the individuals;

(4) Support for the involvement of a parent, a family member, a guardian, an advocate, or an authorized representative if an individual with a disability requests, desires, or needs such support; and

(5) Support for individual and systemic advocacy and community involvement.

Table 3. Scope of vocational rehabilitation services

The Rehabilitation Act will fund any goods and services necessary to render an individual with a disability employable including, but not limited to:

- Assessment for determining eligibility and vocational rehabilitation needs
- Counseling, guidance, and work-related placement services
- Postemployment services to assist individuals to advance in employment as well as to maintain or regain employment
- On-the-job or other related personal assistance services while an individual is receiving vocational rehabilitation services
- Vocational and other training services
- Physical and mental restoration services including corrective surgery or therapeutic treatment, prosthetic and orthotic devices, eyeglasses and visual services, diagnosis and treatment for mental and emotional disorders
- Interpreter services
- Rehabilitation teaching and orientation and mobility services
- Occupational licenses, tools, equipment, and initial supplies
- Transportation in connection with any vocational rehabilitation service
- Telecommunications, sensory, and other technological aids and devices
- Rehabilitation engineering services

Adapted from the Rehabilitation Act Amendments of 1992, Section 723(a).

work, 1993c). Key components of the Rehabilitation Act and their implications for employment of persons with the most challenging disabilities are briefly summarized in the following sections.

Eligibility for Services An ongoing concern for individuals with severe disabilities has been the lack of access to VR services (Mank, 1994). In a recent survey of United Cerebral Palsy Association (UCPA) affiliates, more than a third of the affiliates found that people with substantial disabilities were nonfeasible for employment (Simpson & Button, 1991). By far the most significant change in the Rehabilitation Act is the *presumption of eligibility*. Section 102(a) of the 1992 amendments states that "it shall be presumed that an individual can benefit in terms of an employment outcome from vocational rehabilitation services, unless the designated state unit can demonstrate by clear and convincing evidence that such individual is incapable of benefiting from vocational rehabilitation services." Previously, it was the responsibility of the individual with a disability to demonstrate a capacity to benefit from rehabilitation services in order to be deemed eligible for services (Kiernan, McGaughey, Lynch, Morganstern, & Schalock, 1991). This new standard shifts the responsibility to the state rehabilitation agency to provide "clear and convincing evidence" that a person is not capable of achieving employment.

Supported Employment The 1986 amendments to the Rehabilitation Act (PL 99-506) provided a definition of supported employment, established a funding stream for demonstration projects, and dedicated funding on the state level for VR services. This state-level funding is commonly known as "Title VIc" services, the section of the act in which it is contained. Some states have interpreted this use of dedicated funds to mean that supported employment could *only* be funded under title VIc, creating an artificial limitation on supported employment services. The 1992 Rehabilitation Act clarifies the intent of the legislation that supported employment may be funded under Title I, the major source of funding in the VR system, and that Title VIc is only supplemental to encourage the development of supported employment services.

Short-Term versus Long-Term Supports   VR provides short-term support for entry into employment, typically for a period of up to 18 months, although funding and follow-up support may last longer. Because supported employment by definition involves ongoing support, and because long-term involvement of a professional source of support is likely for persons with severe disabilities, it is necessary that plans be made to *transfer* funding for supports to other state or local sources such as the state mental retardation or mental health systems. This contingency does not require that the service provider change but that the source of funding change.

VR regulations require that a source for ongoing support be identified in an individualized written rehabilitation plan (IWRP) for individuals in supported employment. The 1992 amendments specify that follow-up supports may include such natural support resources as family, friends, or co-workers. While a strength of the 1992 amendments is the clear recognition of the role of natural supports in successful employment, it would be inappropriate to assume that natural supports alone will be a sufficient level of ongoing support for many individuals. Ongoing involvement of an employment specialist or job coach may be critical to facilitating continued involvement of natural support resources.

Choice   The IWRP establishes the agreement for services and funding support between the state VR agency and an individual. As noted earlier, the 1992 act establishes a clear policy for individual choice and empowerment. Particularly for individuals with severe disabilities, who in the past have been either excluded or routed into facility-based services such as sheltered workshops, this increased attention to the role of choice establishes clear opportunities. In addition to representing the individual's choices, the IWRP must contain a statement in the words of the individual (or, if appropriate, a parent, family member, or other representative) describing the individual's role in being informed about and choosing among alternative goals, objectives, services, and methods. There is also a strengthened mandate to include family and others in helping to identify choices and assisting in the development of plans.

The Rehabilitation Act's emphasis on choice is also reflected in the individual's ability to define an acceptable employment outcome. The original supported employment regulations developed in 1986 limited the access of some people to VR funds by requiring that individuals in supported employment work a minimum of 20 hours. Current regulations have loosened this requirement and allow the hours of work to be determined on an individual basis through the IWRP.

Summary and Challenges   Despite the sometimes limited access to VR services in the past, current legislation provides a clearer right to VR services for persons with severe disabilities. While these changes may take time to become institutionalized, individuals and advocates should be more aggressive about requesting VR supports for individual goals related to employment. The VR system offers an appeals process for reviewing disputes about eligibility or service provision, and an independent Client Assistance Program is available in each state to provide support and advocacy assistance when necessary. Inherent in the new law is also a greater emphasis on identifying individual choices and greater flexibility in defining employment outcomes for the individual.

Individuals with Disabilities Education Act of 1990 (PL 101-476)

The Individuals with Disabilities Education Act (IDEA) refocuses the emphasis of education on the inclusion of students with disabilities in the regular classroom setting whenever possible and changes the language of the legislation to reflect a recognition of the person rather than the disability. IDEA also mandates services for youth with disabilities and families to facilitate the transition from school to adult life and clearly places the responsibility for transition planning on the school district.

Recognizing that about one quarter of a million students with disabilities exit school annually, IDEA addresses the need for transition planning and preparation for the time that the student will no longer be in school by requiring that transition planning begin well before the traditional graduation date for students with disabilities (mandatory at age 16 with a preference for planning to begin at age 14). Perhaps the most significant change is that IDEA establishes a broad scope for the school's role in facilitating and supporting transition to adult life. The law states that transition services must reflect a "coordinated set of activities designed within an outcome oriented process, that promotes movement from school to post-school activities, including post-secondary education, vocational training, integrated employment (including supported employment), continuing and adult education, adult services, independent living, or community participation" (Section 1401[a][19]). The individualized education program (IEP) must address four areas in relation to transition services: instruction, community experiences, employment, and other post-school living objectives (National Transition Network, 1993a).

The role of both the student and the family member in the transition planning process is strengthened, with additional emphasis placed on broad participation and attention to the student's preferences. Special notification of the transition meeting must be sent to the student and family. In addition, linkages to appropriate adult service agencies are to be made by the school, and representatives of adult service agencies are expected to attend meetings that address transition. The family has leverage in asking for a transition planning meeting and expecting that key adult service agency representatives would be present at the time of this meeting (Kahn, Moroldo, Maloney, & Walsh, 1991).

While it is the responsibility of the school to offer a curriculum that will assist the student in achieving individual life goals, IDEA seeks to involve a broad coalition including the student, family, school, and outside agencies in the planning process (National Transition Network, 1993a). IDEA addresses the problem of plans not being implemented by requiring that the school reconvene the team to develop alternative strategies if plans are not proceeding properly (Section 1401[a][20]).

Summary and Challenges Changes to IDEA have placed on the school clear responsibility and accountability for both transition planning and appropriate preparation of students with disabilities for adult life. There remains a need for clarification of several sections of the law, particularly the requirement that schools address failure to implement the transition plan by reconvening the IEP team to develop alternative strategies. However, it is clear that schools are accountable for addressing a wide range of transition needs that include providing direct employment supports in community settings (including supported employment), rehabilitation counseling services, and functional vocational evaluation.

Carl D. Perkins Vocational and Applied Technology Education Act of 1990 (PL 101-392)

There is a growing interest in the generic problem of the transition of all students, particularly students who are not college bound, from school to employment. The Perkins Act, originally enacted as the Carl D. Perkins Vocational Education Act in 1984, is the primary generic source of legislation and federal funding for vocational and technical training, and it provides funding on a per-pupil basis to support state and local vocational education activities, including vocational–technical training programs. It emphasizes vocational preparation, transition from school to work, and education. The act calls for the provision of services to students with disabilities under the heading of special populations, with the definition of *disability* reflected as a physical or mental impairment that substantially limits the person in some major life activity (the same definition used in the Americans with Disabilities Act).

The Perkins Act is unclear about its requirement for full access by students with disabilities. While using the term *full participation* in some sections, the core language affecting eligibility uses the terminology *equitable participation*. The meaning of this contradictory language is still being resolved. Despite the confusion, there is a clear indication that supplementary and other services, including curriculum and equipment modifications, supportive personnel, classroom modifications, and instructional aids and devices, must be provided to ensure student success. The act links the activities of vocational education to those noted in IDEA by requiring vocational education to assist in meeting the IDEA transition requirements. Local schools are also required to provide information to all students with disabilities and their families about vocational education opportunities and the support services available no later than 1 year prior to the customary start of vocational education (but never later than the beginning of ninth grade).

The goal, as in the case of IDEA, is successful completion of a vocational education program in the most integrated setting possible with a clear emphasis on student outcomes rather than the content areas of training. Counseling and guidance supports are to be made available for students as they move through a vocational education program (American Vocational Association, 1990).

Summary and Challenges Vocational education provides a useful option for students who do not intend to pursue higher education. Vocational education programs should include specific career-focused vocational training, academic training, and community-based work experiences (often referred to as cooperative work experiences). Like the vocational rehabilitation system, vocational education has not always been effective at including students with severe disabilities. While the mandate for this in the Perkins Act is unclear, other sources, such as the ADA, provide a more generic requirement for inclusion and accommodation.

Job Training Reform Amendments of 1992 (PL 102-367)

The broad need to prepare both youth and adults to enter a skilled labor force is addressed by the Job Training Reform Amendments (amendment of the Job Training Partnership Act, commonly known as JTPA). The JTPA is also a common source of employment support and training for persons with disabilities. Perhaps most familiar is the Summer Youth Employment Program, which provides paid work experiences in nonprofit and government organizations to disadvantaged youth, although JTPA provides considerable flexibility in how funds are used. In FY 1991, 10.9% of adults and 14.9% of youth served by JTPA funds were individuals with disabilities (National Transition Network, 1993b).

Eligibility JTPA has had as its primary focus serving individuals who are economically disadvantaged and who have significant barriers to employment. The new act, while preserving the economic means test, revises the eligibility criteria for participation such that SSI income is not counted as income in determining eligibility. More notably, the new act recognizes that a person who is disabled but over the age of 18 years should be viewed as an adult and thus a "family of one" even though he or she may still be in a school setting. With this change in accounting for assets, the income of the family is not taken into consideration in determining eligibility for such applicants (National Transition Network, 1993b).

Services JTPA funds can be used for a wide range of training activities and employment supports. Unique to JTPA is that local or regional private industry councils or regional employment boards have considerable authority over the specific programs they fund or offer. This local control provides flexibility to address local economic conditions and needs. While not typically used as a resource for persons with severe disabilities, changes in the act make JTPA-funded programs more useful as a resource. Federal JTPA funds may now be used to support job coaching services. JTPA funding can also be used for other supplemental supports and accommodations to enable the participation of persons with disabilities in program activities. Finally, the act requires that states develop linkages between JTPA services and education services at local and state levels.

Summary and Challenges JTPA funding is primarily managed through local or regional private industry councils or regional employment boards. Because these local councils have a wide range of authority over the specific programs they fund or offer, schools or individuals can initiate or influence the development of programs on a local level. For example, communities have been successful in modifying the Summer Youth Employment Program to emphasize individually designed work experiences and supports rather than group- or crew-based work.

Technology-Related Assistance for
Individuals with Disabilities Act of 1988 (PL 100-407)

Since the mid-1980s, there has been increasing recognition that the development and implementation of assistive technology services have been inconsistent and often confusing. Access to assistive technology services is often difficult, particularly for individuals with limited ability to self-advocate and clearly define their needs and preferences. The result has been both limited use of assistive technology, a high rate of abandonment of assistive devices, and confusion about assessment and identification of appropriate assistive technology interventions (Gradel, 1991; Williams, 1991). In general, the term *assistive technology* refers both to "high-tech" alternatives, such as computer modifications or communication devices, and "low-tech" solutions, such as replacing a manual stapler with an electric stapler.

The Technology-Related Assistance for Individuals with Disabilities Act of 1988 established systems change and demonstration projects to address both access to and quality of assistive technology services. The Tech Act brought into the employment process a view of individual capacities and the creation of work opportunities through the use of assistive technology devices and services at a systemic level. Statewide Tech Act projects have been established to provide information and referral assistance for identifying assistive technology resources and to effect systems change on a state level in the organization and funding of technology services.

The Tech Act calls for an assessment of the needs for technology, a review of the policies related to the use of technology, and identification of funding strategies for technology within a state. Both IDEA and the Rehabilitation Act also address access to assistive technology. For example, IDEA stipulates that local schools must provide assistive technology services and devices that can be used at home and in the work setting as well as in the school. The combined effects of the Tech Act, IDEA, and the Rehabilitation Act bring the application of low and high technology into the transition planning and employment development processes (Aasland, 1992).

Summary and Challenges   Services provided by Tech Act projects vary widely based on the individual state's proposal and priorities. These projects provide an important source of support for information and services that can support individuals with challenging disabilities in employment and are working to influence policy development on a state level. Assistive technology is a critical resource in developing employment opportunities for some individuals with disabilities.

School-to-Work Opportunities Act of 1994 (PL 103-239)

The growing recognition of the role that the workplace plays in the educational process for all students was highlighted in the *Scans Report for America 2000,* a review of work and school preparation for work conducted by the Secretary's Commission on Achieving Necessary Skills at the U.S. Department of Labor (1991b). This report noted that the most effective way of learning skills is in the context within which those skills are to be used. This is a recognition of the need to place learning objectives within a real environment rather than insisting that students first learn in the abstract that which they will be expected to apply in the future in a work setting. Although this report did not specifically address the issue of students with disabilities, there was an acknowledgment that practical learning and application of knowledge is a much more effective way to learn that focusing on prerequisite learning.

The movement toward a more generic system of service delivery continues to be reflected in the School-to-Work Opportunities Act of 1994 (PL 103-239). This legislation considers the problem of movement from school to work for all students and proposes initiatives that would be flexible, locally driven, and require multiple sources and levels of support (federal, state, local, and private). The core areas of activity for the act include *school-based learning* related to career options; *work-based learning* including work experiences, job training, job shadowing, and job mentoring; and *connecting activities* that address participation of employers, parents, community-based organizations, and other entities (Sections 102–104). The act requires that programs be developed by local community-based partnerships that must include schools, postsecondary institutions, employers, organized labor, teachers, and students.

Summary and Challenges As illustrated by the School-to-Work Opportunities Act, employment legislation has moved from proscribing a service in detail through extensive regulations, as in the case of earlier rehabilitation and education legislation, to recognizing the need for individualizing programs such that they meet specific person-centered and community-based needs. This change recognizes that effective development and implementation of services requires involvement of a broad array of community resources. Grassroots efforts are taking a more prominent place in recent legislation.

Generic State and Local Employment Programs

Generic employment training and support are also provided through state departments of employment services. There is a need to incorporate these state and local resources into the employment processes for persons with disabilities. The maintenance of a separate and specialized employment service for persons with disabilities is a practice that should be closely reviewed if the emphasis is on the use of existing structures for persons with disabilities. The focus on individual service delivery in natural settings will require that outcomes for persons with disabilities more closely approximate those for all persons.

CONFLICTING POLICIES IN EMPLOYMENT OF PERSONS WITH DISABILITIES

Along with the growing recognition of the effectiveness of community-based instruction and the acknowledgment that integrated employment is a realistic outcome for persons with the most challenging disabilities, there continue to be related policies and practices that inhibit access to integrated employment. There is continuing confusion over standards for differentiating between an employment relationship that requires wage payment, as defined under the Fair Labor Standards Act (FLSA), and unpaid vocational educational experiences (Simon & Halloran, 1994). A recent memo from the U.S. Department of Education and the Department of Labor has started to clarify this issue by indicating guidelines for community-based training, including vocational exploration, assessment, and training, and providing seven standards that work experiences must meet to waive the wage requirement (U.S. Department of Education, 1992) (also see Simon & Halloran, 1994, for a detailed discussion). However, schools and adult service programs continue to use unpaid work experiences and volunteer experiences that violate the FLSA standards. This problem may be most prevalent with individuals with severe disabilities, where negotiation of wages may be difficult because of productivity and other concerns.

Similar conflicting administrative guidelines exist within the Social Security Administration for Supplemental Security Income (SSI) and even more so for Social Security Disability Insurance (SSDI). SSI and SSDI represent important sources of income support for many individuals with disabilities. Most individuals with severe disabilities are recipients of SSI and/or, more rarely, SSDI. Eligibility for both SSI and SSDI require that a person have a disability and be either not working or earning at a level that is less than what the Social Security

Administration defines as substantial gainful activity.[1] In addition, eligibility for SSI is based on limited income and resources, while SSDI is a disability insurance program provided to people who have paid Social Security taxes (FICA) as a worker for enough years to be covered under Social Security. In most cases, persons with disabilities receive SSDI because they are the dependent of a mother or father who was eligible for SSDI. Eligibility for SSI and SSDI also provides for automatic eligibility for Medicaid (SSI) or Medicare (SSDI) coverage in most states.

Students become eligible for SSI without considering parental income as a family of one at age 18 and possibly earlier, based on family income and resources. It is important to emphasize application for SSI as early as possible, since a substantial work history at a level above the level of substantial gainful activity may demonstrate a capacity to work.

For those persons with disabilities who are already eligible for SSI or SSDI, a major concern is the continuing availability of income supports and medical insurance. Programs commonly known as *work incentive programs* have been developed to encourage individuals to return to work, but the programs are confusing and vary in their availability for SSI and SSDI recipients. (Detailed information on SSI and SSDI work incentive programs is available in the *Red Book on Work Incentives,* available from the Social Security Administration or any local Social Security office [Social Security Administration, 1991].) Those receiving SSI have income support protection and continuing Medicaid eligibility from Sections 1619a and 1619b. Section 1619a allows SSI recipients to continue to receive cash payments even when earned income exceeds the substantial gainful activity level, and it provides for permanent eligibility for SSI even if a recipient is no longer receiving a monthly check so that benefits can be reinstituted at any time if an individual's income changes. SSI is reduced at a rate of $1 for every $2 of earned income. Section 1619b provides ongoing Medicaid eligibility until an individual's annual earned income exceeds the established level or threshold for his or her state (currently over $23,000 in Massachusetts, for example). Several other work incentive programs (Impairment Related Work Expenses—IRWE, and Plans for Achieving Self-Support—PASS) provide opportunity to reduce the impact of earned income on SSI benefits by excluding certain

---

[1]"Performance of significant duties over a reasonable period of time in work for pay or profit (generally earnings) averaging more than $500 per month for non-blind (both SSI and SSDI) and more than $810 per month for those who are blind (SSDI only) in 1991" (Social Security Administration, 1991).

work-related income from SSI calculations and by having specific amounts of funds set aside to accomplish a plan for independence.

Unfortunately, the work incentives for those receiving SSDI are both more complex and less flexible. The IRWE program is available to control the impact of earned income, but there are no programs that guarantee long-term access to eligibility and medical insurance. The SSDI program provides this protection only for a time-limited transition period as individuals enter the workforce.

The federal Medicaid program is intended to meet the health care needs of low-income individuals and families. Medicaid funding has been extended to support residential services for persons with mental retardation since 1971 and to support day services since 1981. Because approximately 50% of Medicaid-covered costs are reimbursed with federal dollars, there has been a strong incentive for states to maximize their use of the Medicaid program for day and residential services. As Medicaid regulations have become more liberal, they have played an increasing role in supporting day and employment services. In fiscal year 1990, 9% of day and employment services provided through state MR/DD agencies were funded through the Medicaid program, and the majority of these funds were used for nonvocational day programs (McGaughey et al., 1993). Because of their origin, and the presumption that the funds are being used to fund active treatment or therapy, Medicaid funds are most often used for individuals with the most challenging disabilities and to support nonwork programs.

The use of Medicaid funds for day and employment services sends a confusing message about persons with challenging disabilities. As a health care service, these funds were originally intended to be medical in nature. States have been able to include vocational services such as supported employment under their Medicaid Waiver only since 1986, and not all states have done so. In fact, data suggest that the greater availability of Medicaid funds for nonvocational services reinforces continued segregation and access to vocational services (McGaughey, Kiernan, Lynch, Schalock, & Morganstern, 1991). Individuals who live in Medicaid funded residences—and, in particular, nursing homes—also are the victims of inconsistent policy. Medicaid regulations restrict the access of these individuals to earned income, attaching income over a small amount to support residential expenses. As a consequence, the individual may, after work-related expenses, have less disposable income than if not working.

Finally, state-level policies have been slow to address significant change in the level of segregated day services. Community rehabilitation providers, having a much longer history of providing segregated programs (both work and nonwork), are sometimes reluctant to change, and staff are often ill prepared to assume the role of a support resource in an integrated setting (Agosta, Brown, & Melda, 1993). Family members and some consumers are likewise apprehensive about having no place to go or nothing to do and thus hold onto less optimal placements in segregated settings in adult years.

These dilemmas are not at all inconsistent with a system of supports and services that is in transition. The following section presents strategies that can be used to overcome some of the problems that providers and consumers face in operationalizing the values and principles espoused in the more recent federal legislation.

PROMISING PRACTICES IN EMPLOYMENT SUPPORTS

Major changes in the approaches to the provision of employment support are beginning to have an impact on access to employment for persons with severe disabilities. A variety of support and funding issues affect an individual's ability to be employed. Even with reasonable accommodation, many individuals are unlikely to be able to perform a significant number of the critical functions of jobs available on the open labor market. These individuals require intensive long-term support to maintain employment. For community employment to be an option, alternatives to 1:1 support from an employment specialist will need to be designed to make that support affordable. Finally, creative approaches meant to clearly identify preferences are necessary to implement opportunities for choices in employment.

Several practices are developing that address these issues. Person-centered planning approaches have emerged as a strategy for clearly identifying an individual's preferences and for engaging a broad range of resources in planning and problem solving. Flexible approaches to job development that emphasize job creation and job restructuring provide a broader focus for the job search. Finally, increasing attention to the role of assistive technology and an increasing recognition of the capacity and role of natural support resources in job training and support have each contributed to expanding access to the full range of community employment opportunities.

Person-Centered Planning

Achieving meaningful employment outcomes for persons with disabilities requires careful attention to both the choices and preferences of the individual, as well as creative use of personal and professional resources and networks to identify opportunities and establish sufficient supports. Traditional approaches to vocational evaluation and service planning have not been effective at supporting the movement of individuals with challenging disabilities into employment or other major life areas. Vocational evaluation often takes place in a simulated environment and is viewed as a separate activity from the job-seeking process (Rogan & Hagner, 1990). Individuals with the most challenging disabilities are frequently found ineligible for employment services (Simpson & Button, 1991). Service planning processes such as the IEP or the IWRP have also not been effective at involving family members or enhancing an individual's connection to a network of supportive community members (Gallivan-Fenlon, 1994; Smith, 1990; Turnbull & Turnbull, 1982) and tend to create linkages to formal, paid resources within the service system rather than to natural support resources or nontraditional resources (Irvin, Thorin, & Singer, 1993; Wesiolowski, 1987).

A variety of alternative approaches to planning, commonly referred to as person-centered planning, have evolved in recent years to provide a more effective forum for the development of person-specific goals and the provision of opportunities for choice and the expression of preferences (O'Brien & Lovett, 1993; Steere, Gregory, Heiny, & Butterworth, 1995). These planning approaches have been referred to variously as whole life planning (Butterworth et al., 1993), MAPS (Vandercook, York, & Forest, 1989), personal futures planning (Mount & Zwernik, 1988), essential lifestyle planning (Smull & Harrison, 1992), and outcome-based planning. These approaches share common principles that include 1) an emphasis on preferences, talents, and dreams of the individual rather than needs or limitations; 2) participation by the person with the disability and family, friends, or other significant people in an ongoing group planning process; 3) defining a vision of the lifestyle the individual would like to have and the goals needed to achieve that vision; 4) identifying the supports and/or services an individual needs to reach personal goals; and 5) organizing resources and supports for the individual that are as local, informal, and generic or nonprofessional as possible to implement plans.

Person-centered planning is designed to lead the individual and participants to an unrestricted vision for a positive future and to develop creative action plans to address personal goals. Organizing a person-centered planning process involves establishing a partnership with a student and his or her family, identifying a structure and format for planning that respects individual preferences, and recruiting participants. It is the personal commitment of each participant that defines a successful process. An organizer or facilitator sets the tone for the dynamic interaction but cannot set the level of commitment; this is up to each of the members of the planning group.

Data suggest that such variables as location and time of meetings will affect participation by family and friends. Attendance at meetings held in the evening or on weekends and in the family home have much greater participation (Butterworth et al., 1993). The facilitator leads the group by setting the agenda and ground rules and by managing interactions among participants so that each person has input and the group maintains a focus on dreams, capacities, and opportunities. The facilitator helps spark creativity and projects a relaxed, comfortable style. The facilitator may be a professional, a friend, a family member, or perhaps an individual in the community skilled in group facilitation or career planning.

Job Creation and Job Restructuring

Many individuals with challenging disabilities require substantial assistance with personal care, social interactions, mobility, and/or job performance. Detailed skill-based approaches to assessment and job matching tend to highlight these limitations and do not effectively emphasize the impact of job-site supports and job accommodations on an individual's ability to perform job tasks. Traditional evaluation also matches individuals to existing job categories as identified in resources such as the Dictionary of Occupational Titles (U.S. Department of Labor, 1991a). A job development approach that emphasizes job creation allows a broader approach to identifying job positions.

Much of the job development in supported employment has followed a job-centered model (Hagner & Daning, 1993). This approach emphasizes identifying an existing job and then using strategies to match a person to the job requirements (cf. Moon, Inge, Wehman, Brooke, & Barcus, 1990). While the job-centered approach is effective for many individuals, it has several disadvantages for individuals with multiple disabilities:

- Existing jobs contain a wide range of duties and require a variety of skills that will often match only some of the skills and physical abilities of the job candidate. In particular, even with the requirement of reasonable accommodations as stated in the ADA, persons with challenging disabilities will rarely be able to perform the essential functions of an existing job.
- Existing jobs have established specifications and production standards as well as employer expectations.
- Competition for jobs often includes a pool of qualified applicants who are interviewing for the same position.

Job creation and job restructuring are methods that combine a company-centered approach (Hagner & Daning, 1993) to job development with a person-centered approach. The company-centered approach looks at the specific needs of a company rather than at existing job openings and offers a flexible approach to meeting those needs. Person-centered job development is guided by individual preferences as defined during the whole life planning process.

Through job creation, a position is created by identifying unmet or poorly met needs in a company and combining them to create a new position. Through job restructuring, existing jobs are modified by eliminating certain tasks or reassigning those tasks to others who have the relevant skills and interests. Job restructuring can also involve modifying working conditions, such as work schedules, task sequences, or work area organization. Job creation and job restructuring are strategies that both require a more skillful and systematic approach to job development. The process often takes longer than traditional job development and entails developing a relationship with the employer and understanding the specific needs and culture of the business. Once positive relationships have been established, employers are often more willing to explore and discuss business needs, and they are more flexible about considering innovative ways of meeting those needs.

Assistive Technology

Assistive technology refers to objects or devices that assist an individual in completing a task or activity more effectively or independently. Included is a wide range of possible solutions, from generically available tools and devices such as electric staplers or a high-intensity light, to specialized adaptive equipment such as augmentative communication devices or computer adaptations. The majority of assistive devices are readily available and inexpensive, and current data suggest that the cost to employers of providing accommodations has not been high (Button & Wobschall, 1994).

Access to related employment supports such as assistive technology is a problem for persons with challenging disabilities. In a survey conducted by United Cerebral Palsy Associations, two thirds of the affiliates reported problems in including assistive technology in IWRPs (Simpson & Button, 1991). Considerable attention has been paid in recent years to expanding access to assistive technology for persons with disabilities. However, approaches to assistive technology intervention continue to emphasize the functional limitations of individuals with disabilities rather than modifying environmental variables. Assistive technology service providers also often emphasize high-technology solutions such as computers and custom-designed devices such as workstations. These interventions require highly specialized service providers, tend to be center based, and often require long waiting periods that are not responsive to the needs of a job opportunity.

Natural Supports

An important recent development in employment services for individuals with severe disabilities has been an increased emphasis on involving natural sources of support in the process of finding and maintaining employment. Natural sources of support include an individual's network of family and friends, co-workers and supervisors, and generic community resources such as churches, employment agencies, or service clubs (Nisbet, 1992). Such natural supports may occur spontaneously or may be facilitated through human service facilitation or consultation (Hagner & DiLeo, 1993; Murphy et al., 1993).

Initially, the primary approach to community employment support for persons with severe disabilities was the use of a job coach or employment specialist (Powell et al., 1991; Wehman & Moon, 1988). The job coach assumed responsibility for employment training and ensured that a job was being performed to company standards. Once the job was mastered, the job coach reduced the amount of support to a level designed to ensure the individual's continued employment. Recent data suggest that, in some instances, the very presence and role of the job coach may distance the individual with disabilities from co-workers, creating an aura of separate status for the individual and interfering with naturally occurring social relationships in the workplace (Curl & Chisholm, 1991; Hagner, 1992; Udvari-Solner, 1990). At the same time, there is increasing documentation of the capacity of internal workplace resources to provide a greater level of support than was originally assumed (Baumgart & Askvig, 1992; Fabian & Luecking, 1991; Mank, Oorthuys, Rhodes, Sandow, & Weyer, 1992).

Having a well-developed social network that includes friends and membership in social groups is an important outcome of special education and rehabilitation services (DeStefano & Wagner, 1993). Social relationships play an essential role in the personal and work adjustment of individuals with and without disabilities, and they have important implications for job satisfaction and stability (House, 1981; Kiernan, Schalock, Butterworth, & Sailor, 1993; O'Connor, 1983; Romer & Heller, 1983). In the context of employment, for example, the majority of typical jobs are obtained through personal resources such as family, friends, or acquaintances (Silliker, 1993).

Family involvement is an important contributing factor to an individual's employment status (Lichtenstein & Michaelides, 1993). Family and friend networks contribute in concrete ways to employment success through such supportive activities as assisting with career planning, providing job leads, supporting job search efforts, and providing support to maintain employment (Knox & Parmenter, 1993; Lin & Dumin, 1986; O'Brien & Lovett, 1993; Silliker, 1993). On the job, co-worker involvement can play a role in learning a job and achieving social acceptance (Hagner, Cotton, Goodall, & Nisbet, 1992; Park et al., 1991). Employers possess knowledge and resources that can be effective sources of support for employees (Baumgart & Askvig, 1992; Rhodes, Sandow, Mank, Buckley, & Albin, 1991). Social inclusion and natural workplace support may also influence co-worker and supervisor satisfaction with an employee (Butterworth & Strauch, 1994). In addition, the workplace can be an important source of new social relationships (Barber & Hupp, 1993).

While adequate support may develop spontaneously in some situations, intervention of some kind may be required in other situations in order to maximize the support potential of families, co-workers, and others in the community. The importance of the role of natural supports to employment has been recently emphasized in the Rehabilitation Act Amendments of 1992. These amendments specifically address the role of family and friends in the rehabilitation process and establish natural supports as a recognized source of follow-up support.

A number of strategies have been proposed to facilitate involvement of families and workplace personnel in transition and job support (e.g., Brotherson et al., 1988; Gallivan-Fenlon, 1994; McDonnell, Hardman, & Hightower, 1989). Person-centered planning approaches that emphasize the involvement of family and friends have been applied to transition and career planning (Butterworth et al., 1993; O'Brien & Lovett, 1993). And several strategies have been proposed for involving natural supports in the workplace. For example, Fabian, Edelman, and Leedy (1992) described a project that incorporates both direct and indirect intervention strategies to secure employer support, and Rogan, Hagner, and Murphy (1993) documented several case examples of natural supports facilitation strategies. Taliaferro, Sandow, and Rhodes (1993) described a training and problem-solving support process for co-workers in a manufacturing company to provide job supports to workers with severe disabilities. Selected strategies that have been proposed for involving natural workplace resources in employment support are summarized in Table 4.

Despite the availability of examples of companies providing substantial supports to workers with severe disabilities (Sowers, 1991; Taliaferro et al., 1993), severity of disability is seen by some as precluding the use of natural supports or as more appropriate for individuals with mild or moderate disabilities (Smith, Belcher, Juhrs, & Nabors, 1994; Hagner, Butterworth, & Keith, 1995). Further expansion of the use of

Table 4. Strategies for facilitating natural supports

	Direct strategies	Indirect strategies
Individual	Create, restructure, or modify job for social inclusion	Train to use effective self-advocacy in the workplace
	Teach participation in informal routines (e.g., sharing in coffee making)	Use personal connections to identify jobs
Individual co-worker/supervisor	Adopt a consultant role: facilitate problem solving by workplace staff	Facilitate mentor assignment
	Arrange for co-workers and supervisor to provide orientation and job training	Seek jobs with a social culture compatible to the individual
	Train co-workers to use systematic instruction	Foster understanding of employee
	Identify commonalities (matchmaking), assist employee to share hobbies and interests	
Job design/environment	Reorganize work tasks/job to ensure time for co-worker/supervisor training and support	Analyze workplace culture
	Build in overlapping or intersecting (cooperative) tasks	Choose high status, low turnover workplaces (stable workforce for support continuity)
	Allow flexibility in job duties	Target shared or similar positions
	Incorporate social times into work schedule	
Group or corporate interventions	Consult regarding adaptation of company training programs	Provide training to address attitude changes (e.g., communication skills training, discussion groups regarding myths and stereotypes regarding disability in the workplace)
	Provide funding to company to compensate for additional training and support responsibilities	Include systematic instruction training in generic workplace training programs (indirect)
	Assess company training and support resources during job development	Expand role of employee assistance programs
		Expand scope of company-sponsored diversity initiatives

Adapted from Fabian, Edelman, and Leedy (1993). See also Fabian et al. (1992); Hagner and DiLeo (1993); Hagner, Rogan, and Murphy (1992); Mank et al. (1992); Murphy and Rogan (1994).

natural support resources will be essential to ensuring that individuals with the most challenging disabilities can gain access to employment in a manner that both provides high-quality outcomes to the individual and is affordable and manageable for the human services system.

Promising practices in supported employment for persons with disabilities include an emphasis on person-centered planning and the use of natural support. For those with more challenging disabilities, there is a greater need to look at the use of assistive technology approaches as well as such strategies as job creation and job restructuring, given the unique skills, interests, and needs of these persons. With more creative use of existing resources and the development of adaptations that will both modify the tasks and enhance the abilities of the individual to perform the essential functions of the job, the role of supported employment for persons with challenging disabilities will grow. The final section presents some of the challenges to expanding the use of supported employment for persons with challenging disabilities.

ISSUES AND FUTURE DIRECTIONS

Federal legislative intent clearly encourages personal choice, consumer control, and inclusion of persons with disabilities at all levels. Strategies for assisting persons with challenging disabilities in gaining access to and maintaining employment have been demonstrated. However, the data continue to note the lack of persons with challenging disabilities in integrated employment. This section considers some of the issues and challenges that need to be addressed if employment options are to become a reality for all persons with disabilities.

This section is divided into two subsections: individually focused issues and systemic challenges. These issues and challenges must be addressed if the full intent of the legislation noted earlier in this chapter is to be realized.

Individual Issues in Employment

Limited Expectations and Lack of Experience Because individuals with the most challenging disabilities have had limited experiences in integrated settings, the identification of true personal interests is often difficult. In the 1980s, the expectations were that a caring and protective setting would be the most appropriate, so there was little effort to provide opportunities for persons with challenging disabilities to develop work experiences. With the individual who is disabled as the central element in the development of a life plan, there needs to be an acknowledgment of this absence of previous work experience and the development of strategies that will provide individuals with opportunities to gain firsthand work experiences. This does not mean that prior to placement in a job there must be a series of work experiences, but rather in the planning process there must be a recognition that personal dreams and wishes may be limited and expressed interests may change as additional experiences in employment are developed. Any planning process must thus be dynamic and person focused. Review and revision of the goals of a whole life plan should be done as needed with the involvement of the individual and other interested parties.

With the recognition of the importance of the employment experience for persons with challenging disabilities, educational curricula often will include experiences in work settings prior to leaving school. The mandates of IDEA require that transition planning begin no later than 16 years of age and preferably as young as 14 years of age, and encourage the adoption of secondary curricula that provide real employment experiences as part of the school experience. Those students who are exiting schools or have exited schools over the past decade have benefited from such community-based work curricula. Their expectations and those of their parents and family members reflect work as an anticipated outcome of the school-to-adult-life transition process.

Consumer-Focused Planning Past planning efforts, as in the case of the IWRP and the individualized service plan (ISP), while focusing on the individual, frequently do not have the individual present and often look at fitting the needs of the individual into the available service options in the area. Such plans reflect a narrow focus and are viewed as a one-time or an annual planning effort. The whole life or futures planning effort is a dynamic process that involves nontraditional participants in the planning effort (family, friends, and other invited community participants) and considers interests and aspirations rather than needs and limitations. The outcome of such a planning process is one that is comprehensive and individually designed, not around what is available in the current service delivery system, but around what resources exist in the community and how these resources can be used or redesigned to meet an individual interest.

Flexibility in Resources Person-centered planning efforts can serve to reinforce the issue of consumer choice and also involve naturally occurring supports in the implementation of the plan. What is often lacking is the flexibility in the use of monies to support nontraditional outcomes. Discussions about the use of vouchers or payment to consumers who in turn seek out desired supports have been a topic of interest in many states. Vouchers are a way of creating supports that are more flexible and can be used in ways that will meet individual interests rather than fill community program slots. Although much investigation relative to the use of more flexible supports and the outcomes realized through the use of such strategies is necessary, for the person with significant disabilities the impediment to realizing a dream or interest is often a reflection of inflexible monies to support individual choice and preference. There is also a growing interest in the use of direct payment to co-workers and employers to compensate for training and support expenses (Nisbet & Hagner, 1988).

Coordination of Interests Across Major Life Areas Concern about the coordination of the major life area interests as in the case of community living, employment, and recreation is often expressed by family members and consumers. Frequently, the needs in one life area are addressed apart from other needs. For those individuals in community living settings, there is often little coordination of programs and supports across life areas. The support resources in the community living setting have no knowledge of the nature or extent of the support services being provided in the work setting. More integration of both the planning and service implementation effort is required if we are to be successful at responding to the needs and interests of the whole person.

Loss of Benefits A major concern on the part of family members and consumers is the possible loss of health and cash benefits. The security of these benefits received under SSI and SSDI through Social Security has served to discourage persons with disabilities from entering employment. The work incentives available through the SSI program are one strategy for reducing the risk of loss benefits should the individual become employed. Unfortunately, as was noted earlier in this chapter, the work incentives available in the SSDI program are less effective. It is not uncommon to find that jobs sought for persons with disabilities do not provide benefits, so the concern about loss of Medicaid is a real concern. Expansion of work incentives to include those on SSDI would go a long way in reducing some of the concern about loss of Social Security benefits when a person with disabilities enters work.

The concerns noted are those that are often raised by consumers and family members when considering employment. In many ways these concerns reflect the fragmented system of supports and services for persons with disabilities as they enter employment. Many of these concerns could be addressed with a more coordinated planning and implementation process for the individual with disabilities and a more comprehensive system of supports that could be used by the individual. The following section examines some of the systemic challenges to expanding employment options for persons with challenging disabilities.

Systemic Challenges to Employment

Funding Much of the support for employment services from both the federal and state sources is currently used to maintain segregated work and nonwork settings (McGaughey et al., 1993). The use of monies at all levels should reflect the intent of the federal legislation in that resources should be directed at the development and maintenance of integrated employment (competitive and supported). Through the Home and Community Based Waivers under Medicaid, supported employment services are an option, but only for those individuals who are leaving institutions or are at risk of institutionalization. Greater flexibility in the use of Medicaid resources and an expansion of the target audience is needed. As long as the federal government reimburses states for the provision of segregated outcomes, there is minimal incentive for state governments to develop real work options for persons with challenging disabilities at a time when state budgets are shrinking.

State support, in the form of purchase of service, likewise has and continues to focus on the role of segregated day and employment outcomes (McGaughey et al., 1994). Through performance contracting, where a percentage of persons are to be served in integrated settings, state MR/DD agencies can significantly influence the practices of community-based rehabilitation providers. If the intent of the ADA and the Rehabilitation Act is to be realized, state agencies must develop strategies for requiring providers of services to develop integrated employment and must have a mechanism for reimbursing those providers in more flexible fashions (hourly or daily rather than on an annual "slot" basis). In addition to a direct payment to individuals through the voucher system noted previously, there is a need to have a way of reimbursing providers and co-workers for actual costs of supports provided in real work settings. This more flexible reimbursement and the requirement of integrated employment, as in the case of performance contracting, provides sufficient flexibility and incentive to develop and maintain integrated employment options for persons with challenging disabilities.

A number of individuals who enter supported employment will exit this service at some point in time. McGaughey et al. (1994) noted that those who exit (about 40% of those who entered supported employment in 1991) will exit either as a result of no longer needing the supports (25%) or as a result of quitting or job termination (70%). For those individuals, about one third will return to integrated employment, one third will enter sheltered employment, and one third will become unemployed. For those individuals who need job site supports or job placement assistance but are "closed" to rehabilitation services or not in a funded "slot" from the state MR/DD agency, 7 out of 10 served received services through the provider funds rather than through the state agency funds. More flexibility is critical in providing supports to those already employed who need some on-site assistance or job development as a result of a job termination.

Flexibility in funding can create an incentive for consumers and providers to look to the use of natural supports in employment. Gaining access to those supports and resources available to all employees can aid the development of a more inclusive setting for the worker with a disability as well as more creatively use fiscal resources. While reduction in support costs may in some cases be a product of successful involvement of natural support resources, the primary role of natural supports is as a strategy for creating a more inclusive environment for the employee. Direct payment to compensate co-workers, employers, or family and friends for providing work-related supports may also be a cost-effective way of meeting the extraordinary support needs of some individuals with challenging disabilities. Providing long-term 1:1 (or higher) levels of staffing at a job site will provide a strong disincentive for supporting individuals in community jobs. Alternative support structures will need to be developed.

Funding remains one of the major concerns that must be addressed if consumer involvement, choice, and community inclusion are to be outcomes of the employment process. It is not an issue of more monies but rather a redirection of resources and a more creative utilization of natural supports that must be addressed. Monies currently allocated to support segregated outcomes must be redirected toward integrated employment, and flexibility in the use of fiscal resources is essential if persons with challenging disabilities are to be supported in real work.

Staff Training The limited experience and capacity of supported employment staff have also served to restrict the employment options for persons with severe disabilities. Direct support staff working in community-based employment support often have little training in integrated employment for persons with severe disabilities, and they receive limited compensation. Agosta et al. (1993) found that of those individuals who have taken on the role of job coach or employment training specialist, less than half received more than 8 hours of training before assuming responsibilities in a supported employment setting. Over a third of these staff list high school as their highest level of education, and about 40% earn less than $16,000 per year (Agosta et al., 1993). With minimal orientation to the principles of supported employment and little training in the strategies of on-site training and job modification, many persons who are filling the role as job coaches are ill prepared. Formal training and ongoing supervision and support are essential for staff who are often asked to be independent, creative, and knowledgeable in both job duties and disability issues. Although training competencies for such a position have been identified, little formal training is provided to these front-line staff.

Training is not necessarily a one-sided issue. There is a need to support persons with disabilities as they assume the role of managing their support systems. Preparing persons with disabilities to take over the management of their support services will be necessary. This concept is not new and has been identified as a need in the area of personal assistance services for persons with physical disabilities. If consumers are to be provided opportunities to develop, implement, and manage those plans relating to their future goals, then a more formal process of preparing and at times assisting persons with disabilities in accomplishing this task will need to be developed.

Quality of Life   As we move toward person-centered planning, consumer control, natural supports, and inclusion, there will be a need to examine the impact of these processes on the consumer and the quality of life that the consumer realizes. Much of the investigation in the areas of employment has considered such issues as earnings, benefits, hours worked, and occupational activities with little investigation of the changes in the quality of life of the individual as a result of employment. In addition, no studies to date have examined the impact of person-centered planning processes on the consumer either quantitatively or qualitatively. Consideration of the impact of approaches and interventions on the individual will be a thrust for research in the years to come.

The research agenda for the future must identify strategies for facilitating the inclusion and social acceptance in the workplace of the person with challenging disabilities. The simple presence in an integrated work setting does not ensure that the worker will become part of the social network. Strategies that demonstrate effective ways of including co-workers and the person with a disability in the culture of the workplace will need to be developed, evaluated, and disseminated. There is a growing awareness that effective job placement must include not only the matching of the skills and interests of the individual to the duties and expectations of the job but also to the culture of the workplace.

The recognition of the use of those resources and supports that are inherent in work and community settings, referred to as natural supports, has opened up a new and growing area of investigation. The role of natural supports and the strategies for developing support networks are areas that research is just beginning to examine. The principles associated with inclusion require that access is gained to the natural supports and typical resources and that there be a concerted effort at incorporating those supports into the adjustment and social acceptance of persons with severe disabilities in the work setting.

From a systemic perspective, there is a growing need to look at what factors contribute to the development of programs or services directed at enabling persons with severe disabilities to move from school to real work, segregated settings in sheltered workshops to regular jobs, and from nonwork day habilitation programs into paid employment. The issues of program conversion have been discussed for some time, yet little has been done to examine on a more systematic basis what factors will influence the program conversion process.

The research agenda for the future will reflect the efforts of agencies, programs, family members, and, most important, persons with disabilities in identifying ways to focus the efforts on the interests and goals of the individual while incorporating the community resources into both the planning and implementation process. Better strategies for creating inclusive settings for persons with disabilities must be developed through more systematic investigation of approaches, strategies, and methods of empowering persons with disabilities to take control of those events and activities that will influence their lives in the years to come. The concepts of inclusion, choice, and empowerment must be taken in the context of reasonable risk, flexible resources, and individual service delivery.

SUMMARY

This chapter presented an overview of the status of employment of persons with disabilities and a perspective on the employment of persons with the most severe disabilities. Despite legislative mandates, the current system continues to focus on how to fit the person into an existing slot rather than the identification of a unique approach to responding to an expressed interest on the part of the individual. The emphasis on choice, inclusion, and person-specific planning will require that the current system revise the way monies are allocated, plans are developed and implemented, and impacts are assessed. The use of a person-centered planning approach, the adoption of flexible funding patterns, and the recognition of qualitative outcomes such as issues of individual satisfaction and changes in quality of life are the challenges that the system will face as it moves toward the values articulated in the ADA.

For the family and the individual with disabilities, the future holds opportunity and choice but also responsibility and a level of risk. A more flexible person-centered system using all available community resources with the intent of creating a more inclusive life for the person with a disability is the outcome that must be sought. The employment future for persons with the most severe disabilities can and will be substantially increased when the planning is driven by the interests and needs of the individual, when the implementation approaches reflect the use of those natural resources within the community and the workplace, and when the utilization of assistive technologies and flexible supports is common practice rather than the exception. Persons with severe disabilities can be employed in real jobs when effective planning and adequate supports are available.

REFERENCES

Aasland, E. (1992). Transition to postsecondary opportunities and assistive technology: Policy overview and recommendations. *Technology and Disability, VI*(2), 73–77.

Agosta, J., Brown, L., & Melda, K. (1993). *Job coaching and community integrated employment: Present conditions and emerging directions*. Salem, OR: Human Services Research Institute.

American Vocational Association (AVA). (1990). *The AVA guide to the Carl D. Perkins Vocational and Applied Technology Education Act of 1990*. Alexandria, VA: Author.

Americans with Disabilities Act of 1990 (ADA), PL 101–336. (July 26, 1990). Title 42, U.S.C. 12101 et seq: *U.S. Statutes at Large, 104*, 327–378.

Barber, D., & Hupp, S. (1993). A comparison of friendship patterns of individuals with developmental disabilities. *Education and Training in Mental Retardation, 28*(1), 13–22.

Bates, P. (1989). Vocational training for persons with profound disabilities. In F. Brown & D. Lehr (Eds.), *Persons with profound disabilities: Issues and practices* (pp. 265–293). Baltimore: Paul H. Brookes Publishing Co.

Baumgart, D., & Askvig, B. (1992). Job-related social interventions: Suggestions from managers and employees. *Education and Training in Mental Retardation, 27*, 345–353.

Bellamy, G.T., Rhodes, L., Bourbeau, P., & Mank, D. (1986). Mental retardation services in sheltered workshops and day activity programs: Consumer benefits and policy alternatives. In F.R. Rusch (Ed.), *Competitive employment issues and strategies* (pp. 257–271). Baltimore: Paul H. Brookes Publishing Co.

Brotherson, M.J., Turnbull, A.P., Bronicki, G.J., Houghton, J., Roeder-Gordon, C., Summers, J.A., & Turnbull, H.R. (1988). Transition into adulthood: Parental planning for sons and daughters with disabilities. *Education and Training in Mental Retardation, 23*, 165–174.

Butterworth, J., Hagner, D., Heikkinen, B., Faris, S., DeMello, S., & McDonough, K. (1993). *Whole life planning: A guide for organizers and facilitators*. Boston: Institute for Community Inclusion, Children's Hospital.

Butterworth, J., & Strauch, J. (1994). The relationship between social competence and success in the competitive work place for persons with mental retardation. *Education and Training in Mental Retardation, 29*(2), 118–133.

Button, C., & Wobschall, R. (1994). The Americans with Disabilities Act and assistive technology. *Journal of Vocational Rehabilitation, 4*(3), 196–201.

Carl D. Perkins Vocational and Applied Technology Education Act of 1990, PL 101–392. (September 25, 1990). Title 20, U.S.C. 12301 et seq: *U.S. Statutes at Large, 104,* 753.

Cullen, J.P., & Pappanikou, A.J. (1992). Postsecondary transition to employment and the Americans with Disabilities Act: An annotated bibliography. *Journal of Postsecondary Education and Disability, 10*(1), 24–28.

Curl, R., & Chisholm, L.A. (1991). *Unlocking co-worker potential in competitive employment: Keys to a cooperative approach.* Unpublished manuscript. Utah State University, Logan.

DeStefano, L., & Wagner, M. (1993). Outcome assessment in special education: Implications for decision making and long term planning in vocational rehabilitation. *Career Development for Exceptional Individuals, 16*(2), 147–158.

Developmental Disabilities Act of 1984, PL 98-527. (October 19, 1984). Title 42, U.S.C. 6000 et seq.: *U.S. Statues at Large, 98,* 2662–2685.

Fabian, E.S., Edelman, A., & Leedy, M. (1993). Linking workers with severe disabilities to social supports in the workplace: Strategies for addressing the barriers. *Journal of Rehabilitation, 58,* 29–34.

Fabian, E.S., & Luecking, R.G. (1991). Doing it the company way: Using internal company supports in the workplace. *Journal of Applied Rehabilitation Counseling, 22*(2), 32–35.

Gallivan-Fenlon, A. (1994). "Their senior year": Family and service provider perspectives on the transition from school to adult life for young adults with disabilities. *Journal of The Association for Persons with Severe Handicaps, 19*(1), 11–23.

Gradel, K. (1991). Customer service: What is its place in assistive technology and employment services? *Journal of Vocational Rehabilitation, 1*(2), 41–54.

Hagner, D. (1992). The social interactions and social supports of supported employees. In J. Nisbet (Ed.), *Natural supports in school, at work, and in the community for people with severe disabilities* (pp. 217–239). Baltimore: Paul H. Brookes Publishing Co.

Hagner, D., Butterworth, J., & Keith, G. (1995). Strategies and barriers in facilitating natural supports for employment of adults with severe disabilities. *Journal of The Association for Persons with Severe Handicaps, 20*(2), 110–120.

Hagner, D., Cotton, P., Goodall, S., & Nisbet, J. (1992). The perspectives of supportive coworkers: Nothing special. In J. Nisbet (Ed.), *Natural supports at home, work, and in the community for people with severe disabilities* (pp. 241–256). Baltimore: Paul H. Brookes Publishing Co.

Hagner, D., & Daning, R. (1993). Opening lines: How job developers talk to employers. *Career Development for Exceptional Individuals, 16*(2), 123–134.

Hagner, D., & DiLeo, D. (1993). *Working together: Workplace culture, supported employment, and persons with disabilities.* Brookline, MA: Brookline Books.

Hagner, D., Rogan, P., & Murphy, S. (1992). Facilitating natural supports in the workplace: Strategies for support consultants. *Journal of Rehabilitation, 58*(1), 29–34.

Halpern, A.S. (1992). Transition: Old wine in new bottles. *Exceptional Children, 58*(3), 202–211.

House, J.S. (1981). *Work stress and social support.* Reading, MA: Addison-Wesley.

Individuals with Disabilities Education Act of 1990, PL 101-476. (October 30, 1990). Title 20, U.S.C. 1400 et seq: *U.S. Statutes at Large, 104* (Part 2), 1103–1151.

Irvin, L., Thorin, E., & Singer, H. (1993). Family-related roles and considerations: Transition to adulthood by youth with developmental disabilities. *Journal of Vocational Rehabilitation, 3*(2), 38–46.

Job Training Reform Amendments of 1992, PL 102-367. (Sept. 7, 1992). Title 29, U.S.C. 1501 et seq: *U.S. Statutes at Large, 106*, 1022.

Kahn, K.F., Maroldo, R.A., Maloney, M.H., & Walsh, S. (1991). *Individuals with Disabilities Education Act of 1990.* Horsham, PA: LPR Publishing.

Kiernan, W.E., McGaughey, M., Schalock, R., & Rowland, S. (1988). *National survey on employment of adults with developmental disabilities.* Boston: Training and Research Institute for Adults with Disabilities, Children's Hospital.

Kiernan, W.E., McGaughey, M.J., Lynch, S., Morganstern, D., & Schalock, R. (1991). *National survey of day and employment programs for persons with developmental disabilities.* Boston: Training and Research Institute for People with Disabilities, Children's Hospital.

Kiernan, W.E., Schalock, R.L., Butterworth, J., & Sailor, W. (1993). *Enhancing the use of natural supports for people with severe disabilities.* Boston: Training and Research Institute for People with Disabilities (UAP), Children's Hospital.

Kiernan, W.E., & Stark, J. (Eds.). (1986). *Pathways to employment for adults with developmental disabilities.* Baltimore: Paul H. Brookes Publishing Co.

Knox, M., & Parmenter, T.R. (1993). Social networks and support mechanisms for people with mild intellectual disability in competitive employment. *International Journal of Rehabilitation, 16*, 1–12.

Lichtenstein, S., & Michaelides, N. (1993). Transition from school to young adulthood: Four case studies of young adults labelled mentally retarded. *Career Development for Exceptional Individuals, 16*(2), 183–195.

Lin, N., & Dumin, M. (1986). Access to occupations through social ties. *Social Networks, 8*, 365–385.

Mank, D. (1994). The underachievement of supported employment: A call for reinvestment. *Journal of Disability Policy Studies, 5*(2), 1–24.

Mank, D., Oorthuys, J., Rhodes, L., Sandow, D., & Weyer, T. (1992). Accommodating workers with mental disabilities. *Training and Development Journal, 46*(1), 49–52.

McDonnell, J., Hardman, M.L., & Hightower, J. (1989). Employment preparation for high school students with severe handicaps. *Journal of The Association for Persons with Severe Handicaps, 27*(6), 396–405.

McGaughey, M., Kiernan, W., McNally, L., & Gilmore, D. (1993). *National perspectives on integrated employment: State MR/DD agency trends.* Boston: Training and Research Institute for People with Disabilities, Children's Hospital.

McGaughey, M., Kiernan, W.E., Lynch, S.A., Schalock, R.L., & Morganstern, D.R. (1991). *National survey of day and employment programs for persons with developmental disabilities: Results from state MR/DD agencies.* Boston:

Training and Research Institute for People with Disabilities, Children's Hospital.

McGaughey, M.J., Kiernan, W.E., McNally, L.C., Gilmore, D.S., & Keith, G.R. (1994). *Beyond the workshop: National perspectives on integrated employment.* Boston: Institute for Community Inclusion (UAP).

Moon, M.S., Inge, K.J., Wehman, P., Brooke, V., & Barcus, J.M. (1990). *Helping persons with severe mental retardation get and keep employment.* Baltimore: Paul H. Brookes Publishing Co.

Mount, B., & Zwernik, K. (1988). *It's never too early, it's never too late: A booklet about personal futures planning.* Mears Park Centre, MN: Metropolitan Council.

Murphy, S., & Rogan, P. (1994). *Developing natural supports in the workplace: A manual for practitioners.* Saint Augustine, FL: Training Resource Network, Inc.

Murphy, S., Rogan, P., Olney, M., Sures, M., Dague, B., & Kalina, N. (1993). *Developing natural supports in the workplace: A manual for practitioners.* Syracuse, NY: Center on Human Policy, Syracuse University.

National Transition Network. (1993a). IDEA: Its impact on transition regulations. *Policy Update, Winter.*

National Transition Network. (1993b). Job Training Reform Amendments of 1992: Expanded opportunities for youth and adults with disabilities. *Policy Update, Spring.*

National Transition Network. (1993c). Rehabilitation Act Amendments. *Policy Update.*

Nisbet, J. (Ed.). (1992). *Natural supports at home, work, and in the community for people with severe disabilities.* Baltimore: Paul H. Brookes Publishing Co.

Nisbet, J., & Hagner, D. (1988). Natural supports in the workplace: A reexamination of supported employment. *Journal of The Association for Persons with Severe Handicaps, 13*(4), 260–267.

O'Brien, J., & Lovett, H. (1993). *Finding a way toward everyday lives: The contribution of person centered planning.* Harrisburg: Pennsylvania Office of Mental Retardation.

O'Connor, G. (1983). Social support of mentally retarded persons. *Mental Retardation, 21,* 187–196.

Park, H., Simon, M., Tappe, P., Wozniak, T., Johnson, B., & Gaylord-Ross, R. (1991). Effects of a coworker advocacy program and social skills training on the social interaction of employees with mild disabilities. *Journal of Vocational Rehabilitation, 1*(4), 73–90.

Powell, T.H., Pancsofar, E.L., Steere, D.E., Butterworth, J., Itzkowitz, J., & Rainforth, B. (1991). *Supported employment: Developing integrated employment opportunities for persons with disabilities.* White Plains, NY: Longman.

Rehabilitation Act Amendments of 1986, PL 99-506. Title 29, U.S.C. 701 et seq: *U.S. Statutes at Large, 100,* 1807–1846.

Rehabilitation Act Amendments of 1992, PL 102-569. (October 29, 1992). Title 29, U.S.C. 701 et seq: *U.S. Statutes at Large, 100,* 4344–4488.

Rehabilitation Act of 1973, PL 93-112. (September 26, 1973). Title 29, U.S.C. 701 et seq: *U.S. Statutes at Large, 87,* 355–394.

Revell, W.G., West, M., Wehman, P., & Kregel, J. (1994). *Programmatic and administrative trends affecting the future of supported employment.* Richmond: Virginia Commonwealth University, Supported Employment Technical Assistance Center.

Rhodes, L., Sandow, D., Mank, D., Buckley, J., & Albin, J. (1991). Expanding the role of employers in supported employment. *Journal of The Association for Persons with Severe Handicaps, 16*(4), 213–217.

Rogan, P., & Hagner, D. (1990). Vocational evaluation in supported employment. *Journal of Rehabilitation, 56*(1), 45–51.

Rogan, P., Hagner, D., & Murphy, S. (1993). Natural supports: Reconceptualizing job coach roles. *Journal of The Association for Persons with Severe Handicaps, 18*(4), 275–281.

Romer, D., & Heller, T. (1983). Social adaptation of mentally retarded adults in community settings: A socio-ecological approach. *Applied Research in Mental Retardation, 4,* 303–314.

Rusch, F.R., & Hughes, C. (1990). Historical overview of supported employment. In F.R. Rusch (Ed.), *Supported employment: Models, methods, and issues* (pp. 5–14). Sycamore, IL: Sycamore.

School-to-Work Opportunities Act of 1994, PL 103-239. (May 4, 1994).

Shafer, M., Revell, G.W., & Isbister, F. (1991). The national supported employment initiative: A three year longitudinal analysis of 50 states. *Journal of Vocational Rehabilitation, 1*(1), 9–17.

Silliker, S.A. (1993). The role of social contacts in the successful job search. *Journal of Employment Counseling, 30,* 25–34.

Simon, M., & Halloran, W. (1994). Community-based vocational education: Guidelines for complying with the Fair Labor Standards Act. *Journal of The Association for Persons with Severe Handicaps, 19*(1), 52–60.

Simpson, J., & Button, C. (1991). *Results of survey on "rehabilitation service under the Rehabilitation Act."* Unpublished manuscript, United Cerebral Palsy Associations, Governmental Activities Office, Washington, DC.

Smith, M., Belcher, R., Juhrs, P., & Nabors, K. (1994). Where people with autism work. *Journal of Vocational Rehabilitation, 4*(1), 10–17.

Smith, S.W. (1990). Individualized education programs (IEPs) in special education—from intent to acquiescence. *Exceptional Children, 57*(1), 6–14.

Smull, M., & Harrison, S.B. (1992). *Supporting people with severe reputations in the community.* Alexandria, VA: NASMRPD.

Social Security Administration. (1991). *Red book on work incentives: A summary guide to social security and supplemental security income work incentives for people with disabilities.* Washington, DC: Author.

Sowers, J. (1991). Employment for persons with physical disabilities and related technology. *Journal of Vocational Rehabilitation, 1,* 55–64.

Steere, D.E., Gregory, S.P., Heiny, R.W., & Butterworth, J. (1995). Lifestyle planning: Considerations for use with people with disabilities. *Rehabilitation Counseling Bulletin, 38*(3), 207–223.

Taliaferro, W., Sandow, D., & Rhodes, L. (1993). Using company support to employ people with disabilities: One company's story. *The Oregon Conference Monograph, 5,* 126–133.

Technology-Related Assistance for Individuals with Disabilities Act of 1988, PL 100-407. (August 19, 1988). Title 29, U.S.C. 2201 et seq: *U.S. Statutes at Large, 102,* 1044–1065.

Turnbull, A.P., & Turnbull, H.R. (1982). Parent involvement in the education of handicapped children: A critique. *Mental Retardation, 20*(3), 115–122.

Udvari-Solner, A. (1990). *Variables associated with the integration of individuals with intellectual disabilities in supported employment settings* Unpublished doctoral dissertation, University of Wisconsin, Madison.

U.S. Department of Education. (1992). *Guidelines for implementing community-based educational programs for students with disabilities.* (OSEP Memorandum 92-20). Washington, DC: Office of Special Education Programs.

U.S. Department of Labor. (1991a). *Dictionary of occupational titles* (4th ed.). Washington, DC: U.S. Department of Labor, Employment and Training Administration.

U.S. Department of Labor. (1991b). *What work requires of schools: A scans report for America 2000.* Washington, DC: Author.

Vandercook, T., York, J., & Forest, M. (1989). The McGill Action Planning System (MAPS): A strategy for building the future. *Journal of The Association for Persons with Severe Handicaps, 14*(3), 205–215.

Wehman, P. (Ed.). (1993). *The ADA mandate for social change.* Baltimore: Paul H. Brookes Publishing Co.

Wehman, P., & Kregel, J. (1994). *At the crossroads: Supported employment ten years later.* Unpublished manuscript, Virginia Commonwealth University, Supported Employment Technical Assistance Center, Richmond, VA.

Wehman, P., Kregel, J., & Shafer, M.S. (Eds.). (1989). *Emerging trends in the national supported employment initiative: A preliminary analysis of twenty-seven states.* Richmond: Virginia Commonwealth University, Rehabilitation Research and Training Center.

Wehman, P., & Moon, M.S. (Eds.). (1988). *Vocational rehabilitation and supported employment.* Baltimore: Paul H. Brookes Publishing Co.

Wesiolowski, M. (1987). Differences in sizes of social networks of rehabilitation clients vs. those of nonclients. *Rehabilitation Counseling Bulletin, 31,* 17–27.

West, M., Revell, W.G., & Wehman, P. (1992). Achievements and challenges I: A five-year report on consumer and system outcomes from the supported employment initiative. *Journal of The Association for Persons with Severe Handicaps, 17*(4), 227–235.

Williams, R. (1991). Assistive technology in the eye of the beholder. *Journal of Vocational Rehabilitation, 1*(2), 9–14.

11

Meaningful Work and People Who Are Deaf-Blind

LORI GOETZ, NICHOLAS J. CERTO,
KATHY DOERING, AND MELLANIE LEE

PARTICIPATION IN MEANINGFUL activities is a frequently recognized component of quality of life for all persons, regardless of age or disability status (cf. Dennis, Williams, Giangreco, & Cloninger, 1993; Giangreco, Cloninger, Mueller, Yuan, & Ashworth, 1991; Goode, 1990; Halpern, 1993). Work—performing a real job for real wages—is one dimension of this component that is particularly relevant to adults. Work is a commonly valued activity (Super, 1984; Terkel, 1972), and the absence of appropriate employment services for persons with disabilities has had a negative impact in terms of human dignity, family concerns, earning power, and economic benefits to society, as well as having a negative impact on business and industry (Wehman, Moon, Everson, Wood, & Barcus, 1988). While work, or the pursuit of vocation, career, and employment opportunities, is only one of the variety of adult roles that contribute to quality of life (Halpern, 1993), it is a role in which persons with multiple disabilities have had reduced opportunities for participation (Barrett & Smith, 1986; Wehman, 1992).

This chapter identifies emerging practices that help to enable participation of all adults in meaningful employment, specifically individuals with multiple disabilities and who are deaf-blind. After a brief review of the existing database addressing participation of these individuals in supported employment, the chapter reviews promising

Preparation of this chapter was supported in part by grants from the U.S. Department of Education, Office of Special Education and Rehabilitative Services/Special Education Program (Grant #HO25D30013), and U.S. Dept. of Health and Human Services (Grant #91ASPE249A). No official endorsement is intended or should be inferred.

practices that have emerged from this database. The second major section of the chapter discusses natural supports as a concept common to many of these promising practices. The changing role of the employment specialist that is required when natural supports are used is the third major section of the chapter. The chapter concludes with suggestions for needed future research and evaluation.

The supported employment initiative heralded the inclusion of persons with severe and profound disabilities in integrated competitive employment (cf. Wehman, 1988), but analyses to date suggest that the outcomes have fallen short of expectations. Kregel and Wehman (1989) and Wehman, Kregel, and Shafer (1989) present data indicating that persons with severe and profound disabilities—as well as specific disabilities including autism, cerebral palsy, and sensory impairments—are, in general, not being served in supported employment programs.

Supported employment provides persons with disabilities paid work in integrated settings accompanied by support both to the employer and the employee. Supported employment would appear to be a particularly promising service delivery option for persons who experience profound cognitive disabilities and for persons who are deaf-blind, particularly if these persons experience other multiple disabilities, including cerebral palsy, health impairments, and behavioral disorders (Fredericks & Baldwin, 1987; Riggio, 1992). Nevertheless, the published literature has addressed largely sheltered options (e.g., Busse, Romer, Fewell, & Vadasy, 1985; Gerner, 1986).

However, a small database is beginning to emerge. Gaylord-Ross et al. (1989) and Goetz, Lee, Johnston, and Gaylord-Ross (1991) reported successful placement of individuals who were deaf-blind into work settings that were integrated, including restaurants, retail stores, a public library, and an insurance corporation. Doering, Usilton, Farron-Davis, and Sailor (1989) and Gee and Goetz (1990) report successful participation of young adults with multiple profound disabilities in the transition from high school to integrated employment. Everson and Burwell (1991) present case studies documenting successful supported employment individual placements for two young adults who were deaf-blind, and they note that supported employment placements of Helen Keller clients increased from 10% in 1987 to 45% in 1990. Downing, Shafer, Brahm-Levy, and Frantz (1992) report case study outcomes for three young adults who were deaf-blind and had been placed into supported employment in an enclave. Reports such as these, combined with a growing literature addressing both the broader service delivery issues in employment for persons with disabilities (cf. Rusch, Chadsey-Rusch, & Johnson, 1991) and specific adult service and transition support needs of persons experiencing severe cognitive delays (Moon, Inge, Wehman, Brooke, & Barcus, 1990) and deaf-blindness (Everson, Burwell, & Killam, 1995; Griffin & Lowry, 1989), suggest several promising practices in achieving participation in meaningful work.

PROMISING PRACTICES

Dispersed Heterogeneous Clusters

Goetz et al. (1991) report that heterogeneous grouping, or the grouping of persons with differing degree and disability types within or throughout one work setting, was a strategy that enabled Howard, a young man with congenital rubella and associated mental retardation and seizure disorder in addition to legal blindness and deafness, to work for 1 1/2 hours daily at a wage determined in accord with state or federal standards (Lee & Johnston, 1990). The local pizza parlor where Howard worked also functioned as the employment setting for two other co-workers with moderate and severe disabilities who worked for longer hours. All three employees were supported by one employment specialist who was better able to support Howard's unique means of communication (design and implementation of a portable tactile calendar [Roland & Schweigert, 1990]) because Howard's co-workers with disabilities required less direct support. Nietupski, Chappelle, and Murray (1994) discuss similar advantages of the model of dispersed heterogeneous placement in supported employment, particularly in large business (100-plus employees) settings such as hospitals, where supported employees may be dispersed across several subenvironments, such as the cafeteria, laundry, and equipment assembly areas.

Moon et al. (1990) discuss in detail the implementation and outcomes of dispersed group placements for persons with severe cognitive disabilities. Working within the Federal Rehabilitation standards that have defined supported employment as working for pay for at least 20 hours per week, they articulate that "the point of a group placement . . . is to meet the needs of persons who may not be able to achieve vocational independence" (p. 37). Goetz et al. (1991) further argue that, in addition to development of innovations such as dispersed heterogeneous group placement, the existing four major supported employment models of individual placement, enclaves, mobile work crews, and small businesses are insufficient. Additional support options for community employment must continue to emerge if persons with profound and multiple disabilities are to be participants (cf. Nisbet & Hagner, 1988; Sowers & Powers, 1989).

Dispersed heterogeneous clusters provide a number of practical and logistical advantages, including more efficient use of the employment specialist's expertise (Goetz et al., 1991) and positive co-worker interaction outcomes between workers with and without disabilities (Moon et al., 1990). Co-workers may more readily see the individual as a person versus "one of the group." However, disability-specific mentoring, in which peers who share a specific disability such as deaf-blindness participate in a common work site and provide both technical expertise and social support to one another, is lost when this option is pursued (Haring & Romer, 1995; Lipton, 1993).

Job Restructuring

Lee, Lynch, and Goetz (1988) and Sowers (1989) identify specific innovations in the larger process of task redesign and adaptations (cf. Martin, 1986; York & Rainforth, 1991) that contribute to supporting adults with multiple support needs. Lee et al. (1988) found job restructuring to be an effective strategy in achieving integrated work participation. Job restructuring extends the concept of adaptation beyond individual tasks to the relationship among tasks. In job restructuring, the employer first specifies and identifies all the company's needs. The employment specialist then visits the site and does or observes the multiple jobs to identify how current employees are completing them. Based on the job skills of the target employee, restructured jobs are created by identifying one task currently performed by many different individuals as a distinct description of a separate job for the target employee's position or by recombining elements of several different job descriptions into new jobs that use the specific job skills of the target employee. In a large architectural firm, for example, maintenance of several pots of coffee at diverse locations was left to any employee who happened to reach the coffee maker when it was empty. Maintaining an adequate supply of ready coffee throughout the firm was consolidated into a job that was part of a supported employee's responsibilities.

In job sharing (Sowers, 1989), a job that has traditionally been performed by one employee may be restructured into two or more parts, each performed by a different employee. Teresa, a young woman with a severe bilateral hearing loss and functional vision in only one eye, worked 15 hours a week and earned one half the prevailing minimum wage at a restaurant near her home. Part of her job was washing and chopping eight different vegetables for the restaurant's salad bar. Before Teresa was hired, the job description for salad bar preparation included washing and chopping vegetables, putting them in containers, and placing the containers in the salad bar located in the center of the restaurant. When Teresa was hired, the job was restructured into two different parts: 1) Teresa prepped the vegetables, which a co-worker had set up for her each morning in a fixed sequence; and

2) the co-worker then set up the completed containers that Teresa had prepared in the salad bar. By restructuring the salad bar prep into two separate tasks, Teresa was able to avoid the need for complex mobility skills within and around several confined spaces as a routine component of her work.

Social and Communicative Skill Instruction

The fundamentally social nature of the workplace has been widely discussed (cf. Nisbet & Hagner, 1988), and data suggest that for persons with mild and moderate disabilities, job terminations are often related to social factors rather than poor performance of discrete job tasks per se (Greenspan & Shoultz, 1981). Sisson, Van Hasselt, and Hersen (1987) addressed the significant challenges that persons who are deaf-blind face in achieving social integration into any natural environment, and they noted that few published examples of effective strategies to enhance interactions were available.

Gaylord-Ross, Park, Johnston, Lee, and Goetz (1995) reported a combination of social enhancement procedures that was used in accomplishing social integration of two employees who were deaf-blind. Systematic instruction for the employees on how to initiate and respond to social interactions and a co-worker training packager, in which an employment specialist participated with selected co-workers in brief rap sessions on ways to include the two employees, were used to increase both direct social interactions among co-workers and the inclusion of the two employees in social networks.

For example, Tanya was a 22-year-old nonverbal woman in the Gaylord-Ross et al. (1995) study who experienced severe low vision and a functional hearing loss; hemiplegia and low muscle tone affected her gait and speed in accomplishing fine motor tasks. She worked 10 hours a week at a local department store hanging and tagging merchandise on the floor and pricing merchandise in the warehouse. After Tanya had been on the job nearly 5 months but still experienced few social initiations, despite her competent job performance, Tanya's employment specialist suggested a consistent greeting routine. Co-workers were informally asked to greet Tanya each morning by approaching her within 2 feet and extending their hands. Tanya learned to respond to this greeting by grasping and shaking the extended hand while orienting her face toward the employee. After several weeks, Tanya was known by name to all her co-workers, who included her in activities outside the workplace, such as purchasing a Mother's Day card or going to a baseball game.

The other woman in this study was Teresa, a 27-year-old woman who was legally deaf and blind and who worked at a Pizza Hut. Informal co-worker advocacy suggestions by the employment specialist, such as proposing that a co-worker invite Teresa along for after-work pizza and beer, led to little alteration in social exchanges. Teresa was then taught to check in and check out from her workplace. She greeted a co-worker by activating an audiocassette, which played a tape saying hello and requesting her card. The co-worker then greeted and gave Teresa the card, which she subsequently punched in. The training led to consistent interactions with co-workers.

A growing literature has documented innovations in both technology and instructional technologies that enable all persons to communicate (Gee, Graham, Oshima, Yoshioka, & Goetz, 1991; Meisel, 1994; Wacker, Wiggins, Fowler, & Berg, 1988; see Mirenda & Iacono, 1990, for review). Both Tanya's nonverbal greeting routine and Teresa's microswitch-adapted tape recorded message enabled these women to have a personal voice in the workplace. The instructional strategies used to increase the competence of these two persons in *using* these communication systems included prompt fading and time delay (Snell, 1993). These strategies are well documented in the literature (cf. Touchette, 1971) and are straightforward and easily applied.

The data presented by Gaylord-Ross et al. (1995) do not allow an analysis of the relative effectiveness of informal co-worker advocacy training and social skills instructional training for the employee who is deaf-blind. However, the instructional strategies used by Gaylord-Ross et al. have been documented to be effective in teaching persons with profound multiple disabilities, including deaf-blindness, to initiate requests using a variety of communicative means. Gee et al. (1991) present data demonstrating the existence of instructional technology that establishes persons who are deaf-blind as competent communicators even when these persons have multiple profound disabilities in addition to deaf-blindness. The employment specialist may play a critical role in both creating and facilitating use of specific equipment and adaptations (although the need for highly specialized communication systems does not necessarily preclude alternative models of support). Provision of the resources needed to enable all employees to participate in the social context of the workplace is an essential feature of meaningful work.

Communication Technology

Growth in high-technology adaptations for communication continues at an impressive pace. Mirenda and Iacono (1990) have discussed and reviewed innovations that enable all persons to be effective communicators. Huebner, Prickett, Welch, and Joffee (1995) present detailed information addressing the range and variety of multimodal systems available to persons who are deaf-blind. What all high-tech communication options and systems have in common is the provision of a personal voice that is easily accessed, easily understood, and reflective of the user's interests and capacities. The importance of a personal voice in establishing a person as part of a sustained social network in the workplace cannot be overlooked. For example, recent data (Meisel, 1994) suggest that such a personal voice may, in fact, be crucial in establishing social interaction. Meisel instructed three young adults with severe disabilities (though without sensory impairments) in the use of a picture communication system during participation in regular classroom activities and monitored social interactions among students and their peers using the educational assessment scale for social interaction (EASI) (Goetz, Haring, & Anderson, 1983). When a voice output system was added to the picture system in a time-logged, multiple baseline across participants, social interactions showed dramatic increases in frequency and duration for all three participants.

People who are deaf-blind, by the very nature of their disability, often lack a personal voice that is readily accessible and readily understood (cf. Smithdas, 1995). The growth of high-tech options that meet the fundamental requirements of accessibility, portability, ease of partner comprehension, and responsivity to the user's capacities and interests (cf. Siegel-Causey, 1995), coupled with evidence presented earlier that all persons can be taught to use these systems (cf. Gee et al., 1991), suggests that the tools needed to ensure social and communicative participation of people who are deaf-blind do already exist.

NATURAL SUPPORTS

Heterogeneous grouping, job restructuring, social and communication skill instruction, and use of communication technology are all strategies developed within the context of supported employment as it is traditionally defined (Moon et al., 1990): "Supported employment offers paid work in integrated community settings with permanent follow-along or supervision. . . ." (p. 1). The implication is, of course, that the permanent follow-along or supervision is provided by paid personnel trained in rehabilitation services. However, Nisbet and Hagner (1988) first suggested that paid support staff might not be necessary or that their role might be very different. For a variety of reasons, ranging from practical implementation constraints to the larger values base in support of including persons with disabilities in all components of community life, they proposed the use of natural supports in the work-place.

Natural supports were, by definition, naturally available internal supports who were persons not paid to specifically train, supervise, or support an employee with a disability. Basing their analysis on traditional roles naturally occurring in business and industry, Nisbet and Hagner (1988) proposed at least three available support roles: 1) mentor roles, in which a co-worker or supervisor supervises on an ongoing basis an employee with disabilities who is already trained in the job requirements; 2) training consultant roles, in which an employment specialist trains a co-worker(s) who then, in turn, trains and supervises an employee with disabilities (with or without compensation); and 3) job-sharing roles, in which an employee with disabilities divides job responsibilities with an employee without disabilities, and this co-worker provides ongoing support to the employee with disabilities and receives added compensation from an external source. Natural supports were any one of these roles, or a combination of roles based on the unique features of the particular business setting. Nisbet (1992) has more recently added "broker" to the roles that human service providers can fill: The broker assists the client in acquiring the natural supports that are necessary for inclusion in all aspects of community life.

Certo and Doering (1993) have provided the following working definition of natural supports as related to employment:

> Natural supports refers to a person (or people) who agree(s) to provide assistance or feedback, or provide companionship to facilitate independent or partially independent performance in employment settings, for or with an individual with severe disabilities, and for whom the provision of such assistance, feedback, contact, or companionship is not their primary responsibility, regardless of whether or not they are compensated. (p. 7)

Both Goetz (1989) and Everson and Burwell (1991) provide examples of how a training consultant role was used to achieve natural supports for employees who were deaf-blind. Lizbeth was a 26-year-old woman who lived by herself in an apartment in a bustling university town. Lizbeth was legally blind and had a profound hearing loss in one ear and moderate-to-severe loss in the other ear; she communicated through spoken language. Lizbeth worked 20 hours a week in the records department of a large national corporation, having expressed a preference for office work in her ITP (individualized transition plan). She earned $5.50 an hour. An employment specialist taught Lizbeth her first job, which was using an electronic scanning system to log documents. Lizbeth was also responsible for daily cleaning of the employee break room. In her initial 1 1/2 years on the job, her co-workers trained her to perform two additional jobs as part of her responsibilities, with only brief consultation with the employment specialist, who then started checking in with Lizbeth and the employer approximately once a month.

Everson and Burwell (1991) similarly report that after an initial month-long training effort, supervision for a supported employee who was deaf-blind was transferred directly to the actual supervisor within the hotel laundry and follow-along services lowered to once-a-week contacts.

The support needs of persons who are deaf-blind may, in fact, be considerable (cf. Downing et al., 1992; Smithdas, 1995), encompassing specialized communication systems, orientation and mobility services, and idiosyncratic expression of preferences and desires (cf. Billingsley, Huven, & Romer, 1995). Downing et al. (1992) conclude that there are at least four challenges in realizing supported employment for people with multiple disabilities that include deaf-blindness: 1) the need for meaningful assessment procedures, including situational assessment (Moon et al., 1990) of sufficient duration to enable consumer choice and preference in making job placements; 2) the need for more effective use of technology and instructional supports to enhance vocational competence on the job; 3) the need for effective alternative modes of communication that are easy for co-workers to use and understand, but flexible enough to be responsive to changing consumer needs; and 4) the need to develop effective interagency funding configurations that provide financial incentives (rather than disincentives) for providing supported employment placements.

Natural supports would appear to offer at least one logical solution to some of these challenges. Conceptually, this solution is consistent with the values base underlying the inclusion of persons with severe disabilities in all domains. Diversity is not merely acknowledged but celebrated (Sapon-Shevin, 1992); participation by all persons in the life of the community—at school, at work, at play—contributes to the quality of life of the community as a whole, and exclusion of persons undermines this quality of community life (O'Brien & O'Brien, 1992). Employees with disabilities who are naturally supported and who receive needed supports from co-workers in the workplace through the same process of relationship formation and mutual assistance that all workers rely on become employees like any other employee—each one different and each contributing to the whole.

Practically, the use of natural supports, which rely on already existing internal resources and people, offers the potential for a cost-effective solution to the provision of ongoing necessary support that may be required, for example, for an employee to gain access to and use a tactile calendar box (e.g., Goetz et al., 1991). A values base in the workplace that accepts and celebrates diversity, coupled with a consultant-trainer model of natural support (cf. Nisbet & Hagner, 1988) to ensure that co-workers have technical knowledge needed to use a calendar box, could reduce the cost of providing a full-time employment specialist. Given the highly specialized support needs some persons who are deaf-blind may have (ranging from tactile communication systems to comprehensive functional assessment and positive behavioral intervention plans [e.g., Billingsley et al., 1995; Downing et al., 1992]), the need for paid support staff with technical expertise will vary. However, the capacity of peers in the service environment to generate fruitful and positive solutions to specific problems should not be underestimated (cf. Salisbury, Palombaro, & Evans, 1993).

Finally, natural support strategies may well contribute directly to achieving the valued outcome of membership in a sustained social network. Giangreco et al. (1991) interviewed parents of children who were deaf-blind and identified several quality-of-life indicators that parents wished for their children, including participation in meaningful activities in multiple environments; health; a safe, stable home environment; and membership in a sustained social network of caring persons. Carr (1995) interviewed five adults with deaf-blindness and similarly found the need for friendships and socialization to be one of four recurring important needs that consumers identified.

Natural support strategies appear to be one way in which these valued outcomes can be at least partially realized, although further data are needed to test this assumption. Hagner, Cotton, Goodall, and Nisbet (1992) interviewed 16 co-workers identified as supportive by supervisor nomination at 12 different community work settings. Using an iterative analysis process (cf. Patton, 1987), they reported findings in relation to three areas: roles, support, and relationships. Of particular interest are themes that emerged in characterizing relationships between supported employees and supportive co-workers. A sense of mutual commitment and a sense of pride in accomplishments of the supported employee characterized these relationships. Comments such as "the guy's (supported employee) always there. He's incredible" (p. 252) or "She (supported employee) has a secure job as long as she wants it" (p. 252) suggest that participation in real work, with real co-worker support, contributes to each employee's sustained social network.

Further empirical data are provided by Murphy (1991), who analyzed job performance and social interactions of four young adults with severe disabilities who each participated in two different work experiences: one as a supported employee with a job coach, and one as an employee supported through natural co-worker supports. She found no differences in job performance, suggesting that natural supports need not result in decreased job performance. She also found an increase in social interactions for all four employees when they began the job context in which they were naturally supported, but internal validity constraints suggest caution in interpretation. Lee (1994) compared social interactions of three groups of 10 persons each: 1) persons supported by a job coach, 2) persons supported by a mentor, and 3) a randomly selected group of workers without disabilities. Results indicated that workers who were supported by a mentor initiated a significantly larger number of interactions than workers in the other two groups. Both the Murphy (1991) and Lee (1994) data are preliminary, but do suggest differences in valued outcomes when natural support strategies are used.

The emergence of natural support strategies cannot, and should not, occur at the expense of the specialized service needs that individuals who are deaf-blind may need in order to benefit from increased participation in the workplace. Goetz (1993) identified a similar concern for students who are deaf-blind in models of inclusionary schooling, and identified at least three areas that inclusive schools need to address in terms of serving students who are deaf-blind: 1) curricular adaptations, or the determination of relevant content (academic skills vs. functional life skills vs. experiential learning) and instructional strategies; 2) specialized service provision, or the availability of services, including Braille, Orientation & Mobility, Tadoma, etc.; and 3) social inclusion, or participation as a valued member of the social context.

Goetz (1995) identified a number of potential solutions in these areas, including specialized curriculum development strategies such as contextual analysis (Gee, 1993); the use of collaborative teams (Bruner, 1991; Rainforth, York, & Macdonald, 1992) to ensure delivery of any needed specialized services, and use of support circles (Forest & Lusthaus, 1989) in promoting social inclusion. Each of these potential solutions, however, is predicated upon a school-based model of service delivery. As young adults with severe disabilities make the transition out of school and into adult life, the system of service delivery is vastly different and poorly integrated (cf. Gerry & Mirsky, 1992). The emergence of alternative support strategies such as those suggested by Goetz et al. (1991) and Everson and Burwell (1991), and the emergence of natural supports as a practical and conceptual model that is receiving initial empirical support, suggest fundamental changes in the approach of the key personnel associated with implementation of meaningful work roles: job coaches and employment specialists. These changes

may be particularly critical in establishing meaningful work participation for persons typically excluded from supported employment services due to the nature of their disabilities (cf. Kregel & Wehman,
1989).

CHANGING ROLES OF THE EMPLOYMENT SPECIALIST

An initial set of data, as cited previously, is emerging that suggests the
usefulness of natural supports in achieving supported employment
outcomes. Co-workers and others in job settings have been used successfully to provide assistance, information, and companionship for
workers with disabilities. Such a concept is not revolutionary when
one examines it from a broader context. Natural supports simply represent equal treatment for workers with disabilities. Workers with severe disabilities, including individuals who have profound multiple
disabilities or who are deaf-blind, should be provided training and
orientation opportunities just as any other worker. This should not be
construed as a statement indicating that disability-related needs of an
individual worker are ignored, or dealt with solely by co-workers with
little formal training. Rather, it is a statement that accommodation to
disabilities should not be the sole focus of a placement. Introducing a
worker with severe disabilities as an individual who needs orientation
and training, rather than someone who cannot do a variety of things,
emphasizes similarities rather than differences.

This act of equal treatment represents a fundamental change in
the workplace. It provides the potential for these individuals to be
fully included in work and social networks—that is, the total culture
or ecology of the workplace. It accomplishes this outcome by shifting
the responsibility for supporting workers with disabilities from paid
professionals in special education and rehabilitation to the workers or
managers who orient, train, and manage all employees. Within traditional supported employment models, the employment specialist in-
vestigates employment possibilities with employers; develops the job
and related adaptations, if needed; trains the new worker; and moni-
tors performance on site, according to a fixed schedule. Typically, the
individual with disabilities is not involved in the process of selection
and development until the training begins. Training techniques and
adaptations are not necessarily developed to be compatible or unobtrusive within the work and social ecology of the job setting. In addition, the amount of effort expended to assist the individual with disabilities to identify job preferences is limited.

Establishing natural supports is a process of facilitation and consultation, rather than direct training (Hagner, Rogan, & Murphy, 1992).
For natural supports to be effective, they must be compatible with the

work routines and social ecology of the particular employment setting and be as unobtrusive as possible (Rogan, Hagner & Murphy, 1993). All of the activities listed previously may be necessary in order to ensure a successful outcome on the job for an individual with specific disabilities. Within a natural supports approach, how they will occur, who will provide the support, and the direct involvement of the individual with severe disabilities will be very different in comparison to traditional job coaching in supported employment. These differences have a direct impact on how the employment specialist's role is defined, and on the skills needed to be effective in this role.

Person-centered planning [PCP] (Hobbs & Allen, 1989; Mount & Zwernik, 1988) provides a clear example of how a natural supports process can be developed and of how the employment specialist role becomes one of facilitation and advocacy, rather than one of direct training. PCP is a process in which the individual with disabilities directly participates in 1) gathering relevant information that addresses strengths, capacities, interests, and experiences; 2) developing a vision of what the individual considers to be a desirable and fulfilling future in relation to employment, community living, and social relationships; 3) identifying and implementing a series of actions for the individual to engage in to attain this vision; and 4) securing the commitment of friends, relatives, co-workers, and so on, who agree to function as natural supports to assist the individual to achieve his or her vision.

The PCP process generally involves a series of meetings that include the individual with disabilities and significant others, such as family, friends, co-workers, employers, neighbors, teachers, and rehabilitation staff. Each meeting could involve a large group or be distributed over several days with different participants giving input at a number of smaller meetings. The input of various people can be presented on audiotape or videotape, if needed. The statements of individuals, including the individual upon whom the meeting will focus, can be prepared or outlined in advance to facilitate discussion at the meeting. The frequency of the meetings is typically determined by the need for more input into the ongoing action plan, need to identify new choices, or the need to solicit the commitment of participants to function as new natural supports. PCP meetings are one important source of soliciting individuals to function as natural supports. The logistics and organization of initial or ongoing PCP meetings may, in fact, be a new component of the employment specialist's job description, although responsibility for initiating PCP currently varies from agency to agency.

Vision is a key word in PCP. It indicates that the intent of this process is to examine an individual's life from a broad perspective that considers both immediate and future goals. In addition to immediate job, community living, and recreation goals, PCP should assist in identifying more long-term lifestyle objectives. For example, an individual might state a preference to work in retail sales at a major department store. However, honoring this preference should not stop with job selection; goals for forming social relationships at work and extending beyond the workday should also be set. Therefore, the vision might be to work in retail sales, to have lunch with and attend birthday parties during work hours with co-workers, and to go to movies, bars, picnics, ball games, and/or classes with fellow workers during nonwork hours.

The following quote is an excerpt from a personal journal entry written (with assistance) by a young woman who had just graduated from public school and was receiving supported employment services through an adult service agency. This excerpt was written in her own words, in preparation for a PCP meeting, and gives an example of the breadth of the vision that should be encouraged through the PCP process. This meeting occurred after she had provided job preference input, and clearly emphasizes her social expectations from work:

> I will like work on taking a bus to Kelly's house; someday on the week-end go shopping at Nordstrom's (her place of employment); have lunch at the mall and I will take the bus home.
> . . . This is my dream about me. I would like to go out for a date.
> This is my dream about me. I would like to stay up late on Saturday night.
> . . . I will ask my friend (at work) for lunch sometime.
> . . . This is my dream for me. I would like to go out with different people . . . go out dancing and drink on Saturday night. (Toney et al., 1993, p. 2)

Based on PCP information, the next steps include locating a place of employment that matches stated preferences, being hired, and developing a job based on the individual's skills and strengths. These steps do not necessarily happen in a particular sequence. When engaging in these activities, the employment specialist offers to help the employer work out needs or problems through regular consultation, but refrains from offering training or assistance on the job site to the worker with disabilities.

The following example is provided from Toney et al. (1993) to illustrate how this process worked for another individual, "Lisa," who is being supported:

> The employment specialist met with the department store's Personnel Director, explained the goals of natural supports, and stated that she would be the liaison to the company and would assist in training Lisa as needed. She stated further that her services would be available indefinitely, but that typically she would not be physically present at the job site. With this information, the Personnel Director assumed the responsibility of de-

veloping a job for Lisa. She circulated a survey to the different departments, asking each manager to identify a combination of job tasks that included both physical and academic skills (e.g., pricing, hanging, making boxes). She then developed a skills list and reviewed it with the employment specialist.

Next, the Personnel Director scheduled an interview with Lisa, and the employment specialist supported her during the interview. . . . Lisa was hired that day to work part-time, nine hours each week, distributed across three days.

In preparation for Lisa's start date, the Personnel Director called a meeting with managers from six targeted departments to inform them that Lisa would be hired as a "floater" between departments. Lisa's responsibilities would be determined from the skills list compiled earlier, and Lisa would receive direct assignments from the Personnel Director each day. The employment specialist attended this meeting to answer questions informally, and described the meeting as follows:

> Most of the questions were about what Lisa could and could not do. Managers were afraid that if they asked her to make a box or gave her directions and she was not able to do it, they would feel embarrassed.

> . . . The Personnel Director and a second employee from the store's Personnel Department became responsible for providing Lisa's initial support at the store. Lisa began work at a busy time one week before a big sale. The employment specialist primarily supported Lisa by "hanging out" in the employee break room during breaks and at lunch, and made herself available to Lisa's co-workers to answer any questions and facilitate the interactions. Since Lisa had a hard time remembering people's names, the employment specialist developed a simple adaptation to help her. She provided Lisa with a list of names of each of her co-workers so that she could practice them throughout the day. Over time Lisa learned the names and was able to stop using the list. The employment specialist also developed another adaptation to help Lisa in performing her work duties. She designed a calendar and date book that listed Lisa's work duties in a table or grid so that she had an easy visual reference of her duties across each day. (pp. 5–6).

A few working strategies for the role of employment specialists emerge from this example. First, the services offered by the employment specialist and the length of time those services will be available are clearly delineated in advance to the employer. These services should fall under the category of *technical assistance* and should be *available to the employer and other relevant employees,* not directly to the worker with disabilities. Second, job development and direct training are left to the formal or informal mechanism(s) used by the employer for any new employee. If the employer feels that the employment specialist should provide direct training for the employee with disabilities, then this training is short term and limited to demonstrating a particular technique. Third, and of special significance, direct involvement by the employment specialist at the place of employment focuses on activities that will assist the employee with disabilities function within the social milieu of the workplace. Providing Lisa with a list of names of co-workers and having Lisa rehearse that list enabled her to exchange greetings and to secure the attention of other employees when needed. Providing Lisa with a table that gave her an easy visual reference of her different duties ensured that she would complete them and arrive at designated workstations on time. Co-workers thus viewed her as reliable and competent, in much the same way that Gaylord-Ross et al. (1995) facilitated inclusion of employees who were deaf-blind through the use of adapted communication systems.

Five additional strategies were cited by Rogan et al. (1993) to facilitate natural supports:

1. Use of personal connections to enhance social support
2. Matching employee preferences and attributes to work-site social climates
3. Collaboration with work-site personnel in developing adaptations and modifications
4. Facilitation and support by the employment specialist of the involvement of work-site personnel
5. Consultation on the person–environment fit to benefit the individual and setting

PCP strategies have been used in supporting persons who are deaf-blind (Perlroth, Pumpian, Hesche, & Campbell, 1993) as well as persons with other severe and/or multiple disabilities (Vandercook, York, & Forest, 1989). For those persons who may not express preferences in conventional or readily understood ways, the role of family members (Ford, 1992; O'Donnell, 1992) as well as peers (Haring, Haring, Breen, Romer, & White, 1995) in both advocacy and interpretation of behavior is critical. Indeed, the multiple perspectives available from a divergent group of individuals who share common esteem for the focus person in a PCP meeting may ultimately contribute to a richer understanding of that person's dream and needs (cf. Perlroth et al., 1993).

Many of the practices described here have been used in the past in supported employment and are not unique to a natural supports approach. Providing a table that delineates the worker's duties, as mentioned for Lisa, is one example. However, without the constant presence of the employment specialist, such activities take on a different meaning. They constitute an important method of facilitating the development of relationships that can evolve into natural supports on the job and beyond the workday.

In addition, they are an important component of developing self-advocacy skills for individuals who have severe disabilities. Over time, if Lisa is to make the dreams she lists in her journal become a reality, she will need to ask co-workers to go to lunch, or to go out drinking on a Saturday night; that is, she will need to advocate for herself. Without self-advocacy (cf. Gonsalves & Harp, 1994), the outcome of natural supports may only be the transfer of responsibilities from employment specialists to individuals outside of the fields of special education or rehabilitation. Such a shift may improve job maintenance and the quality of life for individuals with disabilities—a highly significant outcome. But without self-advocacy, which ensures the active participation of the individual with disabilities in this equation, he or she may still remain the passive recipient of services.

SUMMARY

Much remains to be learned about how persons who challenge the system, such as people with deaf-blindness and multiple disabilities, can become valued members of the workforce. Some of the specific promising practices reviewed here—heterogeneous grouping, job restructuring, social skill instruction, use of adaptive communication technology—are consistent with a natural support model, while some are not. For example, job restructuring can readily occur on the part of co-workers who are providing natural support, and it is in fact a natural support strategy identified by Rogan et al. (1993). Direct social skill instruction to an employee with disabilities is not consistent with a natural support model, yet data suggest that this practice can be effective in accomplishing social inclusion at the workplace (cf. Gaylord-Ross et al., 1995).

These divergent databases suggest that establishing dichotomies between natural supports and other validated practices—natural supports "versus" supported employment, natural supports "versus" structured instruction—may result in practices that ultimately hinder, rather than support, people who have individualized service needs. People with multiple disabilities, including deaf-blindness, may, for example, require an interpreter in order to communicate. This type of support role is highly specialized, requiring technical training and expertise. Meeting this need does not, and should not, preclude using a strategy of natural supports as well. The challenge that faces us is to create a system in which these diverse support needs are valued and responded to equally.

Ongoing evaluation of all strategies for providing employee support is clearly needed. Given the desired quality-of-life outcomes for all people—participation in both job activities and the social context of the workplace—and given the heterogeneous and highly individualized service needs of the target population, appropriate methodologies for answering questions about effectiveness may include both qualitative and small-sample, time-series methodologies. Both have much to offer, and the challenge of combining qualitative "variables" (such as friendship or mentor relationships) with quantitative methodologies (such as a time series design) is one that must be addressed (cf. Goetz & Hunt, 1993). However, sufficient data already exist to state with confidence that the valued outcome of participation in meaningful work is possible for all people with multiple disabilities. Future empirical study must identify the ways in which this possibility can become a reality for everyone.

REFERENCES

Barrett, S., & Smith, A. (1986). *Employment options for young adults with deaf-blindness.* Washington, DC: Helen Keller National Center Technical Assistance Center.

Billingsley, F., Huven, B., & Romer, L. (1995). Behavioral supports in inclusive school settings. In N. Haring & L. Romer (Eds.), *Welcoming students who are deaf-blind into typical classrooms: Facilitating school participation, learning, and friendships* (pp. 251–275). Baltimore: Paul H. Brookes Publishing Co.

Bruner, C. (1991). *Thinking collaboratively: Ten questions and answers to help policy makers improve children's services.* Washington, DC: Education and Human Services Consortium.

Busse, D., Romer, L., Fewell, R., & Vadasy, P. (1985). Employment of deaf-blind rubella students in a subsidized work program. *Journal of Visual Impairment and Blindness, 79,* 59–64.

Carr, T.S. (1995). Consumers speak out. In J. Everson (Ed.), *Supporting young adults who are deaf-blind in their communities* (pp. 71–85). Baltimore: Paul H. Brookes Publishing Co.

Certo, N., & Doering, K. (1993, February). *Strategies to facilitate effective transition from school to adult life.* Paper presented at 3rd annual integration institute of the Integrated Resources Institute, Costa Mesa, CA.

Dennis, R., Williams, W., Giangreco, M., & Cloninger, C. (1993). Quality of life as a context for planning and evaluation of services for people with disabilities. *Exceptional Children, 59*(6), 499–512.

Doering, K., Usilton, R., Farron-Davis, F., & Sailor, W. (1989). *Comprehensive transition system: Preparing people with severe disabilities to move from school to work and independent living.* San Francisco State University, Department of Special Education, San Francisco. (USDOE/OSERS Grant #G008530143).

Downing, J., Shafer, M., Brahm-Levy, A., & Frantz, M. (1992). Supported employment for individuals with dual sensory impairments and mental retardation: Current practices and future challenges. *Journal of Vocational Rehabilitation, 2*(1), 28–38.

Everson, J., Burwell, J., & Killam, B. (1995). Working and contributing to one's community: Strategies for including young adults who are deaf-blind. In J.

Everson (Ed.), *Supporting young adults who are deaf-blind in their communities* (pp. 131–158). Baltimore: Paul H. Brookes Publishing Co.

Everson, J.M., & Burwell, J.B. (1991). Transition to work: Addressing the challenges of deaf-blindness. *Journal of Vocational Rehabilitation, 1*(4), 39–45.

Ford, J. (1992, March). Reflections and future directions (reaction paper). In *Proceedings of the National Conference on Deaf-Blindness: Deaf-blind services in the 90s* (pp. 58–61). National Conference on Deaf-Blindness, sponsored by the Hilton/Perkins National Program, Washington, DC.

Forest, M., & Lusthaus, E. (1989). Promoting educational equity for all students: Circles and maps. In S. Stainback, W. Stainback, & M. Forest (Eds.), *Educating all students in the mainstream of regular education* (pp. 43–57). Baltimore: Paul H. Brookes Publishing Co.

Fredericks, H.D., & Baldwin, V.L. (1987). Individuals with dual sensory impairments: Who are they? How are they educated? In L. Goetz, D. Guess, & K. Stremel-Campbell (Eds.), *Innovative program design for individuals with dual sensory impairments* (pp. 3–14). Baltimore: Paul H. Brookes Publishing Co.

Gaylord-Ross, R., Lee, M., Johnston, S., Lynch K., Rosenberg, B., & Goetz, L. (1989). Supported employment for youth who are deaf-blind and in transition. *Career Development for Exceptional Individuals, 14*(2), 77–89.

Gaylord-Ross, R., Park, H.S., Johnston, S., Lee, M., & Goetz, L. (1995). Individual social skills training and co-worker training for supported employees with dual sensory impairment. *Behavior Modification, 19*(1), 78–94.

Gee, K. (1993, May). *An experimental and qualitative investigation into the motivation and competence of peer interactions involving students with severe multiple disabilities in middle school classrooms.* Unpublished doctoral dissertation, San Francisco State University–University of California, Berkeley, Joint Doctoral Program.

Gee, K., & Goetz, L. (1990). *Integrated education for students with the most severe disabilities* (final report). (OSERS/SEP Model Demonstration Grant #G008730421). San Francisco State University, Department of Special Education, San Francisco.

Gee, K., Graham, N., Oshima, G., Yoshioka, K., & Goetz, L. (1991). Teaching students to request the continuation of routine activities by using time delay and increasing physical assistance in the context of chain interruption. *Journal of The Association for Persons with Severe Handicaps, 16,* 154–167.

Gerner, M. (1986). Vocational training of individuals who are deaf-blind at the Elwyn Institutes. In S. Barrett & A. Smith (Eds.), *Employment options for young adults with deaf-blindness: Philosophy, practice, new directions* (pp. 143–164). Washington, DC: Helen Keller National Technical Assistance Center.

Gerry, M.H., & Mirsky, A. (1992). Guiding principles for public policy on natural supports. In J. Nisbet (Ed.), *Natural supports in school, at work, and in the community for people with severe disabilities* (pp. 341–346). Baltimore: Paul H. Brookes Publishing Co.

Giangreco, M., Cloninger, C., Mueller, P., Yuan, S., & Ashworth, S. (1991). Perspectives of parents whose children have dual sensory impairments. *Journal of The Association for Persons with Severe Handicaps, 16*(1), 14–24.

Goetz, L. (1989). *Supported employment for deaf-blind youth* (Bay Area Personnel Systems) (Continuation proposal). (OSERS/SEP Model Demonstration Grant #G00873047). San Francisco State University, Department of Special Education, California Research Institute, San Francisco.

Goetz, L. (1993). Can inclusive education work for students who are deaf-blind? *Deaf-Blind Perspectives, 1*(2), 3–5.

Goetz, L. (1995). Inclusion of students who are deaf-blind: What does the future hold? In N. Haring & L. Romer (Eds.), *Welcoming students who are deaf-blind into typical classrooms: Facilitating school participation, learning, and friendships* (pp. 3–16). Baltimore: Paul H. Brookes Publishing Co.

Goetz, L., Haring, T., & Anderson, J. (1983). *The educational assessment scale for social interaction* (EASI). San Francisco State University, Department of Special Education, San Francisco.

Goetz, L., & Hunt, P. (1993). *Development of optimal learning and social environments in full inclusion settings* (OSERS/SEP Grant #H086D3001). San Francisco State University, Department of Special Education, California Research Institute, San Francisco.

Goetz, L., Lee, M., Johnston, S., & Gaylord-Ross, R. (1991). Integrated work for persons with dual sensory impairments: Strategies for inclusion. *Journal of The Association for Persons with Severe Handicaps, 16*(3), 131–139.

Gonsalves, J., & Harp, H. (1994, April). *Why go to all these boring meetings?* Presentation at 12th annual Cal-TASH Conference, Oakland, CA.

Goode, D. (1990). Thinking about and discussing quality of life. In R. Schalock & M. Bogale (Eds.), *Quality of life: Perspectives and issues* (pp. 41–58). Washington, DC: American Association of Mental Retardation.

Greenspan, S., & Shoultz, B. (1981). Why mentally retarded adults lose their jobs: Social competence as a factor in work adjustment. *Applied Research in Mental Retardation, 2,* 23–38.

Griffin, S.L., & Lowry, J. (1989). Supported employment for persons with deaf-blindness and mental retardation. *Journal of Vision Impairment & Blindness, December,* 495–499.

Hagner, D., Rogan, P., & Murphy, S. (1992). Facilitating natural supports in the workplace: Strategies for support consultants. *Journal of Rehabilitation, 58*(1), 29–34.

Hagner, D.C., Cotton, P., Goodall, S., & Nisbet, J. (1992). The perspectives of supportive coworkers: Nothing special. In J. Nisbet (Ed.), *Natural supports in school, at work, and in the community for people with severe disabilities* (pp. 241–256). Baltimore: Paul H. Brookes Publishing Co.

Halpern, A.S. (1993). Quality of life as a conceptual framework for evaluating transition outcomes. *Exceptional Children, 59*(6), 486–498.

Haring, N., & Romer, L. (Eds.). (1995). *Welcoming students who are deaf-blind into typical classrooms: Facilitating school participation, learning, and friendships.* Baltimore: Paul H. Brookes Publishing Co.

Haring, T., Haring, N., Breen, C., Romer, L., & White, O. (1995). Social relationships among students with deaf-blindness and their peers in inclusive settings. In N. Haring & L. Romer (Eds.), *Welcoming students who are deaf-blind into typical classrooms: Facilitating school participation, learning, and friendships* (pp. 231–247). Baltimore: Paul H. Brookes Publishing Co.

Hobbs, T., & Allen, W. (1989). *Preparing for the future: A practical guide for developing individual transition plans.* Napa: California Institute on Human Services.

Huebner, K.M., Prickett, J.G., Welch, T.R., & Joffee, E. (Eds.). (1995). *Hand in hand: Essentials of communication and orientation and mobility for your students who are deaf-blind.* New York: AFB Press (The American Foundation for the Blind).

Kregel, J., & Wehman, P. (1989). Supported employment: Promises deferred for persons with severe disabilities. *Journal of The Association for Persons with Severe Handicaps, 14,* 293–303.

Lee, M. (1994). *The effective co-worker vs. job coach training on inclusion in supported employment settings.* Unpublished master's thesis, California State University–Hayward, Department of Special Education.

Lee, M., & Johnston, S. (Directors). (1990). *Now is the time: Supported employment for persons with dual sensory impairments* [Videotape]. Seattle: The Association for Persons with Severe Handicaps.

Lee, M., Lynch, K., & Goetz, L. (1988). *Supported employment for individuals with dual sensory impairments.* Paper presented at the 15th annual TASH Conference, Washington, DC.

Lipton, D. (1993). Inclusion in the 90s: Advocacy, family, and curriculum issues. Keynote address, annual Cal-TASH Conference, Burbank, CA.

Martin, J. (1986). Identifying potential jobs. In F. Rusch (Ed.), *Competitive employment issues and strategies* (pp. 165–174). Baltimore: Paul H. Brookes Publishing Co.

Meisel, C. (1994). *Increasing interactions with voice output augmentative communication systems.* Unpublished master's thesis, San Francisco State University, Department of Special Education, San Francisco.

Mirenda, P., & Iacono, T. (1990). Communication options for persons with severe and profound disabilities: State-of-the-art and future directions. *Journal of The Association for Persons with Severe Handicaps, 15,* 3–21.

Moon, S., Inge, K., Wehman, P., Brooke, V., & Barcus, J.M. (1990). *Helping persons with severe mental retardation get and keep employment: Supported employment issues and strategies.* Baltimore: Paul H. Brookes Publishing Co.

Mount, B., & Zwernik, K. (1988). *It's never too early, it's never too late—a booklet about personal futures planning* (Publ. No. 421-88-109). St. Paul: Minnesota Governor's Planning Council on Developmental Disabilities.

Murphy, S. (1991). *The effects of using co-workers in training workers with severe disabilities.* Unpublished master's thesis, San Francisco State University, Department of Special Education, San Francisco.

Nietupski, J., Chappelle, S., & Murray, J. (1994). *A dispersed heterogeneous placement SE model: An innovative alternative for transitioning students with mental retardation from school to work.* Iowa University Affiliated Program, Iowa City, IA.

Nisbet, J. (1992). Introduction. In J. Nisbet (Ed.), *Natural supports in school, at work, and in the community for people with severe disabilities* (pp. 1–10). Baltimore: Paul H. Brookes Publishing Co.

Nisbet, J., & Hagner, D. (1988). Natural supports in the workplace: A reexamination of supported employment. *Journal of The Association for Persons with Severe Handicaps, 13,* 260–267.

O'Brien, J., & O'Brien, C.L. (1992). Members of each other: Perspectives on social support for people with severe disabilities. In J. Nisbet (Ed.), *Natural supports in school, at work, and in the community for people with severe disabilities* (pp. 17–63). Baltimore: Paul H. Brookes Publishing Co.

O'Donnell, M.M. (1992, March). Population trends and life span issues for individuals with deaf-blindness (reaction paper). In *Proceedings of the National Conference on Deaf-Blindness: Deaf-Blind Services in the 90s* (pp. 17–19). National Conference on Deaf-Blindness, sponsored by the Hilton/Perkins National Program, Washington, DC.

Patton, M.Q. (1987). *How to use qualitative methods in evaluation.* London: Sage.

Perlroth, P., Pumpian, I., Hesche, S., & Campbell, C. (1993). Transition planning for individuals who are deaf and blind: A person-centered approach. *OSERS News in Print,* Winter, 24–30.

Rainforth, B., York, J., & Macdonald, C. (1992). *Collaborative teams for students with severe disabilities.* Baltimore: Paul H. Brookes Publishing Co.

Riggio, M. (1992). A changing population of children and youth with deaf-blindness: A changing role of the deaf-blind specialist/teacher (reaction paper). *Proceedings of the National Conference on Deaf-Blindness: Deaf-blind services in the 90s—Revitalization and future directions* (pp. 20–27). Sponsored by Hilton/Perkins National Program, Washington, DC.

Rogan, P., Hagner, D., & Murphy, S. (1993). National supports: Reconceptualizing job coach roles. *Journal of The Association of Persons with Severe Handicaps, 18*(4), 275–281.

Roland, C., & Schweigert, P. (1990). *Tangible symbol systems: Symbolic communication for individuals with multisensory impairments.* Tucson: Communication Skill Builders.

Rusch, F.R., Chadsey-Rusch, J., & Johnson, J.R. (1991). Supported employment: Emerging opportunities for employment integration. In L. Meyer, C. Peck, & L. Brown (Eds.), *Critical issues in the lives of people with severe disabilities* (pp. 145–169). Baltimore: Paul H. Brookes Publishing Co.

Salisbury, C.L., Palombaro, M.M., & Evans, I. (1993). *Collaborative problem solving: Instructor's manual.* Binghamton: State University of New York–Binghamton.

Sapon-Shevin, M. (1992). Celebrating diversity, creating community: Curriculum that honors and builds on differences. In S. Stainback & W. Stainback (Eds.), *Curriculum considerations in inclusive classrooms: Facilitating learning for all students* (pp. 19–36). Baltimore: Paul H. Brookes Publishing Co.

Siegel-Causey, E. (1995). Choosing systems and modes of communication. In K.M. Huebner, J.G. Prickett, T.R. Welch, & E. Joffee (Eds.), *Hand in hand: Essentials of communication and orientation and mobility for your students who are deaf-blind* (pp. 367–409). New York: AFB Press (The American Foundation for the Blind).

Sisson, L., Van Hasselt, V.B., & Herson, M. (1987). Psychological approaches with deaf-blind persons: Strategies and issues in research and treatment. *Clinical Psychology Review, 7,* 303–328.

Smithdas, J. (1995). Foreword. In J. Everson (Ed.), *Supporting young adults who are deaf-blind in their communities* (pp. xii–xiv). Baltimore: Paul H. Brookes Publishing Co.

Snell, M.J. (Ed.). (1993). *Instruction of students with severe disabilities* (4th ed.). New York: Merrill.

Sowers, J. (1989). Supported employment models and approaches for persons with physical and multiple disabilities. In J. Sowers & L. Powers (Eds.), *Vocational preparation and employment of students with physical and multiple disabilities* (Chapter 2). Portland: Oregon Research Institute.

Sowers, J., & Powers, J. (1989). Job design strategies for persons with physical and multiple disabilities. In J. Sowers & L. Powers (Eds.), *Vocational preparation and employment of students with physical and multiple disabilities.* Portland: Oregon Research Institute.

Super, D.E. (1984). Perspectives on the meaning and value of work. In N. Gysbers & Associates (Eds.), *Designing careers* (pp. 27–53). San Francisco: Jossey-Bass.

Terkel, S. (1972). *Working*. New York: Pantheon.

Toney, L., Lee, M., Certo, N., Markey, L., Belanger, D., & Toney, K. (1993). *Natural supports case study: Assisting Lisa to connect with her dreams*. Unpublished manuscript, San Francisco State University, Department of Special Education, San Francisco.

Touchette, P. (1971). Transfer of stimulus control: Measuring the moment of transfer. *Journal of Experimental Analysis of Behavior, 15,* 347–354.

Vandercook, T., York, J., & Forest, M. (1989). The McGill Action Planning System (MAPS): A strategy for building the vision. *Journal of The Association for Persons with Severe Handicaps, 14*(3), 205–215.

Wacker, D., Wiggins, B., Fowler, M., & Berg, W. (1988). Training students with profound or multiple handicaps to make requests via microswitches. *Journal of Applied Behavior Analysis, 18,* 331–343.

Wehman, P. (1988). Supported employment. Toward zero exclusion of persons with severe disabilities. In P. Wehman & M.S. Moon (Eds.), *Vocational rehabilitation and supported employment* (pp. 3–16). Baltimore: Paul H. Brookes Publishing Co.

Wehman, P. (1992). *Life beyond the classroom: Transition strategies for young people with disabilities*. Baltimore: Paul H. Brookes Publishing Co.

Wehman, P., Kregel, J., & Shafer, M. (1989). *Emerging trends in the national supported employment initiative: A preliminary analysis of 27 states*. Richmond: Virginia Commonwealth University, Rehabilitation Research and Training Center.

Wehman, P., Moon, M.S., Everson, J., Wood, W., & Barcus, J. (1988). *Transition from school to work: New challenges for youth with severe disabilities*. Baltimore: Paul H. Brookes Publishing Co.

York, J., & Rainforth, B. (1991). Developing instructional adaptations. In F. Orelove & D. Sobsey, *Educating children with multiple disabilities: A transdisciplinary approach* (2nd ed., pp. 259–295). Baltimore: Paul H. Brookes Publishing Co.

12

People with Challenging Behavior in Integrated Work Environments

CAROLYN HUGHES AND FRANK R. RUSCH

PEOPLE WORK FOR many different reasons. They work for wages because money provides a degree of independence, they work because they form close relationships with their co-workers, and they work to obtain the satisfaction that results from being valued by employers. Edgerton (1967) observed that some employees with mental retardation work because they believe that work "cloaks" their disabilities. For employees with chronic mental illness, work, even when not "symptom free" (e.g., free from episodic agitation or aggression), may produce a measure of acceptance from society (Cook, 1990).

However, employment outcomes for many individuals with challenging behavior are not favorable (Cook, Solomon, & Mock, 1989; Frank, Sitlington, & Carson, 1991; MacDonald-Wilson, Mancuso, Danley, & Anthony, 1989). In general, research indicates that persons associated with the rubric "challenging behavior" experience the highest school dropout and unemployment rates of all disability groups (Edgar & Levine, 1988; Frank et al., 1991; Linden & Forness, 1986; Neel, Meadows, Levine, & Edgar, 1988; Wagner, 1993), in addition to substantial economic dependence and extensive involvement in social welfare services (Edgar & Levine, 1988). Furthermore, individuals with challenging behavior are not engaged in community activities to nearly the same extent as their peers with other disabilities who do not have challenging behavior (Wagner, 1993).

The work performance literature indicates that unemployment and job loss typically are attributed to social or personal behaviors rather than behaviors associated with task performance, such as rate of production or acquisition of job skills (Anthony & Blanch, 1987; Bullis & Gaylord-Ross, 1989; Cook et al., 1989; Greenspan & Shoultz, 1981; Kochany, Simpson, Hill, & Wehman, 1982). For example, Meyer and Evans (1989) identified an array of challenging behaviors associated with employment termination. These behaviors, followed by an illustrative example of each, include stereotypic behavior (e.g., rocking in one's seat while entering data into a computer), self-injury (e.g., biting one's hand when approached by a customer), aggression (e.g., hitting a co-worker who is standing "too close"), inappropriate social behavior (e.g., talking aloud to imaginary people while waxing floors), physical regulatory disorders (e.g., drooling on pizza boxes while folding them), and specific emotional disturbance (e.g., being afraid to enter a closed storeroom to get supplies). Other challenging behaviors identified as interfering with job success include temper tantrums (e.g., yelling while throwing instead of stacking boxes), excessive activity (e.g., stacking wire hangers repeatedly), off-task behavior (e.g., staring at members of the dish crew instead of loading the dishwasher) (Smith & Coleman, 1986), prompt dependency (e.g., waiting for a supervisor's request before starting the photocopy machine), ritualistic behavior (e.g., insisting on stacking the washcloths on only one particular shelf), and destructive behavior (e.g., tearing the wrappers off cans while shelving them) (McCarthy, Fender, & Fender, 1988).

Challenging behavior becomes a problem in a work environment when co-workers react to performance that does not meet their expectations. Cook (1990) suggested that the stigma of challenging behavior may alarm or frighten potential employers or co-workers. Anthony and Blanch (1987) concurred that an employee with challenging behavior is more likely to be stigmatized, blamed, or feared than an employee with, for example, mental retardation and no challenging behavior. Isbister and Donaldson (1987) reported that employer attitudes toward workers with challenging behavior may be unfavorable and that community service providers such as mental health workers may be inflexible in accommodating work schedules or may not be convinced of the value of work for their clients. Furthermore, the community's or worksite's demands for "appropriate" behavior may exceed an employee's skill repertoire.

One response to challenging behavior in the workplace is supported employment. Supported employment is a new vocational option for persons with severe disabilities, including challenging behavior (Rusch & Hughes, 1989). As defined by the Developmental Disabilities Assistance and Bill of Rights Act Amendments of 1987 (PL 100-146), supported employment provides paid work (working for wages) in integrated settings (places where employees without disabilities also work vs. sheltered employment) and support (including supervision, training, and transportation) for individuals who, because of their disabilities, require ongoing assistance to remain employed. Employment specialists provide an array of services to supported employees such as assistance in task completion, physical modification of job demands, or behavior management strategies. Typically, however, employment specialists have not been taught strategies to assist employees with challenging behavior, such as aggression, self-injury, or destructive behavior (Hughes & Rusch, 1992; Smith, 1994). Instead, an employment specialist is more likely to be at a loss as to what to do if a supported employee begins tearing off his or her clothes or sits in the middle of the employee lunchroom and begins screaming.

This chapter discusses strategies and solutions that employment specialists, teachers, direct service providers, employers, and administrators may use to improve employment outcomes for people with challenging behavior. Specifically, we describe 1) how to assess challenging behavior using a "systems approach" to functional analysis, and 2) how to support behavior by modifying the environment or teaching alternative behaviors. Throughout the chapter, in order to demonstrate application of these strategies to actual employees, we introduce two case examples typical of employees with challenging behavior, those of Stacy Hawkins and Albert Trotter. Our intent is to illustrate, by example, how practitioners may apply solutions to problems they may encounter in employment situations. Furthermore, we present examples and information derived from both the psychiatric and the developmental disabilities literature, because the technology for maintaining workers with challenging behavior in employment largely has been implemented by the mental health field. Consequently, in order to include relevant literature from multiple fields, we discuss findings related to individuals identified under a variety of nomenclature, including 1) students or adolescents with serious emotional disturbance or behavior disorders, 2) adults with psychiatric disabilities or chronic mental illness, 3) persons with dual diagnoses, and 4) individuals with autism.

STRATEGIES AND SOLUTIONS

A Systems Approach to Functional Analysis of Challenging Behavior in the Workplace

A growing body of literature supports the use of a functional analytic approach to assessing challenging behavior (Carr & Durand, 1985; Favell & Reid, 1988; Horner & Billingsley, 1988; Horner, O'Neill, & Flannery, 1993; O'Neill, Horner, Albin, Storey, & Sprague, 1990; Remington, 1991). This approach is based on establishing a causal relationship among environmental events and identifying the external variables of which behavior is a function (Skinner, 1938, 1953). Methods used to identify controlling variables include interviewing the individual and significant others, direct observation, and systematic manipulations of environmental events. (See O'Neill et al. [1990] for a complete description of procedures for conducting functional analyses of challenging behavior.) To illustrate functional analytic methods as applied to employment, we introduce supported employee Stacy Hawkins, our first case example:

> Stacy Hawkins, who works as a part-time clerk in a public library, demonstrates behavior that probably would be considered challenging by most people. When she runs out of books to stamp or process, for example, Stacy frequently picks at her face or hands with her fingernails, producing open lesions on her skin. Admonishments from her supervisor or co-workers to stop have been ineffective. Instead, Stacy yells and swears angrily at anyone who mentions her face picking, often while folding her arms and pressing her thumbs tightly against her forearms. Stacy is usually a good worker if no one comes too near or if nothing is out of place in her immediate area. If a co-worker comes close by, especially unexpectedly, Stacy usually becomes noticeably shaky and agitated, shields her face with the back of her hands, and repeatedly screams "Don't want to." When she notices something missing at her desk area such as the paper towels, she hollers "Put back towels now!" Unwanted items are quickly pushed to the floor. As a result of her behavior, people have learned to shy away from Stacy. She consequently spends most of her time at work alone, in the corner of her desk and shielded by stacks of books.

Using a functional analytic approach to Stacy's behavior, an employment specialist may use the interviewing strategy and ask Stacy what is bothering her if she is screaming or ask a co-worker what items, if missing, seem to prompt Stacy's screaming. A co-worker may use direct observation to determine what events precede Stacy's periodic instances of extreme agitation and when these instances are most likely to occur. Or Stacy's supervisor may use systematic manipulations to vary the amount of Stacy's work demands to determine whether Stacy's face picking and verbal outbursts relate to not having enough work to stay busy. The value of a functional analysis is that we may be able to determine the events that are associated with the occurrence of challenging behavior and then use this information to develop a behavior support plan.

The functional analytic approach to assessing problem behavior has been typically investigated in nonemployment settings such as schools (Haring & Kennedy, 1990), group homes (Horner, Day, Sprague,

O'Brien, & Heathfield, 1991), and institutional settings (Steege et al., 1990). We propose an adaptation of the functional analytic approach to employment that regards challenging behavior as a *systems* problem (Bronfenbrenner, 1977; Rusch & Mithaug, 1985). As displayed in Table 1, we suggest applying functional analysis strategies (O'Neill et al., 1990) to challenging behavior across the multiple environmental systems (levels) that may affect an employee (i.e., individual, small group, worksite or agency, community) in order to locate the sources that are influencing behavior.

According to our proposed systems approach to analyzing challenging behavior, events that influence a person's actions may originate from multiple sources or environmental levels. With respect to employment, levels of influence may include the individual employee (e.g., an employee gets little sleep the night before coming to work), the small group of individuals with which the employee has frequent contact (e.g., an employee gets his or her co-workers' attention by talking too loudly), the worksite (e.g., a new manager reassigns job tasks and gives an employee a job that he or she has difficulty completing), and the community (e.g., a neighborhood doughnut shop that an employee frequents with friends closes down). Our systems approach to functional analysis applies the strategies recommended by O'Neill et al. (1990) (e.g., interviewing, direct observation, systematic manipulation) to the array of environmental spheres that may influence an employee's behavior. Table 1 demonstrates the range of application of these strategies across the four suggested environmental levels, using a variety of possible workplace scenarios. We now provide an in-depth application of the systems approach to Stacy's challenging behavior.

On the individual employee level, Stacy's transition teacher may 1) ask Stacy if the lesions on her face are irritating and if she would like to apply some salve to reduce the irritation (interview), 2) check to see when Stacy's face picking is most likely to occur (direct observation), or 3) vary the amount of co-workers' attention directed at Stacy's face picking to determine if this attention is maintaining the behavior (systematic manipulation). On the small group level, the employment specialist may 1) ask Stacy's family what happens at home if she is approached unexpectedly (interview), 2) observe Stacy as people come and go in the lunchroom (direct observation), or 3) announce to Stacy that someone is entering her work area to see if prior knowledge of someone's presence reduces her agitation (systematic manipulation). On the worksite or agency level, Stacy's supervisor may 1) ask the rehabilitation counselor if Stacy became agitated at her previous job when items were missing from her desk and what had been done to alleviate the problem (interview), 2) observe to determine

Table 1. Systems approach to a functional analysis of challenging behavior in the workplace

Functional analysis strategy	Environmental levels				
	Individual	Small group	Worksite or agency	Community
Interview	Interview employee to identify function of challenging behavior. Example: The transition teacher asks a young man employed in a doughnut shop to point to a picture that indicates how he was feeling prior to hitting his hand against the wall.	Interview significant others (e.g., co-workers, family, employer) to identify function of challenging behavior. Example: The supervisor calls a car wash attendant's mother to determine if an event at home may be the cause of the attendant's crying as she punched in for work.	Interview direct service providers and agency administrators to identify function of challenging behavior. Example: A high school student's father calls the adult service agency serving his son to find out if a change in job coach may be the source of his son's refusal to go to work.	Interview community members (e.g., bus driver, store clerk, neighbor) to identify function of challenging behavior. Example: Employer asks the bus driver if a change in bus routes may be causing a recycling plant employee to come to work late every day.
Direct observation	Observe employee over time to identify function of challenging behavior. Example: A co-worker observes a factory worker to see if his verbal outbursts usually occur when there is a sudden loud noise near the assembly line.	Observe employee in small group interaction (e.g., with co-workers or family) to identify function of challenging behavior. Example: The employment specialist at a floral shop notices that a worker makes faces every time co-workers initiate conversation in the breakroom.	Observe employee in worksite and agency interaction to identify function of challenging behavior. Example: The owner of a Mexican restaurant observes that the new pots and pans man works hard only when his transition teacher is in the kitchen.	Observe employee in community interaction to identify function of challenging behavior. Example: A mental health counselor observes that the new neighbors next to an office clerk's group home have been inviting the clerk over for frequent beer parties. The interaction of the alcohol and the clerk's medication causes him to be listless and irritable at work each day after a party.

Systematic manipulation

Systematically manipulate environmental events on individual employee level to identify function of challenging behavior.

Example: The kitchen supervisor in a cafeteria asks an employee to bus tables instead of washing dishes to determine if her spitting is related to her not liking to get her hands wet.

Systematically manipulate environmental events on group level to identify function of challenging behavior.

Example: The head librarian in a public library moves a clerk's desk closer to a co-worker's to find out if the clerk's hand biting is due to wanting to get her co-worker's attention.

Systematically manipulate environmental events on worksite and agency level to identify function of challenging behavior.

Example: The rehabilitation counselor asks a work supervisor to change a food service worker's shift from breakfast to lunch to determine if working in the early morning is what is causing the worker to verbally abuse her co-workers.

Systematically manipulate environmental events on community level to identify function of challenging behavior.

Example: The transition teacher asks a fellow student to ride the bus to work with a preschool aide to find out if the aide's agitation when leaving school to go to work is caused by fear of changing buses alone.

if Stacy's agitation varies due to the presence of the employment specialist (direct observation), or 3) change the location of Stacy's desk to see if having a full view of the door through which co-workers enter decreases her agitation when someone approaches (systematic manipulation). Finally, on the community level, Stacy's rehabilitation counselor may 1) ask the bus driver if there are any passengers with whom Stacy interacts on the bus (interview), 2) observe if Stacy has neighbors with whom she is friends (direct observation), or 3) arrange for a co-worker to bring Stacy to a social event at the library (systematic manipulation). The purpose of conducting a functional analysis on each of these levels is without a systems-analytic approach, we do not know which sphere(s) of influence may be affecting an employee's behavior. The systems approach to functional analysis may help pinpoint the exact source of events contributing to challenging behavior.

In addition, we recommend using social validation measures (Wolf, 1978) in conjunction with the systems-analytic approach when assessing challenging behavior. Social validation is a method that may be used to assess the extent to which an employee with disabilities is socially accepted within an environment. (See White [1986] for guidelines for using social validation measures, such as subjective evaluation and social comparison, in employment.) To illustrate, let us return to Stacy, the library clerk. We suggest using subjective evaluation (i.e., soliciting the opinions of participants in a setting) on the individual level to determine if Stacy considers her behavior at work to be a problem (e.g., does she really want to change, or is she "happy" the way she is?); the small group level to see if her co-workers or family consider Stacy's behavior a problem (e.g., would her fellow clerks like to interact socially with Stacy or like to see her stop picking her face?); the worksite or agency level to find out if Stacy is creating a problem for her boss, the library, or the adult service agency that serves her (e.g., does Stacy's screaming result in frequent complaints by library patrons?); and the community level to discover if Stacy's employment-related behavior in the community is considered a problem (e.g., does Stacy also scream on the bus, producing complaints from other riders?).

We also recommend using social comparison (i.e., comparing a worker's behavior to that of other employees to determine if performance is substantially different) to identify environments in which an employee's typical performance is not considered acceptable when compared to that of others. By identifying the environmental systems (individual, small group, worksite or agency, and community) in which Stacy's behavior is considered by others to be a problem, we develop a case for designing a support plan to change the behavior. By contrast, if Stacy's behavior is not considered problematic, we cannot justify intervening to change it within a particular environment.

Intervening with Challenging Behavior in the Workplace

Conducting a functional analysis, whether through interviews, observations, or systematic manipulation, allows us to pinpoint potential environmental causes of challenging behaviors and to determine the effect of these behaviors on individuals demonstrating them. For example, we may determine that what probably causes Stacy to behave as she does at work is that 1) picking her skin provides sensory stimulation that is unavailable when she runs out of work, 2) yelling and swearing keep people from instructing her not to pick at her skin, 3) shielding her face and screaming keep people away from her and prevent social interaction, and 4) shouting and throwing items allow her to control the placement of objects in her immediate environment.

The benefits of determining the function of Stacy's behaviors are that we may find new, more acceptable ways to teach Stacy to achieve the same functional goals. In addition, social validation methodology gives us the means for establishing whether a challenging behavior is considered enough of a problem to warrant intervention. If we determine that challenging behavior presents a problem in the work environment, we recommend intervening to modify the behavior by introducing environmental support strategies or teaching alternative, competent behaviors. The next two sections of this chapter describe such strategies.

Introducing Environmental Support Strategies

In this section, we discuss strategies that have been used to support people with challenging behavior at work. Specifically, we review 1) providing personnel support, 2) modifying the work environment, 3) promoting social acceptance, and 4) job matching. We also provide examples of these strategies as used by Community Services for Autistic Adults and Children, Rockville, Maryland, by introducing Albert Trotter, a supported employee.[1] (Buckley, Mank, and Sandow [1990], Chadsey-Rusch and Rusch [1988], and Karan and Knight [1986] discuss additional support strategies that relate to work settings [e.g., advocacy training, agenda setting for service coordination, awareness training].)

> Albert Trotter is a 25-year-old man with autism. He has mental retardation and limited verbal skills (speaks in one- and two-word phrases). He is employed by a retailer. His job is to unbox merchandise, use a price gun

[1]Special thanks are extended to Dr. Marcia D. Smith and the staff of Community Services for Autistic Adults and Children, Rockville, Maryland, for providing this case example.

to put price stickers on merchandise, and otherwise prepare the merchandise for display on the floor. He has severe behavior problems at work, including refusing to work, lying on the floor and refusing to get up, stripping, spitting, grabbing food from co-workers, making loud ongoing demands for candy, running from the work area, occasional aggression (hitting others), and practicing self-injury (hitting himself). Albert is supervised by an employment specialist, and he participates with one other worker with autism at the job. The rest of Albert's co-workers (approximately 40) are persons who are not receiving disability services.

Providing Personnel Support Co-workers are a potential source of support for workers with challenging behavior. Rusch and his colleagues (Rusch, Hughes, Johnson, & Minch, 1991; Rusch, Johnson, & Hughes, 1990; Rusch & Minch, 1988; Rusch, Wilson, Hughes, & Heal, 1995), Shafer (1986), and others have studied the roles that co-workers play in the workplace in relation to persons with disabilities. Although the research literature on persons with challenging behavior is limited, findings suggest certain guidelines to follow when considering these individuals' behaviors.

Rusch and Minch (1988) and Shafer (1986) identified co-worker roles in the empirical literature, including advocating (optimizing and supporting an employee's employment status), associating (interacting socially), befriending (becoming someone's close associate and interacting away from the workplace), evaluating (appraising an employee's work behavior), and training (providing on-the-job skill training). For example, Rusch, Weithers, Menchetti, and Schutz (1980) taught co-workers to provide feedback to an employee who talked to himself often and repeated topics during interactions with co-workers. Training was provided to co-workers during 10-minute in-service sessions during daily breaks. The co-workers were taught to give feedback when a topic was reported.

Peer mentoring has been identified as a strategy associated with the successful employment of adolescents with severe behavior disorders (Bullis & Gaylord-Ross, 1989). Recommendations made by Bullis and Gaylord-Ross (1989) include involving peers who 1) are the same age or slightly older and 2) are "good citizens." They also suggested the possibility of having peer mentors with similar problems provide support to each other.

Supervisors at the worksite may be a source of support for workers with challenging behavior. By interviewing 10 job-site supervisors who employed persons with mental retardation, Rusch, Minch, and Hughes (1989) found that supervisors made several accommodations to promote continued employment of these workers. For example, they offered additional incentives, provided training, and modified job tasks. In addition, they instituted disciplinary procedures, recognized good work behavior, and monitored the quality of the job being performed.

Albert Trotter, the retail store worker, provides an illustration of the use of personnel support strategies. Based on a functional analysis of Albert's challenging behavior, the employment specialist determined that Albert's refusal to work typically occurred when he was required to unbox merchandise and rarely when he priced the merchandise. A simple solution to this problem was found when Lannie Jackson, Albert's co-worker, agreed to unbox all the merchandise while Albert did all the pricing. Soon, Albert's lying on the floor, spitting, and refusing to work occurred only rarely, and Albert and Lannie together completed their merchandising job daily. Albert's supervisor made a point of visiting the merchandising area, complimenting the two men on the quality of their work. In addition, Lannie and a few other co-workers started accompanying Albert to break, joking and sharing their snacks with him.

Modifying the Environment   Settings influence behavior. For example, if co-workers are placed in areas that are distant from each other, we can expect less interaction or sharing of job tasks as they work. Alternately, we can assume that loud noises created by one worker are less likely to distract another if that second worker is located "out of earshot." Therefore, if an employee's behavioral repertoire includes bizarre verbalizations, an appropriate work setting might be the laundry service of a large hotel, where much vocalization is "drowned out" by the sound of industrial washers and dryers.

Physical variables deserve careful attention when employment involves a person with challenging behavior. The work environment poses certain demands on all employees, including those with challenging behavior. Accordingly, it is recommended that a careful job analysis be conducted and that the work setting be restructured as much as possible to coincide with the unique characteristics of employees (Bailey & Pyles, 1989; Meyer & Evans, 1989).

Fortunately, a growing literature has addressed many of the physical variables that influence work behavior. For example, the U.S. Office of Personnel Management (1984) recommended considering the following factors when analyzing work requirements: 1) the way the tasks are accomplished, 2) the physical movements and mental processes involved in the work activity, 3) the degree of physical effort and the complexity of mental processes involved in the job, 4) the time involved in performing each task, and 5) the frequency with which each activity is performed.

Albert's employment specialist was sensitive to the physical variables in Albert's environment that might affect his behavior. Since the functional analysis that the specialist conducted revealed that Albert worked better in areas that were quiet, enclosed, and uncluttered, it was determined that a small storeroom where several co-workers worked would serve as a cue for Albert's appropriate behavior. Because the specialist had observed that Albert's self-injury tended to occur when job materials were lost or unavailable, extra sets of required materials were placed in clearly marked, readily available areas close to where Albert worked.

Promoting Social Acceptance in the Workplace Literature has begun to emerge that provides guidelines for promoting the social acceptance of persons with challenging behavior by their co-workers, supervisors, and employers. The importance of promoting acceptance in the workplace cannot be understated. As offered by Hughes, Rusch, and Curl (1990), "an *integrated workplace* is formed when individual differences are accepted and individual competence is maximized by providing opportunities and support" (p. 190). If individual differences are accepted and the strengths of employees with and without disabilities are capitalized upon, the need for environmental support strategies will be reduced. However, if the expectations of all involved—individuals with challenging behavior, co-workers, supervisors, and employers—are not being met, then the need for environmental support strategies will increase. Recommendations made by Hughes et al. (1990) are helpful in providing direction for managing these expectations. Specifically, they suggest that work performance (social and work behavior) be evaluated routinely (e.g., monthly, bimonthly, every 6 months) by administering work performance evaluations that consider ratings of the work behavior of *all* employees. The results of these work performance evaluations provide information that enables interested parties to determine the extent to which individuals are being accepted on the job. If certain individuals are receiving low ratings in certain areas, then interventions can be devised that may result in higher ratings over time. Alternately, if an individual's behavior cannot be modified, strategies may be designed to assist employees to be more accepting of individual differences, thereby allowing that individual to enjoy some level of acceptance in the employment setting.

Albert's employment specialist promoted social acceptance in the retail store by unobtrusively asking Albert's supervisor and co-workers which of Albert's behaviors were acceptable on the job. The interviews revealed that no one minded much when Albert talked to himself or occasionally lay on the floor. However, no one liked it when Albert hit, grabbed food, or spit. A contingency management system was introduced in which Albert was able to purchase a snack of his choice at break after infrequent occurrences of unacceptable behavior. As Albert's acceptable behavior gradually began to increase, the employment specialist observed that Albert's co-workers were spending more time with Albert and directing more positive remarks toward him.

Job Matching An extensive literature exists on the importance of matching an employee's skills, needs, interests, and preferences to the requirements and opportunities of a job and the expectations of a worksite. Job matching occurs when the employment specialist surveys community job opportunities and analyzes specific job requirements at potential worksites (Rusch & Hughes, 1989). The specialist then matches this information to potential employees' individual characteristics to arrive at an appropriate match between the person and the job. Of particular importance for this discussion is research addressing persons with chronic mental illness (Anthony & Blanch, 1987; Isbister & Donaldson, 1987), autism (Berkell, 1992; Winking, O'Reilly, & Moon, 1993), and severe emotional disturbance (Bullis & Gaylord-Ross, 1989). A complete review of this literature is beyond the scope of this chapter; however, employee preference has been identified as particularly critical to an appropriate job match for persons with challenging behavior (Anthony & Blanch, 1987; Winking et al., 1993) and is discussed in the following paragraphs.

Winking et al. (1993) provided profiles of four young adults with challenging behaviors to illustrate their work performance on jobs that were associated with high (versus low) preference. Work preference assessments were obtained in actual work settings by the transition teacher in order to sample the range of variables, potential reinforcers, and stimuli available in an environment. Winking et al. (1993) inferred that the four individuals had preferences for specific job tasks by the consistency of their behavior associated with "high-preference" tasks (e.g., smiling, attending to task, singing) versus "low-preference" tasks (e.g., noncompliance, bathroom requests, shutting of eyes). Specifically, challenging behaviors associated with low preference tasks such as shrieking, biting, or property destruction decreased systematically for the employees when they performed high-preference job tasks. For example, one person (Hannah) demonstrated fewer challenging behaviors (aggression, grabbing, crumbling materials) when performing a high-preference task (cleaning bathrooms) than when she performed a low-preference task (turning down sheets in a motel). In addition, the validity of the employees' behavior as an indicator of preference was corroborated by interviews with the employees themselves and with others familiar with them.

The importance of considering preference when conducting job matches seems straightforward. If we respect the wishes and desires of individuals as they make choices about employment, they probably will enjoy a higher level of job satisfaction than if we were to ignore their preferences and the relationship of these preferences to problem behaviors. For example, Albert's employment specialist was sensitive to Albert's preferences for tasks at the retail store where he worked.

Having observed that Albert's refusals to work, spitting, and lying on the floor typically occurred when Albert was unboxing rather than pricing merchandise, the specialist reassigned Albert to pricing. Because Albert's challenging behaviors decreased, we can assume that he preferred to price rather than unbox merchandise. Respecting Albert's job preference was a relatively simple way to alleviate challenging behavior.

Teaching Alternative Competent Behaviors

Providing support for employees is an effective strategy to prevent or ameliorate problems associated with challenging behavior on the job. A related approach to challenging behavior involves teaching an employee a socially acceptable alternative behavior that serves a similar function for the employee (Carr, 1988; Horner & Billingsley, 1988; Horner et al., 1993). Horner and Billingsley (1988) observed that an individual has a higher probability of adopting an alternative behavior if that behavior is equally or more efficient at producing reinforcement than the challenging behavior is.

Based on a functional analysis, we should learn what function a particular behavior may be serving for an employee. For example, a functional analysis might indicate that Albert strips to avoid social interaction that he finds aversive. His outbursts allow him to escape from the aversive stimulus of co-workers talking to him. If Albert can learn an alternative behavior that will achieve the same reinforcer (i.e., escape from an aversive situation) more effectively and quickly than stripping, it is likely that he will learn to perform the alternative behavior. If social interaction is aversive to Albert primarily because he lacks social skills, teaching him some conversational phrases may make social interaction less aversive and even result in positive attention. For example, Albert might be taught a few short phrases that he could use to respond to co-workers' social initiations, such as "I'm fine," "Good," and "Yes." Alternately, Albert might be taught how to escape appropriately from social situations by expressing a simple phrase such as "Not now."

Positive behavioral support may help increase an employee's repertoire of competent, acceptable behaviors that replace challenging behavior (Haring, 1989; LaVigna, Willis, & Donnellan, 1989). Evans and Meyer (1985) argued that perhaps all challenging behavior is a problem of insufficient instruction. For example, an employee may never have learned socially acceptable behavior that would be functionally equivalent to a challenging behavior. Therefore, teaching an effective, competent behavior to replace the challenging behavior gives an employee the option of behaving differently. Accordingly, Wehman and

Kregel (1988) argued that the issue is not whether employees with challenging behavior have the ability to work, but whether we have the ability to teach critical skills necessary for an individual to be successfully employed. In this section, we introduce strategies that may be used to teach alternative behaviors in the following areas: 1) communication, 2) problem solving, 3) self-management and coping strategies, 4) social skills, 5) making choices and expressing preferences, 6) generalized skills building, and 7) compliance with work demands.

Communication Employees with challenging behavior often demonstrate limited language and communication skills (McCarthy et al., 1988; Smith, Belcher, Juhrs, & Nabors, 1994; Wehman & Kregel, 1988). Deficient language and communication skills as well as bizarre verbalizations have been associated with low levels of social integration in integrated work settings (Smith & Belcher, 1994). Carr and Durand (1985) and others have hypothesized that challenging behavior may serve a communicative function for individuals who have limited skill in communicating through more socially acceptable forms such as conversation. For example, rather than politely asking co-workers not to stand too close to her desk, Stacy, the library clerk, yells and swears at them.

Functional communication training has been used successfully to teach alternative responses to challenging behavior in employment settings (Burt, Fuller, & Lewis, 1991; McCarthy et al., 1988; Smith & Coleman, 1986; Wehman & Kregel, 1988). To illustrate, Burt et al. (1991) used role play to teach a clerical worker to say "Excuse me" and other appropriate phrases, rather than interrupting or abruptly terminating conversations, and to ask for a 5-minute walk when she became angry, rather than throwing a tantrum. Similarly, Smith and Coleman (1986) taught an employee in a book bindery to ask for assistance with difficult tasks rather than throwing a tantrum or engaging in verbal outbursts. Stacy, the library clerk, could have been taught to ask her co-workers to sit in a chair several feet from her desk when addressing her rather than standing too close.

Problem Solving D'Zurilla and Goldfried (1971) defined "problems" as situations that occur frequently in our everyday life to which we must respond in order to function effectively but to which a correct response is not immediately known or available. Problem solving may provide an alternative to challenging behavior for employees who are faced with a difficult situation on the job to which they must respond (Cook, 1990; D'Zurilla & Goldfried, 1971; Haring, 1989; Hughes & Rusch, 1989). Some instances of challenging behavior such as aggression or property destruction may represent ineffective or inappropriate responses to a problem situation. For example, a parking lot attendant may have misplaced the key to the money drawer, and a customer may be waiting impatiently for change. Instead of looking on the floor or through his pockets for the keys, the parking attendant begins yelling and banging his fist against the drawer. While this behavior may serve the function of silencing the impatient customer, it does not solve the problem of the lost key or the locked money drawer.

Problem-solving techniques have been implemented in employment as alternatives to challenging behavior. For example, Hughes and Rusch (1989) taught two employees in a soap-packaging plant who were self-injurious, were aggressive, and failed to comply with work demands to solve task-related problems by stating the problem, identifying a solution, and praising themselves. Problem solving was associated with decreases in aggression and self-injury and increases in task performance and compliance with task demands. Stacy, who became upset when items were missing from her desk, could have been taught strategies for finding the items, such as checking her desk drawers, asking her supervisor, or looking in the storage cabinet.

Self-Management and Coping Strategies Gardner and Cole (1989), Meyer and Evans (1989), and others have suggested that a lack of self-management or coping skills may increase the likelihood of challenging behavior by an employee who is confronted with a provoking or stressful situation. The emphasis of employment training since the late 1980s has focused on teaching employees to control their own reactions to situations likely to produce inappropriate behavior rather than relying on others to address the problem (Carr, 1991; Cook, 1990; Gardner & Cole, 1989; Hughes & Rusch, 1989; Rusch, Hughes, & Wilson, 1995). The shift from external to self-managed approaches to challenging behavior is likely a result of 1) the realization that employment specialists could not be present consistently or control all the variables throughout an employee's workday and 2) the increasing value placed on independent performance (Hughes & Agran, 1993; Rusch et al., 1995).

Self-management and coping strategies have been applied successfully in employment across a variety of challenging behaviors. For example, Cook (1990) reported teaching employees with mental illness to control their symptomatology at work and to discuss their anxiety, confusion, or disturbing thoughts outside the workplace with their case manager or support group. Smith (1985) taught employees to use picture schedules to stay on task and decrease aggressive episodes. Smith and Coleman (1986) taught a recycling plant worker to self-monitor in an effort to decrease wandering from his work area, hitting co-workers, destroying property, and remaining off-task. Self-management strategies also have been used to increase relaxation and to cope with anxiety and anger in employment training situations (Cole, Gardner, & Karan, 1985; Lindsay, Baty, & Michie, 1989; McPhail & Chamove, 1989). Self-management might have been used in conjunction with Albert's contingency management system, which was introduced in response to his hitting, grabbing food, and spitting at his retail job. Albert could have been taught to monitor occurrences of these behaviors by marking squares on a tally sheet. If fewer than a predetermined number of squares were marked, Albert would know that he could purchase his favorite snack at break.

Social Skills Some forms of challenging behavior may be caused by an employee's lack of social interaction skills. LaPaglia (1982), MacDonald-Wilson et al. (1989), and others have suggested that inappropriate social behavior such as "talking to voices," disturbing others, displaying a lack of hygiene and grooming, and talking excessively about problems may be alleviated by teaching employees social skills considered appropriate in the workplace. Examples of social skills valued by employers in integrated worksites include 1) asking for assistance, 2) responding to criticism, 3) following directions, 4) offering to help co-workers, 5) providing information about the job, 6) answering questions, 7) greeting co-workers, 8) conversing with others, 9) using social amenities, and 10) giving positive comments (Chadsey-Rusch, 1990).

Teaching employees appropriate social skills has been associated with decreases in challenging behavior. To illustrate, LaPaglia (1982) taught a young office cleaner to greet co-workers politely and to knock quietly on office doors before entering and cleaning offices. Learning appropriate entry behavior was accompanied by decreases in disruption and emotional outbursts. Similarly, Rusch et al. (1980) taught co-workers to instruct a food service employee to decrease his topic repetitions, which were annoying to the co-workers when they conversed at break. Decreases in the employee's topic repetitions were accompanied by increases in novel conversational topics. Shafer, Brooke, and Wehman (1985) taught a janitor who had difficulty getting along with co-workers and supervisors to use appropriate social skills when responding to criticism or sarcastic remarks delivered by co-workers. Albert, the retail worker, could have been taught to replace his loud, ongoing demands for candy with a request for a co-worker's assistance in using the vending machine to purchase his own snack at lunch.

Making Choices and Expressing Preferences Unless an employee has learned more appropriate alternatives, challenging behavior may be the only way he or she knows to express choice or preference (Casey-Black & Knoblock, 1989; McCarthy et al., 1988; Meyer & Evans, 1989). For example, Albert may lie on the floor and refuse to get up because he cannot express his preference for a break and lacks the verbal or social skills to tell his supervisor. Research indicates that, like all employees, persons with challenging behavior experience more success on the job if they believe that they are partly in control of their schedule and can express their own interests, values, and choices (Anthony & Blanch, 1987; Isbister & Donaldson, 1987; MacDonald-Wilson et al., 1989). However, persons with challenging behavior rarely are given opportunities to learn to make choices and personal decisions or to express their preferences (Bannerman, Sheldon, Sherman, & Harchik, 1990; Kishi, Teelucksingh, Zollers, Park-Lee, & Meyer, 1988).

Fortunately, respecting an individual's choices and preferences for specific employment options has been mandated by the Individuals with Disabilities Education Act (IDEA) of 1990 (PL 101-476). The IDEA legislation requires that schools take into account students' needs, preferences, and interests in the development of their employment goals and educational programs. It is critical that teachers and employment specialists respect a student's vocational choices when placing a student at a particular job site because, once on the job, work demands may limit an individual's opportunity for choice related to job requirements. Potential problems may be alleviated by allowing students to "sample" different types of jobs through high school work experiences in order to match their preferences with available jobs in the community (Hutchins & Renzaglia, 1990). For example, some of Stacy's and Albert's challenging behaviors may have been alleviated by different employment placements that would have incorporated their choices and preferences.

Sometimes individuals may not know how to make choices related to their employment. Although models for teaching choice do exist (cf. Meyer & Evans, 1989), few studies have investigated procedures for teaching choice making in employment settings (Schaller & Szymanski, 1992; Wehmeyer, 1992). Yet, as mentioned, studies conducted in work settings have shown that persons with challenging behavior can demonstrate task preferences and that their work performance is affected by their preference (Mithaug & Hanawalt, 1978; Mithaug & Mar, 1980). Clearly, a critical area warranting future investigation is choice making and providing opportunities for choice in employment.

Generalized Skills Building Challenging behavior may relate to an employee's impoverished skill repertoire in responding to everyday work-related situations (Casey-Black & Knoblock, 1989). For example, a warehouse worker who does not know how to "punch in" his time card may lose the card instead, a soap packager who does not know how to replace tape in a dispenser may wander away from his work area looking for assistance, or a furniture finisher who does not know which kind of sandpaper to use on a chair may curse herself repeatedly. In each case, the challenging behavior may be mitigated by teaching the employee skills that are critical to functioning successfully in the work environment (Berkell, 1992; Carr, 1991; Casey-Black & Knoblock, 1989; McCarthy et al., 1988; O'Neill et al., 1990). Furthermore, strategies that promote maintaining newly learned skills should be incorporated into instruction to enable employees to use these skills in the absence of the teacher or the job coach (Favell & Reid, 1988; Horner & Billingsley, 1988; Hughes & Rusch, 1992). For example, Albert's refusing to work, lying on the floor, and spitting occurred when he was required to unbox merchandise. His behavior may have been due to his inability to use a utility knife to cut the tape that sealed the boxes. Teaching Albert an efficient way to hold the knife may have made the task easier and eliminated his challenging behavior.

Compliance with Work Demands   Ideally, we would have much opportunity to practice choice at work; in reality, workplace demands and job requirements frequently inhibit our opportunity to choose. Although tasks may be modified to some extent, because our jobs exist as part of the workplace environment or system, sometimes we must learn to comply with job demands even when it is not our own choice. For example, a waitress on the morning shift in a coffee shop must arrive at 6:00 A.M. to take breakfast orders even if it is not her preference.

Occurrences of challenging behavior may relate to an employee's limited number of opportunities to learn how to comply with workplace demands (McCarthy et al., 1988; O'Brien, 1989). Conversely, an employee may have a long history of noncompliance that has been reinforced by the environment's response to the challenging behavior. For example, an electrical component assembler may be reinforced by being left alone and escaping from an assigned task after yelling at a co-worker who instructed her how to wire a printed circuit. Or a mail clerk may be reinforced by the attention (scolding) he gets whenever he refuses to follow his supervisor's instructions. If it can be determined that these employees' job placements represent appropriate job matches (i.e., ones that respect employee preference) and that by learning to comply with job demands the employees would have access to reinforcers such as supervisor praise or satisfaction from job completion, an appropriate strategy may be to teach the employees to comply to workplace demands. For example, if Albert's stripping off his clothes had been approached as a compliance issue, he would receive a consequence (e.g., a snack at break) for not removing clothes at work and be praised by his supervisor and co-workers for keeping his clothes on.

Several researchers have investigated teaching compliance in employment settings. For example, Rusch and Menchetti (1981) observed that a food service assistant was not complying with his supervisors' task-related requests to help during meal preparation and was in danger of losing his job. Subsequently, the employee was taught how to respond appropriately to requests, given repeated practice in responding appropriately, and provided with praise when he did follow through on requests. Following compliance training, both task performance and compliance to demands increased, and supervisors' ratings of the employee's performance at work improved as he learned to comply. In addition, as his behavior changed, the employee was observed by his supervisor to take increased "pride in his work" (p. 110).

SUMMARY

This chapter introduced several strategies to consider when addressing the challenging behavior of persons in the workplace. The discussion of recent advances in assessing behavior and its causes emphasized the importance of interviewing the employee and significant others, direct observation in the workplace, and systematic manipulation of environmental events. Furthermore, social validation procedures were reviewed from a systems-analytic perspective in order to identify the multiple sources of influence within an environment that may affect an employee's behavior. The systems-analytic perspective was introduced because of our growing understanding of the influence that varying levels of interactions may have on maintaining challenging behavior.

Finally, two broad categories of support strategies were reviewed: 1) strategies that can be introduced to increase environmental support and 2) strategies that can be used to teach alternative, competent behaviors. Both of these strategies are important because they may help decrease unacceptable workplace performance of individuals with challenging behavior, promote appropriate employee behavior, and encourage more congenial work environments.

REFERENCES

Anthony, W.A., & Blanch, A. (1987). Supported employment for persons who are psychiatrically disabled: An historical and conceptual perspective. *Psychosocial Rehabilitation Journal, 11*, 5–23.

Bailey, J.S., & Pyles, D.A. (1989). Behavioral diagnostics. In E. Cipani (Ed.), *The treatment of severe behavior disorders: Behavior analysis approaches* (pp. 85–107). Washington, DC: American Association on Mental Retardation.

Bannerman, D.J., Sheldon, J.B., Sherman, J.A., & Harchik, A.E. (1990). Balancing the right to habilitation with the right to personal liberties: The rights of people with developmental disabilities to eat too many doughnuts and take a nap. *Journal of Applied Behavior Analysis, 23,* 79–89.

Berkell, D.E. (1992). Transition issues for secondary school students with autism and developmental disabilities. In F.R. Rusch, L. DeStefano, J. Chadsey-Rusch, L.A. Phelps, & E. Szymanski (Eds.), *Transition from school to adult life: Models, linkages, and policy* (pp. 459–472). Sycamore, IL: Sycamore.

Bronfenbrenner, U. (1977). Toward an experimental ecology of human development. *American Psychologist, 32,* 513–531.

Buckley, J., Mank, D., & Sandow, D. (1990). Developing and implementing support strategies. In F.R. Rusch (Ed.), *Supported employment: Models, methods, and issues* (pp. 131–144). Sycamore, IL: Sycamore.

Bullis, M., & Gaylord-Ross, R. (1989). *Moving on: School-to-community transition for adolescents and young adults with behavioral disorders.* Unpublished monograph.

Burt, D.B., Fuller, S.P., & Lewis, K.R. (1991). Brief report: Competitive employment of adults with autism. *Journal of Autism and Developmental Disorders, 21,* 237–242.

Carr, E.G. (1988). Functional equivalence as a mechanism of response generalization. In R.H. Horner, G. Dunlap, & R.L. Koegel (Eds.), *Generalization and maintenance: Life-style changes in applied settings* (pp. 221–241). Baltimore: Paul H. Brookes Publishing Co.

Carr, E.G., & Durand, V.M. (1985). Reducing behavior problems through functional communication training. *Journal of Applied Behavior Analysis, 18,* 111–126.

Carr, J. (1991). Recent advances in work with people with learning difficulties. *Behavioural Psychotherapy, 19,* 109–120.

Casey-Black, J., & Knoblock, P. (1989). Integrating students with challenging behaviors. In R. Gaylord-Ross (Ed.), *Integration strategies for students with handicaps* (pp. 129–148). Baltimore: Paul H. Brookes Publishing Co.

Chadsey-Rusch, J. (1990). Teaching social skills on the job. In F.R. Rusch (Ed.), *Supported employment: Models, methods, and issues* (pp. 161–180). Sycamore, IL: Sycamore.

Chadsey-Rusch, J., & Rusch, F.R. (1988). Ecology of the workplace. In R. Gaylord-Ross (Ed.), *Vocational education for persons with handicaps* (pp. 234–256). Mountain View, CA: Mayfield.

Cole, C.L., Gardner, W.I., & Karan, O.C. (1985). Self management training of mentally retarded adults presenting severe conduct difficulties. *Applied Research in Mental Retardation, 6,* 337–347.

Cook, J.A. (1990). *Issues in supported competitive employment for youth with mental illness: Theory, research and practice.* Chicago: Thresholds.

Cook, J.A., Solomon, M.L., & Mock, L.O. (1989). What happens after the first job placement: Vocational transitioning among severely emotionally disturbed and behavior disordered adolescents. In S.L. Braaten, R.B. Rutherford, T.F. Reilly, & S.A. DiGangi (Eds.), *Programming for adolescents with behavioral disorders* (pp. 71–93). Reston, VA: Council for Children with Behavioral Disorders.

Developmental Disabilities Assistance and Bill of Rights Act Amendments of 1987, PL 100-146. (October 29, 1987). Title 42, U.S.C. 6000 et seq: *U.S. Statutes at Large, 101,* 840–859.

D'Zurilla, T.J., & Goldfried, M.R. (1971). Problem solving and behavior modification. *Journal of Abnormal Psychology, 78,* 107–126.

Edgar, E., & Levine, P. (1988). A longitudinal study of graduates of special education. *Interchange, 8,* 3–5.

Edgerton, R. (1967). *The cloak of competence.* Berkeley: University of California Press.

Evans, I.M., & Meyer, L.H. (Eds.). (1985). *An educative approach to behavior problems: A practical decision model for intervention with severely handicapped learners.* Baltimore: Paul H. Brookes Publishing Co.

Favell, J.E., & Reid, D.H. (1988). Generalizing and maintaining improvement in problem behavior. In R.H. Horner, G. Dunlap, & R.L. Koegel (Eds.), *Generalization and maintenance: Life-style changes in applied settings* (pp. 171–196). Baltimore: Paul H. Brookes Publishing Co.

Frank, A.R., Sitlington, P.L., & Carson, P. (1991). Transition of adolescents with behavioral disorders—is it successful? *Behavioral Disorders, 16,* 181–191.

Gardner, W.I., & Cole, C.L. (1989). Self-management approaches. In E. Cipani (Ed.), *The treatment of severe behavior disorders: Behavior analysis approaches* (pp. 19–35). Washington, DC: American Association on Mental Retardation.

Greenspan, S., & Shoultz, B. (1981). Why mentally retarded adults lose their jobs: Social competence as a factor in work adjustment. *Applied Research in Mental Retardation, 2,* 23–28.

Haring, N.G. (1989). Foreword. In E. Cipani (Ed.), *The treatment of severe behavior disorders: Behavior analysis approaches.* Washington, DC: American Association on Mental Retardation.

Haring, T.G., & Kennedy, C.H. (1990). Contextual control of problem behavior in students with severe disabilities. *Journal of Applied Behavior Analysis, 23,* 235–243.

Horner, R.H., & Billingsley, F.F. (1988). The effect of competing behavior on the generalization and maintenance of adaptive behavior in applied settings. In R.H. Horner, G. Dunlap, & R.L. Koegel (Eds.), *Generalization and maintenance: Life-style changes in applied settings* (pp. 197–220). Baltimore: Paul H. Brookes Publishing Co.

Horner, R.H., Day, H.M., Sprague, J.R., O'Brien, M., & Heathfield, L.T. (1991). Interspersed requests: A nonaversive procedure for reducing aggression and self-injury during instruction. *Journal of Applied Behavior Analysis, 24,* 265–278.

Horner, R.H., O'Neill, R.E., & Flannery, K.B. (1993). Effective behavior support plans. In M.E. Snell (Ed.), *Instruction of students with severe disabilities* (pp. 184–214). New York: Macmillan.

Hughes, C., & Agran, M. (1993). Teaching persons with severe disabilities to use self-instruction in community settings: An analysis of applications and issues. *Journal of The Association for Persons with Severe Handicaps, 18,* 261–274.

Hughes, C., & Rusch, F.R. (1989). Teaching supported employees with severe mental retardation to solve problems. *Journal of Applied Behavior Analysis, 22,* 365–372.

Hughes, C., & Rusch, F.R. (1992). Behavior-management strategies for school-work-community. In F.R. Rusch, L. DeStefano, J. Chadsey-Rusch, L.A.

Phelps, & E. Szymanski (Eds.), *Transition from school to adult life: Models, linkages, and policy* (pp. 209–218). Sycamore, IL: Sycamore.

Hughes, C., Rusch, F.R., & Curl, R. (1990). Extending individual competence, developing natural support, and supporting social acceptance. In F.R. Rusch (Ed.), *Supported employment: Models, methods, and issues* (pp. 181–197). Sycamore, IL: Sycamore.

Hutchins, M.P., & Renzaglia, A.M. (1990). Developing a longitudinal vocational training program. In F.R. Rusch (Ed.), *Supported employment: Models, methods and issues* (pp. 365–380). Sycamore, IL: Sycamore.

Individuals with Disabilities Education Act of 1990 (IDEA), PL 101-476. (October 30, 1990). Title 20, U.S.C. 1400 et seq: *U.S. Statutes at Large, 104,* 1103–1151.

Isbister, F., & Donaldson, G. (1987). Supported employment for individuals who are mentally ill: Program development. *Psychosocial Rehabilitation Journal, 10,* 45–54.

Karan, O.C., & Knight, C.B. (1986). Developing support networks for individuals who fail to achieve competitive employment. In F.R. Rusch (Ed.), *Competitive employment issues and strategies* (pp. 241–255). Baltimore: Paul H. Brookes Publishing Co.

Kishi, G., Teelucksingh, B., Zollers, N., Park-Lee, S., & Meyer, L. (1988). Daily decision-making in community residences: A social comparison of adults with and without mental retardation. *American Journal on Mental Retardation, 92,* 430–435.

Kochany, L., Simpson, T., Hill, J., & Wehman, P. (1982). Reducing noncompliance and inappropriate verbal behavior in a moderately retarded food service worker: Use of a systematic fading procedure. In P. Wehman & M. Hill (Eds.), *Vocational training and job placement of severely disabled persons* (pp. 128–139). Richmond: Virginia Commonwealth University, School of Education.

LaPaglia, J. (1982). Training and generalization strategy for teaching work-related social skills. *Career Development for Exceptional Individuals, 5,* 122–131.

LaVigna, G.W., Willis, T.J., & Donnellan, A.N. (1989). The role of positive programming in behavioral treatment. In E. Cipani (Ed.), *The treatment of severe behavior disorders: Behavior analysis approaches* (pp. 59–83). Washington, DC: American Association on Mental Retardation.

Linden, B.E., & Forness, S.R. (1986). Post-school adjustment of mentally retarded persons with psychiatric disorders: A ten-year follow-up. *Education and Training of the Mentally Retarded, 21,* 157–164.

Lindsay, W.R., Baty, F.J., & Michie, A.M. (1989). A comparison of anxiety treatments with adults who have moderate and severe mental retardation. *Research in Developmental Disabilities, 10,* 129–140.

MacDonald-Wilson, K.L., Mancuso, L.L., Danley, K.S., & Anthony, W.A. (1989). Supported employment for people with psychiatric disability. *Journal of Applied Rehabilitation Counseling, 20,* 50–57.

McCarthy, P., Fender, K.W., & Fender, D. (1988). Supported employment for persons with autism. In P. Wehman & M.S. Moon (Eds.), *Vocational rehabilitation and supported employment* (pp. 269–290). Baltimore: Paul H. Brookes Publishing Co.

McPhail, C.H., & Chamove, A.S. (1989). Relaxation reduces disruption in mentally handicapped adults. *Journal of Mental Deficiency Research, 33,* 399–406.

Meyer, L.G., & Evans, I.M. (1989). *Nonaversive intervention for behavior problems: A manual for home and community.* Baltimore: Paul H. Brookes Publishing Co.

Mithaug, D.E., & Hanawalt, D.A. (1978). The validation of procedures to assess prevocational task preferences in retarded adults. *Journal of Applied Behavior Analysis, 11,* 153–162.

Mithaug, D.E., & Mar, D.K. (1980). The relation between choosing and working prevocational tasks in two severely retarded young adults. *Journal of Applied Behavior Analysis, 13,* 177–182.

Neel, R.S., Meadows, N., Levine, P., & Edgar, E.B. (1988). What happens after special education: A statewide follow-up study of secondary students who have behavioral disorders. *Behavior Disorders, 13,* 209–216.

O'Brien, R. (1989). Punishment for people with developmental disabilities. In E. Cipani (Ed.), *The treatment of severe behavior disorders: Behavior analysis approaches* (pp. 37–58). Washington, DC: American Association on Mental Retardation.

O'Neill, R.E., Horner, R.H., Albin, R.W., Storey, K., & Sprague, J.R. (1990). *Functional analysis of problem behavior: A practical assessment guide.* Sycamore, IL: Sycamore.

Remington, B. (Ed.). (1991). *The challenge of severe mental handicap: A behavior analytic approach.* Chichester, England: John Wiley and Sons.

Rusch, F.R., & Hughes, C. (1989). Overview of supported employment. *Journal of Applied Behavior Analysis, 22,* 351–363.

Rusch, F.R., Hughes, C., Johnson, J.R., & Minch, K.E. (1991). A descriptive analysis of interactions between co-workers and supported employees. *Mental Retardation, 29,* 207–212.

Rusch, F.R., Hughes, C., & Wilson, P.G. (1995). Utilizing cognitive strategies in the acquisition of employment skills. In W. O'Donohue & L. Krasner (Eds.), *Handbook of skills training with adults* (pp. 363–382). Needham, MA: Allyn & Bacon.

Rusch, F.R., Johnson, J.R., & Hughes, C. (1990). Analysis of co-worker involvement in relation to level of disability versus placement approach among supported employees. *Journal of The Association for Persons with Severe Handicaps, 15,* 29–32.

Rusch, F.R., & Menchetti, B.M. (1981). Increasing compliant work behaviors in a non-sheltered work setting. *Mental Retardation, 19,* 107–111.

Rusch, F.R., & Minch, K.E. (1988). Identification of coworker involvement in supported employment: A review and analysis. *Research in Developmental Disabilities, 9,* 247–254.

Rusch, F.R., Minch, K.E., & Hughes, C. (1989). Evaluating the role of job site supervisors in the long-term employment of persons with severe disabilities. *Journal of Vocational Special Needs Populations, 12,* 9–16.

Rusch, F.R., & Mithaug, D.E. (1985). Competitive employment education: A systems analytic approach to transitional programming for the student with severe handicaps. In K.C. Lakin & R.M. Bruininks (Eds.), *Strategies for achieving community integration of developmentally disabled citizens* (pp. 177–192). Baltimore: Paul H. Brookes Publishing Co.

Rusch, F.R., Weithers, J.A., Menchetti, B.M., & Schutz, R.P. (1980). Social validation of a program to reduce topic repetition in a nonsheltered setting. *Education and Training of the Mentally Retarded, 15,* 208–215.

Rusch, F.R., Wilson, P.G., Hughes, C., & Heal, L.W. (1995). Interaction of persons with severe mental retardation and their nondisabled co-workers in integrated work settings. *Behavior Modification, 19,* 59–77.

Schaller, J.L., & Szymanski, E.M. (1992). Supported employment, consumer choice, and independence. *Journal of Vocational Rehabilitation, 2,* 45–50.

Shafer, M.S. (1986). Utilizing co-workers as change agents. In F.R. Rusch (Ed.), *Competitive employment issues and strategies* (pp. 215–224). Baltimore: Paul H. Brookes Publishing Co.

Shafer, M.S., Brooke, V., & Wehman, P. (1985). Developing appropriate social-interpersonal skills in a mentally retarded worker. *Vocational Evaluation and Work Adjustment Bulletin, 8,* 76–81.

Skinner, B.F. (1938). *The behavior of organisms.* New York: Appleton-Century.

Skinner, B.F. (1953). *Science and human behavior.* New York: Macmillan.

Smith, M.D. (1985). Managing the aggressive and self-injurious behavior of adults disabled by autism. *Journal of The Association for Persons with Severe Handicaps, 10,* 228–232.

Smith, M.D. (1994). Increasing work productivity of employees disabled by autism. *Journal of Vocational Rehabilitation, 4,* 60–65.

Smith, M.D., & Belcher, R.G. (1994). Factors influencing integration of employees with autism. *Journal of Vocational Rehabilitation, 4,* 52–59.

Smith, M.D., Belcher, R.G., Juhrs, P.D., & Nabors, K. (1994). Where people with autism work. *Journal of Vocational Rehabilitation, 4,* 10–17.

Smith, M.D., & Coleman, D. (1986). Managing the behavior of adults with autism in the job setting. *Journal of Autism and Developmental Disorders, 16,* 145–154.

Steege, M.W., Wacker, D.P., Cigrand, K.C., Berg, W.K., Novak, C.G., Reimers, T.M., Sasso, G.M., & DeRaad, A. (1990). Use of negative reinforcement in the treatment of self-injurious behavior. *Journal of Applied Behavior Analysis, 23,* 459–467.

U.S. Office of Personnel Management. (1984). *Handbook of job analysis for reasonable accommodation.* Washington, DC: Selection Placement Programs.

Wagner, M. (1993, June). *Trends in postschool outcomes of youth with disabilities.* Paper presented at the meeting of project directors of the Transition Research Institute at Illinois, Washington, DC.

Wehman, P., & Kregel, J. (1988). Supported competitive employment for individuals with autism and severe retardation: Two case studies. *Focus on Autistic Behavior, 3,* 1–14.

Wehmeyer, M.L. (1992). Self-determination and the education of students with mental retardation. *Education and Training in Mental Retardation, 27,* 302–314.

White, D.M. (1986). Social validation. In F.R. Rusch (Ed.), *Competitive employment issues and strategies* (pp. 199–213). Baltimore: Paul H. Brookes Publishing Co.

Winking, D., O'Reilly, B., & Moon, M.S. (1993). Preference: The missing link in the job match process for individuals without functional communication skills. *Journal of Vocational Rehabilitation, 3,* 27–42.

Wolf, M.M. (1978). Social validity: The case for how applied behavior analysis is finding its heart. *Journal of Applied Behavior Analysis, 11,* 203–214.

V

CHALLENGING THE SYSTEM WITH SELF-DETERMINATION

13

Self-Determination for All Individuals

FREDDA BROWN AND CAROLE R. GOTHELF

> What I choose is my choice . . .
> What I choose is my voice.
> (Corgan/Smashing Pumpkins, 1993)

THE GENERATION OF the 1990s is concerned with its right to make decisions and be heard. Although expressed with a different rhythm, instrumentation, and often volume, this same message has often been echoed by past generations. The members of each new generation seek to control events in their lives, whether the events be political, economic, or personal. Young people rebel at the lack of control they have over events and their helplessness in effecting change in a world full of problems that they have inherited from the prior generation, both globally (e.g., destruction of the environment, economic depression, war) and personally (e.g., high cost of education, unemployment, lack of affordable housing).

The exercise of control over one's personal life, or ability to shape one's own destiny, can be described as self-determination. Brown and Cohen (1994) extensively reviewed definitions and conceptualizations of self-determination, and they conclude that at the center of these conceptualizations is an individual who exerts control over his or her own life. According to their review, the specific skills and behavioral characteristics that have been identified as necessary for self-

Some of the ideas of this chapter are based on a grant proposal developed by Shirley Cohen and Fredda Brown (1993), "Foundations of Self-Determination in Young Children," submitted to the Office of Special Education and Rehabilitative Services, U.S. Department of Education. The authors acknowledge and thank Dr. Cohen for her overall contribution to the development of so many of the basic concepts discussed in this chapter.

determination include initiative, development and awareness of preferences, choice/decision-making, personal goal setting, problem solving, independent thinking, assertiveness, self-advocacy, self-knowledge, self-regulation, self-efficacy, and persistence (Brown & Cohen, 1994). The behaviors that contribute to the development and practice of self-determination vary with such factors as age, level of disability, and setting. Abery (1994) describes this as a complex process of shaping that involves the individual and the environment, each of which change over time.

However, individuals with disabilities often do not participate in the behaviors that allow personal control over their lives (Abery, 1994; Brown & Cohen, 1994; Guess, Benson, & Siegel-Causey, 1985; Wehmeyer & Metzler, 1995). The reason these behaviors fail to be acquired may be attributed to a complex set of variables. For example, inclusion in natural settings provides many challenges for individuals with the most severe disabilities, for events in these settings are less predictable and harder to control (Schloss, Alper, & Jayne, 1993). These challenges may be experienced as obstacles to participation or as natural opportunities for decision making that fundamentally support the development of self-determination skills. However, at this point in time, we must assume that these skills need to be systematically taught (Gothelf, Crimmins, Mercer, & Finocchiaro, 1994). The need for the development of a technology for training and instruction to enable individuals to exercise self-determination is eloquently described by Williams (1991):

> Every person, regardless of the severity of his or her disabilities, has the right and ability to communicate with others, express everyday preferences, and exercise at least some control over his or her daily life. Each individual, therefore, should be given the chance, training, technology, respect and encouragement to do so. (p. 543)

This chapter begins with an analysis of some common misconceptions about self-determination as they relate to individuals with profound disabilities and challenging behaviors. The second section of the chapter discusses the new emphasis on self-determination that can be seen in some current trends in the area of disabilities. Specifically, the interrelationship of self-determination, communication, and problem behaviors is discussed, along with how self-determination is increasingly supported in law and the relationship of the self-advocacy movement to self-determination. The third section of the chapter reviews some current "best practice" strategies and how they might support, as well as inhibit, the development of self-determination.

EXPLODING THE MYTHS

From our many years of providing in-service workshops to professionals and caregivers who support individuals with profound disabilities and/or challenging behavior, we have become familiar with the most common misconceptions and concerns about the application of self-determination to such individuals. Following is a discussion of each of these myths and a review of current literature refuting each. Table 1 lists these common misconceptions along with a corresponding counterpoint based on our personal clinical experiences, the existing research, and current best practice.

Myth 1: Some individuals are too profoundly cognitively disabled or multiply disabled to be self-determining. Professionals may assume that individuals with severe disabilities lack the ability to indicate a

Table 1. Misconceptions about self-determination

Myth	Counterpoint
Some individuals are too profoundly disabled to be self-determining.	Research has shown that individuals with even the most profound disabilities have definite preferences and seek to control their environment.
The presence of disruptive behavior requires increased control of the individual, not self-determination.	Behavior problems are often a way of communicating protest about lack of control. Supporting the individual to have more control over their environment, rather than less, may serve to reduce some problem behaviors.
If given the opportunity to be self-determining, some individuals would make inappropriate choices or choose to do nothing.	All individuals, regardless of presence or level of disability have the right to make "bad" decisions. If an individual frequently chooses to do nothing, ways of creating a more stimulating and personally meaningful environment should be explored.
Some individuals cannot be self-determining because they need a highly structured environment with planned and systematic instructional opportunities.	If extensive physical and cognitive support is needed across many areas of daily life, it should not be assumed that such assistance is also necessary for the individual to make decisions and take control over many elements of life.
Program standards and regulations concerning habilitation prohibit self-determination.	There are no regulations that prohibit individuals from taking control of their lives. Increasingly, regulations are requiring procedures that promote self-determination.

preference and participate in making meaningful choices and decisions (Brown, Belz, Corsi, & Wenig, 1993; Kishi, Teelucksingh, Zollers,
Park-Lee, & Meyer, 1988; Wehmeyer & Metzler, 1995). Current literature and research support the assertion that people with even the most
severe cognitive disabilities have definite preferences and seek to control their environment (e.g., Dattilo & Rusch, 1985; Goode & Gaddy,
1976; Kennedy & Haring, 1993; Pace, Ivancic, Edwards, Iwata, & Page,
1985; Parsons & Reid, 1990; Wacker, Berg, Wiggins, Muldoon, & Cavanaugh, 1985). Although some individuals may express a desire to
control their environments in nontraditional and sometimes inappropriate ways (e.g., self-injurious or stereotyped behavior), such behavior
indicates the importance of control to them. A great challenge for professionals and families is to support the individual in these attempts
to be self-determining and to trust that all individuals do have preferences. There are three basic premises that must be assumed if this
challenge is to be met. First, the individual must be provided with the
appropriate training in communicating preferences. Second, the individual must be provided with opportunities to be self-determining.
Third, caregivers, family, and professionals must accept nontraditional
forms of communication as true expressions of self-determination. (See
Chapter 14 for an in-depth discussion of strategies.)

*Myth 2: The presence of disruptive behavior requires increased
control of the individual, not self-determination.* It is a common reaction of staff to believe that they need to "pull in the reins" when
someone is displaying severe behavior problems. However, this approach may serve only to increase the problem behaviors. There is
increasing evidence that many severe problem behaviors may serve a
general controlling function for the individual. That is, many serious
behavior problems may be attributable to the lack of control in the
individual's daily life (Meyer & Evans, 1989). Current research (e.g.,
Dyer, Dunlap, & Winterling, 1990; Koegel, Dyer, & Bell, 1987; Munk &
Repp, 1994) supports the view that, while behavior problems are often
an individual's way of communicating some very important messages,
these behaviors reflect the individual's lack of control or self-determination.

The goal of functional communication training is to teach an individual to use an appropriate communication form (e.g., sign language, verbalization, gestures, object cues) to express the message that
he or she was attempting to communicate with inappropriate behavior
(Carr & Durand, 1985; Doss & Reichle, 1989; Durand, 1990; Haring &
Kennedy, 1990; LaVigna & Donnellan, 1986; Meyer & Evans, 1989;
Repp, Felce, & Barton, 1988). This strategy supports the development
of self-determination in individuals who are seeking it. Further, in-

creasing involvement by students in the selection of learning activities may foster such characteristics as initiative, independence, decision-making ability, and a sense of control over one's environment, while reducing the incidence of problem behaviors (Brown & Cohen, 1994).

Myth 3: Some individuals would make inappropriate choices, or choose to do nothing, if they were given the opportunity to be self-determining. All people make inappropriate decisions at some points in their lives, and people with disabilities deserve the right to do this as well. In 1972, Perske described this phenomenon in a chapter entitled "The Dignity of Risk." Almost 25 years later, it appears as if professionals are still struggling with balancing this concept of dignity of risk with our concerns about safety and our perceptions of the potential of individuals with severe disabilities. Perske (1972) expresses this point:

> Many who work with the handicapped, impaired, disadvantaged, and aged tend to be overzealous in their attempts to "protect," "comfort," "keep safe," "take care," and "watch." Acting on these impulses, at the right time, can be benevolent, helpful, and developmental. But, if they are acted upon exclusively or excessively, without allowing for each client's individuality and growth potential, they will overprotect and emotionally smother the intended beneficiary. In fact, such overprotection endangers the client's human dignity, and tends to keep him from experiencing the risk-taking of ordinary life which is necessary for normal human growth and development. (p. 195)

If an individual too frequently chooses to do nothing, the types of activities that are being offered and the lifestyle in which he or she is supported must be critically examined. When an individual chooses to do nothing, it must be assumed that the daily routines in which he or she is supported to participate are not motivating. Increasing or changing some artificial reinforcer to increase participation in daily routines is likely to be met with little success. However, supporting the individual to exert more control over the content and timing of these routines (i.e., self-determination) may have a profound effect over the individual's participation (Bambara & Ager, 1992; Bannerman, Sheldon, Sherman, & Harchik, 1990; Brown, 1991). For example, Brown and Lehr (1993) describe a student who, after a period of non-participation and refusal, began participating in physical therapy exercises when given control over where and when these exercises would occur. An apparent lack of motivation must be met with changes in the lifestyle of the individual, not with changes in artificial reinforcers. According to Bannerman et al. (1990), "Client refusals, bad choices, and off-task behavior should signal staff to examine the situation and to determine whether allowing more choice or teaching more choices would be of benefit" (p. 86).

Myth 4: Some individuals cannot be self-determining because they need a highly structured environment with systematic and planned instructional opportunities. Many individuals with the most severe disabilities participate in highly structured and planned environments, with little room for individual diversity and flexibility. Living environments are often limited in decision making and opportunities for autonomy (Bannerman et al., 1990; Brown, 1991; Brown & Rosa, 1994; Kishi et al., 1988; Wehmeyer & Metzler, 1995). Special education settings, especially those for preschool children, are often more teacher directed than child initiated and more focused on the development of isolated skills than their regular early childhood parallels (Brown & Cohen, 1994; Hanline & Fox, 1993).

Perhaps the extent and diversity of supports that are sometimes needed (e.g., cognitive, physical, behavioral) have led professionals to overgeneralize the need for supports. That is, because professionals may need to support a person in multiple areas, we assume support is needed in areas that may not be necessary (e.g., decision making). Encouraging individuals to be self-determining does not mean that supports will be withdrawn, that systematic instruction on specific learning objectives will be abandoned, that chaos will reign, or that a specific vision for the future cannot be designed. Rather, it means that individuals should not just participate in the design of a vision and objectives that reflect this vision but should take the lead in the creation of this vision. Mount (1994) developed the process of Personal Futures Planning as a strategy to assist an individual and his or her team to develop a powerful—and empowered—vision of the future and to identify ways in which the achievement of this vision can be supported and accomplished.

An individual's participation in the formation of this vision might not be accomplished in traditional ways. For example, certain behaviors (e.g., disruptive behavior) may be a form of protest against living with five other individuals or having to sit in one place during work hours. Those supporting this individual must be aware of these behaviors as acts of self-expression and be willing to respect them and offer them as critical input into the team process.

Brown (1991) pointed out that some individuals desire a structured daily routine while others prefer a more flexible day. Regardless of the individual's lifestyle preference, choices and control of daily events can be supported. Opportunities for the individual to control daily events and express preferences can occur within any type of structure. Brown et al. (1993) developed a model that identified seven levels of choice making available within most daily routines. This model allows for increased opportunities to control daily events across the day and within naturally occurring routines (see Chapter 14 for a complete description of this model). Brown, Evans, Weed, and Owen (1987) offer another model that systematically includes behaviors related to self-determination across natural settings. Extension and enrichment components of routines, such as initiating, problem solving, and terminating the activity, allow an individual control within the context of structured routines.

Myth 5: Program standards and regulations concerning habilitation prohibit self-determination. An individual's personal liberties can be compromised by service providers as they attempt to meet the extensive lists of standards designed to evaluate habilitation (Bannerman et al., 1990). Guidelines for monitoring a program's effectiveness often focus on a quantitative analysis of number of goals and objectives identified, implemented, and completed. A qualitative component may also be included but be limited to such variables as age appropriateness, functionality, and range of domains covered. Having the responsibility for the systematic instruction of this precisely prescribed set of objectives leads some staff to believe that there is little room for activities that do not meet this purpose. For example, it may be perceived as inefficient to ask an individual what he or she would like to do when there are 10 task analyses that must be completed each day.

There are no standards or regulations that prohibit individuals from taking control of their own lives. However, there are many standards and regulations aimed at providing individuals the opportunity to plan their future and arrange their daily lives. For example, individualized education programs (IEPs) for students and individualized habilitation plans (IHPs) for adults require participation of the focus individual. Unfortunately, physical participation does not necessarily equate with meaningful participation (Brown & Lehr, 1993). In a study of group homes, Brown and Rosa (1994) found that few residents participated in deciding what to do and when to do it on a daily basis. On a more positive note, Newton, Horner, and Lund (1991) found that when staff were provided with assessment information concerning the individual's preferences, these preferences were likely to be included on the IHP.

CURRENT TRENDS SUPPORTING SELF-DETERMINATION

People with profound disabilities or severe challenging behavior are not typically provided with opportunities to exert social influence, participate in decisions, and exercise control over their lives. As a society we have sought to control individuals by segregating them so that the community cannot hear their voices. As individuals we have sought to control them by forcing our decisions on them.

One of the ways we exercise self-determination is by effectively communicating and, by doing so, influencing others and affecting events. Caregivers, service providers, and funding agencies often limit opportunities for self-determination by deciding, among any number of other things, the program in which a person will be "placed," restricting access to preferred activities (typically in the name of therapy), imposing rigid daily schedules, and determining what rewards individuals may "earn" and how often.

The individual with profound disabilities quickly learns that he or she has little control over his or her life and few ways to influence others. Some people in this situation experience such powerlessness and lack of self-direction that they become passive. Feeling a loss of control over one's life and believing that nothing one does makes a difference can lead to what is referred to as learned helplessness (Guess et al., 1985; Reichle, York, & Eynon, 1989). Still others learn that choice, decisions, and social influence are possible when they express themselves stridently enough and often enough. In a sense, they are forced by the situation to resort to behavior problems as an expression of choice and self-direction.

Fortunately, in recent years, we have witnessed a growing belief that consumers of human services, including people with profound disabilities or severe problem behaviors, should have control over the services that they receive and maintain power over their own lives. Empowerment provides a greater degree of dignity for the individual and results in increased motivation to participate and succeed (West & Parent, 1992). Individuals with disabilities become full partners in planning and effecting changes in their lives (Parent, 1993). Their individual preferences, goals, and choices become preeminent so that their lives may reflect their desires, rather than what is simply available within the system. These beliefs have been translated into legislative mandates with the passage of the Americans with Disabilities Act (ADA) in 1990 (PL 101-336) and the Rehabilitation Act Amendments of 1992 (PL 102-569). Legislation empowered individuals with disabilities to effect change in the issues and actions that influenced their lives (West, Kregel & Revell, 1993/1994; Wolfe, 1993).

The self-advocacy movement (Bowen, 1994; Kitch, 1978) is a prime example of how individuals with disabilities can persistently influence programs and systems to bend, shift, and change so that their preferred lifestyles and choices can be supported. The first step to self-advocacy occurs when the individual recognizes his or her own choices and preferences, effectively communicates them, and takes charge of obtaining them. The second, and equally important step, occurs when caregivers and service providers take responsibility for teaching individuals with disabilities to take control of their lives. Developing interests, making choices, planning for pursuing these interests, and acquiring the communication skills necessary to give effective voice to their own capacity for assertiveness are all critical components of the process of taking control.

According to West and Parent (1992), the individual should have both the opportunity and responsibility to identify his or her own preferences and to express those preferences. Empowerment provides a greater degree of dignity for the individual and results in increased motivation to participate and succeed. However, for many individuals with the most significant disabilities, self-advocacy may be hampered and participation in planning may be restricted by problems occurring in the process of either identifying or expressing preferences. This, in turn, limits the value that service providers, caregivers, and funding sources place on decisions expressed by these individuals. This situation is particularly true in vocational and living opportunities and community involvement, in which persons with profound disabilities and severe problem behavior are typically afforded few choices (Bannerman et al., 1990; Brown, 1991; Kishi et al., 1988).

Learning how to make good choices and express them effectively requires experience with the process of decision making. There are ample opportunities to empower individuals with disabilities by teaching them throughout life to make age-appropriate choices so that when they are old enough to make major decisions, they can participate by making choices in a meaningful way and by following through to achieve their desired goals.

DO CURRENT BEST PRACTICE
STRATEGIES ENCOURAGE SELF-DETERMINATION?

Self-determination is a reflection of an individual's functioning in certain areas in relation to the environment, setting, or context. The degree and quality of the acts of self-determination are governed, in part, by the opportunities available in the setting and by what is permitted, prohibited, or encouraged within each environment. The same individual can behave with greater or lesser self-determination at different times and under different circumstances. Certain environmental factors and instructional strategies may either support or prohibit the development of skills related to self-determination (Brown & Cohen, 1994). The next two sections discuss how certain instructional strategies and behavioral strategies, while effective in accomplishing certain outcomes, may actually prohibit the development of skills associated with self-determination.

Instructional Strategies

One promise of education is qualification for employment. It follows that the effectiveness of education can be measured by the degree to which an individual achieves productivity and independence (Gothelf & Crimmins, 1993). However, researchers have reported that the majority of young adults with disabilities have not made successful transitions from school to adult life in the community (Wagner et al., 1991). They are not attaining employment or community involvement. Schloss et al. (1993) point out that it is likely that these individuals have acquired basic skills within the highly structured setting of school, but when faced with the diverse options of the real world and the need to make appropriate choices in natural settings they lack the self-determination necessary to use these skills functionally. This set of events compels us to support self-determination as a critical educational outcome throughout an individual's school career. The teaching strategies that we use must provide enhanced opportunities to make choices, express preferences, participate in decisions, and exercise control over one's life, and these strategies must do so without exerting excessive external influence and interference (Wehmeyer, 1992).

As a matter of course, the daily lives of individuals with profound disabilities and severe behavior problems are rigidly structured and regulated by caregivers and professionals. Many of the instructional strategies used with these individuals have been designed to assist them in developing specific isolated skills, usually motor or rote skills. Although these strategies may indeed promote participation in the motor component of certain skills and activities, they may be incompatible with the development of self-determination (Brown & Cohen, 1994). Recognition of how the use of certain instructional practices may serve to discourage self-determination is the critical first step in identifying how these approaches must be enhanced to promote self-determination. What follows is a brief discussion of the practices of task analysis and prompting, two procedures commonly used by teachers, and their relationship to the development of self-determination.

Task Analysis Brown et al. (1987) found that most published task analyses focused on the performance of observable motor skills that enable an individual to participate in the environment without engaging in communicative behavior. The task analyses omitted skills such as self-initiating the activity, problem solving, monitoring the quality of the activity, expressing choice or preference within the activity, and terminating the activity before its completion. A critical shortcoming of the traditional task-analytic approach is apparent when applied to an individual with severe multiple disabilities. This individual would be expected to participate in the motor components of the task without regard to the nonmotor aspects that might allow the individual to achieve control over the activity and independence on meaningful components (e.g., initiating, monitoring quality, problem solving, communicating, terminating).

Sigafoos and York (1991) point out that task analyses must be expanded to include steps that target communicative opportunities and demands of the activity. For example, a task analysis of making a bologna sandwich might be expanded to include steps to choose between wheat or rye bread, ask for the mustard if it cannot be located, or ask for more bologna when the package has only one slice remaining in it. A task analysis for making coffee might include steps to ask for assistance if the sugar cannot be located or to offer coffee to others (see Chapter 15). When self-determination is targeted as an educational outcome, task analysis can be thoughtfully expanded to promote self-initiated communication (Rowland & Schweigert, 1993).

Prompting The extensive use of physical prompting strategies may also affect the development of skills contributing to self-determination. Although the pronounced goal of instruction is to teach students to respond spontaneously in the presence of naturally occurring contextual cues, individuals with profound disabilities and severe behavior problems often remain dependent on cues presented in an artificial manner. Extensive levels of physical prompting and manipulation and inadequate fading procedures, along with low expectations of the individual, are likely to foster excessive dependence on the caregiver or service provider (Snell & Brown, 1993), and are unlikely to foster behaviors related to self-determination (Brown & Lehr, 1993; Gothelf, Crimmins, & Woolf, in press). In a study examining a sample of early childhood IEPs, Brown and Cohen (1994) found a heavy emphasis on following teacher's verbal directives and excessive use of physical prompting. Although physical prompting may be a necessary instructional strategy to achieve a future goal of independence for some individuals, the exclusive identification of objectives that never will advance beyond prompting is questionable. This again underscores many professionals' over-reliance on motor components of tasks and the omission of those aspects that may allow independent control of the activity.

Gothelf et al. (in press) point out that instructional prompts need to augment communication in response to natural cues. Natural cues that elicit and maintain communicative behavior need to be identified. Effective prompting may begin with the teacher arranging instructional opportunities in the natural environment. However, the goal is to transfer teacher-directed or -arranged cues to cues in the environment that can occur in the absence of the teacher's presence. For example, a teacher may arrange to have dirty glasses placed in equal amounts on two trays. After loading half the glasses in the dishwasher, a student is asked if she would like to take a break and have a soda in the breakroom or if she wants to continue working. In this example, the teacher is instructing the student that the halfway point in an activity is an appropriate time to communicate that she wants to take the available break. The instructional strategy is twofold. First, the arrangement of the glasses on two trays provides a cue for the student that when one tray is empty, the job is halfway done. The teacher initially encourages the student with verbal prompts to ask for a break in response to emptying one of the trays. The teacher waits for the student to respond before providing additional prompts or cues. Waiting for a response encourages initiation. The teacher's verbal prompts can be gradually faded, leaving the two trays as a natural prompt. The teacher's strategy also includes responding positively if the student communicates a desire for a break before the halfway point is reached. In this way, the student also learns that he or she can respond to internal stimuli as well as to contextual cues. This method of prompt management encourages students to take control over when they ask for a break, thus encouraging independent self-determination. The teacher must structure naturally occurring situations that implicitly prompt the student to evaluate the options and respond by communicating a choice.

Behavioral Strategies

Historically, the establishment of "compliance" in individuals with developmental disabilities has been a valued outcome of many special education and adult programs. Indeed, many professionals and parents often saw "adaptive behavior" as synonymous with conformity (Abery, 1994). Until recently, individually developed behavioral programs to establish these behaviors and decrease disruptive behaviors relied heavily on consequence strategies (e.g., differential reinforcement, time-out, response cost). With this approach, many environmental and motivational variables were ignored. A narrow focus on consequences overlooks critical information such as the individual's preference for the task in which he or she is asked to participate, how long the individual has worked on the skill, the lack of significant relationships the individual has with others, or the physical comfort of the setting. Motivational issues have also been omitted as a contributing factor in behavioral program development. For example, food may be established as a reinforcer for an individual and effectively used to increase participation in an array of activities. However, the strength of this reinforcer may not be able to compete with the strength of the individual's motivation to escape from a nonpreferred activity (negative reinforcement). Rather than focus on altering how the contingent reinforcement is delivered, exploring the broader context in which the individual participates would be more fruitful.

Professionals are now increasingly looking at qualitative outcomes of behavior change rather than at narrow quantitative measures of a single target behavior, such as noncompliance, self-injury, or aggression (Haring & Breen, 1989; Meyer & Evans, 1993; Meyer & Janney, 1989). For example, Meyer and Evans (1989) include outcomes such as acquisition of alternative skills, greater participation in integrated community experiences, happiness, satisfaction, choices, and expanded social relationships as critical in evaluation of program effectiveness. Haring and Breen (1989) focus on the functions of social initiation, social responses, social turn taking, and duration of social interactions as measures of success when students with disabilities are included in regular education settings. Attention to skills related to self-determination are thus becoming increasingly evident within the behavioral approach to the analysis of problem behavior.

That the use of aversive behavioral strategies that cause pain, discomfort, or humiliation is dehumanizing has been adequately documented (cf. Guess, 1988; Evans & Meyer, 1985; Guess, Helmstetter, Turnbull, & Knowlton, 1987; Horner et al., 1990). Helmstetter and Durand (1991) state that "it is arguably immoral to use intrusive procedures on persons who are so communicatively and otherwise behaviorally limited as to be unable to indicate their needs and concerns, or to adequately control their environments" (p. 560). For example, if a person tries to control his or her environment by using self-injury to escape from doing a nonpreferred activity, supporters of a positive approach to behavior management would decry the use of shock to decrease the self-injury. Teaching the individual to control the environment in a more appropriate and less dangerous way (e.g., walking away) would not only decrease the self-injury but would also allow the individual to control his or her environment. (Chapters 8, 11, and 15 provide extensive discussions on this strategy.) However, professionals must also consider that even the use of positive procedures to reduce self-injury (e.g., differential reinforcement) may also ignore the individual's behavior as an expression of self-determination. If an individual is using the self-injury to control his or her environment (i.e., escape from doing a nonpreferred activity), even reinforcement procedures aimed at increasing participation in the activity ignore this self-expression and thus punish self-determination. That is, reinforcing a person to participate in an activity of which he or she has expressed clear avoidance punishes communication and disregards efforts at self-determination.

A conflict may emerge at this point. The individual may be avoiding an activity that reflects a health need (e.g., taking medication, showering, brushing teeth) or a necessary responsibility (e.g., participating in cleaning his or her living quarters). Although there is no simple resolution to this conflict, the following three steps may serve as a guideline. First, it should be assumed that the individual has the right to refuse to do any activity. Second, if this assumption is dangerous because avoiding the activity is unhealthy or unsafe, consider alternative ways in which the individual can participate (e.g., choices of where, when, how, or with whom it is performed). Allowing escape from or avoidance of the activity—that is, control of the activity—may actually serve to increase participation in that activity (Brown, 1991). Third, if the activity is seen as important because it encourages traditional age-appropriate responsibility, consider replacing this activity with a more preferred one and providing choices (e.g., the form of the activity, where, when, how, and with whom it will be performed). It is rare that a particular form of an activity is so important that it cannot be replaced with an alternative; indeed, most responsibilities "assigned" to individuals with severe disabilities are quite arbitrary. Individuals without disabilities frequently negotiate responsibilities to achieve a more preferred routine (e.g., "I'll vacuum and you do the dishes") or to escape a nonpreferred activity (e.g., hire someone to do the cleaning).

Schloss et al. (1993) recommend the use of a three-dimensional continuum when encouraging or limiting an individual's right to make personal decisions. This model weighs input of the individual (from no input to total control of the decision); degree of physical, emotional, economic, or legal risk (immediate or long-term risk); and the degree to which input from others is perceived as required (parent's input regarding clothing style versus physician's input on dietary restrictions for diabetes). These authors state that "the ultimate goal for each choice is for the individual to exercise as much personal freedom as possible while minimizing personal risk" (p. 219).

SUMMARY

This chapter reviewed definitions and conceptualizations of self-determination as it relates to individuals with profound disabilities and challenging behaviors—individuals who are at the most risk for being denied opportunities to be self-determining. The chapter attempted to discredit certain misconceptions about self-determination for these individuals and discussed how certain trends in legislation and service delivery support its development, while many practices may serve to discourage its development. Although we continue to express some of the same concerns today that were expressed years ago about self-determination, dignity, and risk, it is our sense that we have accomplished much.

Many areas need to be explored, researched, and demonstrated. Brown and Cohen (1994) point out that one major area that remains unexplored is the relationship of self-determination to young children. In the area of severe disabilities, we have long acknowledged the need for a longitudinal curriculum (e.g., Brown, Nietupski, & Hamre-Nietupski, 1976). Skills that are identified as important for adults must be considered within the school curriculum. Yet most of the research in the area of self-determination has been conducted on adolescents and adults. Research should focus on identifying the age-appropriate skills of young children that will support the development of self-determination across the life span (Brown & Cohen, 1994). As these students are increasingly included in regular education, we need to examine regular education practices. Which strategies support the development of self-determination, and which strategies discourage this development?

The increased acceptance of a diverse range of research methodologies should support continued research in this complex area. Certainly, the growing awareness of the need for a wide range of outcome measures and the importance of quality of life indicators supports and further ensures a focus on self-determination. Another challenge is to further operationalize the concept of self-determination for individuals whose communication abilities are limited. However, what we do know is that all individuals, regardless of the severity of disability, strive to be self-determining. Professionals, family members, and friends must continue to believe in and respond to their messages and support their endeavors.

REFERENCES

Abery, B.H. (1994). A conceptual framework for enhancing self-determination. In M. Hayden & B. Abery (Eds.), *Challenges for a service system in transition: Ensuring quality community experiences for persons with developmental disabilities* (pp. 345–380). Baltimore: Paul H. Brookes Publishing Co.

Americans with Disabilities Act of 1990 (ADA), PL 101-336. (July 26, 1990). Title 42, U.S.C. 12101 et seq: *U.S. Statutes at Large, 104,* 327–378.

Bambara, L.M., & Ager, C. (1992). Using self-scheduling to promote self-directed leisure activity in home and community settings. *Journal of The Association for Persons with Severe Handicaps, 17,* 67–76.

Bannerman, D.J., Sheldon, J.B., Sherman, J.A., & Harchik, A.E. (1990). Balancing the right to habilitation with the right to personal liberties: The rights of people with developmental disabilities to eat too many doughnuts and take a nap. *Journal of Applied Behavior Analysis, 23,* 79–89.

Bowen, J.H. (1994). The power of self-advocacy: Making thunder. In V. Bradley, J.W. Ashbaugh, & B.C. Blaney (Eds.), *Creating individual supports for people with developmental disabilities: A mandate for change at many levels* (pp. 335–346). Baltimore: Paul H. Brookes Publishing Co.

Brown, F. (1991). Creative daily scheduling: A nonintrusive approach to challenging behaviors in community residences. *Journal of The Association for Persons with Severe Handicaps, 16,* 75–84.

Brown, F., Belz, P., Corsi, L., & Wenig, B. (1993). Choice diversity for people with severe disabilities. *Education and Training in Mental Retardation, 28,* 318–326.

Brown, F., & Cohen, S. (1994). *Self-determination in young children.* Manuscript submitted for publication.

Brown, F., Evans, I.M., Weed, K.A., & Owen, V. (1987). Delineating functional competencies: A component model. *Journal of The Association for Persons with Severe Handicaps, 12,* 117–124.

Brown, F., & Lehr, D. (1993). Making activities meaningful for students with severe multiple disabilities. *Teaching Exceptional Children, 25,* 12–16.

Brown, F., & Rosa, C.J. (1994). *Autonomy and group homes: A survey of New York State.* Unpublished manuscript, Queens College, Educational and Community Programs, Flushing, New York.

Brown, L., Nietupski, J., & Hamre-Nietupski, S. (1976). The criterion of ultimate functioning and public school services for severely handicapped students. In M.A. Thomas (Ed.), *Hey don't forget about me: Education's investment in the severely, profoundly, and multiply handicapped* (pp. 2–15). Reston, VA: Council for Exceptional Children.

Carr, E.G., & Durand, V.M. (1985). Reducing behavior problems through functional communication training. *Journal of Applied Behavior Analysis, 18,* 111–126.

Dattilo, J., & Rusch, F.R. (1985). Effects of choice on leisure participation for persons with severe handicaps. *Journal of The Association for Persons with Severe Handicaps, 10,* 195–199.

Doss, S., & Reichle, J. (1989). Establishing communicative alternatives to the emission of socially motivated excess behaviors: A review. *Journal of The Association for Persons with Severe Handicaps, 14,* 101–112.

Durand, V.M. (1990). *Severe behavior problems: A functional communication training approach.* New York: Guilford.

Dyer, K., Dunlap, G., & Winterling, V. (1990). Effects of choice-making on the serious problem behaviors of students with severe handicaps. *Journal of Applied Behavior Analysis, 23,* 515–524.

Evans, I.M., & Meyer, L.H. (1985). *An educative approach to behavior problems: A practical decision model for interventions with severely handicapped learners.* Baltimore: Paul H. Brookes Publishing Co.

Goode, D.A., & Gaddy, M.R. (1976). Ascertaining choice with alingual, deaf-blind and retarded clients. *Mental Retardation, 14,* 10–12.

Gothelf, C.R., & Crimmins, D.B. (1993, June). *Processes and strategies that enable successful transitions.* Workshop jointly sponsored by New England Center for Deaf-Blind Services, NHESSI, and TRACES, Concord, New Hampshire.

Gothelf, C.R., Crimmins, D.B., Mercer, C.A., & Finocchiaro, P.A. (1994). Teaching choice-making skills to students who are deaf-blind. *Teaching Exceptional Children, 26,* 13–15.

Gothelf, C.R., Crimmins, D.B., & Woolf, S.B. (in press). Transition. In K. Hubner, J. Prickett, & T. Rafalowski-Welsch (Eds.), *American Foundation for the Blind: Deaf-Blind project.* New York: American Foundation for the Blind.

Guess, D. (1988). Problems and issues pertaining to the transmission of behavior management technologies from researchers to practitioners. In R.H. Horner & G. Dunlap (Eds.), *Behavior management and community integration for individuals with developmental disabilities and severe behavior problems* (pp. 19–46). Eugene: Specialized Training Program, University of Oregon.

Guess, D., Benson, H., & Siegel-Causey, E. (1985). Concepts and issues related to choice-making and autonomy among persons with severe handicaps. *Journal of The Association for Persons with Severe Handicaps, 10,* 79–86.

Guess, D., Helmstetter, E., Turnbull, H.R., & Knowlton, E. (1987). *Use of aversive procedures with persons who are disabled: An historical review and critical analysis.* Seattle: The Association for Persons with Severe Handicaps.

Hanline, M.F., & Fox, L. (1993). Learning within the context of play: Providing typical early childhood experiences for children with severe disabilities. *Journal of The Association for Persons with Severe Handicaps, 18,* 121–129.

Haring, T.G., & Breen, C. (1989). Units of analysis of social interaction outcomes in supported education. *Journal of The Association for Persons with Severe Handicaps, 14,* 255–262.

Haring, T.G., & Kennedy, C.H. (1990). Contextual control of problem behavior in students with severe disabilities. *Journal of Applied Behavior Analysis, 23,* 235–243.

Helmstetter, E., & Durand, V.M. (1991). Nonaversive interventions for severe behavior problems. In L.H. Meyer, C.A. Peck, & L. Brown (Eds.), *Critical issues in the lives of people with severe disabilities* (pp. 559–600). Baltimore: Paul H. Brookes Publishing Co.

Horner, R.H., Dunlap, G., Koegel, R.L., Carr, E.G., Sailor, W., Anderson, J., Albin, R.W., & O'Neill, R.E. (1990). Toward a technology of "nonaversive" behavioral support. *Journal of The Association for Persons with Severe Handicaps, 15,* 125–132.

Kennedy, C.H., & Haring, T.G. (1993). Teaching choice making during social interactions to students with profound multiple disabilities. *Journal of Applied Behavior Analysis, 26,* 63–76.

Kishi, G., Teelucksingh, B., Zollers, N., Park-Lee, S., & Meyer, L. (1988). Daily decision-making in community residences: A social comparison of adults with and without mental retardation. *American Journal on Mental Retardation, 92,* 430–435.

Kitch, R. (1978). We are people first. In *President's Committee on Mental Retardation, Report to the President: MR 78* (pp. 53–58). Washington, DC: U.S. Government Printing Office.

Koegel, R.L., Dyer, K., & Bell, L.K. (1987). The influence of child-preferred activities on autistic children's social behavior. *Journal of Applied Behavior Analysis, 20,* 243–252.

LaVigna, G.W., & Donnellan, A.M. (1986). *Alternatives to punishment: Solving behavior problems with nonaversive strategies.* New York: Irvington.

Meyer, L.H., & Evans, I.M. (1989). *Nonaversive intervention for behavior problems: A manual for home and community.* Baltimore: Paul H. Brookes Publishing Co.

Meyer, L.H., & Evans, I.M. (1993). Science and practice in behavioral intervention: Meaningful outcomes, research validity, and usable knowledge. *Journal of The Association for Persons with Severe Handicaps, 18,* 224–234.

Meyer, L.H., & Janney, R. (1989). User-friendly measures of meaningful outcomes: Evaluating behavioral interventions. *Journal of The Association for Persons with Severe Handicaps, 14,* 263–270.

Mount, B. (1994). Benefits and limitations of personal futures planning. In V.J. Bradley, J.W. Ashbaugh, & B.C. Blaney (Eds.), *Creating individual supports for people with developmental disabilities: A mandate for change at many levels* (pp. 97–108). Baltimore: Paul H. Brookes Publishing Co.

Munk, D.D., & Repp, A.C. (1994). The relationship between instructional variables and problem behavior: A review. *Exceptional Children, 60,* 390–401.

Newton, J.S., Horner, R.H., & Lund, L. (1991). Honoring activity preferences in individualized plan development: A descriptive analysis. *Journal of The Association for Persons with Severe Handicaps, 16,* 207–212.

Pace, G.M., Ivancic, M.T., Edwards, G.L., Iwata, B.A., & Page, T.J. (1985). Assessment of stimulus preference and reinforcer value with profoundly retarded individuals. *Journal of Applied Behavior Analysis, 18,* 249–255.

Parent, W.S. (1993). Quality of life and consumer choice. In P. Wehman (Ed.), *The ADA mandate for social change* (pp. 19–44). Baltimore: Paul H. Brookes Publishing Co.

Parsons, M.B., & Reid, D.H. (1990). Assessing food preferences among persons with profound mental retardation: Providing opportunities to make choices. *Journal of Applied Behavior Analysis, 23,* 183–195.

Perske, R. (1972). The dignity of risk. In W. Wolfensberger (Ed.), *Normalization: The principle of normalization in human services* (pp. 195–200). Toronto: National Institute on Mental Retardation.

Rehabilitation Act Amendments of 1992, PL 102-569 (October 29, 1992). Title 29, U.S.C. 701 et seq: *U.S. Statutes at Large, 100,* 4344–4488.

Reichle, J., York, J., & Eynon, D. (1989). Influence of indicating preferences for initiating, maintaining and terminating interactions. In F. Brown & D.H. Lehr (Eds.), *Persons with profound disabilities: Issues and practices* (pp. 191–211). Baltimore: Paul H. Brookes Publishing Co.

Repp, A.C., Felce, D., & Barton, L. (1988). Basing the treatment of stereotypic and self-injurious behavior on hypotheses of their causes. *Journal of Applied Behavior Analysis, 21,* 281–289.

Rowland, C., & Schweigert, P. (1993). Analyzing the communication environment to increase functional communication. *Journal of The Association for Persons with Severe Handicaps, 18,* 161–176.

Schloss, P.J., Alper, S., & Jayne, D. (1993). Self-determination for persons with disabilities: Choice, risk, and dignity. *Exceptional Children, 60,* 215–225.

Sigafoos, J., & York, J. (1991). Using ecological inventories to promote functional communication. In J. Reichle, J. York, & J. Sigafoos, *Implementing augmentative and alternative communication: Strategies for learners with severe disabilities* (pp. 61–70). Baltimore: Paul H. Brookes Publishing Co.

Snell, M.E., & Brown, F. (1993). Instructional planning and implementation. In M.E. Snell (Ed.), *Instruction of students with severe disabilities* (4th ed., pp. 99–151). New York: Merrill.

Wacker, D.P., Berg, W.K., Wiggins, B., Muldoon, M., & Cavanaugh, J. (1985). Evaluation of reinforcer preferences for profoundly handicapped students. *Journal of Applied Behavior Analysis, 18,* 173–178.

Wagner, M., Newman, L., D'Amico, R., Jay, D.H., Butler-Nalin, P., Marder, C., & Cox, R. (1991). *Youth with disabilities: How are they doing? The first comprehensive report from the national longitudinal transition study of special education students.* Menlo Park, CA: SRI International.

Wehmeyer, M. (1992). Self-determination as an educational outcome. *Impact, 6*(4), 6–7.

Wehmeyer, M.L., & Metzler, C.A. (1995). How self-determined are people with mental retardation? The national consumer survey. *Mental Retardation, 33,* 111–119.

West, M.D., Kregel, J., & Revell, W.G. (1993/1994). A new era of self-determination. *Impact, 6*(4), 12–13.

West, M.D., & Parent, W.S. (1992). Consumer choice and empowerment in supported employment services: Issues and strategies. *Journal of The Association for Persons with Severe Handicaps, 17,* 47–52.

Williams, R.K. (1991). Choices, communication and control: A call for expanding them in the lives of people with severe disabilities. In L.H. Meyer, C.A. Peck, & L. Brown (Eds.), *Critical issues in the lives of people with severe disabilities* (pp. 543–544). Baltimore: Paul H. Brookes Publishing Co.

Wolfe, P.S. (1993). Increased access to community resources. In P. Wehman (Ed.), *The ADA mandate for social change* (pp. 241–254). Baltimore: Paul H. Brookes Publishing Co.

14

Instructional Support for Self-Determination in Individuals with Profound Disabilities Who Are Deaf-Blind

Carole R. Gothelf and Fredda Brown

As PROFESSIONALS AND caregivers, when we think about self-determination, the overriding question that comes to mind is "How can we prepare individuals to make the choices that enable them to exert control over their lives?" Historically, individuals with profound disabilities who are deaf-blind have had few opportunities to acquire or use the skills that would allow them to exercise choice in their lives. One of the most fundamental skills necessary for people to exercise self-determination is the ability to appropriately communicate preference and, by so doing, affect events. Individuals with profound disabilities who are deaf-blind are delayed in acquiring standard systems of communication. Their ability to react to auditory and visual stimuli is limited, and they may appear unresponsive. They must rely on alternative sensory modes (e.g., touch, movement, smell) to augment their efforts to understand others and, in turn, communicate with them. Their cognitive and physical limitations make it more difficult for others to perceive their efforts as communication, let alone understand them (Siegel-Causey & Downing, 1987). The ways in which they do communicate may be considered ineffective, problematic, or disruptive; as a result, they may be denied opportunities to gain experience in making the choices that contribute to the development and practice of self-determination.

This chapter is based on the assumptions that a "good life" can be achieved only when individuals participate in age-appropriate decisions that enable increased control over their lives and that individuals with profound disabilities who are deaf-blind have the right to express their own desires and preferences and make choices as a matter of routine. Therefore, it is essential that these individuals be provided with the opportunities, training, and support necessary for them to develop the ability to communicate personal choice. This chapter presents practices that will help the individuals begin to exert control over their lives by making choices, allowing them to come to be recognized by others as "self-determining."

NEED FOR INSTRUCTIONAL SUPPORT

Individuals with the concomitant impairments of profound disabilities and deaf-blindness may not be able to communicate their desires or choices clearly or appropriately, even when provided with opportunities to do so. These individuals may respond appropriately when others communicate directives for them to follow, but they often have significant difficulty developing a conventional system of communication with which to convey their needs and desires to others (Siegel-Causey & Downing, 1987). Rather, they use idiosyncratic, inconsistent, self-selected modes to communicate (e.g., vocalizations, actions, gestures) that may be inefficient, problematic, or disruptive.

Ineffective communication becomes apparent when the communication partner (e.g., peer, caregiver, teacher) does not respond appropriately to the individual's message (e.g., "I want something," "I don't want to do this now," "Leave me alone"), because they have failed to interpret it and have then guessed wrong. Continued unsuccessful attempts to transmit a message thwart the development of the communication processes by which an individual exerts control over his or her life. When an individual's means of communication are not effective in exerting control and causing desired outcomes to occur, the individual's communicative behavior may be extinguished, resulting in learned helplessness (Guess, Benson, & Siegel-Causey, 1985; Reichle, York, & Eynon, 1989; Seligman, 1975). If the individual's intention to communicate and obtain a desired outcome is important enough, the communicative behavior may not be extinguished but may evolve into problematic or disruptive behavior and escalate until the partner's response satisfies the original desired outcome (Crimmins & Gothelf, 1995; Durand, 1990; Durand & Crimmins, 1988; Johnston &

Reichle, 1993; Reichle, Mirenda, Locke, Piche, & Johnston, 1992; Wacker & Reichle, 1993).

Instructional staff can further hinder an individual's opportunities to communicate choices by anticipating his or her needs and desires, and with good intentions, making choices for the individual. Choices can also be constrained by those who believe an individual is unable to meaningfully participate in making choices. For example, during dinner, a child may always be given a second portion because his mother "knows" that he is hungry. At school, lunch is served on trays that are prepared in advance in the kitchen with foods that the staff expects that the students will prefer. In a restaurant, an individual reaches for her cup of water, and the caregiver moves the cup away, more concerned with avoiding a possible spill in a public place than with interpreting the individual's movement as an attempt to communicate her intention.

While the desire to overprotect the individual or the belief that the caregiver knows what the individual wants may motivate the caregiver, it deprives the individual of his or her basic right to choose, experience a sense of accomplishment, or risk failure (Guess et al., 1985). Situations like these deprive individuals of the opportunity to communicate preferences in order to obtain what they want or reject what they do not want. While the self-initiated behavior of someone who has profound disabilities and is deaf-blind may be viewed as disruptive to scheduled or planned events, instructional staff and caregivers must acknowledge the importance of choosing and initiating, and they must engender situations in which self-initiated behavior can take place.

How can we prepare individuals who have profound disabilities and are deaf-blind to make the choices that enable them to exert control over their lives? When we consider this question, we are often required to change the way that we design and implement instructional programs. Programs that have as a focus the development of autonomy and dignity by encouraging individuals to make choices share the following characteristics:

- They include flexible curricula in which individuals have the opportunity to make choices as a matter of routine on a consistent daily basis.
- They teach individuals the power and control that they can exert over their environment by using communicative behavior to indicate choice and preference.
- They reinforce autonomous behavior and the power of clear communication by responding appropriately to the individual's intent in a respectful and nonjudgmental way.

COMMUNICATIVE COMPETENCE AND SELF-DETERMINATION

When self-determination is the focus of instruction, opportunities for individuals who have profound disabilities and are deaf-blind to exercise their own initiative, indicate choices, and shape their daily routine are revealed. Objects, persons, and activities that spark an individual's interest, desire, dislike, or avoidance represent natural opportunities for the individual to learn to effectively and appropriately express wants and needs. Reasons to communicate and opportunities to do so become abundant throughout the course of the day (Siegel-Causey & Ernst, 1989).

For example, consider a classroom situation with Eamon, a 14-year-old who has profound disabilities and is deaf-blind. Eamon has residual hearing and residual vision that can aid the instructional process. (Fredericks and Baldwin [1987] point out that 93.8% of individuals who are classified as deaf-blind have some residual hearing and/or residual vision.) Eamon also has cognitive disabilities and epilepsy. It is 10:30 A.M. and time for Eamon and two of his classmates to go the recycling center with their teacher. At the center, Eamon's job is to put cans into the recycling machine and pull the lever that crushes the cans. The teacher simultaneously uses key word signs (KWS) and speech to direct Eamon to go to his daily schedule board. KWS refers to the technique of total communication in which the speaker speaks in full sentences and signs critical words as they are spoken (Grove & Walker, 1990; Windsor & Fristoe, 1989). The schedule board holds pictures arranged in sequence representing the activities planned for Eamon's day. Eamon uses Picture Communication Symbols (Mayer-Johnson, 1987), simple line drawings that have been enlarged to 3/4" and mounted on dark cardboard in order to accommodate his visual requirements. Using total communication, the teacher directs Eamon to look at the board, signs to him that it is time to go to the recycling center, and points to his picture cue of a crushed can. Eamon is prompted to take his picture cue and walk out of the classroom with his classmates. He then drops the picture cue and begins to wander away and spin aimlessly. The teacher directs him to pick up his picture cue and proceed to the job site. Eamon begins to respond but then reverts to his spinning. At this point the teacher asks an assistant to take the other two students to the recycling center while she goes back to the classroom with Eamon. She directs him, using total communication, to a display of picture cues for available activities and shows it to Eamon, instructing him to choose from these activities (Vaughn & Horner, 1995). He spontaneously removes the picture of the tape recorder from the display, indicating that this is what he prefers to do now. Using KWS, the teacher signs "Listen" and "Music" to Eamon;

she says, "Eamon wants to listen to music now," and Eamon signs "Listen" by tapping his ears. He goes to the tape recorder and puts on headphones; the teacher assists him in putting in a tape. A short time later the teacher signs to Eamon that the music is finished, and says, "Music is finished now. It is time to put the music away." Eamon independently takes off the headphones and puts away the tape recorder with the teacher's assistance. Using total communication, the teacher directs Eamon to his daily schedule and indicates that it is now time for the recycling job. Eamon then takes the job site picture cue and proceeds to the recycling center with his teacher.

This scenario can be analyzed in terms of its communicative and instructional opportunities. According to Rowland and Schweigert (1993), "The ideal communicative interaction is an entirely natural one that is prompted by the demands of the moment" (p. 173), as well as having real consequences in that the interaction influences the environment, "which, in turn, responds in accordance with the intent of the communication" (p. 161). In the previous example, the teacher saw the communicative value of the interaction. She balanced the need to follow scheduled instruction with the need to respond positively and appropriately to the intent of Eamon's communication to escape the planned activity in order to reinforce his communicative behavior (dropping the picture cue for the recycling job). She did not attempt to impose a value judgment that a work activity is more worthwhile than a music activity. She did not attempt to force him to follow the scheduled activity and thereby risk a confrontation that could cause Eamon to become disruptive (and thereby not participate in the recycling job) or cause Eamon to become unresponsive (and passively resist participating). Rather, she recognized his communication as an expression of his choice, supported his attempt at self-determination, and reinforced his spontaneous communication.

With this in mind, consider what could be done if, after listening to music for a few minutes, Eamon communicated that he still did not want to proceed to the job site. This communication might simply be the way in which he continued to hold on to his headphones and refused to stand up when instructed to do so. His teacher could reintroduce the possibility of going to the job site after allowing him to continue listening to music, or she could present him with alternate activity choices. In addition, Eamon's teacher should recognize that frequent rejections of an activity represent a statement of preference and should be acknowledged. An activity may be dropped temporarily or possibly restructured.

The development of communicative competence goes hand in hand with the development of self-determination (Williams, 1991). Real-life, meaningful situations, such as Eamon's, provide the context in which appropriate and effective communication skills can be promoted. Language is embedded in life's activities and routines, and it will be acquired and reinforced to the extent that it enables individuals to control different aspects of their environment (Rowland & Schweigert, 1993). By uncovering opportunities in the daily routine in which self-initiated behavior and choice making can be fostered, caregivers and instructional staff can provide individuals with a powerful motivation to use appropriate communication (Brown, Evans, Weed, & Owen, 1987; Halle, 1982, 1987; Harrell & Strauss, 1986; Peck, 1985; Siegel-Causey & Ernst, 1989).

The tools necessary to achieve communicative competence for self-determination are 1) a vocabulary that corresponds to the individual's personal preferences and desires, and 2) an appropriate mode of communicating through which this vocabulary can be effectively employed. Eamon's teacher was prepared to recognize opportunities for him to communicate choice and engage in self-selected activities. The teacher used a variety of communication modes (Beukelman & Mirenda, 1992) and engaged Eamon in meaningful activities that provided opportunities for true communication (O'Neill, Gothelf, Cohen, Lehman, & Woolf, 1990).

Some individuals who have profound disabilities and are deaf-blind may not appear to have acquired any functional system for communication. They may appear unresponsive, be able to form a few signs when prompted but not spontaneously, or have learned so few signs over the years that they cannot adequately express their needs. While it is tempting to simply strive to teach these individuals a few more signs, such an approach may not be productive. There may be underlying reasons for the absence of spontaneously produced manual signs that will continue to thwart these attempts. A more promising strategy may be to engage these individuals in preferred activities that provide natural opportunities for communication by using a simultaneous communication approach that includes the use of aided alternative and augmentative systems (Durand, 1993; Mirenda, Iacono, & Williams, 1990; Reichle, York, & Sigafoos, 1991; Wacker, Wiggins, Fowler, & Berg, 1988).

Through communicating choice, individuals are given the opportunities to affect their environment and satisfy their desires. Opportunities can be discovered and arranged to allow individuals to communicate their preferences, make choices, and perform for themselves, helping them to be more self-reliant and more in control of their lives.

UNCOVERING OPPORTUNITIES FOR COMMUNICATING CHOICES

Typically, individuals have numerous opportunities to make choices in the natural course of the day. In order for choices to be meaningful to individuals who have profound disabilities and are deaf-blind, choice-making opportunities must also be available across the day, within their normal daily activities and routines. Instructional staff and caregivers must be aware of these opportunities when they occur, and they must also strive to structure routines to present opportunities for choice making. No one would like to be told that his or her time to make a choice was only going to occur every morning between 9:00 and 9:30 A.M.!

Eamon's teacher saw an opportunity to allow Eamon to choose the activity he preferred, and she presented him with a chance to communicate using the tools with which he was fluent (i.e., KWS, picture cues). She recognized the opportunity to communicate his choice as being more valuable to Eamon than anything he would gain by being forced to follow the predetermined schedule. The judgment was not whether the recycling job was more "important" than music; rather, it was a recognition of an opportunity to allow Eamon to communicate his preferences and control his environment. Providing opportunities for choice across daily routines has many benefits:

- The individual may be more motivated to participate in an activity because he or she has more control over it.
- The individual will have multiple opportunities to practice the process of choice making. This practice will aid learning and generalization of "choosing."
- The individual will become more self-determining by learning to exert control over his or her daily activities.
- Others will increasingly perceive this individual as a competent individual who is able to control events in his or her daily life.

The quality of an individual's life may be judged by the frequency with which the individual has the chance to exercise his or her own initiative and make choices as a matter of routine (Gothelf, Crimmins, Mercer, & Finocchiaro, 1993, 1994). However, we need to be careful not to present individuals with choices that are either not very important to them or are very limited. The same limited range of choice-making opportunities can be presented over and over again, causing a potentially meaningful choice to become trivialized. For example, if the only opportunity for choice presented to an individual is the choice of milk or juice at meals or snack, this choice will not remain a meaningful one. In addition, choice making should avoid focusing on nonpreferred options, such as a choice between broccoli and Brussels sprouts or between cleaning the kitchen and folding the laundry. Another situation to avoid is presenting the "choice" between preferred options and nonpreferred options as a real choice-making opportunity. These are not real choice-making opportunities, because they are not opportunities to select between valued alternatives.

Daily routines present many opportunities to make choices. Brown, Appel, Corsi, and Wenig (1993) identified seven types of choices that are available within the context of most activities and routines:

- Choosing *within an activity* (e.g., choosing between a muffin or cereal for breakfast)
- Choosing *between two or more activities* (e.g., choosing to shower or to help set the dinner table)
- Deciding *when to do an activity* (e.g., choosing to shower in the morning rather than in the evening)
- Selecting the individual *with whom to participate* in an activity (e.g., choosing to go to the market with Eva but not with John)
- Deciding *where to do an activity* (e.g., choosing to polish your nails in the bedroom and not in the bathroom)
- *Refusing to participate* in a planned activity (e.g., choosing not to fold the laundry)
- Choosing to *terminate an activity* at a self-selected time (e.g., deciding that you are done riding the exercise bicycle, eating dinner, or using the computer)

In the earlier example, Eamon refused to participate at the onset of the recycling job. His teacher respected his communication and provided him with choices between other activities. Figure 1 is a worksheet that can be used for analyzing choice opportunities across the routines of the day.

PROCEDURES FOR TEACHING INDIVIDUALS TO MAKE CHOICES

The most basic factor for establishing self-determination is the individual's ability to wield control over his or her environment by using effective, appropriate communicative behavior to indicate choice. Because of the essential nature of the ability to communicate choice and the potential barriers to choice making, it is essential to teach individuals the process and skills necessary to make meaningful choices and to develop a flexible curriculum in which individuals have opportunities to practice making choices within the context of their daily routines. Specifically, procedures are provided for teaching individuals to make choices within and between activities; to make choices of where, when, and with whom to participate; to refuse to participate; or to terminate the activity after initially participating.

INSTRUCTOR: _____   LEARNER: _____
DATE OF REVIEW: _____   SETTING: _____

Instructions: Indicate the form(s) of choice that could occur in each box. Leave box blank if choice is not relevant.

ROUTINE	WITHIN	BETWEEN	REFUSED	WHO	WHERE	WHEN	TERMINATE

COMMENTS:

Figure 1. Choice diversity. (From Brown et al. [1993]). Choice diversity for people with severe disabilities. *Education and Training in Mental Retardation, 28,* 321. Reprinted by permission.)

Choice-Making Instruction:
Choosing Within and Between Activities

Table 1 presents a step-by-step instructional model for teaching individuals with profound disabilities who are deaf-blind to make choices within the context of natural routines. The goal is not to simply identify the choices that individuals may prefer or to create curricular models in which the choices are included, but to actually teach the individuals to spontaneously and independently communicate their choices, shape their daily activities, and have control over their lives.

Determining Preferences

Acknowledging personal preferences and including them in day-to-day routines enhances the individual's quality of life and motivates the individual to become an active participant. It is important to identify objects, materials, people, environments, and activities that the

Table 1. Choice-making instruction: Within and between activities

Step	Examples and procedures	Guiding precept
1. Use the Choice Diversity Grid to determine the times and situations throughout the day in which choice-making opportunities can be structured.	Choosing which cereal to eat for breakfast (within).	People typically make choices in the environments in which the outcomes of their choice are available.
	Choosing to listen to music or lie down (between).	Natural routines help the individual understand what is expected of him or her. They help establish correspondence between words and their meanings.
	Choosing to have a catch or walk on the treadmill (within).	
	Choosing to water the plants or return the trays to the cafeteria (between).	
2. Select choice-making alternatives from things that the individual is likely to want.	Observe individual to determine activities frequently engaged in.	Individual preferences play an important role in enhancing motivation for the activity.
	Ask significant others which objects and activities the individual likes.	
	Present individuals with a variety of objects and record their approach to them (e.g., which ones did they manipulate, for how long, what was their effect?).	
3. A first alternative is presented on the individual's left.	A small lunch sample (e.g., 2 teaspoons of macaroni) is placed on the individual's left; identified, smelled, and tasted (with the necessary assistance), using a utensil in the left hand; and then removed.	The boundaries in which the choice-making activity takes place should be defined through the use of appropriate aids and cues. Providing boundaries minimizes the visual/motor and cognitive requirements of orienting and reaching.
Use a nonskid mat to help stabilize objects on surfaces.	A cassette player is placed on the individual's left, identified, manipulated with the left hand, and then removed.	The individual is made aware of the choice through tactile/kinesthetic cues (guided or paired movements between the teacher and the individual), visual, verbal, gestural, and object cues. The teacher must assess the conditions that facilitate communication.
Use adaptive equipment when needed for postural alignment, head control, grasping, manipulating, and so forth.	A ball of yarn, which represents the crafts room, is placed on the individual's left and identified; the individual looks at it and feels it with his or her left hand. The yarn is then removed.	
Position the object(s) in the individual's area of best vision. Use proper lighting and provide visual contrasts between the objects and the surfaces they are on.	A graphic representation of picture symbol of a deck of cards is placed on the individual's left side and identified, and he or she is directed to look at it. It is then removed.	Language input is always provided at a level and in a mode that the individual can understand.
Ensure that the individual is not always choosing an object based on its position.		

4. **A second alternative is presented on the individual's right side.**

(Refer to Step 3.)

- A different small lunch sample (e.g., a small piece of chicken) is placed on the individual's right; identified, smelled, and tasted (with the necessary assistance), using a utensil in the right hand; and then removed.

- A mat to rest on is placed on the floor to the individual's right. It is identified, tactually and visually explored, and then removed.

- A ball, which represents the gym, is placed on the individual's right and identified. The individual looks at it and manipulates it. The ball is then removed.

- A graphic representation or picture symbol of a snack is placed on the individual's right side. It is identified, and the individual is directed to look at it. It is then removed.

- Both alternatives are then presented to the individual.

Choices should be presented consistently in order to reinforce the physical structure within which choosing occurs. Placing the choices in the same locations relative to the individual's body each time they are presented helps the individual anticipate where the alternative is likely to be.

5. **Present both alternatives to the individual and direct him or her to indicate a preference.**

- Provide the individual with the level of support needed to make the choice. The individual may require the instructor to move his or her hands. If this is the case, instructional staff and the individual should cooperatively move their hands together, the individual's hand riding on top. The instructor should pause in the pushing action, implicitly prompting the individual to communicate a desire to continue by moving the instructor's hands.

- The individual smells or touches (with the necessary assistance) the alternative on the left with the left hand, is directed to look at it, and is reminded of each object's name. This is repeated for the alternative on the right side.

- The individual is directed to place both hands in his or her lap and is directed (at a level and in a mode that the individual can understand) that "It is time to pick what you want for lunch." (Other specific circumstances can be indicated instead of lunch.)

Establishing routines within instructional sequences enables the individual to anticipate the next step and encourages self-initiated choice making. A pause or time delay in a sequence (hands in the lap) may serve as a prompt to the individual to initiate an interaction or make a selection (Siegel-Causey & Ernst, 1989).

(continued)

Table 1. (continued)

Step	Examples and procedures	Guiding precept
6. Acknowledge the choice made and provide the individual with the desired object or activity. If the individual indicates that he or she wants both, some of each should be provided (i.e., lay on the mat and listen to music, eat macaroni and chicken).	The individual chooses the preferred object or activity by touching one of the alternatives, by looking, by exhibiting positive affect by vocal sounds and/or body movement, or by gesturing or in any way indicating preference. Alternatively, the individual may indicate preference by rejecting the undesired alternative. If the individual has chosen a class of items, he or she should then be prompted to choose an item from the class. For example, if the individual chooses a snack instead of a deck of cards, he or she may then be asked to choose between fruit or a cookie. If the individual does not respond, then the question should be repeated. If he or she continues not to respond, the staff member should say, "If you don't want ———— or ————, I'll ask you again soon." If no choice is made after three attempts, the staff member should say, "It's OK if you don't want to (eat or play or participate) now." The staff member should accept the individual's lack of response as a refusal. Alternative choices should be offered. The staff member should return with other opportunities and additional prompting if necessary.	Reliable communication of preference depends on a foundation of consistent responses to the individual's nonverbal behaviors. Nonverbal behaviors need to be acknowledged on the assumption that the individual is attempting to communicate meaningful dialogue. This provides a basis for communicating shared meanings (Guess et al., 1985; Williams, 1991).

7. Remove the unselected object.

The individual should be made aware that he or she is not going to get the objects that were not selected. The staff member should say, "You didn't want the _____ now, so we will put (take) it away." The individual should assist the staff in removing the undesired object.

The individual experiences the natural consequences of making a choice.

8. The individual gets what he or she chooses.

The staff member completes the Observation Form for Identifying Preferences (Figure 2). Care must be taken to ensure that the individual is not always choosing the alternative on the right or the alternative on the left. Subsequent opportunites for choosing between the same materials should alternate sides.

Contingent communicative behavior is reinforced by getting the requested item.

Adapted from Gothelf, Crimmins, Mercer, and Finocchiaro (1993, 1994).

individual likes. This can often be a difficult task to accomplish. Individuals with profound disabilities who are deaf-blind may be exposed to a limited number of people, activities, materials, and events on a daily basis. These individuals may not have had access to the natural opportunities from which preferences can develop.

Individuals are more motivated and interested in participating in instruction when it has a direct connection to activities that they prefer (Crimmins, 1994; Dunlap & Kern, 1993; Horner, Sprague, & Flannery, in press; Newton, Horner, & Lund, 1991; Reichle & Sigafoos, 1991). Some methods of instruction attempt to coerce learner participation in activities that are valued because they are considered functional but are unrelated to the individual's desires or preferences. This kind of programming may promote behavior problems and inhibit skill acquisition because the activity has no outcome that the individual values. The interaction between Eamon and his teacher is a good example of how to avoid behavior problems, support communication, respect self-determination, and encourage skill acquisition.

There are several ways to identify an individual's preferences. Collecting and evaluating information on a systematic basis helps determine when an individual is consistently communicating true preferences. The Observation Form for Identifying Preferences is a simple format that can be used to collect and organize information about choices. Identifying preferences must be included as part of program planning. Figure 2 is an example of a completed form for Eamon. In addition, direct observation of the individual may reveal behaviors that indicate a personal preference (e.g., the teacher noticed that Eamon drifted away when it was time to go to the recycling job site). It

NAME: Eamon Stone		AGE: 14
OBSERVER: Susan Dyan DATE: March 15		TIME: 2:45 P.M.
DISPLAY ORIENTATION	**LEFT**	**RIGHT**
ITEMS/ACTIVITIES PRESENTED	Peanut butter & cheese crackers	Bananas
INDICATE CHOICE [x]	X	
HOW DID THE LEARNER APPROACH AND SELECT ITEMS/ACTIVITIES? Eamon smelled and licked the crackers and he smelled the banana and did not want to taste it.		

Figure 2.   Observation form for identifying preferences.

is important to discriminate between casual or arbitrary selections and the actual expression of a preference.

A third way of identifying preferences is by interviewing people who know the individual. Such questions as these may be helpful:

- What are the individual's three favorite activities? How is this communicated? For each, please note how often the person has the opportunity to do each.
- What are the three activities the individual likes least? How is this communicated? For each, please note how often the individual is expected to participate in each.
- What types of activities does the individual begin on his or her own?
- With whom does the individual like to spend time? Describe what they do together. How often do they have the opportunity to spend time together?
- What does the individual do in his or her free time? What kind of support do these activities require? (Gothelf, Crimmins, & Woolf, 1995)

Choice-Making Instruction: Choosing When to Do Activities

Choosing when to do one's daily activities, or what order in which to do them, is a fundamental component of having control of one's life. The order in which things are done may make sense to staff or be convenient for a parent, but the prime consideration is not our convenience but the individual's desire and sense of when things should be done. The relationship between control of when to do activities and the incidence of behavior problems has been noted extensively in the literature (Bambera & Ager, 1992; Bannerman, Sheldon, Sherman, & Harchik, 1990; Brown, 1991; Dyer, Dunlap, & Winterling, 1990; Munk & Repp, 1994).

Instructional staff's main responsibility is to implement strategies that will enable the individual to express his or her intentions effectively. A calendar system can be used to support or display a daily schedule for individuals (Writer, 1987). The calendar can include objects, line drawings, or photographs arranged sequentially to represent the plan for the day or for part of the day. Object or picture cues associated with daily activities are displayed on the calendar to assist the individual in anticipating scheduled events within the day and to schedule his or her own daily routine according to personal preference.

The individual can take the object or picture that represents a preferred activity and move it on the calendar to represent the time at which he or she would like to schedule the activity, or the order in which he or she would like the activities to take place. For example, Noel usually likes to shower in the morning, eat breakfast in his bathrobe, and then get dressed. He will arrange the pictures or object cues representing these activities in this desired sequence on his calendar.

Over time, calendar systems aid the acquisition of the concepts of time, order, and place of events and activities. Individuals must be provided with opportunities throughout the day to organize their own schedule. This has special significance regarding leisure activities, because leisure is by definition something that we do when we choose to do it.

Portable calendar systems should be used in conjunction with fixed calendar displays. This practice is particularly appropriate when out in the community. It allows an individual to make known his or her choice to go to the drugstore and clothing store before going to the ice cream store. Examples of portable calendar/communication systems are a collection of picture cue cards, hole-punched, reinforced, and attached to a key ring; a loose-leaf book with cardboard pages on which the object cues are mounted; a photo wallet with line drawing symbols in it; and such aided augmentative devices as Voice Pal, Intro Talker, Scanmate, or Parrot. (See the Appendix for further information.)

Choice-Making Instruction: Choosing Among Individuals

Individuals with profound disabilities who are deaf-blind are often impeded from participating in the activities through which relationships may develop. These individuals are often placed in segregated, highly structured settings. Even when these individuals do take part in the same activities as others, conditions may still exist that serve as barriers to the formation of relationships. First and foremost is the absence of opportunities to select individuals with whom to participate.

Instructional staff must give considerable time and effort to devising and supporting ways of fostering relationships among individuals. One component necessary to form a relationship is the opportunity and ability to choose individuals with whom one wants to spend time. Staff should encourage individuals to choose others with whom they would like to do things, and staff should observe carefully to determine whether individuals are exhibiting signs of preference for one another. Furthermore, staff should identify specific skills that the individual may need to initiate and sustain interactions with a preferred peer. If such signs are present, staff can support this preference by providing more opportunities for these individuals to choose to be together. Choosing among individuals is another opportunity for choice making.

Eve is one of Eamon's classmates. She is going to the recycling center with her teacher, a teacher assistant, and other students. Eve is asked which student she wants to go with. To facilitate communication, Eve is presented with object cues mounted on cardboard that represent the other students. Eve selects the cue that represents the student with whom she wants to be. (It should be noted that a number of experiences were needed over a substantial period of time before Eve was able to consistently associate each cue with the individual it represented.) Each student and instructional staff member in the class has an identifying object cue. The personal cue for Eve's teacher is a bracelet, because she always wears one. The cue for one of the teacher assistants is a plastic pin that she puts on each day when she arrives at school. Eve's classmates put on their personal cues when they arrive at school each day. A second set of cues is mounted as portable cues to be associated with the ones that are worn.

Choice-Making Instruction: Choosing Where to Do an Activity

The opportunity to choose where to perform an activity is often limited by the nature of the activity itself. For example, we cannot shower in the living room or cook in the bedroom. However, some activities take on a different character if they are done in a different place, and individual preferences play a big part in determining where certain activities are done. Eating in the dining room with the family is different from eating in the living room with a roommate or sibling while watching television or listening to music. Sitting in the garden or in the living room after dinner is different from sitting in your bedroom. Individuals should be provided with the opportunity to choose where to conduct certain activities. As described previously, object cues can be associated with a location.

Choice-Making Instruction: Choosing to Refuse or Terminate Participation in an Activity

An individual's behavior that interferes with the ongoing routine has communicative value. Long before this was established in the literature (Carr & Durand, 1985; Durand, 1990; Durand & Crimmins, 1988), instructional staff and caregivers alike were saying "He's doing that just to get your attention," "She's doing that just because she doesn't want to do her work," and "He's playing with his food and spitting because he doesn't want to eat." Teaching becomes impossible, caregiving becomes unbearable, and learning becomes highly unlikely when individuals are actively disruptive (e.g., throwing materials, kicking, hitting themselves) or offering passive resistance (e.g., giggling, being unresponsive to directions or intervention, wandering around). Eamon's behavior interfered with the ongoing routine of the daily recycling job. His teacher recognized this behavior as Eamon's communicating his desire not to participate. Rather than focusing on his off-task behavior, she proceeded by reinforcing his self-determining behavior.

When these circumstances exist and staff continue to redirect the individual to the activity, a likely outcome is increased resistance to the activity along with acceleration of disruptive behavior. Frustrated staff and caregivers may give up and allow the individual to terminate the activity, thus reinforcing disruptive behavior as a method to communicate self-determination. An alternate, more appropriate, and beneficial intervention is to set up instructional strategies that begin by offering the individual a choice of the activity in which to participate (thereby increasing the chance that the individual will want to take part in it) and thereafter offering the individual 1) a chance to continue the activity (by asking "Do you want to continue working?" or "More work?"), 2) a brief respite from the activity (by asking "Do you want to take a break?" or simply "Break?"), or 3) an opportunity to terminate the activity (by asking "Do you want to stop?" or simply "Finished?"). If the individual has communicated that he or she wants to take a break, an option of choosing from activities appropriate to do on a break (one of which may be choosing to do nothing) should be offered. If the individual has communicated that he or she is truly finished, an option of choosing from other preferred alternatives should be offered. It follows that if individuals are given the option of choosing what they want to do, when they want to do it, and when to stop, that the frequency of disruptive behaviors will be reduced because they now have control over how to spend their time. Although staff may present these opportunities at first, the goal is to have the individual initiate the communication.

Figure 3 is a graphic display of an individual's actions through the course of participating in an activity and, eventually, choosing to terminate the activity. It is important to keep in mind that if an individual consistently becomes disruptive during an activity, communicating that he or she does not wish to participate, instructional staff must consider the relevancy of the activity (as currently structured) to the individual. It may be appropriate to consider restructuring the activity or dropping it for a while.

SUMMARY

Historically, students with profound disabilities who are deaf-blind were at risk for participating in school programs and community experiences that disregard the development of skills associated with

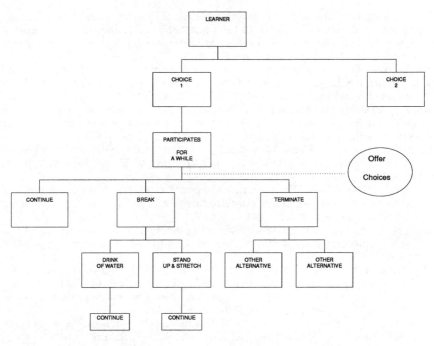

Figure 3. Choice of terminating an activity.

self-determination. This chapter reviewed the concept of self-determination in relation to these individuals and provided direction and guidelines for making self-determination—specifically, choice making, an integral component of the curriculum. Opportunities to participate in choices that enable individuals to exert control over their lives are abundant within naturally occurring routines throughout the day. These choices must be important to the individual and must represent the range of choices available to individuals who are not disabled. Instructional staff must make sure that they create and support environments in which individuals who have profound disabilities and who are deaf-blind can avail themselves of these opportunities. The development of skills associated with self-determination will have a positive impact on the quality of the individual's life, including being recognized by others as someone who is "self-determining."

REFERENCES

Bambera, L.M., & Ager, C. (1992). Using self-scheduling to promote self directed leisure activity in home and community settings. *Journal of The Association for Persons with Severe Handicaps, 17,* 67–77.

Bannerman, D.J., Sheldon, J.B., Sherman, J.A., & Harchik, A.E. (1990). Balancing the right to habilitation with the right to personal liberties: The rights of people with developmental disabilities to eat too many doughnuts and take a nap. *Journal of Applied Behavior Analysis, 23,* 79–89.

Beukelman, D.R., & Mirenda, P. (1992). *Augmentative and alternative communication: Management of severe communication disorders in children and adults.* Baltimore: Paul H. Brookes Publishing Co.

Brown, F. (1991). Creative daily scheduling: A non-intrusive approach to challenging behaviors in community residences. *Journal of The Association for Persons with Severe Handicaps, 16,* 75–84.

Brown, F., Appel, C., Corsi, L., & Wenig, B. (1993). Choice diversity for people with severe disabilities. *Education and Training in Mental Retardation, 28,* 318–326.

Brown, F., Evans, I.M., Weed, K.A., & Owen, V. (1987). Delineating functional competencies: A component model. *Journal of The Association of Persons with Severe Handicaps, 12,* 117–124.

Carr, E.G., & Durand, V.M. (1985). Reducing behavior problems through functional communication training. *Journal of Applied Behavior Analysis, 18,* 111–126.

Crimmins, D.B. (1994). Quality of life for persons with challenging behaviors: Intervention goal, contradiction in terms, or both? In D.A. Goode (Ed.), *Quality of life for persons with disabilities: International perspectives and issues* (pp. 208–217). Cambridge, MA: Brookline Books.

Crimmins, D.B., & Gothelf, C.R. (1995). Examining the communicative purpose of behavior. In K.M. Huebner, J. Glidden-Prickett, T. Rafalowski-Welch, & E. Joffee (Eds.), *Hand-in-hand: Essentials of communication and orientation and mobility for your students who are deaf-blind* (pp. 170–181). New York: AFB Press.

Dunlap, G., & Kern, L. (1993). Assessment and intervention for children within the instructional curriculum. In J. Reichle & D.P. Wacker (Eds.), *Communicative alternatives to challenging behavior: Integrating functional assessment and intervention strategies: Vol. 3. Communication and language intervention* (pp. 177–203). Baltimore: Paul H. Brookes Publishing Co.

Durand, V.M. (1990). *Severe behavior problems: A functional communication training approach.* New York: Guilford Press.

Durand, V.M. (1993). Functional communication training using assistive devices: Effects on challenging behavior and affect. *Augmentative and Alternative Communication, 9,* 168–176.

Durand, V.M., & Crimmins, D.B. (1988). Identifying the variables maintaining self-injurious behavior. *Journal of Autism and Developmental Disorders, 18,* 99–117.

Dyer, K., Dunlap, G., & Winterling, V. (1990). Effects of choice-making on the serious problem behaviors of students with severe handicaps. *Journal of Applied Behavior Analysis, 23,* 515–524.

Fredericks, H.D., & Baldwin, V.L. (1987). Individuals with sensory impairments: Who are they? How are they educated? In L. Goetz, D. Guess, & K. Stremel-Campbell (Eds.), *Innovative program design for individuals with dual sensory impairments* (pp. 3–14). Baltimore: Paul H. Brookes Publishing Co.

Gothelf, C.R., Crimmins, D.B., Mercer, C.A., & Finocchiaro, P.A. (1993). Teaching students who are deaf-blind and cognitively disabled to effectively communicate choices during mealtimes. *Deaf-Blind Perspectives, 1,* 6–8.

Gothelf, C.R., Crimmins, D.B., Mercer, C.A., & Finocchiaro, P.A. (1994). Teaching choice-making skills to students who are deaf-blind. *Teaching Exceptional Children, 26,* 13–15.

Gothelf, C.R., Crimmins, D.B., & Woolf, S.B. (1995). Transition to adult life. In K.M. Huebner, J. Glidden-Prickett, T. Rafalowski-Welch, & E. Joffee (Eds.), *Hand in hand: Essentials of communication and orientation and mobility for your students who are deaf-blind* (pp. 445–480). New York: AFB Press.

Grove, N., & Walker, M. (1990). The Makaton vocabulary: Using manual signs and graphic symbols to develop interpersonal communication. *Augmentative and Alternative Communication, 6,* 15–28.

Guess, D., Benson, H., & Siegel-Causey, E. (1985). Concepts and issues related to choicemaking and autonomy among persons with severe disabilities. *Journal of The Association for Persons with Severe Handicaps, 10,* 79–86.

Halle, J. (1982). Teaching functional language to the handicapped: An integrative model of natural environment teaching techniques. *Journal of The Association for Persons with Severe Handicaps, 1,* 29–37.

Halle, J. (1987). Teaching language in the natural environment: An analysis of spontaneity. *Journal of The Association for the Severely Handicapped, 12,* 28–37.

Harrell, R.L., & Strauss, F.A. (1986). Approaches to increasing assertive behavior and communication skills in blind and visually impaired persons. *Journal of Visual Impairment and Blindness, 24,* 794–798.

Horner, R.H., Sprague, J.R., & Flannery, K.B. (in press). Building functional curricula for students with severe intellectual disabilities and severe behavior problems. In R. Van Houten & S. Axelrod (Eds.), *Behavioral analysis and treatment.* New York: Plenum.

Johnston, S.S., & Reichle, J. (1993). Designing and implementing interventions to decrease challenging behavior. *Language, Speech and Hearing Services in Schools, 24,* 225–235.

Mayer-Johnson, R. (1987). *Picture communication symbols.* Solana Beach, CA: Mayer-Johnson.

Mirenda, P., Iacono, T., & Williams, R. (1990). Communication options for persons with severe and profound disabilities: State of the art and future directions. *Journal of The Association for Persons with Severe Handicaps, 15,* 3–21.

Munk, D.D., & Repp, A.C. (1994). The relationship between instructional variables and problem behavior: A review. *Exceptional Children, 60,* 390–401.

Newton, J.S., Horner, R.H., & Lund, L. (1991). Honoring activity preferences in individualized plan development: A descriptive analysis. *Journal of The Association for Persons with Severe Handicaps, 16,* 207–212.

O'Neill, J., Gothelf, C.R., Cohen, S., Lehman, L., & Woolf, S.B. (1990). *A curricular approach to support the transition to adulthood of adolescents with visual or dual sensory impairments and cognitive disabilities: Handbook for instructional staff.* Albany: New York Department of State Education/Office of Special Education (ERIC Document Reproduction Service, ED 297–506).

Peck, C.A. (1985). Increasing opportunities for social control by children with autism and severe handicaps: Effects on student behavior and perceived classroom climate. *Journal of The Association for Persons with Severe Handicaps, 10,* 183–193.

Reichle, J., Mirenda, P., Locke, P., Piche, L., & Johnston, S. (1992). Beginning augmentative communication systems. In S.F. Warren & J. Reichle, *Causes and effects in communication and language intervention: Vol. 1. Commu-*

nication and language intervention (pp. 131–156). Baltimore: Paul H. Brookes Publishing Co.

Reichle, J., & Sigafoos, J. (1991). Establishing spontaneity and generalization. In J. Reichle, J. York, & J. Sigafoos (Eds.), *Implementing augmentative and alternative communication* (pp. 193–214). Baltimore: Paul H. Brookes Publishing Co.

Reichle, J., York, J., & Eynon, D. (1989). Influence of indicating preferences for initiating, maintaining and terminating interactions. In F. Brown & D.H. Lehr (Eds.), *Persons with profound disabilities: Issues and practices* (pp. 191–212). Baltimore: Paul H. Brookes Publishing Co.

Reichle, J., York, J., & Sigafoos, J. (1991). *Implementing augmentative and alternative communication.* Baltimore: Paul H. Brookes Publishing Co.

Rowland, C., & Schweigert, P. (1993). Analyzing the communication environment to increase functional communication. *Journal of The Association for Persons with Severe Handicaps, 18,* 161–177.

Seligman, M. (1975). *Helplessness: On depression, development, and death.* San Francisco: W.H. Freeman.

Siegel-Causey, E., & Downing, J. (1987). Nonsymbolic communication development: Theoretical concepts and educational strategies. In L. Goetz, D. Guess, & K. Stremel-Campbell (Eds.), *Innovative program design for individuals with dual sensory impairments* (pp. 15–48). Baltimore: Paul H. Brookes Publishing Co.

Siegel-Causey, E., & Ernst, B. (1989). Theoretical orientation and research in nonsymbolic development. In E. Siegel-Causey & D. Guess (Eds.), *Enhancing nonsymbolic communications interactions among learners with severe disabilities* (pp. 17–51). Baltimore: Paul H. Brookes Publishing Co.

Vaughn, B., & Horner, R.H. (1995). Effects of concrete versus verbal choice systems on problem behavior. *Augmentative and Alternative Communication, 11,* 89–92.

Wacker, D.P., & Reichle, J. (1993). Functional communication training as an intervention for problem behavior: An overview and introduction to our edited volume. In J. Reichle & D.P. Wacker (Eds.), *Communicative alternative to challenging behavior: Integrating functional assessment and intervention strategies: Vol. 3. Communication and language intervention* (pp. 1–10). Baltimore: Paul H. Brookes Publishing Co.

Wacker, D.P., Wiggins, B., Fowler, M., & Berg, W.K. (1988). Training students with profound or multiple handicaps to make requests via microswitches. *Journal of Applied Behavior Analysis, 21,* 331–343.

Williams, R. (1991). Choices, communication and control: A call for expanding them in the lives of people with severe disabilities. In L. Meyer, C. Peck, & L. Brown (Eds.), *Critical issues in the lives of people with severe disabilities* (pp. 543–544). Baltimore: Paul H. Brookes Publishing Co.

Windsor, J., & Fristoe, M. (1989). Key word signing: Listener's classification of signed and spoken narratives. *Journal of Speech and Hearing Disorders, 54,* 374–382.

Writer, J. (1987). A movement-based approach to the education of students who are sensory impaired/multi-handicapped. In L. Goetz, D. Guess, & K. Stremel-Campbell (Eds.), *Innovative program design for individuals with dual sensory impairments* (pp. 191–224). Baltimore: Paul H. Brookes Publishing Co.

Appendix: Augmentative Communications Devices

The following list presents a sample of aided augmentative communications devices that have been successfully used by the authors.

VoicePal® and VoicePal Plus® Communications Aids
Adaptivation, Inc.
224 S.E. 16th Street, Suite 2
Ames, IA 50010
1-800-723-2783

IntroTalker® (superseded by AlphaTalker®)
Prentke Romich Co.
1022 Heyl Road
Wooster, OH 44691
1-800-262-1984

Parrot and Macaw
ZYGO Industries, Inc.
P.O. Box 1008
Portland, OR 97207-1008
1-800-234-6006

Say-It-Simply Plus GOLD®, Voicemate 4, Scanmate 4, Switchmate 4
Innocomp
26210 Emery Road, Suite 302
Warrensville Heights, OH 44128
1-800-382-8622

15

Supporting Increased Self-Determination for Individuals with Challenging Behaviors

Daniel B. Crimmins and Denise Berotti

Ivan is a man with a severe cognitive disability and a history of challenging behaviors. He has been known to assault people, throw chairs, tip over large pieces of furniture, and scream—sometimes all of these things within a brief period of time, several times in a day, and for several weeks in a row. It is difficult to plan for a person like Ivan; he does not say what he wants, he hurts people, and he has few apparent interests. In our professional and caregiving roles we have all known people like Ivan and have worked diligently on their behalf. Too often, however, we have supported them poorly—through services that value compliance with rigid programmatic requirements.

We *can* do a better job; we have learned a great deal in the past 10 years that has helped us to do so. The approach is best summarized by a statement that on first consideration may seem paradoxical—we are more likely to gain control over Ivan by having Ivan exert increased control over his own life. However, accomplishing this has required a

Thanks are extended to Carole Gothelf and Mark Durand for comments on earlier sections of this chapter, and to the staff of Community Resource Center of Sullivan County, New York, for their work with the man who is called Ivan in this chapter. Preparation of this chapter was supported in part by grants from the Administration on Developmental Disabilities, Administration for Children and Families (90DD0311), and the Maternal and Child Health Bureau (MCJ36029). The opinions expressed in this paper are solely those of the authors; no official endorsement by the U.S. Department of Health and Human Services should be inferred.

fundamental change in the way in which we view our roles and relationships with individuals with challenging behaviors. This chapter reviews how challenging behaviors can be seen as a response to the environmental and social circumstances associated with having a severe disability, how these behaviors may serve as a means of controlling these circumstances, and how we might support the individual in developing other means of exerting control. These issues are reviewed as part of the process of behavior support planning, with particular focus on assessment and intervention approaches. This chapter places particular emphasis on practices that reflect a new way of "doing business" and supporting people with challenging behaviors in quality lifestyles.

CHALLENGING BEHAVIORS AS A MEANS OF SELF-DETERMINATION

Wehmeyer (1992) describes self-determination as "the attitudes and abilities necessary to act as the primary causal agent in one's life and to make choices and decisions regarding one's quality of life, free from undue external influence or interference" (p. 305). The dilemma in planning for an individual with challenging behaviors is that, although he or she may well be the causal agent in deciding whether to engage in a particular challenging behavior, doing so leads to what most would consider a diminished quality of life. We wish that the individual were far *more* subject to external influences so that he or she would stop the behavior when asked. That is, we want to prevent the individual from exerting control through challenging behaviors because doing so often leads to injury or segregation. As well-intentioned as we are for wanting the individual to do what would be "better" for him or her, we often find ourselves increasing the level of external control in an effort to gain compliance. Thus, although the individual's behavior may reflect a personal choice on some level, it is unclear whether the individual has a more effective means of self-determination. This is the starting point in the planning—to analyze how challenging behaviors can be expressions of self-determination and to determine alternative means of self-determination.

A trademark of challenging behaviors is their persistence. We are forced to ask ourselves why these behaviors persist if the environment really offers a better way to achieve what the individual wants. We are faced with considering two explanations—either the individual is uncontrollable and the behavior is inexplicable *or* the individual is choosing to engage in this behavior for a specific purpose.

The former view was responsible for removing people from the community into segregated facilities. This trend has clearly become philosophically unacceptable with the movement toward integrated schools and community-based programs. However, individuals with challenging behaviors often remain an exception to this movement, continuing to receive specialized supports in segregated environments. Unfortunately, even though it might be done with the best of intentions (e.g., for their own or others' safety), separate services underscore the view that these individuals need to be controlled.

The second explanation, that the individual engages in the behavior for a specific purpose, has become widely acknowledged by the field and leads us in new directions in behavioral planning. Challenging behaviors often reflect a learning history of ineffective communication, and although they may be inefficient they are often effective in obtaining preferred outcomes. That is, some individuals may rely on challenging behaviors as a way of gaining access to favorite events (e.g., social attention, food) or to avoid unpleasant stimuli (e.g., demands) (Carr & Durand, 1985). Even those who are able to communicate often have few opportunities for control, because they may live or work in unresponsive environments (Houghton, Bronicki, & Guess, 1987). In such settings, verbal communication and gestures may be ignored. We also encounter examples where behavior plans systematically limit access to preferred outcomes in order that they may serve as contingent reinforcement for appropriate behavior. Thus, although there may be few opportunities to exert control in the typical manner, individuals may find that their challenging behaviors serve as excellent means of exerting control because they often cannot be ignored. Therefore, these behaviors should be seen as functional in that they may be the only way in which the individual can effect any change in his or her environment. That drive to effect change in the environment leads us to regard the individual with challenging behaviors as someone who is self-determining.

Unfortunately, this explanation is accepted more in theory than in practice. For example, if a behavior serves as a means of gaining another's attention, then clearly we need to teach better ways to request and maintain the attention of others. Or if a different behavior provides sensory stimulation, then the individual needs to have alternative and appropriate means of obtaining this sensory input. Despite the logic of these two examples, many individuals under these very circumstances are expected to be quiet, wait their turn, or keep their hands down, reflecting a paradigm of rigid programming and control rather than of support. Therefore, even though we have become more likely to attribute the characteristic of being self-determining to the individual, this approach does not consistently translate into increased opportunity for exercising that skill.

However, some efforts since the mid-1980s have been directed toward investigating methods for providing individuals with more opportunities to control their environment and toward evaluating the effects of these procedures. The results of these approaches have been very productive in providing educators and clinicians with a variety of procedures to enhance the ability of individuals with developmental disabilities to be more in control of their daily activities. Intervention strategies for increasing self-determination can be divided into two general approaches.

The goal of the first method is to increase opportunities for gaining access to preferred materials, either by presenting materials that have been identified as preferred or by providing the individual with on-the-spot choice-making opportunities. It is important to realize that with these procedures someone other than the individual determines the activities (e.g., tasks, reinforcers) over which he or she will be given control. Although these activities are selected from a set of activities that the individual prefers, they are being presented and used according to what the caregivers believe are the most important at that time. In other words, although the individual may be participating in making choices, the choices are controlled by the caregiver.

In the second method, the individual's behavior guides decisions concerning the selection of activities over which he or she will be provided control. An understanding of the variables that maintain challenging behaviors should guide us as to what is most important to the individual (Durand, 1990; Durand, Crimmins, Caulfield, & Taylor, 1989). For example, if we find that a person behaves well when directed to work but engages in a tantrum when a certain staff member walks out of the room, we may infer that social attention is more critical to the person than the work that is being presented. For this individual, being able to exert control over when, where, and with whom time is spent may relate to a decrease in challenging behaviors. Thus, individuals are less likely to engage in behavior problems when given control over variables that maintain their challenging behavior compared with when they are given control over other variables (Brown, 1991; Carr & Durand, 1985).

Regardless of which of these two general approaches to increasing self-determination for individuals with challenging behaviors might be used, a comprehensive assessment of challenging behaviors, individual preferences, and choice availability should be conducted. The following sections review assessment procedures, with particular emphasis on how the results of these assessments can be used to develop behavior support plans.

ASSESSMENT OF CHALLENGING
BEHAVIORS AS A MEANS OF SELF-DETERMINATION

This chapter examines two particular aspects of assessing environmental and instructional variables related to challenging behaviors. First, we look at ways of viewing challenging behaviors and how an individual's choice to spend time and energy on a behavior may reflect self-determination. Second, we examine the relationship between access to preferred activities and the occurrence of challenging behaviors. This relationship is critical because it suggests ways that we might assess environmental variables in terms of providing individuals with increased control over their environments, thereby providing increased opportunity for self-determination.

Functional Analysis of Challenging Behavior

Persistent challenging behaviors often occur in specific social and environmental contexts, with a presumed probability of being reinforced. Examining these contexts and identifying variables maintaining the behavior are part of the assessment process often referred to as functional analysis (Durand, 1990; Reichle & Wacker, 1993). The process of functional analysis has three outcomes: 1) operational definition of the behaviors, 2) an understanding of the times and conditions in which a behavior is most likely to occur, and (3) an understanding of the function that a behavior serves for the individual (O'Neill, Horner, Albin, Stoy, & Sprague, 1990). These outcomes should assist us in understanding why behaviors persist and what the individual may be trying to accomplish by engaging in these behaviors. Once we have identified the variables maintaining challenging behavior, we can develop interventions that will allow the person to obtain these outcomes without engaging in problem behavior.

Operational Definition of the Behavior Challenging behaviors are generally defined in quantifiable terms that describe their observable topography, their rate or frequency, and their intensity. In community settings, the operational definition generally describes a category of behavior such as self-injury, stereotyped behavior, or aggression, each of which can be further defined (e.g., face slapping, eye poking) should the need occur. Another dimension along which behaviors can be described is the impact they have on the individual or others (e.g., amount of injury the behavior causes, the necessity for restraint procedures, separation from the community, property damage). Using a baseline, counts of incidents of a behavior during a specified unit of time (e.g., per hour, day, or week), the distribution of these incidents over the course of the day, and the impact of the behavior might all be recorded. These assessments of the initial frequency and severity of challenging behaviors are an essential element in implementing any intervention because they allow for an evaluation of the overall success of the plan and they assist in identifying critical variables for follow-up assessment.

Identification of Antecedents and Setting Events The second goal of a functional analysis is the assessment of the situations when the behavior is most likely to occur. In general, occurrences of challenging behavior are not distributed randomly throughout the day or week but rather occur during a limited number of times or under certain conditions. Identifying these situations can assist us in understanding what elicits the challenging behavior and in developing interventions designed to increase the appropriate expression of self-determination. Thus, the next step in the analysis is to identify those events that typically precede the behaviors either immediately or more distally in time—these are generally referred to as antecedents and setting events, respectively. Particular attention is often given to three sets of circumstances: 1) when the individual is faced with nonpreferred stimuli (e.g., difficult tasks, nonpreferred staff), 2) when he or she is faced with preferred stimuli that are not accessible (e.g., favorite foods, toys), or 3) when he or she is left alone with nothing to do. The job of educators and clinicians is to identify those situations that elicit challenging behavior for a particular individual, and there are a number of methods of doing so: Three strategies that are often used in combination are observation, interview, and analog assessment.

A number of different observational strategies are available to assist in identifying antecedents to challenging behaviors. One widely used approach is to record each occurrence of a behavior with a written description of its antecedents and consequences. An analysis of the patterns that exist in the data (if any) can then be conducted. One difficulty with this approach is the range in quality of the data depending on the abilities and motivation of the recorder. In order to streamline the data collection process, different approaches have been suggested that may potentially lead to more direct identification of relevant variables. One such method is termed a *scatter plot* (Touchette, MacDonald, & Langer, 1985), in which caregivers record whether or not a challenging behavior occurred during a specific unit of time (e.g., 30 minutes) during the day. If a pattern is revealed in which the behavior is more likely to occur at specific times of the day or on a certain day, the activities associated with these times can be further analyzed to identify typical antecedents or setting events. Brown (1991) describes another observational method that examines the effect of an individualized activity schedule on assessing challenging behaviors. Variables, such as type of activity, assigned staff, time of day, and prompt level, can be manipulated to determine their effect on the rate of challenging behaviors.

Another approach to assessing the variables that maintain challenging behaviors is through structured interviews or questionnaires. O'Neill et al. (1990) described a method for conducting a functional analysis interview that outlines information that is generally pertinent to understanding the behavior and planning for interventions. The interview process has two potential drawbacks. One is that the quality of information is clearly dependent on who the informants are; the second is that it can be quite time consuming. Another method suggested by Durand and Crimmins (1992) as a relatively quick method of identifying the variables that maintain challenging behavior is the Motivation Assessment Scale (MAS) (Durand & Crimmins, 1992). The MAS provides a series of questions focusing on the relative influences of social attention, demands, sensory stimulation, and access to tangible rewards on the frequency of challenging behaviors.

Often, in order to get a complete picture of the contexts in which challenging behaviors occur, the assessment procedures need to go beyond an examination of immediate antecedents. The assessment may also focus specifically on setting events, which are variables that are more distal in time and do not directly elicit challenging behaviors but are, nonetheless, related to their occurrence (Durand, 1990; O'Neill et al., 1990). For example, an individual may generally be able to perform well on a certain task; the same individual, when tired, may display challenging behaviors when presented with that task. In this case, a disrupted sleep cycle may be considered a setting event. One method for evaluating potential setting events for challenging behaviors was described by Gardner and his colleagues (Gardner, Cole, Davidson, & Karan, 1986). These authors describe a checklist for caregivers to indicate whether any of several events (e.g., receiving bad news, visitors, illness, sleep deprivation) occurred during the previous several hours. If a pattern develops in which the individual tends to display challenging behavior more frequently during the hours following such events, they presumably influence the rate of those behaviors.

Taken together, observation and interview approaches should result in a preliminary understanding of when a given individual is most likely to engage in challenging behaviors. This information can then be confirmed through experimental manipulation of the hypothesized variables. One method is to conduct an analog assessment in which the individual is systematically presented with several situations that potentially elicit the challenging behavior (e.g., difficult demands, a lack of social attention). The frequency of the behavior problems during each of the conditions is then recorded, allowing for an assessment of the condition(s) most related to the occurrence of challenging behaviors. There are a number of sources describing strategies for conducting systematic manipulations of this type (e.g., Derby et al., 1994; Durand, 1990; Iwata, Dorsey, Slifer, Bauman, & Richman, 1982; O'Neill et al., 1990).

Understanding the Function of Challenging Behaviors Challenging behaviors have long been noted as serving a purpose for individuals with developmental disabilities by allowing them to control their environment. To identify the function served by challenging behaviors, in addition to examining the context in which the behavior occurs, it is also critical to identify typical consequences that the behavior has on the environment. Many of the procedures for identifying the antecedents of challenging behaviors described in the previous section can also be used to identify the outcomes that they achieve. Three sets of consequences are commonly encountered in examining the effects that challenging behaviors have on the environment or on the individual: 1) avoidance of or escape from nonpreferred stimuli (difficult tasks, nonpreferred staff), 2) access to preferred stimuli (e.g., attention, food), or 3) an increase in sensory stimulation.

Analysis of Preferred Activities and Choice Making

Preference Often, decisions concerning what activities an individual with severe disabilities engages in are made by others (e.g., teachers, staff) (Houghton et al., 1987; Kishi, Teelucksingh, Zollers, Park-Lee, & Meyer, 1988). Interviews with caregivers have indicated that they often believe that individuals with disabilities lack the ability to make good decisions for themselves (Kishi et al., 1988). Because of such beliefs caregivers might be expected to make decisions for these persons, regardless of whether doing so compromises their personal liberties (Bannerman, Sheldon, Sherman, & Harchik, 1990). For individuals with challenging behaviors, not only does this approach jeopardize personal liberties, but also the presentation of nonpreferred activities has been associated with increased levels of challenging behaviors (Foster-Johnson, Ferro, & Dunlap, 1994; Koegel, Dyer, & Bell, 1987).

Therefore, it is critical for educators and clinicians to determine the preferences of the people whom they support. This situation has historically been viewed as very difficult in that many people with disabilities are unable to communicate their preferences in conventional ways. One method for determining preferences of individuals with severe disabilities is through caregiver interview or completion of different surveys (e.g., Green et al., 1988). Observational methods for identifying the preferences are also used. For example, the inference that materials are preferred can be drawn from the observation that they are regularly selected from a pool of objects (Mithaug & Hanawalt, 1978), that they are manipulated for an extended period of time (Dyer, 1989), or that the individual resists having the materials taken away (Dyer, 1989).

Choice-Making Assessment Choice making, defined as the selection of an activity when two or more alternatives are available (Shevin & Klein, 1984), has come to be viewed as a highly valued activity that enhances personal autonomy, dignity, and self-worth (Guess, Benson, & Siegel-Causey, 1985; Houghton et al., 1987). Despite this, as noted earlier, we realize that people with disabilities often have few opportunities to make choices for themselves and that this lack of freedom may contribute to increased rates of challenging behaviors.

In order to assess the effects of choice availability on the individual's behavior, two conditions are presented—choice and no choice. During the choice condition the individual is able to choose from a variety of tasks and reinforcers. During the no-choice condition the materials are chosen for the individual (e.g., Dunlap, Kern-Dunlap, Clarke, & Robbins, 1991; Dyer, Dunlap, & Winterling, 1990). The conditions can then be contrasted in terms of levels of challenging behaviors or rates of performance during the sessions. A number of recent studies have suggested that choice-making opportunities are associated with reduction in rates of challenging behaviors and enhanced rates of performance (Carr & Carlson, 1993; Dunlap et al., 1994; Dunlap et al., 1991; Dyer et al., 1990).

Distinguishing the Effects of Preference versus Choice We have noted that access to preferred activities and choice making both have been demonstrated to be associated with reductions in levels of challenging behaviors. What is not clear from this research is whether choice making, in and of itself, has unique benefits above and beyond that of gaining access to preferred activities. That is, is choice making beneficial because it allows people access to preferred activities, or is the control that choice making affords beneficial?

In their review of the choice-making research, Bannerman et al. (1990) highlight the importance of making the distinction between the effects of control and the effects of the preferred materials. The decision as to whether an activity or material is preferred is based on the individual's previous behavior or selections, whereas choice making examines the individual's current act of selection. A typical assessment procedure to answer this question is the use of yoked designs, in which the materials or events selected by individuals during a choice condition are then assigned during a no-control or yoked condition. With yoked designs, preference is held constant because the activities are identical in both conditions. Preliminary results of research in this area have revealed that control per se may have advantages above and beyond that of gaining access to preferred activities (Berotti, 1994; Dunlap et al., 1994).

PLANNING FOR INTERVENTION AND LONG-TERM SUPPORTS

Overall, a comprehensive assessment to assist in planning for individuals with challenging behaviors should result in the identification of 1) an understanding of the situations that elicit the challenging behaviors and the function the behaviors serve, and 2) preferred activities and the types of choices that the individual routinely makes. Because people with disabilities often have little control over many events in their lives, the assessment should lead directly to identifying ways to increase opportunities for the expression of self-determination and exercising control over one's life. We want to ensure that individuals with challenging behaviors are exposed to preferred events frequently and that exposure to nonpreferred stimuli be limited to those activities that are vital. Identification of the events that elicit the challenging behaviors must be assessed to determine the activities that should be either eliminated or restricted. Furthermore, the identification of the function(s) that the challenging behaviors serve suggests alternative behaviors that the individual needs to be taught in order to continue to exert control over the environment. Finally, through the assessment procedures, preferred activities should be identified for the purpose of making them more available to the individual.

The strategies reviewed in this section have an intended secondary goal of making challenging behaviors nonfunctional in that they do not lead to increased access to preferred outcomes. If we view the individual as using challenging behaviors as a means of self-determination, we want to make it unnecessary to do so. As noted earlier, we can do this by ensuring that the occurrence of a challenging behavior does not regularly lead to preferred outcomes or that the individual is provided with a more efficient and socially acceptable way to gain access to that variable without having to resort to challenging behaviors (Durand & Crimmins, 1991).

The following sections examine different strategies that have been used to increase opportunities for self-determination. These range from methods that might be used for time-limited periods to others that are likely to be used throughout life. The time-limited strategies may be those that require a great deal of resources (e.g., providing someone with constant attention) or that potentially compromise quality of life (e.g., postponing goals related to community environments). The approaches also vary in the amount of effort required to carry them out successfully—from minimal (e.g., removing a nonpreferred activity from someone's schedule) to intensive (e.g., functional communication training). They are described separately in order to document the research support for their use rather than to suggest that they be single components of a behavior support plan. In practice, we are likely to recommend that they be used in whatever combination proves to be effective.

Changes in the Instructional and Social Environments

Noncontingent Elimination of Maintaining Variables If the functional analysis suggests that a target behavior is most likely to occur during a certain activity, we frequently ask whether that activity can be removed from the person's schedule. Depending on the nature of the situation, this might be short term (e.g., not going to specific community locations) or long term (e.g., not asking the person to do a specific task), considering whether continued termination of this activity would compromise the goal of habilitation. If the demand is nonessential (e.g., swimming), then presumably it can be removed permanently. Touchette and his colleagues (1985) provide two illustrations of this approach. In the first, a young woman frequently displayed significant levels of aggression during group prevocational and community living classes. The initial, short-term intervention was to remove these requirements from her schedule. Over time, however, the demands were reintroduced without a concomitant increase in aggression. In the second example, a young man engaged in high rates of self-injury while working with one particular staff member. Intervention consisted of re-assigning that person to work with others, and reintroduction of the employee was not considered necessary. As can be seen, these interventions responded to the behaviors of the individuals and indirectly gave them control over scheduled activities and assigned staff. This approach requires a commitment to a support plan that incorporates flexible scheduling in order to honor individual interests and preferences.

One desired outcome of the functional analysis is the identification of one or more components of the individual's daily schedule that can be altered in an effort to reduce challenging behaviors and to simultaneously increase control. For example, a setting analysis of the aggression displayed by one young woman determined that high rates of aggression occurred on days when she took a certain route to school that was associated with many stops (e.g., red lights) (Kennedy & Itkonen, 1993). A quick and highly effective intervention consisted of simply avoiding that route to school by taking an alternative route that was not associated with stops (e.g., the highway). This treatment would be considered short term or long term based on the ability and need to continually avoid red lights when this particular student was in the car.

This line of research encourages us to challenge the often-held and well-intentioned belief of professionals that, when working with persons with disabilities, it is our responsibility to develop comprehensive and structured schedules to ensure that people are exposed to a well-balanced array of experiences (e.g., exercise, leisure activities, vocational training) similar to those experienced by persons without disabilities. However, a major difference is that persons without disabilities tend to have a great deal of input into their schedules compared with those without disabilities (Kishi et al., 1988). This raises the issue of balancing the rights of habilitation and the right to personal liberty (Bannerman et al., 1990). When we encounter an individual who informs us through what may be his or her only available means (i.e., via challenging behavior) that he or she does not like a specific activity (e.g., swimming), we must consider whether it is more important for the individual to experience this form of exercise or if it is more critical that he or she be afforded the opportunity to be self-determining.

Noncontingent Presentation of Maintaining Variables A similar approach would be simply to provide the individual with free access to the things he or she is trying to acquire through challenging behaviors. Once again, this has the potential to be either a short-term or a long-term intervention depending on the resources required. For example, if a person bangs her head when left alone, a short-term intervention would be to assign a staff member to be with her at all times. Because this intervention would likely be highly demanding of staff time, an additional treatment plan would be required to reduce the long-term need for this level of support. For example, Vollmer, Iwata, Zarcone, Smith, and Mazaleski (1993) worked with three women whose chronic self-injurious behaviors were all maintained by having access to attention. One of the treatments evaluated in this study consisted of providing the women with constant, noncontingent reinforcement (NCR), which was effective in reducing overall rates of the behaviors. They went on to a condition in which constant attention was reduced slowly until the women were receiving 10 seconds of attention every five minutes, all the while maintaining diminished levels of self-injury. Alternatively, if an individual became disruptive whenever his or her magazines were out of reach, a long-term intervention could be to ensure that the individual always have access to the magazines without the need to discontinue this intervention.

Presentation of Maintaining Variables Contingent upon Occurrence of Alternative Behaviors   An alternative to presenting the variables that maintain challenging behaviors in the manner described previously is to present them contingent upon the occurrence of an alternative, desired behavior (Durand et al., 1989). With this intervention, an assessment of the variables the person is trying to control via challenging behaviors is conducted (i.e., the functional analysis), and these variables (e.g., attention, removal of a task) are used as reinforcers for the desired behavior. The individual is then provided with an alternative means of acquiring these variables. This strategy has been used to increase academic performance and reduce the frequency of problem behaviors (Durand et al., 1989; Vollmer, Iwata, Smith, & Rodgers, 1992). An advantage to this intervention is that it is likely to maximize motivation to participate in the instruction. Because the reinforcers are based on a functional assessment, they are presumably the variables that are important to the individual.

Presentation of Maintaining Variables Contingent upon Nonoccurrence of Challenging Behavior   The variables that maintain challenging behavior can also be presented to the individual contingent upon the nonoccurrence of the identified challenging behavior. This would, of course, fall under the procedure known as differential reinforcement of other behavior (DRO). Historically, the reinforcers used with a DRO procedure were chosen arbitrarily (e.g., M&Ms). More recently, however, this intervention has been extended by using the variables maintaining the challenging behavior as the reinforcers. For example, an individual whose behavior is found to be related to task demands might earn breaks from the task by not exhibiting challenging behaviors for a specified period of time (e.g., Kennedy & Haring, 1993a). This innovative method for conducting a DRO provides individuals an alternative way to control the variables that are presumably most important to them (i.e., by not displaying the challenging behaviors) and has been a successful means of reducing challenging behavior (Kennedy & Haring, 1993a; Vollmer et al., 1993).

Increasing Opportunities for
Preferred Activities and Choice Making

Preferred Activities   Research suggests that educators and clinicians can expect improved behavior from the persons who are provided with increased access to preferred activities. Preference assessment can be conducted with numerous variables (e.g., tasks, reinforcers, metals), and the results can be incorporated into behavior support plans. For example, a preference assessment could be conducted by evaluating the relative value of different assigned tasks, and then only preferred work would be presented to the individual. One study, in which the task preferences were assessed based on the method recommended by Dyer (1987), found that students' challenging behaviors occurred less often while they worked on preferred tasks compared to when they worked on nonpreferred tasks (Foster-Johnson et al., 1994).

Another intervention is to provide increased noncontingent access to preferred tangible items (e.g., food and toys) to people with challenging behaviors. People with disabilities living in group homes often have little control over meals and leisure activities. For example, they may be served meals that are based on a menu developed by a nutritionist. While this may ensure that the individuals are exposed to a balanced diet, it also increases the likelihood that they will receive nonpreferred foods. Ideally, meals should be based on a consideration of both health and preference (e.g., conducting a preference assessment with only healthy foods). Once again, not only does this general practice respect the personal liberties of persons with disabilities, but it is also associated with an improvement in behavior. Students with mental retardation and characteristics of autism have been demonstrated to display decreased levels of social avoidance when prompted to interact with an adult and with materials (e.g., food, conversation, toys) evaluated to be preferred by the students compared to when they were prompted to interact with less-preferred materials (Koegel et al., 1987). Similarly, students have been shown to increase their rate of spontaneous verbal requests when adults sat nearby with toys or food that were assessed to be preferred compared with when the adults sat nearby with nonpreferred materials (Dyer, 1989). Taken together, these results suggest that behavioral concerns commonly associated with developmental disabilities may be partly the result of a lack of motivation to engage in nonpreferred activities and that honoring preferences can have a beneficial effect on these problems.

Choice Opportunities Another approach to increasing opportunities for control is to encourage individuals to make on-the-spot choices for themselves. A potential advantage of choice making over providing preferred activities is that choice making addresses the fact that the preference of individuals may change with time. For example, if individuals are encouraged to choose from a variety of snacks each day, it is more likely that they will get what they want than if they are provided with a snack they preferred several days ago.

Choice-making opportunities can be provided in numerous areas of an individual's life. For example, a person can be encouraged to choose which of several tasks he or she would like to complete; notably, choice making over tasks has been associated with a reduction in problem behaviors (Dunlap et al., 1991; Dunlap et al., 1994). Students who are able to choose reinforcers as well as tasks also display fewer challenging behaviors relative to when they were assigned these activities (Dyer et al., 1990). This type of choice making has also been associated with an increase in communication (Peck, 1985) and on-task responding (Dunlap et al., 1991), although one study did not observe a relationship between choice making and correct responding (Dyer et al., 1990). Other potential areas for choice making include all of the activities that people without disabilities value having control over (e.g., what clothing to wear, where to work, what recreational activities in which to participate) (Meyer & Evans, 1989). Brown and her colleagues describe a model for identifying several ways in which choices can be made within the context of daily routines (Brown, Belz, Corsi, & Wenig, 1993).

Functional Communication Training

One potential problem with many of the previously mentioned procedures is that they depend on changes in caregiver behavior. Thus, generalization across settings or caregivers on the part of the individual would not be expected. To address this issue, procedures have been developed to provide individuals with skills that enhance control over the environment and that are generalizable across situations. One widely researched skill-building intervention for severe behavior problems is functional communication training (FCT) (Carr et al., 1994; Durand, 1990). FCT derives from the position that challenging behaviors are an attempt by an individual to control his or her environment. For example, a man might not know how to initiate a conversation but may have learned very well that, if he bites his arm, people will attend to him. If the individual had an alternative, more efficient means to control the environment, he should no longer need to rely on challenging behavior as a means of control. However, unique to FCT is the fact that the individual is taught to request the variables maintaining his or her behavior by using some form of communication (e.g., speech, sign, use of an augmentative communication system). Once the individual knows how to control the environment by asking for what is wanted, he or she should be able to use this skill in new situations. The man who bit his arm, from the earlier example, would be taught an alternative way to gain attention and influence others; this skill is then available for him to use at various times in which he wishes to get attention. Therefore, generalization across settings is the expected outcome. Indeed, individuals who have learned to request the variables that maintain their challenging behaviors have been observed to make these requests with new teachers with a concomitant reduction in behavior problems, even when the new teachers received absolutely no training (Durand & Carr, 1991).

Another advantage to FCT is that it is likely to be efficient in terms of staff time. With many of the strategies described previously, individuals are provided with the variables that maintain their challenging behavior according to some schedule (e.g., after every 5 minutes or after every correct answer). With FCT, however, once the response has been taught, caregivers do not need to worry about a schedule of reinforcement because the individual receives the variable only when he or she requests it. Because the individual determines when to have access to the variable, there are no instances of it being provided when it is not wanted.

Common Questions in Implementing These Strategies

While these interventions are straightforward and derive from an evolving database, their implementation is often not simple. They require ongoing assessment and adjustment, and more often than not problems will arise. Behavior plans that promote increased individual control over activities do require new ways of structuring services and supports. Because of this, caregivers often raise concerns or objections related to their new role in supporting the individual in decision making instead of controlling that person's behavior. Following are some commonly encountered questions, along with a discussion of potential solutions.

What If She Becomes Too Demanding? One of the most frequent concerns from caregivers is that an individual may, for example, choose to receive attention or take breaks too often. During the planning process there are frequent requests to establish a limit on the amount of attention or the number of breaks that can be requested in a specified period of time. We generally resist this direction for two reasons. First, although there are some examples in the literature of requests occurring at high rates over a prolonged period (e.g., Durand & Carr, 1991), this is relatively rare and is also typically accompanied by a significant decrease in the occurrence of challenging behaviors. We generally anticipate that within a few weeks individuals tend not to request unmanageable amounts of activities once they have control over them (Durand, 1990). Second, fading procedures, such as fading large amounts of attention (Vollmer et al., 1993) or the gradual reintroduction of higher levels of demand, have often been successful

(Bird, Dores, Moniz, & Robinson, 1989; Touchette et al., 1985) and can be used as needed.

What If the Activities He Wants to Control Are Inappropriate? There are at least two possible solutions to this problem. The first is to provide the individual with control over a substitute activity (Durand, 1990). For example, Carr and Carlson (1993) worked with a young man whose challenging behaviors were maintained by giving him access to prohibited snacks. His behavior plan consisted of providing him with a choice over several similar yet healthier snack items. The second potential solution is to reconsider the activity as appropriate. For example, Durand, Berotti, and Weiner (1993) found the challenging behaviors of a woman with autism were provoked when she was prevented from engaging in ritualistic behaviors (e.g., walking down the hallway and tapping the walls and then sitting in a particular chair). The staff members working with her believed that it was inappropriate to allow her to engage in these rituals. During the process of planning behavior supports for this woman, they realized that many people engage in some form of ritualistic behavior and that this woman had a right to engage in such behavior if she so desired. Once they "allowed" her to engage in the ritual, her challenging behaviors decreased substantially.

What If He Does Not Know How to Make Choices? Numerous studies have demonstrated that individuals with even profound disabilities do make choices and requests when taught to do so (e.g., Bambara, Ager, & Koger, 1994; Kennedy & Haring, 1993b; Wacker, Wiggins, Fowler, & Berg, 1988). Since the 1980s, there have been a number of procedures developed to teach people with the most severe disabilities how to make choices (e.g., Dyer, 1989; Gothelf, Crimmins, Mercer, & Finocchiaro, 1994; Meyer & Evans, 1989; Mithaug & Hanawalt, 1978). In addition, the results of the assessment approaches described in this chapter demonstrate how individuals may already be making choices via their challenging behaviors. Thus, choice making is viewed as inevitable for virtually everyone, regardless of level of disability. For those for whom it has been difficult to elicit clear choices, choice making is an important area for instruction.

If I Do This for This One Person, Will I Have to Do It for Everybody? Although our systems of support are supposed to meet the defined needs of an individual, they unfortunately often address the management needs of groups rather than individuals. There has been an increasing recognition that the paradigm of services has shifted from meeting the broad needs of groups to providing flexible and individualized supports (Bradley, 1994). Although there may be real limits on resources, we find that the concern about "everybody" is not critical because the individual with challenging behaviors is already being treated differently from others. Most instructional and living environments accommodate a great range of individual differences and will increasingly be expected to do so. This situation is likely to be particularly important for individuals with challenging behaviors (Foster-Johnson et al., 1994). On a final note, for those times when everybody would truly like to be treated differently, we recommend that the environment be changed to make this possible.

If I Spend All My Time Giving Her Choices, When Will She Do Her Work? The tasks assigned to many people with severe disabilities historically involved completing repetitive or mundane activities that had little long-term value. The strategies described in this chapter are part of broader curricular reform efforts that stress the importance of matching individual interests and preferences with assigned activities. For individuals with challenging behaviors, there has been increased emphasis that assigned activities should naturally lead to outcomes valued by the person (Horner, Sprague, & Flannery, 1993). When participation in preferred activities, making choices, and communicating one's needs occurs throughout the day, we obviously have the beginning of a good behavior support plan. To some this sounds like the description of a vacation, and there is a concern that the individual should do more. The step that we find important to emphasize to caregivers at this point is the continuing development of the behavior support plan to identify opportunities to expand functional routines. This refers to the addition of logical requirements to the process of gaining access to preferred activities. Thus, if the individual communicates that she wants to listen to music, we can expand the routine by having her get headphones from a cabinet or select the type of music that she wishes to hear.

Case Example of Ivan

As a form of a summary, let us return to Ivan, the man introduced in the first paragraph of this chapter. As we noted earlier, Ivan is a man with a severe cognitive disability and a history of challenging behaviors. He was known to assault people, throw chairs, tip over large pieces of furniture, and scream—sometimes all of these things within a brief period of time, several times a day, and for several weeks in a row. The team of caregivers involved in planning for Ivan were concerned that his behaviors had not responded to what they considered extraordinary levels of effort, and they joined together to participate in a behavior support training project. (A more complete description of Ivan and issues related to quality of life appear in Crimmins [1994].)

Ivan is a man in his thirties with a long history of institutional care, followed by a move to a community-based residence serving 15 people. He attends a day treatment program and receives services in an instructional group of 10 people, although he has received large amounts of one-to-one supervision because of his behaviors. Ivan's behavioral concerns were known to occur most often when he was denied requested items or activities—usually coffee or going outside.

There were two incongruities encountered in planning for Ivan. The first of these was that, although the team knew what he wanted (at least some of the time), they believed that they could not give it to him. There were both formal and informal constraints eliciting such denials. The formal constraint was that Ivan was on a DRO system in which he could earn up to four cups of coffee per day contingent on the non-occurrence of his challenging behaviors. This approach had been unsuccessful, and Ivan was receiving very few of these rewards. The informal constraints related to staff attitudes in that they were concerned that Ivan's behaviors served as a form of coercion to make weaker members of the staff "give in" to his behaviors. The second incongruity was that Ivan's behaviors warranted a high level of staff supervision, despite the fact that he appeared to be quite selective about the people with whom he chose to spend time. The result of these incongruities was that both Ivan's behaviors and staff frustration continued.

During the process of behavior support planning, the team agreed on several important findings. First, Ivan had distinct preferences that were communicated but were often ignored because they were not readily available or were believed to be inappropriate at the time he requested them. Second, Ivan tended to be uninterested in the scheduled activities of either the day or residential programs. Third, Ivan was able to communicate both his preferences and his dislike of different activities, largely through his challenging behaviors, but also through the use of informal gestures (e.g., leading others by the hand to the door, holding his coat). These findings had to be addressed in the resulting plan.

The behavioral support plan was developed over a 2-month period with periodic modifications being made throughout the first year. The first intervention was to provide noncontingent access to coffee and to going for a walk. In order to do this, for example, a coffee pot was kept in an accessible location. Ivan could go to it, point, and receive a cup of decaffeinated coffee. These initial interventions did lead to reductions in the level of his challenging behaviors, although some staff members objected to "giving him whatever he wants when he wants it."

The second level of interventions introduced increased effort into gaining access to preferred activities. As Ivan found that coffee, for example, was generally available, the pot was allowed to run out. He then became responsible for assisting in its preparation, making instant coffee at the residence and brewing coffee at the day program. By the end of the year, Ivan also assisted staff members in making fresh coffee during the day for others' consumption. This elaboration of functional routines related to preferred activities became an essential part of his daily life that he clearly appeared to enjoy. The third level of intervention was to introduce a formal means of requesting his preferred items, initially coffee and a walk. This was done through the introduction of tangible cues (e.g., a coffee cup), with the goal of fading to a picture system.

Throughout the year, Ivan's caregivers continued to examine ways in which they could provide him with increased opportunities for self-determination. They surveyed different activities with him for his possible involvement. They also continued to elaborate the functional routines in which he willingly participated, adding steps to going for a walk (e.g., getting his coat from a closet, inviting companions).

The behavior support planning process yielded a number of positive outcomes. Incidents of aggression and property destruction decreased from an average of more than five times per day to less than one time every other day. When these incidents did occur, they were viewed as less intense or of shorter duration. Another outcome was that other people in his house and a broader range of staff members were comfortable spending time with him. In general, Ivan was viewed as more capable than he had been, and there were increased efforts at involving him in community activities because of the reduced threat of behavioral outbursts.

Prior to behavior support planning, it was difficult to see how Ivan might be controlling his own life. His behaviors appeared to be so out of control and dangerous that the overwhelming response of caregivers was to try establish control over him despite the historical ineffectiveness of this approach. Yet Ivan *was* attempting to control his world and needed to have others provide an appropriate means for him to do so. The programs supporting Ivan were willing to do so, but they, in turn, needed support in moving toward a "new way of doing business." This change involved strategies for examining different aspects of Ivan's life to see how his behavior could be seen as self-determining, along with methods for incorporating these findings into an overall plan. They found that, in developing a life plan that makes sense for Ivan, they no longer needed to "control" his behavior.

SUMMARY

Challenging behaviors mark a person as different and historically have served to justify extraordinary means of intervention. In this chapter we reviewed how these behaviors often serve specific functions for an individual and may, in fact, be a means of self-determination. Recognizing this situation has led to the development of a number of intervention strategies that share the underlying themes of increased access to preferred activities and increased control over day-to-day events. An array of literature has begun to emerge supporting the use of these strategies as a means of not only reducing challenging behaviors but also increasing the individual's range of skills.

REFERENCES

Bambara, L.M., Ager, C., & Koger, F. (1994). The effects of choice and task preference on the work performance of adults with severe disabilities. *Journal of Applied Behavior Analysis, 27,* 555–556.

Bannerman, D.J., Sheldon, J.B., Sherman, J.A., & Harchik, A.E. (1990). Balancing the right to habilitation with the right to personal liberties: The rights of people with developmental disabilities to eat too many donuts and take a nap. *Journal of Applied Behavior Analysis, 23,* 79–89.

Berotti, D. (1994, May). *The effects of preference and choice on severe behavior problems.* Paper presented at the meeting of the Association for Behavior Analysis, Atlanta.

Bird, F., Dores, P.A., Moniz, D., & Robinson, J. (1989). Reducing severe aggressive and self-injurious behavior with functional communication training: Direct, collateral and generalized results. *American Journal of Mental Retardation, 94,* 37–48.

Bradley, V.J. (1994). Evolution of a new service paradigm. In V.J. Bradley, J.W. Ashbaugh, & B.C. Blaney (Eds.), *Creating individual supports for people with developmental disabilities: A mandate for change at many levels* (pp. 11–32). Baltimore: Paul H. Brookes Publishing Co.

Brown, F. (1991). Creative daily scheduling. *Journal of The Association for Persons with Severe Handicaps, 16,* 75–84.

Brown, F., Belz, P., Corsi, L., & Wenig, B. (1993). Choice diversity for people with severe disabilities. *Education and Training in Mental Retardation, 28,* 318–326.

Carr, E.G., & Carlson, J.I. (1993). Reduction of severe behavior problems in the community using a multicomponent treatment approach. *Journal of Applied Behavior Analysis, 26,* 157–172.

Carr, E.G., & Durand, V.M. (1985). Reducing behavior problems through functional communication training. *Journal of Applied Behavior Analysis, 18,* 111–126.

Carr, E.G., Levin, L., McConnachie, G., Carlson, J.I., Kemp, D., & Smith, C.E. (1994). *Communication-based intervention for problem behavior: A user's guide for producing positive change.* Baltimore: Paul H. Brookes Publishing Co.

Crimmins, D.B. (1994). Quality of life for persons with challenging behaviors: Intervention goal, contradiction in terms, or both? In D.A. Goode (Ed.), *Quality of life for persons with disabilities: International perspectives and issues* (pp. 208–217). Cambridge, MA: Brookline.

Derby, K.M., Wacker, D.P., Peck, S., Sasso, G., DeRaad, A., Berg, W., Asmus, J., & Ulrich, S. (1994). Functional analysis of separate topographies of aberrant behavior. *Journal of Applied Behavior Analysis, 27,* 267–278.

Dunlap, G., dePerczel, M., Clarke, S., Wilson, D., Wright, S., White, R., & Gomez, A. (1994). Choice making to promote adaptive behavior for students with emotional and behavioral challenges. *Journal of Applied Behavior Analysis, 27,* 505–518.

Dunlap, G., Kern-Dunlap, L., Clarke, S., & Robbins, F.R. (1991). Functional assessment, curricular revision, and severe behavior problems. *Journal of Applied Behavior Analysis, 24,* 387–397.

Durand, V.M. (1990). *Severe behavior problems: A functional communication training approach.* New York: Guilford Press.

Durand, V.M., Berotti, D., & Weiner, J. (1993). Functional communication training: Factors affecting effectiveness, generalization, and maintenance. In J. Reichle & D. Wacker (Eds.), *Communication and language intervention. Vol. 3: Communicative alternatives to challenging behavior* (pp. 317–340). Baltimore: Paul H. Brookes Publishing Co.

Durand, V.M., & Carr, E.G. (1991). Functional communication training to reduce challenging behavior: Maintenance and application in new settings. *Journal of Applied Behavior Analysis, 24,* 251–264.

Durand, V.M., & Crimmins, D.B. (1991). Teaching functionally equivalent responses as an intervention for challenging behavior. In B. Remington (Ed.), *The challenge of severe mental handicap: A behaviour analytic approach.* Chichester, England: John Wiley and Sons.

Durand, V.M., & Crimmins, D.B. (1992). *Motivation assessment scale (MAS) administration guide.* Topeka, KS: Monaco & Associates.

Durand, V.M., Crimmins, D.B., Caulfield, M., & Taylor, J. (1989). Reinforcer assessment I: Using problem behavior to select reinforcers. *Journal of The Association for Persons with Severe Handicaps, 14,* 113–126.

Dyer, K. (1987). The competition of autistic stereotyped behavior with usual and specially assessed reinforcers. *Research in Developmental Disabilities, 8,* 607–626.

Dyer, K. (1989). The effects of preferences on spontaneous verbal requests in individuals with autism. *Journal of The Association for Persons with Severe Handicaps, 14,* 184–189.

Dyer, K., Dunlap, G., & Winterling, V. (1990). Effects of choice making on the serious problem behaviors of students with severe handicaps. *Journal of Applied Behavior Analysis, 23,* 515–524.

Foster-Johnson, L., Ferro, J., & Dunlap, G. (1994). Preferred curricular activities and reduced problem behaviors in students with intellectual disabilities. *Journal of Applied Behavior Analysis, 27,* 493–504.

Gardner, W.I., Cole, C.L., Davidson, D.P., & Karan, O.C. (1986). Reducing aggression in individuals with developmental disabilities: An expanded stimulus control, assessment, and intervention model. *Education and Training of the Mentally Retarded, 21,* 3–12.

Gothelf, C.R., Crimmins, D.B., Mercer, C.A., & Finocchiaro, P.A. (1994). Teaching choice-making skills to students who are deaf blind. *Teaching Exceptional Children, 26*(4), 13–15.

Green, C.W., Reid, D.H., White, L.K., Halford, R.C., Brittain, D.P., & Gardner, S.M. (1988). Identifying reinforcers for persons with profound handicaps: Staff opinion versus systematic assessment of preference. *Journal of Applied Behavior Analysis, 21,* 31–43.

Guess, D., Benson, H.A., & Siegel-Causey, E. (1985). Concepts and issues related to choice-making and autonomy among persons with severe disabilities. *Journal of The Association for Persons with Severe Handicaps, 10,* 79–86.

Horner, R.H., Sprague, J.R., & Flannery, K.B. (1993). Building functional curricula for students with severe intellectual disabilities and severe behavior problems. In R. Van Houten & S. Axelrod (Eds.), *Behavior analysis and treatment.* New York: Plenum.

Houghton, J., Bronicki, B., & Guess, D. (1987). Opportunities to express preferences and make choices among students with severe disabilities in classroom settings. *Journal of The Association for Persons with Severe Handicaps, 12,* 18–27.

Iwata, B.A., Dorsey, M.F., Slifer, K.J., Bauman, K.E., & Richman, G.S. (1982). Toward a functional analysis of self-injury. *Analysis and Intervention in Developmental Disabilities, 2,* 3–20.

Kennedy, C.H., & Haring, T.G. (1993a). Combining reward and escape DRO to reduce the problem behavior of students with severe disabilities. *Journal of The Association for Persons with Severe Handicaps, 18,* 85–92.

Kennedy, C.H., & Haring, T.G. (1993b). Teaching choice making during social interactions to students with profound multiple disabilities. *Journal of Applied Behavior Analysis, 26,* 63–76.

Kennedy, C.H., & Itkonen, T. (1993). Effects of setting events on the problem behavior of students with severe disabilities. *Journal of Applied Behavior Analysis, 26,* 321–327.

Kishi, G., Teelucksingh, B., Zollers, N., Park-Lee, S., & Meyer, L. (1988). Daily decision-making in community residences: A social comparison of adults with and without mental retardation. *American Journal on Mental Retardation, 92,* 430–435.

Koegel, R.L., Dyer, K., & Bell, L.K. (1987). The influence of child-preferred activities on autistic children's social behavior. *Journal of Applied Behavior Analysis, 20,* 243–252.

Meyer, L.H., & Evans, I.M. (1989). *Nonaversive interventions for behavior problems: A manual for home and community.* Baltimore: Paul H. Brookes Publishing Co.

Mithaug, D.E., & Hanawalt, D.A. (1978). The validation of procedures to assess prevocational task preferences in retarded adults. *Journal of Applied Behavior Analysis, 11,* 153–162.

O'Neill, R.E., Horner, R.H., Albin, R.W., Storey, K., & Sprague, J.R. (1990). *Functional analysis of problem behavior: A practical assessment guide.* Sycamore, IL: Sycamore.

Peck, C.A. (1985). Increasing opportunities for social control by children with autism and severe handicaps: Effects on student behavior and perceived classroom climate. *Journal of The Association for Persons with Severe Handicaps, 10,* 183–193.

Reichle, J., & Wacker, D. (Eds.). (1993). *Communicative alternatives to challenging behavior: Vol. 3. Integrating functional assessment and intervention strategies.* Baltimore: Paul H. Brookes Publishing Co.

Shevin, M., & Klein, N.K. (1984). The importance of choice-making skills for students with developmental disabilities. *Journal of The Association for Persons with Severe Handicaps, 9,* 159–166.

Touchette, P.E., MacDonald, R.F., & Langer, S.N. (1985). A scatter plot for identifying stimulus control of problem behavior. *Journal of Applied Behavior Analysis, 18,* 343–351.

Vollmer, T.R., Iwata, B.A., Smith, R.G., & Rodgers, T.A. (1992). Reduction of multiple aberrant behaviors and concurrent development of self-care skills with differential reinforcement. *Research in Developmental Disabilities, 13,* 287–299.

Vollmer, T.R., Iwata, B.A., Zarcone, J.R., Smith, R.G., & Mazaleski, J.L. (1993). The role of attention in the treatment of attention-maintained self-injurious behavior: Noncontingent reinforcement and differential reinforcement of other behavior. *Journal of Applied Behavior Analysis, 26,* 9–21.

Wacker, D.P., Wiggins, B., Fowler, M., & Berg, W.K. (1988). Training students with profound or multiple handicaps to make requests via microswitches. *Journal of Applied Behavior Analysis, 21,* 331–343.

Wehmeyer, M. (1992). Self-determination and the education of students with mental retardation. *Education and Training in Mental Retardation, 27,* 302–314.

VI
FUTURE CHALLENGES

16

Shaping Future Directions

MARTHA E. SNELL

THE PROFESSION OF working with people who have disabilities shares with other fields many of the same forces that shape its future. This field also builds on past practices: the opportunities taken to change and improve conventions and applied procedures along with the demonstrated effects, both successful and failed. While our values may define the boundaries for moving into the future, these lines may not be equally clear to all. We can be swayed by the predominant beliefs, fears, and prejudices (our own and those of others) and by the prevailing political climate. We are stretched by our hopes, our knowledge, and emerging research. We experience the pressures of current limits in fiscal resources and the communal resistance to change.

Thus, to attain improvement amid these forces in any number of issues we hold dear, we must have our goals explicitly defined and the case we make for these goals must be tight. We will present this case to numerous audiences, and as we negotiate the "future shaping maze," we need to be clear-headed, persistent, and clever. Being meaningfully active in shaping the future is demanding; being successful is formidable.

The Power of One Person

We know that the efforts of one individual can be powerful in shaping the futures of many. Think about Robert Gaylord-Ross and Tom Haring and the ripples of force their wisdom has made in our field. Their seemingly simple messages—teach with reference to normalized context, increase the individual's self-control, and promote meaningful social integration—sharply contrast with past messages: Separate students and structure learning to establish teacher control over behavior (Breen, 1995). Their work will continue to influence and motivate. Another singly powerful person is T.J. Monroe and his revolutionary words to others with disabilities on self-advocacy. In 1990 he spoke to a crusade of people, many from the Southbury Training School, who came to the first convention of Connecticut People First: "You have to make thunder. You have to speak for your rights. . . . This is a free country. You can talk for yourself. You might need some help, but you can talk for yourself. . . . I want to hear thunder" (Shapiro, 1993, pp. 184–185, 187). Monroe continues to speak on self-advocacy in disability organizations and to people with disabilities. Ed Roberts was a gutsy crusader who challenged us all into action. Tim Cook pushed so hard on the themes of accessibility that public transportation listened, and Judith Heumann still fights the bureaucracy, but as a leader from within the places where she used to demonstrate.

But people with influential words do not necessarily share common ground with the readers of this book. How many people will be influenced by Singer's *Rethinking Life and Death* (1995), reviewed in the *Washington Post* (Weigel, 1995)? Among Singer's proposals are several stark tenets reflecting the sphere of thinking that rejects "the equity of human life" and replaces it with "the worth of human life varies" (Weigel, 1995, p. 10), a view akin to Shaw's quality of life formula for determining what treatment is given infants born with myelomeningocele, discussed in Chapter 1 of that text. According to Singer, believing in this tenet allows parents to wait for 28 days after the birth of a child, a time during which "responsible decision-makers" could select infanticide for a " 'life that has begun very badly,' and he specifically mentions Down's syndrome children in this respect" (Weigel, 1995, p. 10). Weigel rightfully accuses Singer of having a profound fear of freedom of choice and having an obsession for control; "read this book," Weigel (1995) warns, not to gain insight, but "to remind yourself of the enormities of which putatively civilized human beings are capable" (p. 10). But even in the shadow of the Americans with Disabilities Act of 1990 (PL 101-336), many so-called able-bodied persons will agree with Singer's plan to "purify" humankind.

Resistance to Change

In the midst of powerful voices lies the human tendency to maintain the status quo and to resist change. Within the field of education, this tendency has been noted by Fullan (1991) and Sarason (1990). Resistance to change can have persuasive power over our recognition of problems, our willingness to make improvements, and our tolerance of things as they are. Why have schools been intractable in the area of reform? The failure to adopt change even in the full view of problems is motivated by fear (distrust of the unfamiliar) and a lack of motivation (anticipated dislike of changing familiar patterns). In the context of schools and adult service systems, planning for change and implementing it become complicated by the organizations themselves: "their structure, their dynamics, their power relationships, and their underlying values and axioms" (Sarason, pp. 4–5). Sarason holds that changing power relationships in schools is an essential but still insufficient condition for reaching needed school reform. Teachers (and students) need to share the power and the responsibility for reform, and reform must build on children's natural curiosity and interest in learning. Reformers like Sarason and Fullan call for significant systems change in systems noted for failed change.

Solutions and Challenges

We will continue to discover "cures" or solutions for some of the conditions that lead to developmental and physical disabilities. Genetic detection and prevention, in-utero treatments, and improvements in birth conditions that lead to low birth weight and the possibility of brain damage are some examples of this progress in prevention. But there will always be children who are born with disabilities and those who acquire disabilities during their lifetimes. There will be new threats to health and to human development. For example, today's ordinary use of cars and motorcycles by young drivers has led to many more persons newly disabled with traumatic brain injury, and the HIV virus has led to dramatic threats to the health of many young individuals. Thus, the demand for solutions to those who challenge the system is not anticipated to change, while the challenges and the solutions will shift, evolve, and expand over time.

WHERE WE HAVE BEEN

For much of the recent past, the focus in our field has been on describing labels that prescribe services and establishing locations to provide those services. Labels have been gates through which many have passed, leaving their peers and communities behind in order to receive special education services, to fill "slots" in workshops and day activity centers, and to occupy "beds" in residential facilities.

Cascades and Least Restrictive Environments

In the 1960s, professionals advocated the development of "least restrictive environments" (LRE) instead of institutions and for laws mandating public school services. About this same time, the concept of a continuum of services or placements may have first been published by Reynolds (1962) and later seconded by Deno (1970), but it was not really a new concept. Continuum logic states that the intensity of one's disability should co-vary with the restrictiveness of the placement and the specialized nature of the services needed (Snell & Drake, 1993). Even the trend to replace almshouses with institutions in the early 1800s, while motivated in part by a sense of charity, also appears to have been inspired by a desire to restrict the contact that people with disabilities had with their communities (Shapiro, 1993). Deno (1970) set forth a cascade service system that acted like a filter to allow those needing more specialized services to trickle out of regular classes into the increasingly tapered end of the cascade: from part- to full-time special classes, to special stations and homebound education, and then into "in-patient programs" where instruction was received in hospitals or "noneducational" settings (p. 235).

Our follow-up data on persons with mental retardation indicate that many who trickled down the cascade in the 1960s and 1970s stayed there. Most follow-up studies of students with special education labels during high school indicate that only about one third of the total group is working full time, although most indicate that they would like to work (Hasazi, Johnson, Hasazi, Gordon, & Hull, 1989; Peraino, 1992; Schloss, Alper, & Jayne, 1993). Those with severe disabilities who "aged out" of schools or "graduated" have typically stayed home, while some attend day activity centers or workshop settings where they spend time without pay among others with difficulties (Peraino, 1992). As one mother said, "My child is not a salmon. She can't swim upstream . . . she can't get up your cascade . . . if she tries, she'll drown" (Lusthaus & Forest, 1987, p. 5).

In U.S. public schools today, many more children with severe and multiple disabilities and labels of mental retardation are served in separate or part-time special education placements than are supported with accommodations and supplementary aids and services within the mainstream. Table 1 indicates the percentage of educational environments in which students received special education services during the 1992–1993 school year (U.S. Department of Education, 1994) by several disability areas commonly associated with severe disabilities (mental retardation, multiple disabilities, other health impairments, autism, deaf-blindness, and traumatic head injury). These current placement data indicate minimal integration for persons with mental retardation or those with other labels often designated as "severe disabilities" (approximately 2.26% of the total group served in special education). While Table 1 does not report the quality of services in any setting, one measure of quality is outcome—what happens to these students when they exit school. As previously mentioned, outcome data for this group bring into question the efficacy of our special education system.

Table 1. The number and percentage of children ages 6–21 with labels associated with severe disabilities served under IDEA, Part B, and Chapter 1 of ESEA (SOP) during 1991 and 1992 by educational environment

Educational environment	All disabilities	Mental retardation	Multiple disabilities	Other health impairment	Autism	Deaf blindness	Traumatic brain injury
Total no.	1,559,598	26,535	5,731	19,211	472	82	148
Percent of total[a]	100	1.7	.4	.12	.03	.005	.01
Percent in class	34.9	5.04	6.20	35.30	4.68	5.99	7.82
Percent in resource room	36.3	25.44	18.05	27.61	6.92	6.14	8.93
Percent in separate class	23.52	59.20	47.11	21.45	48.52	36.45	23.61
Percent in separate public/ private facility	3.92	8.85	22.65	3.29	35.88	21.48	53.52
Percent in public/ private residential facility	.89	1.16	3.74	.51	3.11	28.12	3.70
Percent home based	.48	.31	2.24	11.85	.87	1.83	2.43

[a]This row indicates the percentage of children age 6–21 in each disability category out of a total of 1,559,598 children served under IDEA and Chapter 1.

From U.S. Department of Education. (1994). Sixteenth annual report to Congress on the implementation of the Individuals with Disabilities Education Act. Washington, DC: U.S. Government Printing Office.

Underlying Assumptions

Taylor (1988) discussed seven assumptions underlying the LRE principle that drives many service systems in our field: schools, work/
activity programs, and residential programs. First, the LRE principle
justifies restrictive environments because they are on the continuum.
Second, LRE confuses service intensity with segregation. Third, the
LRE principle depends on professional decision making about progress
and labels, not on self-determinism, personal preference, or family
choice. Fourth, both progress and a lack of progress mean movement
to another setting. Fifth, movement to less restrictive settings means
being ready, having the right skills, or getting a label change. Sixth,
the focus within an LRE model is the physical setting rather than what
individualized supports a person needs in order to function. Finally,
the LRE principle authorizes restrictions on people's basic rights and
freedoms to a degree beyond those infringements imposed on people
without disabilities. These assumptions—which are woven into laws,
funding formulas, ways of thinking about people with disabilities, job
descriptions, and organizational structures—beg to be replaced with a
system of support.

Separation and isolation, not support, have been the primary outcomes of the LRE philosophy for students with disabilities. As others
have also concluded, the longitudinal and pervasive effect of cascade
thinking and LRE logic on the evolved structure in schools and in
community living and work programs appears to be the biggest tragedy.
Many authors writing within this book and elsewhere are in agreement
that the LRE model needs to be replaced with a portable system of
individualized supports that would operate across service systems: in
schools, in vocational rehabilitation programs, and in community living (e.g., Ferguson & Ferguson, 1993; Luckasson et al., 1992; Singer &
Irvin, 1989; Smull & Donnehey, 1993).

WHERE WE SEEM TO BE GOING

What are the current themes of best practices for those who challenge
the system? The theme of support, just mentioned, stretches like an
umbrella over many other best practices we are advocating for and
continue to refine. The support theme requires a shift from labels and
places where services are provided to individualized supports that accompany individuals in schools, in neighborhoods, and in towns—
that is, in any of the places where they live their lives.

The Support Model

Support is a vital concept currently woven into all of the best practices of our field and into many of the chapters of this book. Support can be conceptualized as part of the relationship among a person's capabilities, the demands made on the person in different environments (home, school, work, and the community), and the way the person functions (Figure 1). The way in which a person functions is determined by the interaction of that person's capabilities with the demands made on her or him in different environments. For the most part, you and I respond to these demands in adaptive ways without extraordinary supports, simply by applying our capabilities. If our functioning is not up to par, we may seek additional skills or broaden our capabilities in order to function acceptably. For example, if I take a new job, I may be required to attend training sessions to learn computer applications for that job or to learn how to work with customers. If a couple chooses to have children, they are likely to read books or attend classes on childbirth and parenting; they will seek medical advice, learn about their insurance coverage, and plan ahead in many ways. In short, we adapt and extend our capabilities to meet the changing needs of our environment.

We all require the basic supports of food, shelter, and love, along with the supports most societies offer: an education, safety, and eco-

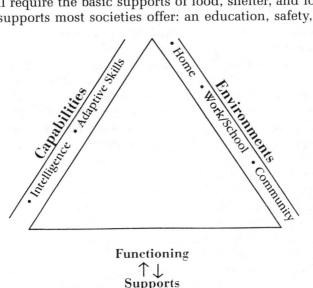

Figure 1. The general structure of the definition of mental retardation showing the relationship between an individual's capabilities, the environments in which that person functions, and how supports bolster the individual's functioning. (From Luckasson et al. (1992). *Mental retardation; Definition, classification, and systems of support* (9th ed.) (p. 10). Washington DC: American Association on Mental Retardation; reprinted by permission.)

nomic and political provisions (e.g., the fire department, an income, a judicial system). We rely on basic supports to function acceptably, and usually we do not require extraordinary supports. When we are dependents as young children and our capabilities are underdeveloped, we require a different intensity of supports than we do during most of our lives. If our health deteriorates to a point where our capabilities are reduced, we also will require supports. Ordinarily, however, we function acceptably within many environments simply by applying our capabilities (and often by adapting and expanding our capabilities) to meet the day-to-day demands of home, school, or work and the demands that are involved in living within a community.

People with significant disabilities, by definition, need support beyond the ordinary in order to function adequately in various parts of their lives or in many or all dimensions of their lives. Just like you and I, people with disabilities often require extra supports in some dimensions of their lives. These needs may not be directly related to their cognitive limitations. The psychological effects of losing a loved one will be experienced by everyone at some time; threats to physical health such as cancer or heart disease may occur regardless of a cognitive disability or the presence of deaf-blindness; and everyone who grows up hungry, lives in an abusive atmosphere, or is homeless shows the effects. A need for having supports may extend beyond support in the traditional dimension of capability (e.g., adaptive abilities) into medical, mental health, and environmental decisions.

Our understanding has broadened concerning the interrelationship among a person's capabilities, the environmental demands she or he experiences, and the resultant functioning. For example, follow-up studies have documented the effects of institutionalization and community placement and are currently examining the relationship between separate special education services and support in the mainstream. These findings lend strength to a general principal: integration among peers is a primary means for reducing functional disabilities in people who challenge the system, but individualized supports are the key for advancing and enriching the success of integration. The reverse of this principle is that many persons with disabilities will not be successful in integrated environments unless they have the needed supports.

This book explores the amazing range of supports that are possible. But the key is that supports must not be selected from a catalogue but designed by a team that includes the person, committed friends, family members, and professionals. Supports are designed to match the current abilities and needs of an individual. Supports come from a variety of sources, take many forms, and fill many functions; their intensity or the degree to which they are experienced varies widely. How much support is needed and for how long are issues that must be addressed. Adults like Lisa, whose deaf-blindness confused her co-workers in a department store (Chapter 11), or Stacy, whose challenging behavior kept library co-workers at a distance (Chapter 12), may require extensive support during the first month on a new job, with the intensity shifting to less support as they are successful. The actual job supervisor may take on more responsibility for supervision and the worker may become acquainted with and better known by her co-workers, who learn how to lend natural forms of needed support.

The 12 women and men described by Horner and his colleagues (Chapter 9) are suitable examples of this process: each had individualized support plans that surrounded them as they moved from institutions to small community residences. Their major behavior problems of aggression, self-injury, tantrums, property destruction, and ingestion of nonedible substances were studied in order to understand the antecedents and consequences controlling these behaviors. Within each person's support team of family and professionals, other data relevant to designing supports were gathered: activity patterns and social contacts, medical needs, and a personal futures plan specifying features critical for successful inclusion. Support plans were designed before the men and women moved so that physical and staff accommodations would be ready. The implementation phase focused on making the daily routines of these men and women more active and linked to the communities to which they moved; teaching them to communicate and maintain their health; developing social networks beyond staff, school, or job opportunities; and creating "systematic strategies for presenting and responding to problem behaviors." Implementation was balanced with ongoing evaluation so that support could be adjusted, added, shifted, or deleted.

As emphasized by Taylor (1988), supports must not be equated with staff members or with places along the continuum of restrictiveness. Instead, supports have to be portable so that they can follow those who need them or be available when and where they are needed. A second serious error in understanding the concept of supports is to confuse support levels with levels of disability or with the old concept of levels of mental retardation. Support intensity is not the same as level of functioning or degree of disability. Using an averaged intensity level of support to describe a person's support is meaningless because it fails to portray an individual's support needs across the many facets of adaptive skills or the supports that may be needed in the other dimensions: psychology, health, and environment. A person's profile for supports is not static; it will change as the person grows older and life circumstances, abilities, and preferences change. A profile of supports is suited to an individual's strengths and needs at a distinct point in life. Table 2, based in part on Luckasson et al. (1992), summarizes these important characteristics of a system based on individualized support.

Most of the 12 men and women described by Horner and his colleagues in Chapter 9 achieved outcomes often credited to the receipt of individualized supports: 1) their capabilities were enhanced, 2) their community presence and participation were fostered, 3) their choices were recognized, 4) their competence was improved and respected, and 5) they obtained opportunities to make personal contributions.

Themes of Best Practices

Consistent with the overarching theme of support, other themes voiced in the chapters of this book will guide our future directions:

1. Person-centered planning, not system-centered planning, should direct our efforts at training and supporting people with disabilities.
2. The individual and people closest to the individual should have the greatest influence on design and changes through a personal futures plan.
3. The individual preferences and choices of the individual need to be consistently solicited and included as part of all decisions.
4. Self-determination, or learning to exert control over one's personal life, involves initiative, awareness of preference, making choices, goal setting, problem solving, assertiveness, self-advocacy, self-regulation, and persistence. People with disabilities are capable of learning these skills.
5. When individuals with disabilities learn and practice self-determination in settings that value these characteristics, problem behaviors seem to decline. Much of our traditional instructional strategies and scheduling practices are designed to be controlled by staff and not designed to emphasize natural cues or to promote self-control; thus, many current teaching approaches are not conducive to self-regulation and may maintain problem behavior.
6. Multiple support procedures "tailored to the person/problem/behavior/setting," not single strategies, are needed to resolve serious behavior problems.
7. While ongoing performance assessment and revision of support procedures are still essential activities, these processes must be socially valid, with linkage back to the persons at the center and to their hopes for themselves.

8. People must be provided with functional ways to communicate, ways that can be understood and are viewed as acceptable by peers.
9. Collaborative teaming is the "glue that holds it all together"; maintaining and improving the team's interactive process enables teams to function successfully.

These practices contrast with teaching strategies typical of the past 30 years in our field that place an emphasis on behavioral control by the teacher and therapist. Lending needed supports while placing the person at the center of the team, understanding the person's preferences and communication, building skills that improve communication and contribute to self-determination, and crafting environments and learning experiences to tap the individual's self-control are orientations new to the current decade. We discovered these orientations because "other-control methods" have not been effective against serious behavior problems or effective in building long-term skills. These new themes will require a new mindset in our organizations and in our professional and institutional staff. Transition to this new mindset will be accompanied by increases in the tension Fredericks describes (Chapter 8) that exists between staff philosophy and residents' rights/ choices and health/safety.

MAPPING THE ROUTE

Discrepancy as a Stimulus for Change

When the discrepancy between what we know and what we practice gets too broad, we must look to sources of organizational change and people barriers. For example, consider the things we know about en-

Table 2. What are supports?

Support Levels Are NOT Substitutes for Levels of Disability
1. Supports are chosen to complement a person's capabilities at any given point in life.
2. Supports enhance capabilities and adaptive functioning possible in many environments: at home, in school, at work, and in the community.
3. Supports are not the same as a place or synonymous with paid staff; supports follow a person, potentially come from numerous sources, fill a range of possible functions, and can fluctuate in their intensity.
4. Support levels do not describe a fixed characteristic but are based on an individual's capabilities: the strengths and limitations across many life dimensions.
5. Support needs are related to the demands in existing environments balanced by natural supports and accommodations.
6. Supports assessment is person centered and involves many views, family, friends, and professionals from relevant disciplines.
7. Support needs for one person will vary across life dimensions.
8. Support needs will change over time.

Adapted from Luckasson et al., 1992.

abling the development of social relations in young children with disabilities:

1. Teach social skills in context.
2. Teach interaction partners.
3. Socially validate skill selection with peers.
4. Teach children to deal with rejection.
5. Begin integration early.
6. Promote horizontal relationships over teaching relationships.
7. Use mutually enjoyable intervention strategies. (Snell & Vogtle, in press)

These statements rest securely on a foundation of 15 years of intervention research with young children with disabilities. When these statements are coupled with the placement data in Table 1, it becomes clear that separate education for children with severe disabilities is widely practiced across all school ages. There is a discrepancy between what we know and our current practices. It is necessary to ask, Why have schools placed so many barriers to allowing these children to be educated alongside their peers? (I will answer this after posing a second, related question.)

Butterworth and Kiernan (Chapter 10) describe equally disturbing statistics on adults with disabilities that exist despite the laws for supported employment; there has been little change in the network of segregated day activity, day treatment, and sheltered employment programs. Supported employment has not replaced these restrictive services. Of the day and employment services provided by MR/DD agencies in 1990, 82% were segregated, and the number of adults entering these segregated services is greater than those newly entering integrated employment. A similar question can be posed for this discrepancy between what we know and current practices: Why have adult service agencies placed so many barriers to integrated employment? There are at least three similar answers to both questions about isolated school programs and adult vocational programs. First, those who established systems (and built structures) for these programs serving children and adults with disabilities did so prior to knowing the value of integration and inclusion. Second, both types of programs were established under the assumption of continuum or cascade thinking, which probably originally was influenced by prejudice toward people with disabilities (Shapiro, 1992). Third, the human tendency to maintain the status quo and to resist change operates in schools, vocational rehabilitation systems, and in agencies responsible for adult services. In other words, adults with disabilities face a situation that is very similar to the one facing children with disabilities.

Phases of Thinking About Disability

Based loosely on Shapiro's (1993) work, four phases of thinking about people with disabilities can be described:

- Survival of the Fittest: Those who cannot meet demands, use too many resources, or cannot contribute in typical ways should not survive or do not deserve resources.
- Pity and Protect: Move people with disabilities out of demanding settings, reduce demands made on them, provide protection, and care for or maintain their basic needs because these people are incapable and deserve sympathy.
- Separate and Remediate: Move people with disabilities to specialized settings where their label determines the location and the specialized treatment provided.
- Support and Respect Remaining Differences: Define and add individualized supports to enable learning and development; to enable living, participating, and working in the community among nondisabled peers; and to maintain physical and psychological health. Then adjust individualized supports as needed.

Inherent in the first three perspectives is the "fearsome possibility" that Shapiro identified: People with disabilities represent that fearful possibility that, while without disabilities now, we are always vulnerable. Since these thoughts are unpleasant, people with disabilities frequently are distanced and treated as "social inferiors," a move that only prolongs ignorance and prejudice.

Although some might characterize these four viewpoints as an evolution of thinking in today's world, there are still many who hold fast to each viewpoint: The earlier views have not been successively replaced with the later views. Parts of our society are organized in ways that maintain each perspective. For example, those advocating a survival-of-the-fittest perspective may be less vocal in our democratic society, but Singer's (1995) philosophy—"the worth of human life varies"—exemplifies this view well. The appeals made for the poster child and "Jerry's Kids" as well as much of the traditional Special Olympics approach have relied on the pity-and-protect perspective. Most special education and vocational rehabilitation services are well rooted in the separate-and-remediate view. The newer support phase is gaining a research and methods basis and a patronage.

Strategies of Change

Before change can occur, enough people must recognize the need for change as well as the direction for change. For example, when a society is characterized by daily struggle for subsistence or by extensive poverty and injustice, the mistreatment of people with disabilities will go unrecognized by many. Making the effort to change requires both awareness of a problem and motivation to resolve it.

Even with the recognition and the motivation present, change is difficult. We have all experienced the tension of trying new ideas and the fear of failing. Knowing what changes will lead to desired outcomes is a key element of planning change, but often the motivation and need for change in education and social welfare precedes a solid database. The complexity of these types of changes greatly increases the difficulty of their success. School reform, even if focused primarily on making schools more inclusive of students with disabilities, is multifarious by nature. Also, when changes are imposed on people, resistance is frequent, but when those who are to experience change are part of its design, participation in change is more acceptable and the outcomes have more potential for success.

Probably the central factor making change difficult is fear: the fear of things unknown and unexperienced and the fear of failure. Large differences in people or in practices are often misunderstood and found to be strange and rejected. Direct positive experiences with the unknowns are often the best way to overcome ignorance and reduce prejudice, but this approach tends to require the presence of models or guides and people or programs that illustrate vision and knowledge about the proposed changes.

Many have described the move to integrated environments for persons with disabilities as a significant social change within a political context and involving political processes (e.g., Meyer & Kishi, 1985; Peck, Furman, & Helmstetter, 1993; Snell & Eichner, 1989). Beyond the space limitations of this chapter are extensive recommendations for planning, initiating, and sustaining change in schools and adult service organizations. For example, the array of outside forces that can be applied to schools regarding integration is portrayed in Figure 2 (Snell & Eichner, 1989). Yet unless the multiple layers of decision makers within a school district (central rectangle in the figure) are involved as the stimulus for change, change will be minimal, if at all, and hard-fought. This approach would seek to identify central office administrators or school leaders (school board members, principals) who are supportive of integration and then design a campaign promoting integration with facts and supportive documentation: Integration is an approach with supportive research, is ethically correct, is required by law, is cost-effective, and is feasible in this locality. Federal and state monitoring agencies, like the courts, are typically heavy-handed, po-

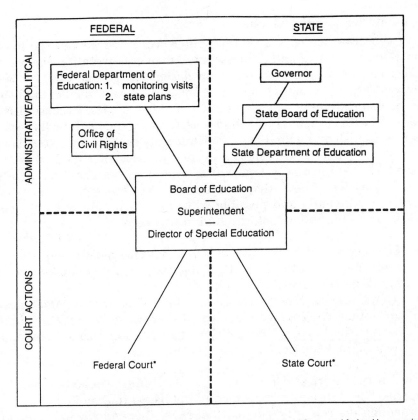

Figure 2. Political forces pertinent to integration in local public schools. (*State and federal law requires that, absent special circumstances, the party exhaust his or her administrative remedies prior to filing an action in court.) (From Snell & Eichner, 1989, p. 125.)

litical approaches to change, but they may be the only way to initiate a reversal of ingrained practices in some localities.

The most important lesson to be learned regarding implementation efforts, according to Peck et al. (1993), is that "the outcomes of *any* approach to program development and change are mediated by local context factors" (p. 199). Change efforts must be flexible plans and general strategies, not rigid formulae to be followed in a lockstep manner. A broad representation of stakeholders must participate. The process must let participants express their worries and explore their concerns. Those who are involved in planning for the larger organization need to make their ideas public and solicit reactions from the whole. Communication and planning must be ongoing as new concerns and issues about each change arise.

Communicating the Themes

For centuries, we have used the written word. We are so used to this medium that we often fail to use more than one modality, and we are so used to taking our messages to designated groups that we often forget to speak to more than just a few audiences. Consider audience. A book for professionals may sell about 3,000 copies. Because it is in English with a relatively small market, the audience will be those who speak English and who live in the United States. Like most good books for professionals, it will show a decline in sales after the first year or two and then gradually taper off as time goes on. However, if other modalities were used, dissemination of the book's messages would proceed differently and possibly with more vigor. For example, consider several individual stories told in this book:

- Eleven-year-old Becky, whose labels included autism and behavior problems and who was not being successfully included in her fourth-grade class (Chapter 6).
- Ivan, a man with cognitive disabilities and no conventional means for communicating, who was regarded as dangerous to others in the community-based residence where he lived along with 14 other de-institutionalized persons (Chapter 15).

The success stories of these two people could be reported within a single-subject design framework and published in a reputable journal, providing the scientific context that researchers would find convincing. Scientific presentation and publication of these "stories" can add to the pool of findings and can influence the direction of other researchers. Ultimately, even single studies can contribute to the momentum that a larger collective body of research has for influencing the ways in which we understand problem behavior and the professional advice we pass down to teachers on discipline and to parents on child rearing. However, for 99.9% of the potential audience that Ivan's and Becky's stories could influence, this presentation would have no direct impact.

Becky's story as shown could be filmed as a documentary, just as Peter's story was in *Educating Peter* (Home Box Office, 1993). Alternately, Becky's and Ivan's story could be narrated by their parents, friends, and support staff on National Public Radio. Basic human messages of justice, communication, or social relationships could be converted to song and put to music by a popular group. When the story's medium shifts from one modality to another, the audience may grow quickly. But with the retelling, the original message may be threatened because of the conventions for retelling stories in different modalities to different audiences.

We need to broaden our research/intervention teams so that a broader set of findings can be gathered to enrich the telling. Economists and politicians want to know the cost of these best practices and the cost compared to current treatments. Ordinary folks in the audience want to hear part of the story from other ordinary folks so that it is believable. Parents and relatives of people with disabilities want to know the long-term results and will question the practices' safety. Parents and relatives of peers without disabilities want to know if the procedures will hurt their own children's schooling, safety, or opportunity.

Successful communication means translating our findings so that they reach multiple audiences. Story retelling strategies include the following:

1. Creating terminology bridges from one audience to another.
2. Adding theme enhancers that enable common themes to be evident as a story is told across audiences. Although a businessperson may be interested primarily in cost factors and a parent interested in the story's emotion, the common-ground themes (e.g., fair and humane treatment) must remain visible without evoking pity or overemphasizing cost savings, etc.
3. Telling true stories so that the outcome is less likely to be modified.
4. Adding "So What" clauses that, like a discussion at the end of a research report, connect the story results back to ordinary lives and answer the question "How does this relate to me and to current practice?"
5. Dealing with the "This is not my problem" reaction by finding ways to convince the audience that the Ivans and the Beckys are part of us and the solutions to their problems are consistent with solutions to more familiar or prevalent problems (i.e., fairness and justice; the need we all have to "be a part," to have friends, to communicate).

If we wish to enlighten others to the powerful themes of best practice woven throughout this book, we must attend to our audience and to our means for communicating these themes. With care, we can build on the compelling power of our message and share it beyond our small professional circles.

SUMMARY

The task of influencing the future in our field involves not only knowledge of the discipline but also an understanding of the socio-political forces relevant to change in schools and agencies, a belief in the power of small numbers and the influence of effective communication, and comprehension of the phenomenon of resistance to change and the tactics needed to overcome it. Our recent past has led us into a maze built on the belief that separation is necessary for serving individuals with disabilities. "Separate and remediate," a principle based on the LRE and the continuum, is still active in placing the vast majority of school-age individuals with more extensive disabilities in separate classes and schools and placing adults into workshops, day training centers, and unnaturally large residences where classmates, co-workers, and roommates also all have disabilities. The best practices described and illustrated in this book rest on a different principle: Support the individual and respect any remaining differences. The concept of individualized supports fits into the relationship that human capabilities have with environmental demands. Supports have the potential to shore up the functioning of those who need it.

The many discrepancies that exist between what we know about people with severe disabilities and what we do with and for them in our society will map the routes that we must take to shape the future of our field. All of us have a role in developing and setting in motion the plans for navigating those routes and monitoring our progress along them.

REFERENCES

Americans with Disabilities Act of 1990, PL 101-336. (July 26, 1990). Title 42, U.S.C. 12101 et seq: *U.S. Statutes at Large, 104,* 327–378.

Breen, C.G. (1995). Thomas G. Haring (1953–1993). *Journal of Behavioral Education, 5,* 1–9.

Deno, E. (1970). Special education as development capital. *Exceptional Children, 37,* 229–237.

Ferguson, P.M., & Ferguson, D.L. (1993). The promise of adulthood. In M.E. Snell (Ed.), *Instruction of students with severe disabilities* (4th ed., pp. 588–607). Columbus, OH: Merrill/Macmillan.

Fullan, M.G. (1991). *The new meaning of educational change* (2nd ed.). New York: Teachers College Press.

Hasazi, S., Johnson, R., Hasazi, J., Gordon, L., & Hull, M. (1989). Employment of youth with and without handicaps following high school: Outcomes and correlates. *Journal of Special Education, 23,* 243–255.

Home Box Office (Producer). [Goodwin, T.C., & Wurzburg, G. (Directors)]. (1993). *Educating Peter* [Videotape]. New York: Ambrose Video Publishing.

Luckasson, R., Schalock, R.L., Coulter, D.L., Snell, M.E., Polloway, E.A., Spitalnik, D.M., Reiss, S., & Stark, J.A. (1992). *Mental retardation: Definition, classification, and systems of support* (9th ed.). Washington, DC: American Association on Mental Retardation.

Lusthaus, E., & Forest, M. (1987). The kaleidoscope: A challenge to the cascade. In M. Forest (Ed.), *More education integration* (pp. 1–17). Downsview, Ontario, Canada: G. Allan Roeher Institute.

Meyer, L.H., & Kishi, G.S. (1985). School integration strategies. In K.C. Lakin & R.H. Bruininks (Eds.), *Strategies for achieving community integration of developmentally disabled citizens* (pp. 231–252). Baltimore: Paul H. Brookes Publishing Co.

Peck, C.A., Furman, G.C., & Helmstetter, H. (1993). Integrated early childhood programs: Research on the implementation of change in organizational contexts. In C.A. Peck, S.L. Odom, & D.D. Bricker (Eds.), *Integrating young children with disabilities into community programs* (pp. 187–205). Baltimore: Paul H. Brookes Publishing Co.

Peraino, J.M. (1992). Post-21 follow-up studies: How do special education graduates fare? In P. Wehman (Ed.), *Life beyond the classroom: Transition strategies for young people with disabilities* (pp. 21–70). Baltimore: Paul H. Brookes Publishing Co.

Reynolds, M.L. (1962). A framework for considering some issues in special education. *Exceptional Children, 28,* 367–370.

Sarason, S.B. (1990). *The predictable failure of educational reform.* San Francisco: Jossey-Bass.

Schloss, P.J., Alper, S., & Jayne, D. (1993). Self-determination for persons with disabilities: Choice, risk, and dignity. *Exceptional Children, 60,* 215–225.

Shapiro, J.P. (1993). *No pity.* New York: The New York Times Company.

Singer, G., & Irvin, L.K. (1989). *Support for caregiving families.* Baltimore: Paul H. Brookes Publishing Co.

Singer, P. (1995). *Rethinking life and death: The collapse of our traditional ethics.* New York: St. Martin's.

Smull, M.W., & Donnehey, A.J. (1993). Increasing quality while reducing costs: The challenges of the 90's. In V.J. Bradley, J. Ashbough, & B. Bailey (Eds.), *Creating individual supports for people with developmental disabilities: A mandate for change at many levels* (pp. 59–78). Baltimore: Paul H. Brookes Publishing Co.

Snell, M.E., & Drake, G.P., Jr. (1993). Replacing cascades with supported education. *Journal of Special Education, 27,* 393–409.

Snell, M.E., & Eichner, S.J. (1989). Integration for students with profound disabilities. In F. Brown & D.H. Lehr (Eds.), *Persons with profound disabilities: Issues and practices* (pp. 109–138). Baltimore: Paul H. Brookes Publishing Co.

Snell, M., & Vogtle, L.K. (in press). Interpersonal relationships of school-aged children and adolescents with mental retardation. In R.L. Schalock (Ed.), *Quality of life: Conceptualization, measurement, and use.* Washington, DC: American Association on Mental Retardation.

Taylor, S.J. (1988). Caught in the continuum: A critical analysis of the principle of the least restrictive environment. *Journal of The Association for Persons with Severe Handicaps, 13,* 41–53.

U.S. Department of Education. (1994). *Sixteenth annual report to Congress on the implementation of the Individuals with Disabilities Education Act.* Washington, DC: U.S. Government Printing Office.

Weigel, G. (1995, March 26). Are humans special? [Review of the book *Rethinking life and death: The collapse of our traditional ethics*]. *The Washington Post,* pp. 1, 10 (Book World supplement).

Index

Page numbers followed by "t" or "f" indicate tables or figures, respectively.